Writing and Radicalism

Crosscurrents

General Editors:
Professor J B Bullen, University of Reading
Dr Neil Sammells, Bath College of Higher Education
Dr Paul Hyland, Bath College of Higher Education

Writing and Radicalism

Edited by John Lucas

Longman
London and New York

Addison Wesley Longman Limited,
Edinburgh Gate,
Harlow, Essex CM20 2JE, United Kingdom
and Associated Companies throughout the world.

*Published in the United States of America
by Addison Wesley Longman, New York*

©Addison Wesley Longman Limited 1996

All rights reserved; no part of this publication may be reproduced, stored in a retrieval system, or transmitted in any form or by any means, electronic, mechanical, photocopying, recording, or otherwise without either the prior written permission of the Publishers or a licence permitting restricted copying in the United Kingdom issued by the Copyright Licensing Agency Ltd.,
90 Tottenham Court Road, London W1P 9HE

First published 1996

ISBN 0 582 214149 CSD
ISBN 0 582 214157 PPR

British Library Cataloguing-in-Publication Data
A catalogue record for this book is
available from the British Library

Library of Congress Cataloging-in-Publication Data
A catalog record has been applied for

Set by 7 in 10/12 Sabon
Produced by Longman Singapore Publishers (Pte) Ltd.
Printed in Singapore

Contents

Notes on the contributors		*vii*
General editors' preface		*x*
Acknowledgements		*xii*

1 Introduction
  John Lucas — 1

2 Milton's radical epic
  Michael Wilding — 19

3 Women and the opposition press after the Restoration
  Maureen Bell — 39

4 Two sansculotte poets: John Freeth and Joseph Mather
  Charles Hobday — 61

5 'Beware of reverence': writing and radicalism in the 1790s
  Paul O'Flinn — 84

6 Four Jacobin women novelists
  Loraine Fletcher — 102

7 Chartism and popular fiction
  Steve Devereux — 128

8 Collaboration and co-operation: a contextured-political reading of Edith Simcox's *Autobiography of a Shirtmaker*
  Pauline Polkey — 150

9   The 1920s: radicals to the right and to the left
    John Lucas   178

10 Literature, lying and sober truth: attitudes to the work of
    Patrick Hamilton and Sylvia Townsend Warner
    Arnold Rattenbury   201

11 '... itself irradiated by the thing it attacks'. Lawrence
    Ferlinghetti's 'One Thousand Fearful Words for Fidel Castro'
    and its political contexts
    R.J. Ellis   245

12 Home alone: re-thinking motherhood in contemporary
    feminist theatre
    Elaine Aston   281

Appendix: Documents   301
Selected bibliography   353
Index   355

Notes on contributors

Elaine Aston is author of *An Introduction to Feminism and Theatre* (London, 1995), co-author of *Theatre as Sign-System* (London, 1991), and co-editor of *Herstory: Plays By Women for Women: vols 1 and 2* (Sheffield, 1991). She has published a number of articles and essays on feminist theatre studies and is a senior lecturer at Loughborough University.

Maureen Bell is a lecturer in the School of English at the University of Birmingham. As well as publishing on the role of women in the seventeenth-century book trade, she has worked on women writers of the period and is co-editor with George Parfitt and Simon Shepherd of *A Biographical Dictionary of English Women Writers 1580–1720* (London, 1990). She is currently working on material for the *History of the Book in Britain* Project and on related aspects of book production and the economics of the trade. Her most recent publication (with John Barnard) is *The Early Seventeenth-Century York Book Trade and John Foster's Inventory of 1616* (Proceedings of the Leeds Philosophical and Literary Society, Vol XXIV, pt. II)

Steve Devereux was born in Beccles and, after failing his 11+ and receiving a Secondary Modern School education, worked as a printer, meat porter, cleaner, assembly line worker, textile machinist and farm labourer for twelve years. He was a shop steward at eighteen, an activist in SOGAT, TGWU, AEU and became a mature student at the University of East Anglia in the eary 1980s. Since 1991 he has been a lecturer at Liverpool Institute of Higher Education and is currently editing a collection of chartist fiction. He holds an MPhil from Manchester University.

R.J. (Dick) Ellis is Head of English at Nottingham Trent University where he teaches American and English Literature. Recent work has focused on the study of little magazines and on post-war American writing, including articles on Alice Walker, Kathy Acker, Jack Kerouac and William Burroughs. He was co-editor of the volume, *Science Fiction: Roots and Branches* (London, 1990).

Loraine Fletcher's first degree was from Reading University. She has an MA from Arizona State University and a doctorate from Birkbeck College, London on the works of Charlotte Smith. She teaches in the English Department at Reading University, has reviewed for *The Guardian* and the *New Statesman* and is at present preparing her doctoral thesis for publication.

Charles Hobday is the author of *Edgell Rickword: A Poet at War* (Manchester, 1989) and the editor of *The Collected Poems of Edgell Rickword* (Manchester, 1991). He has also contributed essays, mainly on Shakespearian themes, to *Shakespeare Survey*, *Renaissance and Modern Studies* and other literary journals.

John Lucas is Professor of English at Loughborough University. Among his many books are studies of England and Englishness, Dickens, Arnold Bennett, Elizabeth Gaskell, John Clare, and Twentieth-Century Poetry. He is also the author of several collections of poetry, the most recent of which is *Flying to Romania* (1992). His versions of the poems of *Egils Saga*, first published in 1975, is now a Dent/Everyman Classic.

Paul O'Flinn has taught English at Ibibio State College, Nigeria and at Trent University, Ontario and has also taught sociology at the University of Reading. He is currently Principal Lecturer in English at Oxford Brookes University. Previous publications include *Them and Us in Literature* (London, 1975) and *How to Study Romantic Poetry* (London, 1988).

Pauline Polkey was born in Liverpool in 1958 to working-class parents, both of whom were active in socialist politics. After returning to full-time education as a mature student in 1988, she has recently completed her doctoral thesis on British women's autobiographies, 1870–1900 and is currently preparing an edition of Edith Simcox's *Autobiography of a Shirt-Maker*. She lectures in English and Women's Studies at the Nottingham Trent University.

Arnold Rattenbury. After early demobilisation in the Second World War Arnold Rattenbury returned as an editor to *Our Time*, an approximately communist journal he had helped to found before conscription. There he worked with left-wing authors and artists of the 1920s and 1930s too old or disabled for war service. He has published four collections of poetry, a fifth and sixth will be published in 1996.

Michael Wilding is the author of *Milton's Paradise Lost* (Sydney, 1969), *Political Fictions* (London, 1980), *Dragons Teeth: Literature in the English Revolution* (Oxford, 1987), and *Social Visions* (Sydney, 1993). His fiction includes *Living Together* (Brisbane, Queensland Press, 1974), *Pacific Highway* (Hale & Iremonger, 1982), *The Paraguayan Experiment* (Harmondsworth, 1985), *Under Saturn* (Black Swan, 1988) and *Great Climate* (London, 1990). He holds a personal chair at the University of Sydney and is a Fellow of the Australian Academy of the Humanities.

General Editors' Preface

Crosscurrents is an interdisciplinary series which explores simultaneously the new terrain revealed by recently developed methodologies while offering fresh insights into more familiar and established subject areas. In order to foster the cross-fertilisation of ideas and methods the topic broached by each volume is rich and substantial and ranges from issues developed in culture and gender studies to the re-examination of aspects of English studies, history and politics. Within each of the volumes, however, the sharpness of focus is provided by a series of essays which is directed to examining that topic from a variety of perspectives. There is no intention that these essays, either individually or collectively, should offer the last word on the subject – on the contrary. They are intended to be stimulating rather than definitive, open-ended rather than conclusive, and it is hoped that each of them will be pithy, and thought-provoking.

Each volume has a general introduction setting out the scope of the topic, the various modes in which it has been developed and which places the volume as a whole in the context of other work in the field. Everywhere, from the introduction to the bibliographies, pointers will be given on how and where the ideas suggested in the volumes might be developed in different ways and different directions, and how the insights and methods of various disciplines might be brought to bear to yield new approaches to questions in hand. The stress throughout the books will be on crossing traditional boundaries, linking ideas and bringing together concepts in ways which offer a challenge to previously compartmentalised modes of thinking.

Some of the essays will deal with literary or visual texts which are well-known and in general circulation. Many touch on primary material which is not easily accessible outside major library collections, and where appropriate, that material has been placed in a portfolio of documents collected at the end of each volume. Here again, it is hoped that this will provide a stimulus to discussion; it will give readers who are curious to explore further the implications of the arguments an opportunity to develop their own initiatives and to broaden the spectrum of their reading.

The authors of these essays range from international writers who are established in their respective fields to younger scholars who are bringing fresh ideas to the subjects. This means that the styles of the chapters are as various as their approaches, but in each case the essays have been selected by the general editors for their high level of critical acumen.

Professor Barrie Bullen
Dr Paul Hyland
Dr Neil Sammells

Acknowledgements

We are grateful to the following for permission to reproduce copyright material:

New Directions Publishing Corp. for the poem 'One Thousand Fearful Words for Fidel Castro' by Lawrence Ferlinghetti in *Starting From San Francisco*. Copyright ©1961 by Lawrence Ferlinghetti; Random House UK Ltd/The Estate of Sylvia Townsend Warner for poems from *Whether a Dove or a Seagull* by S.T. Warner & V. Ackland and *OPUS 7* by S.T. Warner; the Dean and Chapter of Worcester for 'The Worcester Cathedral Misericord' postcard (Document 1); The British Library for the two photographs in Document 2, shelfmarks 444a21(3), Mirabilis Annus, 1661.

Whilst every effort has been made to trace the owners of copyright material, in a few cases this has proved impossible and we take this opportunity to offer our apologies to any copyright holders whose rights we may have unwittingly infringed.

1 Introduction

John Lucas

Radical: 'Forming the root, basis, or foundation; original, primary'. That is how the *Oxford English Dictionary* defines the word. But it then goes on: 'Advocating thorough or far-reaching change; representing or supporting an extreme section of a party.' For this definition it offers as example, 'seeking extreme action against the South at the time of the Civil War'. Presumably extreme action required the use of any necessary means to rid the South of slavery. What some label radicalism others might well regard as common-sense behaviour. But that is to say no more than that the word is a loaded one. Hence the fact that early in the nineteenth century it acquired the meaning of 'left-wing, revolutionary'; and in this inflection it is inevitably connected to the republican egalitarianism that inspired the French revolution. ('Left-wing' refers to the fact that in the early years of the Revolution, before they were overthrown by the Jacobins, the Girondists – the moderate Republicans – sat on the left of the Legislative Assembly.) From this develops a further range of meanings: 'characterised by departure from tradition; progressive, unorthodox'. Radical, in short, is a word within history as well as being a word with a history.

Nowadays radicalism is associated with oppositional forces. It means resistance to orthodoxy, to the accepted. It is therefore a term that implies marginality. Radical groups are minority groups, radical opinion is a departure from the norm, from the everyday, from common sense. It gathers to itself a frisson of the disreputable, the *outré*. As such, it can become fasionable. It then enters the world of non-kosher bohemianism or what has latterly been called radical chic. It's a way of making the headlines or at least the gossip columns. The 1960s phrase 'way out' implied that radicalism offered an exit to a world elsewhere for all the beautiful people. And so it did, at all events, until the cold winds of the 1970s began to blow, whereupon the beautiful people, as was famously said at the time, got their hair cut and went to law school.

Radical behaviour, whether genuine or ersatz, has its fascination and probably deserves a study to itself. (There are several good accounts of dandyism but that isn't quite the same thing, or rather dandyism is one kind of radical behaviour, although no more essential than, say, bohemian or anarchist behaviour.) In what follows, however, the concern is specifically with radicalism and writing, or rather writing as part of print culture. 'When Adam delved and Eve span, Who was then the Gentleman?' John Ball's great rhetorical question was radical in just about every sense. It looked back to the very origins of society and at the same time urged a far-reaching change in English society of the late fourteenth century and proposed what its opponents saw as extreme action in order to bring that change about. Given that those opponents were the men of power there was little chance that the Peasants' Revolt would succeed. Nor did it. As Dickens commented in his radical *Child's History of England*:

> The end of this rising [against the poll tax] was the then usual end. As soon as the King found himself safe, he unsaid all he had said, and undid all he had done; some fifteen hundred of the rioters were tried ... with great rigour, and executed with great cruelty. Many of them were hanged on gibbets, and left there as a terror to the country people ... The King's falsehood in this business makes such a pitiful figure, that I think Wat Tyler appears in history as beyond comparison the truer and more respectable man of the two.[1]

Dickens's written approbation of Tyler's radical behaviour was published in 1851, the year of the Great Exhibition, that glorification of monarchical as well as industrial Britain. Among the benefits of the industrialising process were the many improvements made to printing presses, so much so that we can fairly say that the book industry is part of the process. But when Ball and Tyler stood up to oppose the poll tax there were no printing presses at all. If they were prompted by any writing it seems likely to have been Wycliffe's English bible, on which he and his followers, the Lollards, had been labouring for some time prior to 1381. The writing of that bible was, then, a key radical moment. Control of reading and writing matter had hitherto been very largely in the hands of the church and as the church was governed from Rome that meant such writing was by and large unavailable to the laity, the majority of whom couldn't read. And of those few who could, most were unable to read church Latin. Wycliffe's bible was therefore dangerous because it threatened to take the power of understanding and interpretation away from churchmen and give it to lay people. Protestantism begins with Wycliffe and the Lollards (the name derives from the Dutch "lollen" – to sing in a low voice), and includes a denial of the doctrine of transubstantiation and an attack on the wealth and indolence of the clergy. Not surprisingly the Lollards were much persecuted, especially after the 1381 rising. Wycliffe himself escaped punishment for heresy because he was a friend of John of Gaunt, but without stretching a term too far it seems reasonable to say that his doctrines were both censured and censored.

This wasn't difficult to do. Wycliffe's bible had to be painstakingly copied by hand so that even if word of it spread there would be comparatively few who, for one reason or another, were in a position to read it.

Nearly a hundred years later, in 1476, William Caxton produced the first book to be printed in England and from then on the history of writing and censorship would become intertwined. With the advent of printed material the widespread dissemination of writing unfavourable to those in power became not merely likely but inevitable. The history of the book is therefore also the history of book-burning. There is no opportunity to follow that contention through here, but we need to note that censorship is Authority's tool and that it should be so is proof of the power of the written/printed word. Here, we might note Isaiah Berlin's remark that Alexander Herzen's

> celebrated periodical, which he called *The Bell (Kolokol)* . . . dealt with anything that seemed to be of topical interest. He exposed, he denounced, he derided, he preached, he became a kind of Russian Voltaire of the mid-nineteenth century . . . during the heyday of his fame Herzen exercised a genuine influence within Russia itself . . . by exposing abuses, naming names, but, above all, by appealing to liberal sentiment . . .[2]

In our own day it would be difficult to overestimate the importance of *samizdat* writing.

Once you can read you read on your own. That is what makes reading so potentially subversive, so dangerous as a radical activity and as a prelude to further, collective radical activity. The state's agents can't be looking through every window, hiding under every bed. Of course, bookprinters and sellers and those who make newspapers – printers, editors, journalists, distributors – can be prosecuted; and such censorship has always had state sanction. In the United Kingdom this sanction is said to be justified in the name of national security, or of the public interest, it being the state's argument that 'the public interest' precludes the public from having access to what might interest it. In earlier ages, the state – i.e. whoever held power – feared that 'factions' (those without power but who might want to challenge the ones who held it) were a threat to stability. Either way, the arguments for censorship usually turn out to be examples of self- interest masquerading as *pro bono publico*. This is a worldwide phenomenon.

The fear of public assembly is also widely shared by those who hold state power. To permit public assembly is in all probability to sanction factional interest. So runs the argument. Hence, stage censorship. Plays bring people together for what may well be dangerous (radical) purposes, as the famous playing of *Richard II* the night before the Essex rebellion in 1599 reminds us. The history of stage censorship in England is a fascinating one, especially in that prolonged period from 1624 when the Lord Chamberlain took over from the Master of the Revels the duty of supervising stage activities, down until 1968, when the responsibility was finally taken away from his office. It is not, however, a history to be traced in these pages, and with the exception of Elaine Aston's chapter on post-Lord Chamberlain times (Chapter 12), we have on the whole kept away from what is a vast and perhaps separate subject. Instead, we have chosen to interpret 'writing' as non-dramatic material.

Chapter 2 is on Milton. Early in his career Milton wrote the masque usually known as *Comus* which brilliantly subverted the politics of court masque. Where that had endorsed the power and authority of the throne, Milton provides an image of profligacy, false authority and licentiousness. In his study, *The Golden Age*

Restor'd: The Culture of the Stuart Court, 1603–42, Graham Parry notes that the refined cult of love at Court was bound to have damaging consequences because it highlighted

> the unreal atmosphere that prevailed at the heart of a kingdom that was becoming steadily more agitated about questions of political and religious authority. It was an exclusive cult, restricted to the inner circle of courtiers and literary wits. It haunted the plays of the period, and attained its fullest manifestation in the platonic subject matter of the masques, where the King and Queen in person expressed their mutual love.[3]

As D.J. Gordon has shown in his magisterially definitive essays on Court Masque, collected together as *The Renaissance Imagination* (1975), the amount of money spent on individual masques was part of their propaganda: the riches of the Stuart court were lavished on extolling its virtues. Yet the Castlehaven scandal revealed that such virtues were always liable to be more show than reality. In Christopher Hill's words:

> A major scandal of the early thirties concerned Lord Castlehaven, who was executed for buggery, for connivance at the rape of his wife by a servant who was also his lover, and for the prostitution of his daughter-in-law to another servant. Milton would certainly be aware of this *cause célèbre*; but it was brought forcibly to his notice when he was asked to write a masque for the Earl of Bridgewater, whose wife was Lady Castlehaven's sister.[4]

It is clear enough that Milton loaded onto the figure of Comus much that he detested and feared about the English Court, and that Comus's night-time world of rape and excess anticipates a great deal that goes into the figure of Satan in *Paradise Lost*. Hence Michael Wilding's powerfully argued contention that 'a consistent radical vision is present from [Milton's] earliest work'.

The *Masque* (1634/7) and *Paradise Lost* (1667) are separated by thirty years and were written either side of the Revolution and the Commonwealth period. It is therefore not surprising that Milton needed to exercise cunning in his attacks on the Court and this has sometimes misled commentators into thinking that Comus is no more to be identified with monarchical institutions, their abuse of power and privilege, than is Satan. Blake and

Shelley both thought Satan was Milton's secret hero. But that is because neither of these great Romantic poets could believe in the divine goodness of Milton's God. They therefore impose a Manichaean reading on Milton's poem. What is 'officially' good turns out to be bad and vice versa. That Satan has his real attractions is not to be denied. Without them how could he have hoped to succeed in gathering together so large a following? The same goes for Comus. But this is to pay tribute to Milton's imaginative understanding of the attractiveness of power and its silver-tongued plausibility. It isn't to question the intensity of his radicalism.

During the Commonwealth period Milton the radical became committed to pamphleteering. With the toppling of the monarchy freedom of speech and writing had suddenly become a reality. Out poured every kind of opinion, from sane to entirely crazy. That's how it always is at times of sudden liberty. Post-1917 Russia provides an obvious parallel, as does post-1789 France. And in all three cases the carnivalesque moment of joyous freedom is followed by a return to authority, censorship, repression. Revolution turns into its opposite. Milton was passionately opposed to censorship, as he makes plain in his 1644 pamphlet, *Areopagitica*. (The Areopagus is a hill to the north west of the Athenian acropolis where the members of the judicial council met.) But as the Commonwealth period lengthened so did the shadow of censorship. And with the restoration of Charles II censorship once again became a standard device of government, a means of law enforcement in the interest of the State. Those who fell foul of the law could expect imprisonment or worse. Bunyan, who from his long incarceration was entitled to be heard with respect, urged the cause of valiancy against disaster.

The cause was taken up by women, as Maureen Bell shows in her deeply informed Chapter 3 on the role of women in keeping opposition presses going after the restoration. She begins by quoting Serjeant Morton in 1664, for whom the 'Dispersing seditious books is very near a-kin to raising of tumults.' Books are dangerous. Women who print books are dangerous. But as Bell points out, 'women's status in law as marginal figures – creatures incapable, technically, of crimes – may have worked to protect them.' It didn't always do so but that radical, oppositional writing continued to be printed and dispersed under the most adverse conditions is at least partly due to the law's being an ass. It is even more owing to the courage of women who, during the Commonwealth period, had begun to find their voices (literally, in that they preached in certain communions as well as speaking at public assemblies); and the restoration was unable to return them to silence. I regret that *Writing and Radicalism* doesn't include a chapter on women's writing during the latter half of the seventeenth century or the first half of the eighteenth: there simply wasn't the space for it. But recent work by feminist literary historians means we are now in a much better position to recognise just how much good writing by women there was at that time and how it challenges and subverts Pope's implicit claim that women's writing was typically that of 'A maudlin Poetess'.

That phrase comes from the 'Epilogue to the Satires' where Pope betrays a deep discomfort with much contemporary writing. At least some of that would be writing by women, for as Roger Lonsdale remarks, 'From the 1730s, for various reasons, women began to find it easier and more acceptable to publish their verse.'[5] Male reaction to this was, for the most part, reactionary. Certainly, the three great names with whom Augustan values are conventionally identified – Swift, Pope and Johnson – were at one in making plain their customary opposition to women writers. This is not to deny that on occasions they could be affable, even supportive: Swift was friendly with the poet Mary Barber and Boswell records Johnson's approval of Fanny Burney's *Cecilia* and Anna Seward's 'Ode on the Death of Captain Cook'. But these were exceptional cases and did nothing to shake the widely shared conviction that women were meant for a life of married subservience. Even when a woman did publish a volume of poems it was likely to be by subscription and, in Lonsdale's words, 'The aim of such subscription was often less to encourage a woman writer to embark on a precarious literary career than to reward a "deserving" wife or mother and her family with some degree of financial security.'[6]

The hundred-year period between the restoration of Charles II and the accession to the throne of George III in 1760 was, so older literary historians were accustomed to telling us, the age of 'Tragic toryism'. The Augustans were of a piece in doing their damnedest to shore up a culture threatened by hostile forces. So ran the argument. And for 'hostile' it seems natural to read 'radical'. But where *were* these forces? There is a problem here. With the exception of Methodism it is difficult to locate any movement or moment which produces radical writing or which prepares the way for that radical energy which explodes in the last decade of the eighteenth century. And yet the tragic tories weren't taking up arms against a ghost army. Perhaps the best way to characterise what was happening is by thinking of a number of underground streams converging on one fault-line as a result of which, suddenly and wholly unexpectedly, they cause a gigantic landslip. There are inevitably limits to the usefulness of this image, but it does at least help us to understand that radicalism was not so much dead during the eighteenth century as finding ways back to the light after the disasters of 1660 and all that followed from it. Methodists, Unitarians, Free Thinkers, other Dissenters; anti-monarchists, whig (and Wilkite) democrats, sympathisers with the cause of American independence; anti-classicists, Gothicists, 'inspirationalists' who believed a Scottish ploughman (or even woman) might as easily be a great poet as someone from orthodox circumstance – these and others formed the hidden, half-heard streams converging on the faultline of century's end.

There had been earlier moments when the ground seemed, if not about to give way, then at least to shift a little. Ireland caused some tremors. Jonathan Swift's Irish Tracts, especially his great 'Modest Proposal', of 1729, and his 'Drapier's Letters', gathered together for pseudonymous publication in 1725, when it was described by Lord Wharton as 'this damned libellous pamphlet', were, in Walter Scott's words, vindications of 'Ireland's rights against the aggressions' of England. And I have suggested elsewhere that later in the century Goldsmith wrote not so much as tame Poll but as a subtly subversive Irish patriot. 'The Deserted Village' radicalises the sentimental genre of pastoral.[7]

But these and other minor shocks were absorbed by those in power who, as Linda Colley argues in *Britons*, were intent on 'forging the nation'. One way of doing this was to invoke Franco-phobia. Colley makes excellent use of Hogarth's 'Calais Gate, or the Roast Beef of Old England', executed in 1749, in order to help build her case:

The fat monk salivating over a newly roasted joint of imported English beef; the singularly unattractive nuns, bare-footed and fatuously pleased because they think they have found Christ's image in the features of a skate fish; the French soldiers, at once scrawny and ragged and curiously effeminate; even the forlorn Scottish Highlander, forced into exile and garlic-eating because he has rebelled against his Protestant sovereign George II: all these are rather ritualised figures of fun, an array of centuries-old Protestant stereotypes. Only after a time do we notice the really deadly and innovative part of Hogarth's satire. By the mere act of looking at the print we have come within the arch of a French prison. All of a sudden, we – the spectators – have become unfree, just like the French.[8]

Franco-phobia lasted for most of the century and would later re-emerge as a powerful element in the cement to bind Englishness into a unifying concept. But it was at least temporarily dissolved by the French Revolution. For with the events of 1789 France was no longer the nation of the *ancien régime* and Catholicism. Liberty, equality, fraternity: these were the watchwords of the new order. No wonder young and not-so young English people should be ecstatic at the prospect of realising that utopian vision in perfide Albion. Wordsworth's recollection of the moment is well known;

> Bliss was it in that dawn to be alive,
> But to be young was very heaven!

And because it is so well known, as are the radical writings of other Romantic Poets, all of whom were in different ways responsive to events in France, there seems no good reason to devote space to them in the present collection of essays. It isn't at all difficult to find good accounts of radical Blake, Shelley, and the rest. An essay on the sansculottists John Freeth and Joseph Mather is, however, a rarity in that it introduces us to the existence of writing that has been persistently overlooked by literary historians of the period.

Charles Hobday in Chapter 4 hints at an especially teasing question, of just how popular or otherwise George III was during the late 1780s and 1790s. Colley argues that by then 'Farmer George' had transformed public perception of the monarchy and in the process had saved it: he had ceased to be reviled, had indeed become widely venerated, even loved. Hobday remarks that radical in some ways though Freeth was, his references to George were 'almost all respectful'. This may seem to support Colley's argument. Yet against it we have to set the passionate republicanism of Blake who, as E.P. Thompson and others have shown, was speaking out of a London of artisanal popular culture. It is worth noting that the government of the day was sufficiently alarmed by republican tendencies among radicals to use every means at its disposal to oppose them. Hence, the hatred and fear of Tom Paine, especially given his claim in *The Rights of Man* (1791) that the monarchy was incapable of lasting more than a few more years. The repressions of the 1790s are every bit as important as the upsurge in radical writing, and are, it hardly needs to be said, a direct, brutal response to such writing. They have been studied by, among others, David Worrall, in *Radical Culture: Discourse, Resistance and Surveillance, 1790–1820* (London, 1992, Ian McCalman, in *Radical Underworld: Prophets, Revolutionaries, and Pornographers in London, 1795–1840* (Oxford, 1992), and by E.P. Thompson, in his classic *The Making of the English Working Class* (London, 1963).

It is always possible to argue that repression was out of all proportion to threat, that it was an over-reaction to imagined fears of what went on 'under the vast smug surface' of ordinary life, to use Henry James's formulation. But Paul O'Flinn's cheering Chapter 5 reminds us that throughout the 1790s a wholly energised and energising amount of radical writing really *was* being produced; and he is surely correct in saying that 'What we have in the writing of the 1790s is a glimpse of men and women, impelled by brave curiosity, involved in ... system-making and system-breaking, inspiring examples of Marx's dictum that in transforming the world we transform ourselves.'

It is therefore important that O'Flinn's contribution should be followed by Loraine Fletcher's pioneering essay on Four Jacobin women novelists (Chapter 6). If working-class writers have been little written about, the same is true, perhaps even truer, of women writers of the period. Where they have received attention it is usually, Fletcher tartly notes, as precursors of Jane Austen and Mary Shelley. Yet they were formed by very different circumstances. Fletcher points out that in 1789 her chosen writers were already mature women who were 'defining for themselves feminist attitudes that were just starting to be called "radical"'. This requires of them that they 'blur the line between life and fiction', and I suggest that in so doing they contribute to the radicalising of autobiography that will prove so crucial in nineteenth-century writing, where it becomes a way of testing to the limit notions of selfhood, and thus calls into question assumptions of gender, class, and the very concept of an ontologically secure identity.

Class begins to emerge as an issue of the first importance as the years round into the nineteenth century and as Britain moves slowly towards the possibility of a democratically elected government. The Reform Act of 1832, fiercely opposed though it was by much of the aristocracy – and for that matter, by William IV – enfranchised large numbers of people but kept still more from possessing the power of the vote. These were mostly working-class people. Because they came together to labour in factories, mills and mines, it was inevitable that they should develop a collective consciousness – a working-class consciousness – of their withheld rights. From this came the Chartist movement, including Chartist poets and novelists. In his chapter on Chartism and popular fiction (Chapter 7), Steve Devereux argues that we cannot and should not try to accommodate chartist fiction within the conventional formal modes or to judge it by standards of cultural orthodoxy. It isn't intended to be 'art'. Quite the contrary, in fact. Chartist writers, Devereux argues, 'appear to have made a conscious decision to move away from ... heroic writing and towards a more recognisably popular form of fiction'. But this imposes its own limits: it even de-radicalises what writers attempt to do. Concern for what their readers will expect interferes with the integrity of the writing.

This touches on an important point. By the middle years of the nineteenth century the novel had become the dominant literary form, overwhelmingly so indeed. Fortunes could be made from writing fiction, and the book industry saw to it that novelists were promoted as readily as cures for ailments. But this meant that writers had a keener sense of audience than ever before. State censorship might have eased off but other forms were quick to take its place. In *Our Mutual Friend* Dickens wonderfully satirises middle-class prurience in Podsnap's insistence that nothing should be allowed to bring a blush to the cheek of a young person; but, mindful perhaps of the power of the temperence movement, his later novels backed off from scenes of genial drunkenness which had been such a feature of his early work. I would not say that this seriously compromised his radicalism, but he undoubtedly had to find new strategies, and this was true of other writers.

Sex in particular was a problem. To understand why this should have been so we need to note the conditions of book making and selling during the period. Most novels came in two- or three-volume form. That made them expensive, which was good for the writer and even better for the publisher, assuming sales were satisfactory. But it put books beyond the pocket of many readers. Some paid a subscription to join a circulating library and selected their fiction from that (often the back shelves of a shop). This gave the libraries enormous power, because a refusal to stock a certain novel would seriously damage its sales. Publishers were alert to this. They saw no point in publishing a novel they couldn't hope to sell to the libraries. Meredith's *The Ordeal of Richard Feverel* (1861) provided the test case. According to Jack Lindsay, 'many parsons seem to have banned it from the parish book-clubs';[9] and he quotes a letter from Meredith to a friend, in which Meredith comments mordantly on the decision of Mudie, the non-conformist head of the main lending library, to withdraw the novel 'in consequence of the urgent remonstrances of several respectable families who objected to it as dangerous and wicked and damnable'. Not surprisingly, other publishers took care not to repeat Chapman and Hall's mistake.

Well, so what? Censorship of any kind is no doubt very undesirable, but what has the kind I have just been discussing to do with radicalism? A great deal, as it happens. Meredith was deeply sympathetic to women's causes. Feminist historians have shown that during the latter half of the nineteenth century women's increasingly powerful struggles to assert themselves were opposed by increasingly oppressive methods. The 'sensation' novels of the 1860s in various ways explored the problems of the hysterical woman. (The term 'hysteria' is derived from the Greek for 'womb'.) And 'neurasthenia' became identified as a newly fashionable illness for middle-class women. Neurasthenia signified a mental and physical collapse, the kind of illness that we are likely to call 'breakdown'. But both hysteria and neurasthenia were troublingly related to middle-class women's perceived social roles and functions: as wives, mothers and upholders of family values. Feminist historians have persuasively argued that both 'hysteria' and 'neurasthenia' were terms created by a male-controlled medical profession in order to explain the pathology of women's behaviour – specifically, the behaviour of women discontented with and protesting against the image in which a patriarchal society imprisoned them.

To put matters this way is, I realise, seriously to foreshorten. It is even to come close to parody. On the other hand, the panicky (hysterical?) response of some men to the importation of French fiction in the 1870s and 1880s serves to show how much had been repressed in the years before. In his 'Familiar Colloquy', published in the journal *The Nineteenth Century* (August, 1878), W.H. Mallock described Gautier's *Mme de Maupin* as 'the foulest and filthiest book that ever man put pen to. It is the glorification of nameless and shameless vice.' Any man who gave it to his sister to read ought to be horse-whipped, Mallock said. Presumably it might give her the wrong ideas. (The association of French novels with a new 'loose' morality is made much of in Henry James's *The Awkward Age*, whose cast of adulterers and adulteresses are addicted to French paperback fiction.) But once French novels began to arrive it was difficult to stop them. They not only had the allure of the forbidden, they were also cheap to buy. The publisher Henry Vizetelly, who did much to make them available, had hit on the simple idea of issuing them as paperbacks, which at a stroke took away the all-but-in-name censorship of the circulation libraries. Most people could afford to buy from Vizetelly's list of novels, which were marketed in their distinctive yellow paper covers. (Hence, the term 'yellow period', sometimes used of the period otherwise known as the decadence or *fin de siècle*.)

There were setbacks. Vizetelly served a prison sentence for publishing 'obscene' literature – that of Zola. In 1885 George Moore persuaded Vizetelly to issue his risqué novel *A Mummer's Wife*, in one volume, which partly offset the loss of sales to circulating libraries; and Moore then put out a furious pamphlet,

Literature at Nurse, attacking the role of such libraries: 'Into this nursery none can enter except in baby clothes; and the task of discriminating between a divided skirt and a pair of trousers is performed by the librarian . . . it is certain that never in any age or country have writers been asked to perform under such restricted conditions.'[10] The vicious, vengeful trial of Oscar Wilde has to be seen in the context of the late nineteenth-century struggle to re-impose the authority of moral 'norms', as does the subsequent persecution of Aubrey Beardsley, whose artwork for the provocatively titled journal, *The Yellow Book*, was held to be tainted by association with Wilde-like perversions.

Wilde was not only homosexual. He was, as Tom Paulin has called him, 'an aesthetic fenian'. He had also written a typically mordant, searching essay on socialism as the ideal for the future. With the abolition of private property, Wilde said, 'nobody will waste his life in accumulating things, and the symbols for things. One will live. To live is the rarest thing in life. Most people exist, that is all.'[11] Wilde is here very close to much that William Morris argued in *News from Nowhere*, 1891, and the essays he published in his journal *Commonwealth*. In the closing years of the nineteenth-century, socialism – whether of the Fabian or Marxist variety – was beginning to exert a most powerful influence on men's political thinking, one that entailed a re-thinking of the family and of women's roles both there and in the workplace. That is well enough known. Far less well known is how this affected women. Pauline Polkey's important Chapter 8 shows that Edith Simcox's much-referred to but scarcely known autobiography can be read as, among other things, evidence of how she and other women chose to find ways of acting – intervening – in political matters and as such necessarily rejected their 'given' roles. Here, Simcox's account of the setting up of the shirt-making firm, Hamilton & Co., as a co-operative venture, is of the greatest significance, as is Polkey's own self-conscious use of the term co-operative as 'gender-specific and politically-specific'.

In the opening years of the twentieth century, radical writing is often buoyant with the hopes of making a new world. Yet underneath the surface confidence of, say, Shaw and Wells, runs a wide, dark counter-current. E.M. Forster's *Howard's End*, with its famous epigraph 'Only Connect', more than hints at the possibility of disconnection, of the coming of an outer world of 'telegrams and anger' which duly materialised in August, 1914. And though some young men rushed eagerly to join in what they thought of as a crusade, it soon became apparent that they were not 'swimmers into cleanness leaping', as Rupert Brooke put it. The First World War was not an escape from modernity. It was the confirmation of modernity. The 'war to end all wars' did not lend itself to swift-footed cavalry and acts of individual heroism. It was a machine war and those who supplied the machines to which millions of lives were fed were, of course, capitalists.

Post-war attitudes have therefore often been characterised as dominated by a world-weary cynicism, the joyless hedonism of 'The Bright Young Things'. But my own contribution to *Writing and Radicalism* (Chapter 9) challenges this reading of the post-war decade. Radical politics not only survive into the 1920s, in both activity and writing they are sharpened by an angry awareness of the sham of established, 'orthodox' values which had led to war, had supported it, and whose upholders now proposed that there should be 'business as usual'. For an important number of young writers the business of the future had to be very different.

Among such writers were Sylvia Townsend Warner and Patrick Hamilton, the subjects of Arnold Rattenbury's impassioned Chapter 10. Both came to Marxism through their experience of the 1920s and their contempt for habits of thought and social modes which, though all-too obviously moribund, appallingly wasteful of human lives and destructive of creative energies, nevertheless still claimed and in some measure enjoyed authority. In 'The Soul of Man Under Socialism', Wilde had remarked that 'Agitators are a set of interfering, meddling people, who come down to some perfectly contented class of the community, and sow the seeds of discontent among them. That is the reason why agitators are so absolutely necessary.'[12] As hunger marches and the General Strike of 1926 make very plain, in no sense could the British working class of the 1920s or 1930s be called perfectly content. But Townsend Warner and Hamilton certainly saw their writing as the work of agitators, in the all-important sense that they directed it towards investigating and exploring the endemic injustices and rottenness of capitalist society, though hardly ever in a propagandist way. Both writers characteristically go 'deeper' than the study of social manners or deployment of political allegory with which they are sometimes (dis)credited.

Doing justice to Townsend Warner and Hamilton requires Rattenbury to tear off the cold war wrappers which hid their Marxism and made it possible for them to be re-shelved among the odds-and-sods. Unofficial censorship again. Censorship of a more formal kind saw to it that certain Communist Party members had a hard time getting published. Rattenbury supplies the evidence and reminds us that 'so superior have the English always been about McCarthyism in the States, that the politeness of his counterpart McSh-sh and Lists of the Damned in their own country has gone largely unremarked'. The difficulties that faced radical writers in America during the McCarthy period I assume to be well enough known to require no comment here. But R.J. Ellis's detailed study in Chapter 11 of Lawrence Ferlinghetti's 'One Thousand Fearful Words for Fidel Castro' very persuasively shows how such a poem comes out of a specific set of conditions, including west-coast anarchism and other elements in what Ellis calls 'the particular socio-political climate created by then recent events in political history', which inevitably include the cold war and its attendant politics of paranoia.

Ellis provides a fascinating, extremely detailed study of a particular poem which could have been written at no other time. The plays about which Elaine Aston so interestingly writes are also necessarily of their moment. She begins with the Tory government's 1993 attack on single mothers, looks back on developing feminist arguments about 'the politics of motherhood', and then considers a number of contemporary feminist plays which explore issues to do with motherhood. She ends by noting that during the fifteen-year period she covers, from 1979–94, her chosen plays have, whether explicitly or otherwise, testified to a regime of ' "us and them" – a "major" record of achievement of which the Tories can be "dead proud".' As with all the other contributors to the present collection, Aston's own radicalism is very properly written into her Chapter 12.

I recognise that to say this is to lay myself open to the charge that *Writing and Radicalism* lacks impartiality. Of course it does. On the other hand, the individual chapters, whether wide-ranging or closely focused on a single text, attend to the social, political and historical contexts out of which radical writing comes and to which it makes its response, diagnostic, exploratory, corrective. That is why those who claim impartiality for themselves are always ready to censor radical writing. Its partiality for getting to the root of the matter endangers the interests of those who derive their authority from mystificatory claims to be charged with responsibility for holding close to 'truths' which it can profit nobody else to possess. A certain kind of critic will undoubtedly want to dismiss this as irrational prejudice or, as it is sometimes called by the upholders of impartiality, 'the politics of paranoia'. In which case – in *any* case – I recommend a quick glance through copies of *Index on Censorship* or the files of Amnesty International. And we should not forget that 'being economical with the truth' is accepted tactics for a government which, in the early 1980s, put pressure on the BBC not to allow E.P. Thompson to give the Richard Dimbleby Memorial Lecture because he planned to attack the official nuclear arms policy and because his lecture would not only be witnessed by millions but would be read by countless others when, as was bound to be the case, it was published in *The Listener*. Mindful, no doubt, of its role as the voice of the nation – or should that be the state – the BBC caved in. That's impartiality for you.

Notes

1. There being no standard edition of *A Child's History of England* there is not much point in giving a page reference to the edition I have used. The quotation comes from Ch. XIX, 'England Under Richard the Second'.
2. Isaiah Berlin, Introduction. In A. Herzen, *Childhood, Youth and Exile* (Oxford, 1980), p. xvi.
3. G. Parry, *The Golden Age Restor'd: The Culture of the Stuart Court, 1603–42*, (Manchester, 1981), p. 206.
4. C. Hill, *Milton and the English Revolution* (London, 1977), p. 43.
5. Roger Lonsdale, *Eighteenth-Century Women Poets: An Anthology* (Oxford, 1989), p. xxvi.
6. Ibid., p. xvii.
7. See J. Lucas, *England and Englishness* (London, 1990), ch. 3.
8. Linda Colley, *Britons: Forging the Nation, 1707–1837* (New Haven, 1992), p. 33.
9. Jack Lindsay, *George Meredith: His Life and Work*, (London, 1956), p. 94.

10. Quoted in Graham Owens (ed.), *George Moore's Life and Art* (Edinburgh, 1968), p. 48.
11. Oscar Wilde, *De Profundis and Other Writings* (Harmondsworth, 1987), p. 26.
12. Ibid., p. 23.

2 Milton's radical epic

Michael Wilding

John Milton's commitment to social justice, to a primal egalitarianism, is basic throughout his literary production. A consistent radical vision is present from his earliest work. The indictment of the unequal distribution of wealth in *A Maske Presented At Ludlow Castle, 1634* (*Comus*) is one of the great dramatic utterances of the English literary heritage. The Lady declares:

> If every just man that now pines with want
> Had but a moderate and beseeming share
> Of that which lewdly-pampered Luxury
> Now heaps upon some few with vast excess,
> Nature's full blessing would be well-dispensed
> In unsuperfluous even proportion,
> And she no whit encumbered with her store;
> And then the giver would be better thanked
> His praise due paid . . . (768–76)[1]

The radicalism is unambiguous and incontrovertible.[2]

Three years later, in 'Lycidas', he denounces the corrupt clergy of the reactionary church of England, indicting their careerism, greed and idleness.[3] 'The pilot of the Galilean lake' (St Peter) 'stern bespake':

> 'How well could I have spared for thee, young swain,
> Enow of such as, for their bellies' sake,
> Creep, and intrude, and climb into the fold!
> Of other care they little reckoning make
> Than how to scramble at the shearers' feast,
> And shove away the worthy bidden guest;
> Blind mouths! That scarce themselves know how to hold

> A sheep-hook, or have learned aught else the least
> That to the faithful herdman's art belongs!
> What recks it them? What need they? They are sped;
> And, when they list, their lean and flashy songs
> Grate on their scrannel pipes of wretched straw;
> The hungry sheep look up, and are not fed,
> But, swoll'n with wind and the rank mist they draw,
> Rot inwardly, and foul contagion spread . . . '(113–27)

As well as clergy the indictment of bad shepherds includes academics and poets,[4] all of those whose teaching lacks substance and leaves their listeners 'swoll'n with wind'.

With the outbreak of the revolution, Milton became a prolific and increasingly radical pamphleteer and polemicist.[5]

It is often said that Milton took a radical step in writing his epic *Paradise Lost* in English rather than in Latin. But the vernacular epic was well established with Dante, Camoens and Spenser. To have published a Latin epic at this late stage, 1667, would have been absurd. One of the major projects of the English revolution had been to complete the access to major texts begun with the introduction of the English language bible into churches in 1532. The publishing explosion consequent upon the breakdown of censorship in the 1640s resulted in the large-scale availability in English translation of works previously restricted to a privileged elite educated in Latin.

The radical aspect of *Paradise Lost* resides in the choice of theme and in the redefinition of epic values. The epic characteristically celebrated the tribal group or nation. A narrow, local patriotism informs Homer's *Iliad* and Virgil's *Aeneid*. Milton rejects that tradition and chooses the theme of the Fall of Adam and Eve. It is a foundation myth but what is founded is the human race, not a particular nation. The focus is on the loss of Paradise rather than on the establishment of a dynasty. Milton had once considered writing an epic on King Arthur; but the collapse of the English republic and the restoration of the monarchy in 1660, the failure of the English revolution, made him disinclined to celebrate his native land.

But as always with Milton it is dangerous to make too dogmatic or simplistic an assertion. It is tempting to say that his choice of the theme of Paradise represents a refusal to write about Britain. At the same time, however, to write of Paradise was also to write of Britain. The slogan of the English Peasants' Revolt of 1381 took Paradise as its touchstone:

> When Adam delved and Eve span
> Who was then the gentleman?

The restoration of primal social equality and just distribution of wealth was the aim of these pioneering English revolutionaries. The image of honest labour – Adam with spade, Eve with distaff – survives in woodcarvings in English churches. The slogan underpins *Paradise Lost*.

England as Paradise – spoiled or potential – was given a new currency by John of Gaunt in Shakespeare's *Richard II*: 'This other Eden, demi-paradise' (II. i.42). Again the context is revolutionary. *Richard II* dramatizes the overthrow of a monarch. Queen Elizabeth took the point: 'Know that I am Richard.' The play was contracted to be performed the day before Essex's unsuccessful rebellion. Later, in the 1650s, Marvell uses the concept in 'Upon Appleton House', the poem he wrote commemorating the estate of the retired commander-in-chief of the Parliamentary army.

> Oh Thou, that dear and happy Isle
> The Garden of the World ere while,
> Thou *Paradise* of four Seas,
> Which *Heaven* planted us to please,
> But, to exclude the World, did guard
> With watry if not flaming Sword;
> What luckless Apple did we tast,
> To make us Mortal, and Thee Wast? (321–8)[6]

England as a lost Paradise is a potent image for the English radical. There is no doubt it is a calculated subtext in *Paradise Lost*. When Satan proposes a mission from Hell to search out Paradise, Eden is paraphrased as 'The happy isle' (II. 410). England is clearly denoted.

Milton, then, rejected a nationalist commemoration of Britain in favour of a cosmic epic, preceding and transcending nationalism. Yet simultaneously he inscribed a potent British radical image that suggests England could have been, indeed once was, a Paradise; and he indicates in the course of the poem the forces that have spoiled it (the abandonment of common ownership, the development of the value systems he identifies with Satan and Hell). So the English radical theme is reasserted in the cosmic epic.

The radical departure from traditional epic practice here is significant. Compare Milton's practice with Bakhtin's definition of the epic:

> The epic as a genre in its own right may, for our purposes, be characterized by three constitutive features: (1) a national epic past – in Goethe's and Schiller's terminology the 'absolute past' – serves as the subject for the epic; (2) national tradition (not personal experience and the free thought that grows out of it) serves as the source for the epic; (3) an absolute epic distance separates the epic world from contemporary reality, that is, from time in which the singer (the author and his audience) lives.[7]

The nationalist past and tradition of (1) and (2) are significantly absent. And rather than preserving an absolute epic distance, Milton pointedly introduces contemporary reference: in the way the world of Hell parallels his contemporary world, in the references to parliamentary practice, gunpowder, and imperial trading adventures which we shall discuss later, and in the explicit references to contemporary and near contemporary historical figures like Galileo, whom Milton had visited ('the Tuscan artist,' I. 288) and Columbus ('such of late / Columbus found,' IX. 1115–16).

Milton's systematic redefinition of epic is characteristic of his strategy. He removes the nationalist component, redefining his epic as cosmic, and then reinserts a contemporary nationalist reference to England as the paradisal 'happy isle'. In a similar way he opens the poem with a vision of splendid epic rebellion, only to redefine the nature of rebellion, deepening our thinking about rebellion and epic.

At first glance Satan is the archetypal rebel, resisting the arbitrary authoritarianism of God. This was the reading of *Paradise Lost* that appealed to the Romantic poets – Blake and Shelley especially – and that continued through to William Empson.[8] The poem records Satan's rebellion in Heaven; it opens with Satan and his followers in defeat in Hell, and follows their revenge on God in Satan's destruction of Adam and Eve.

It is the destruction of Adam and Eve and the ensuing human race that is markedly less admirable than the heroic speeches of resistance, and it is this that requires our rethinking of Satan's epic heroism. Satan as the master of lies is characteristically and inevitably ambiguous, and Milton exploits this ambiguity to make the reader rethink. And by an extraordinary, outrageous and absolutely persuasive reversal of received thinking, Milton redefines revolution. He confronts the established, ruling-class ideology head on; you are the rebels, he declares, you are the perpetrators of revolution against divine authority, against the good. The radical activists on earth are not rebels, they are the emissaries of divine truth attempting to restore the primal state.[9] So the poem opens:

> Of man's first disobedience, and the fruit
> Of that forbidden tree whose mortal taste
> Brought death into the world, and all our woe,
> With loss of Eden, till one greater man
> Restore us, and regain the blissful seat,
> Sing, heavenly Muse . . . (I. 1–6)

The emphatic positioning of 'Restore us' at the poem's beginning is an extraordinary assertion. The word 'restore' had been appropriated by the monarchical reaction that had destroyed the English revolution and brought the 'Restoration' of 1660. Milton seizes it back. The true restoration is to the primal paradisal state. Monarchy is the rebellion against God.

In the course of the poem Milton spells this out. Satan is unambiguously identified as 'The monarch' (II. 467) who uses 'The tyrant's plea' (IV. 394). He sits 'on a throne of royal state' (II. 1) in parody of 'the almighty Father . . . High throned above all height' (III. 56–8).

Satan is traditionally the first, the archetypal rebel. Milton simultaneously presents him as the archetypal monarch. Monarchy is the fruit of Satan's rebellion, an institution invented in a futile attempt to imitate the divine. It was not something established by God. Humanity was established as equal in Paradise; there were no social ranks. This is spelled out in the culminating book of the epic when Adam is shown a vision of the career of Nimrod (XII. 24–37).

The ideal social model is 'fair equality, fraternal state'. But Nimrod 'will arrogate dominion undeserved / Over his brethren', (XII: 27–28) just as Satan aspired 'To set himself in glory above his peers' (I. 39). It is a rebellion against the divinely instituted egalitarianism. Nimrod's name derives from the Hebrew verb 'to rebel'; but this arch rebel, like every ruling elite, accuses others of rebellion.

Adam's response to this vision is to reassert the original divine establishment of human equality:

> O execrable son, so to aspire
> Above his brethren, to himself assuming
> Authority usurped, from God not given;
> He gave us only over beast, fish, fowl,
> Dominion absolute; that right we hold
> By his donation: but man over men
> He made not lord – such title to himself
> Reserving, human left from human free. (XII. 64–71)

The assertion has a further radical resonance. Milton is here offering the same socio-political interpretation of Genesis as the Diggers made in 1649. The Diggers attempted to found a communist society. Their manifesto *The True Levellers' Standard Advanced: or the State of Community Opened and Presented to the Sons of Men* declared:

> In the beginning of time, the great creator Reason made the earth to be a common treasury, to preserve the beasts, birds, fishes and man, the lord that was to govern this creation, for man had domination given to him, over the beasts, birds and fishes; but not one word was spoken in the beginning, that one branch of mankind should rule over another.[10]

In the same year Milton wrote in *The Tenure of Kings and Magistrates,* his defence of the judicial execution of Charles I:

> No man who knows ought, can be so stupid to deny that all men naturally were born free, being the image and resemblance of God himself, and were by privilege above all the creatures, born to command and not to obey: and that they liv'd so. Till from the root of Adam's transgression, falling among themselves to doe wrong and violence, and foreseeing that such courses must needs

tend to the destruction of them all, they agreed by common league to bind each other from mutual injury, and joyntly to defend themselves against any that gave disturbance or opposition to such agreement. Hence came Citties, Townes and Common-wealths. And because no faith in all was found sufficiently binding, they saw it needful to ordaine som authoritie, that might restraine by force and punishment what was violated against peace and common right. . . . [11]

Mankind was not born to dominion over mankind. Structures of rule and control were established after the Fall, as a direct consequence of the Fall, of Satan's destruction of the original paradisal state.

Milton's strategy here is important. He is asserting that a radical vision is primary, not reactive. It has always been the argument of the ruling class that they are the natural rulers and that any radical challenge is reactive, disruptive, subversive. Milton resolutely confronts this position. As he wrote in *Areopagitica* (1644):

> There be who perpetually complain of schisms and sects, and make it such a calamity that any man dissents from their maxims. 'Tis their own pride and ignorance which causes the disturbing, who neither will hear with meekness, nor can convince; yet all must be suppressed which is not found in their syntagma. They are the troublers, they are the dividers of unity, who neglect and permit not others to unite those dissevered pieces which are yet wanting to the body of Truth. (p. 608)

The revolutionary programme, the radical agenda, is the restoration of primal unity, primal truth, primal equality.[12]

Like the Diggers' settlement, Paradise was communist.[13] There was no private property, earth was 'a common treasury'. Celebrating the institution of marriage, Milton wrote:

> Hail, wedded love, mysterious law, true source
> Of human offspring, sole propriety
> In Paradise of all things common else. (IV. 750–2)

The Ranters of the English Revolution had extended their communism to sexuality.[14] Milton, like the Diggers, opposed this. But he emphatically asserts that in every other sphere there was no private possession, 'all things common else'. It is a brief assertion, half a line in an epic, but it is unambiguously stated and at no point retracted. Unobtrusive enough to slip past the censors, who carefully scrutinised this work of a high profile revolutionary, it spells out unassailably the social model of Paradise.[15]

Moreover, it is not a property obsessed, materialist life in Paradise. The emphasis is on simplicity. When the archangel Raphael visits, Adam

> walks forth, without more train
> Accompanied than with his own complete
> Perfections; in himself was all his state,
> More solemn than the tedious pomp that waits
> On princes, when their rich retinue long
> Of horses led and grooms besmeared with gold
> Dazzles the crowd and sets them all agape. (V. 351-7)

Paradisal existence is defined in contrast with earthly ruling-class corruptions, with the 'tedious pomp' designed to mystify the ruled. Milton's contempt for this political show is caught in the way the grooms are 'besmear'd' with gold. In contrast, when Adam and Eve entertain Raphael the emphasis is on nature rather than artifice:

> Raised of grassy turf
> Their table was, and mossy seats had round,
> And on her ample square, from side to side,
> All autumn piled, though spring and autumn here
> Danced hand-in-hand. A while discourse they hold –
> No fear lest dinner cool. . . . (V. 391-6)

The stress is on the advantages of paradisal primitivism. The food is freshly, freely on hand and does nopt need to be cooked. As for utensils, Adam and Eve simply pick fruits and use the shells:

> The savoury pulp they chew, and in the rind,
> Still as they thirsted, scoop the brimming stream. (IV. 335-6)

There is no unnecessary commodity production. There are no markets, no vanity fair.

Importantly, Adam and Eve are vegetarian. There is no death, no killing in Paradise till after the Fall. They live in friendship and harmony with the animals:

> About them frisking played
> All beasts of the earth, since wild, and of all chase
> In wood or wilderness, forest or den. (IV. 340–2)

It is a vision of primal harmony, the peaceable kingdom. Humanity's relationship with nature is an indicator of its relationship with itself. Political radicalism has at various times tended to forget this holistic vision; the vegetarianism of numerous radical writers – Shelley, George Bernard Shaw, Jack Lindsay – has tended to be marginalized, though the emergence of an environmental politics, the green movement, has brought these issues back into focus. They are all part of a whole – freedom, equality, environmental concern, vegetarianism, anti-militarism, common ownership.

After the Fall flesh-eating is introduced. Death declares:

> such a scent I draw
> Of carnage, prey innumerable, and taste
> The savour of death from all things there that live. (X. 267–9)

The introduction of death is in terms associated with eating: 'prey', 'taste', 'savour':

> So saying, with delight he snuffed the smell
> Of mortal change on earth. As when a flock
> Of ravenous fowl, though many a league remote,
> Against the day of battle, to a field
> Where armies lie encamped come flying, lured
> With scent of living carcasses designed
> For death the following day in bloody fight;
> So scented the grim feature, and upturned
> His nostril wide into the murky air,
> Sagacious of his quarry from so far. (X. 272–81)

Flesh eating is one human activity alien to Paradise before the fall. The other associated activity likewise alien is warfare, and Milton's rejection of militarism is one of the most radical features of his epic, and it is here closely linked with Death's carnivorousness.

The possibilities for presenting Paradise are various; they all clearly depend on a vision of social good. The Old Man of the Mountains offered a paradise of flowing drinks and enticing young women to the hashish-entranced assassins he trained. Milton's paradise is markedly not a place of rest and recreation leave for killers. It is not a paradise of idleness and indulgence. There was sexuality; that is stressed in radical opposition to those who would deny it. And centrally there is work. It is not exploitative, alienated labour; it is work without undue pressures, work that is part of the totality of their existence, work that stimulates the appetite and that makes rest a delight rather than a tedium.

> They sat them down, and after no more toil
> Of their sweet gardening labour than sufficed
> To recommend cool Zephyr, and made ease
> More easy, wholesome thirst and appetite
> More grateful, to their supper-fruits they fell. . . (IV. 327–31)

It is work, but it is not burdensome: this point is reiterated in IX (235–9).

In Milton's radical vision work is central to human life. Paradise is a place of work. He does not offer an aristocratic ideal of indulgence and diversion. It is not a leisure-class vision of idleness. There are no servants in Paradise, no handmaidens, no slaves, no robots, no labour-saving devices. Labour is a central part of Paradise. As Marx wrote in *Capital*:

> As creator of use-values, as useful labour, labour is a necessary condition of human existence, and one that is independent of the forms of human society; it is, through all the ages, a necessity imposed by nature itself, for without it there can be no interchange of materials between man and nature – in a word, no life.[16]

In contrast to Paradise, Milton presents Hell as materialist, technological, sophisticated, hierarchical and militaristic. Pandemonium is established:

> Built like a temple, where pilasters round
> Were set, and Doric pillars overlaid
> With golden architrave; nor did there want
> Cornice or frieze, with bossy sculptures graven;
> The roof was fretted gold. Not Babylon
> Nor great Alcairo such magnificence
> Equalled in all their glories. . . . (I. 713–19)

The stress is on architectural splendour, on the intimidating buildings of an absolutist regime. The inspiration for such achievement is Mammon (whose name is the Aramaic word for riches)

>   Mammon led them on –
> Mammon, the least erected spirit that fell
> From heaven; for even in heaven his looks and thoughts
> Were always downward bent, admiring more
> The riches of heaven's pavement, trodden gold,
> Than aught divine or holy else enjoyed
> In vision beatific; by him first
> Men also, and by his suggestion taught,
> Ransacked the bowels of their mother earth
> For treasures better hid. Soon had his crew
> Opened into the hill a spacious wound,
> And digged out ribs of gold. Let none admire
> That riches grow in hell; that soil may best
> Deserve the precious bane. (I. 678–92)

Milton's critique is unambiguous. It is greed for material riches, represented by Mammon, that inspires the mining enterprises. He presents earth as a sensate being – 'their mother earth' – an ancient conception that is once again part of an environmental politics. Rifling the bowels is what the executioners did when hanging, drawing and quartering. Digging out ribs of gold represents a Hellish parody of the creation of Eve. Once seen as benightedly anti-technological, Milton's concerns here at the destruction and desecration of 'mother earth' can now be properly resituated as prescient radical environmentalism. The first mining enterprises are Hellish. It might be objected that these represented episodes of mining occur in Heaven, when the first cannon are made, and in Hell, when Pandemonium is constructed, rather than on earth. But Milton stresses a continuity throughout his cosmos. And whereas the Paradise he shows us is an unspoiled primal state, Hell represents a pre-vision of what the earth was to become, with its mines, buildings, parliament, military and false philosophers. Hell is consistently presented in comparison with earthly civilisations; the epic similes serve to introduce Fiesole, Valdarno, Norwegian hills, Pelorus, Etna, the Red Sea, the Rhine, the Danube, Egypt, Gibraltar, Libya, and so on. The analogies and comparisons serve to indicate that Hell is the site of Milton's critique of the modern world.

Hellish technology is closely associated with repressive and destructive aims. Pandemonium is the venue for the puppet parliament of Satan's archetypal tyranny, in which the imperialist conquest and exploitation of Paradise is proposed and approved. Before their fall, Satan's crew develop cannons and gunpowder in heaven. They are the first armaments manufacturers.

Raphael spells out the parallel between Satanic and human military technology to Adam:

> In future days, if malice should abound,
> Some one, intent on mischief, or inspired
> With devilish machination, might devise
> Like instrument to plague the sons of men
> For sin, on war and mutual slaughter bent. (VI. 502–6)

The cannon are first used in the war in heaven. Backed by this weapons technology Satan launches his archetypal imperialist adventure from Hell, the conquest of 'this new world' (II. 403). Beelzebub proposes the scheme as a revenge on God for their defeat:

>   either with hell-fire
> To waste his whole creation, or possess
> All as our own, and drive, as we were driven,
> The puny habitants; or if not driven
> Seduce them to our party. . . . (II. 364–8)

As it happens, seduction rather than force is the successful methodology. Satan is situated firmly in that interface of disinformation, arms, and drug trading so familiar in the late twentieth century. Setting off on his mission of destruction, his voyage is compared to that of a trading fleet

> Close sailing from Bengala, or the isles
> Of Ternate and Tidore, whence merchants bring
> Their spicy drugs. . . . (II. 638–40)

The association with the colonial ventures of European powers is spelled out.[17] Both East and West Indies are specified: after the Fall, conscious of their nakedness, Adam and Eve

>   choose
> The fig-tree – not that kind for fruit renowned,
> But such as at this day to Indians known,
> In Malabar or Decan spreads her arms
> Branching so broad and long . . .
>   those leaves
> They gathered, broad as Amazonian targe,
> And with what skill they had together sewed,
> To gird their waist – vain covering, if to hide
> Their guilt and dreaded shame; O how unlike
> To that first naked glory! Such of late
> Columbus found the American, so girt
> With feathered cincture, naked else and wild,
> Among the trees on isles and woody shores. (IX. 1100–18)

This epic that deals with the events of the very beginnings of human history now firmly locates its reference in the present time – 'at this day', 'such of late / Columbus found'. The fallen Adam and Eve are identified with the newly colonised peoples of India and America. And if Adam and Eve are to be compared to Indian and American peoples, then the invading coloniser Satan is implicitly but unavoidably to be identified with the Spanish, Portuguese, Dutch and English merchant adventurers, and the values of those adventurers are to be registered as Satanic. Satan reaches earth from Hell by flight, but the recurrent images describing his progress are of a sea voyage. This – in an era before air travel and space travel – locates him pointedly in contemporary analogies: the European voyages of trading and colonisation.

    The decision to make the attack on earth was ratified by the parliament of Hell. At one level the motivation is revenge on God for the defeat in the war in heaven; the barbarous revenge values of primitive epic are alluded to here. But at the same time Milton presents it as a thoroughly political decision, approved by the decision of a modern parliament.

The political context offers yet another radical indictment of contemporary practice. The parliament of Hell is a sham, the democratic institution a mystifying illusion. The first indication of this is given at the end of Book I when the fallen angels swarm to the 'solemn council' (I. 755). In order for them all to enter they have to reduce their size:

> Thus incorporeal spirits to smallest forms
> Reduced their shapes immense, and were at large,
> Though without number still amidst the hall
> Of that infernal court. But far within,
> And in their own dimensions like themselves,
> The great seraphic lords and cherubim
> In close recess and secret conclave sat,
> A thousand demi-gods on golden seats,
> Frequent and full. (I. 789–97)

The members of the council retain their full size and consult in secret; the crowd remains outside, reduced; a physical reduction that expresses the reduction of their significance to the political decision making. As for the council of a thousand – far too many for any meaningful consultation – only four get to speak: Moloch, Belial, Mammon and Beelzebub. It is a blatant travesty of decision making, and a powerful indictment of parliamentary practice.[18] Moreover, of those speakers, Beelzebub was merely proposing what Satan himself had already decided – the attack on Paradise:

> Thus Beelzebub
> Pleaded his devilish counsel – first devised
> By Satan, and in part proposed. (II. 378–80)

Critical attention has tended to focus on the rhetorical splendour of the individual speeches. This has its appropriateness, for they are splendid; but their objective function is to divert attention from the realities of the decision-making process. The decision has already been made secretly, in a private deal. The parliamentary debate is a theatrical masquerade. Such is Milton's radical analysis of contemporary political practice.

The epic poem traditionally has a hero, a powerful protagonist on whose adventures the action revolves. Satan is the obvious candidate for the role in *Paradise Lost,* but how can the embodiment of evil be the hero? Milton's strategy, of course, is to re-evaluate the nature of heroism.[19] Satan, with his great physical strength, his undoubted military courage, his commitment to revenge and his refusal to surrender, embodies a large part of the traditional heroic qualities. Verbal and metaphorical parallels and allusions to *The Iliad* and *The Aeneid* are recurrent.[20] But how admirable are these traditional heroic qualities? Is military might something we want to admire and enshrine? Satan responds to Abdiel in the war in heaven, defending

> The strife which thou call'st evil, but we style
> The strife of glory. . . (VI. 289-90)

It is Milton's strategy to present this traditional 'strife of glory' in a questioning way, to show it clearly as the 'strife of evil'. By giving the role of epic hero to Satan, Milton redefines that traditional celebration of military might as the commemoration of military atrocities.

It is a radical rewriting of the epic, a confrontation of the whole cultural tradition, and a refusal of contemporary social practice. It is a rejection of conventional, official values towards militarism as challenging today as it was when written. The rejection is explicit in the invocation to Book IX, where Milton describes himself as

> Not sedulous by nature to indite
> Wars, hitherto the only argument
> Heroic deemed, chief mastery to dissect
> With long and tedious havoc fabled knights
> In battles feigned (IX. 27-31)

He is not only not 'skilled' in the militarism and ruling-class pageantry of the traditional heroic poem, he is not 'studious' in it either (IX. 42); it is not something on which he has spent time or in which he intends to develop his skills.

There is indeed 'long and tedious havoc. . . In battles feigned' in *Paradise Lost*, but it is grotesque.[21] The war in Heaven begins with full epic clichés:

> Now waved their fiery swords, and in the air
> Made horrid circles; two broad suns their shields
> Blazed opposite, while Expectation stood
> In horror. . . (VI. 304–7)

But it soon becomes mock epic or anti-epic. Satan introduces the cannon 'scoffing in ambiguous words' (VI. 568):

> ' "Vanguard, to right and left the front unfold,
> That all may see who hate us how we seek
> Peace and composure, and with open breast
> Stand ready to receive them, if they like
> Our overture, and turn not back perverse:
> But that I doubt; however, witness heaven;
> Heaven, witness thou anon, while we discharge
> Freely our part; ye who appointed stand
> Do as you have in charge, and briefly touch
> What we propound, and loud that all may hear." ' (VI. 558–67)

After the onslaught Belial remarks:

> "Leader, the terms we sent were terms of weight,
> Of hard contents, and full of force urged home". . . . (VI. 621–2)

The punning on the technical terms of cannonry, on the firing procedures and on the cannon balls help bring the episode close to burlesque. The response of the good angels increases that tendency: they throw back hills.

> They plucked the seated hills with all their load,
> Rocks, waters, woods, and, by the shaggy tops
> Uplifting, bore them in their hands. . . (VI. 644–6)

The episode has moved beyond epic splendour to excess – an excess of technology, an excess of punning, an excess of sheer brute force:

> So hills amid the air encountered hills,
> Hurled to and fro with jaculation dire,
> That underground they fought in dismal shade... (VI. 664–6)

There is a deliberately grotesque aspect to this, an absurdist critique of epic warfare. The focus of this epic has moved from the traditional single combat encounter, with all its alleged nobility, to absurdity: an absurdity of laboured puns, an absurdity of child-like mud-throwing, an absurdity of overkill. This is not an episode that ennobles military conflict. And Milton's final point is that nothing is achieved, nothing is proved. Even though the good angels have right on their side, warfare resolves nothing. The Almighty Father says to the Son:

> sore hath been their fight,
> As likeliest was when two such foes met armed:
> For to themselves I left them; and thou know'st
> Equal in their creation they were formed,
> Save what sin hath impaired – which yet hath wrought
> Insensibly, for I suspend their doom:
> Whence in perpetual fight they needs must last
> Endless, and no solution will be found:
> War wearied hath performed what war can do... (VI. 687–95)

This is no war to end all wars, for there never was such. This is the archetypal war in which nothing is resolved, nothing is achieved. There is nothing admirable, nothing noble, nothing glorious. It is just 'long and tedious havoc', the stuff of traditional epic poetry.

Just as Satan's archetypal monarchical tyranny is shown in its first earthly manifestation in Nimrod, so his archetypal militarism is shown in its first earthly manifestation with the giants. This thematic reiteration firmly locates Milton's critique as applicable to earthly issues. The cosmic evil of Satan is something re-enacted continually on earth; its manifestations are there in ruling-class practice – in monarchical tyranny, parliamentary fraud, military slaughter. We are shown the giants in battle and Michael interprets the episode to Adam:

> Such were these giants, men of high renown;
> For in those days might only shall be admired,
> And valour and heroic virtue called;
> To overcome in battle, and subdue
> Nations, and bring home spoils with infinite
> Manslaughter, shall be held the highest pitch
> Of human glory, and for glory done,
> Of triumph, to be styled great conquerors,
> Patrons of mankind, gods, and sons of gods –
> Destroyers rightlier called, and plagues of men.
> Thus fame shall be achieved, renown on earth,
> And what most merits fame in silence hid. (XI. 688–99)

The rejection of militarism and military solutions is explicit and unambiguous. Milton's position was consistent on this. In *Paradise Regained* the Son tells Satan:

> They err who count it glorious to subdue
> By conquest far and wide, to overrun
> Large countries, and in fields great battles win,
> Great cities by assault; what do these worthies
> But rob and spoil, burn, slaughter, and enslave
> Peaceable nations. (III. 71–6)

In his rejection of traditional epic military values, Milton's concerns are both social and literary. There is no separation between the two. In challenging and rewriting literary tradition in its privileging of militarism, he is at the same time challenging prevailing social attitudes and ruling-class assumptions. He is a revolutionary in the literary sphere and in the political sphere, for each involves the other. This can be seen in his prefatory note to *Paradise Lost* on 'The Verse'. It concludes:

> This neglect then of rhyme so little is to be taken for a defect, though it may seem so perhaps to vulgar readers, that it rather is to be esteemed an example set, the first in English, of ancient liberty recovered to heroic poem from the troublesome and modern bondage of rhyming. (p. 148)

The terms are the terms of his political radicalism – the recovery of 'ancient liberty' from 'modern bondage'. Liberty is what humanity began with, and lost, and must now struggle to restore; and *Paradise Lost* was written as 'an example' of what had been lost, and what can be done.

Notes

1. All quotations from John Milton, *Complete English Poems, Of Education, Areopagitica*, ed. Gordon Campbell (London, 1993).
2. See Saad El-Gabalawy, 'Christian Communism in *Utopia*, *King Lear*, and *Comus*', *University of Toronto Quarterly*, 47 (1978), 228-38.
3. 'An expression of the same spirit which had long been making itself heard in the Puritan pulpit and which was at the moment clamoring in the reckless pamphlets of Prynne and Lilburne' – William Haller, *The Rise of Puritanism* (1938) (Philadelphia, 1972), p. 288. On the radicalism of Milton's early poetry see David Norbrook, *Poetry and Politics in the English Renaissance* (London, 1984) and Michael Wilding, *Dragons Teeth: Literature in the English Revolution* (Oxford, 1987).
4. David Daiches, *Milton* (London, 1957), pp. 76-92; Catherine Belsey, *John Milton: Language, Gender, Power* (Oxford, 1988), p. 28.
5. The best account of Milton's political career is in Christopher Hill, *Milton and the English Revolution* (London, 1977). Recent discussions of the prose works can be found in David Loewenstein and James Grantham Turner (eds), *Politics, Poetics and Hermeneutics in Milton's Prose* (Cambridge, 1990) and Thomas N. Corns, *Uncloistered Virtue: English Political Literature, 1640-1660* (Oxford, 1992).
6. *The Riverside Shakespeare*, ed. G. Blakemore Evans (Boston, 1974). *The Poems and Letters of Andrew Marvell*, ed. H.H. Margoliouth, revised by Pierre Legouis with E.E. Duncan-Jones (Oxford, 1971).
7. 'Epic and Novel'. In M.M. Bakhtin, *The Dialogic Imagination*, ed. Michael Holquist, trans. Caryl Emerson and Michael Holquist (Austin, 1981), p. 13.
8. John T. Shawcross, *Milton 1732-1801: The Critical Heritage* (London, 1972) and William Empson, *Milton's God*, 2nd ed. (London, 1965).
9. Fredric Jameson, 'Religion and Ideology'. In Francis Barker et al. (eds), *1642: Literature and Power in the Seventeenth Century* (Colchester, 1981), p. 329.
10. Christopher Hill (ed.), *Winstanley: The Laws of Freedom and Other Writings* (Harmondsworth, 1973), p. 150.
11. *The Complete Prose Works of John Milton*, ed. Don M. Wolfe et al., 8 vols (New Haven and London, 1953-82), vol. 3, pp. 198-9.
12. Michael Wilding, 'Milton's *Areopagitica*: Liberty for the Sects.' In Thomas N. Corns (ed.), *The Literature of Controversy: Polemical*

Strategy from Milton to Junius, (London, 1987), pp. 7–38 (reprinted from *Prose Studies*, vol. 9, no. 2).
13. On the Diggers and other radical groups of the English revolution, see Christopher Hill, *The World Turned Upside Down* (Harmondsworth, 1975); Eduard Bernstein, *Cromwell and Communism: Socialism and Democracy in the Great English Revolution* (1930) (Nottingham, 1980); David W. Petergorsky, *Left-Wing Democracy in the English Revolution* (London, 1940).
14. I have discussed the issue of gender equality in 'Their Sex not equal seemed', in P.G. Stanwood (ed.), *Of Poetry and Politics: New Essays on Milton and His world* (Binghamton, NY, 1994).
15. 'Censorship and English Literature'. In *The Collected Essays of Christopher Hill: Volume 1. Writing and Revolution in Seventeenth Century England* (Brighton, 1985).
16. Karl Marx, *Capital*, trans. Eden and Cedar Paul (London, 1930), vol. I. p. 12.
17. See J. Martin Evans, 'Milton's Imperial Epic'. In P.G. Stanwood (ed.), *Of Poetry and Politics*.
18. Merrit Y. Hughes, 'Satan and the "Myth" of the Tyrant'. In Hughes, *Ten Perspectives on Milton* (New Haven, 1965), p. 187.
19. John M. Steadman, *Milton and the Renaissance Hero* (Oxford, 1967); Michael Wilding, *Milton's Paradise Lost* (Sydney, 1969).
20. Davis P. Harding, *The Club of Hercules: Studies in the Classical Background of Paradise Lost* (Urbana, 1962).
21. Arnold Stein, *Answerable Style* (Minneapolis, 1953).

3 Women and the opposition press after the Restoration

Maureen Bell

'Dispersing seditious books is very near a-kin to raising of tumults; they are as like as brother and sister: raising of tumults is the more masculine; and printing and dispersing seditious books, is the feminine part of every rebellion.'

(Serjeant Morton, at the trial of Thomas Brewster, 1664)[1]

In July 1679 the bookseller and publisher Francis Smith was accused of publishing a 'scandalous libel' directed at Lord Chief Justice Scroggs. The case came to trial in February of the following year, and he was found guilty in his absence. In *An impartial account of the tryal of Francis Smith*, Smith offers a transcript of the trial proceedings.[2] The account is, indeed, 'impartial', in that Smith adds no commentary of his own: the proceedings of the court are recorded verbatim and the prejudices of the court, from Smith's point of view, speak for themselves. On the last page of the pamphlet is another transcript, of the case which followed Smith's at the Sessions of the King's Bench on 7 February 1680: *The tryal of Jane Curtis. Upon an information brought against her for publishing and putting to sale a scandalous libel, called A Satyr upon Injustice: or Scroggs upon Scroggs*. This second transcript is particularly interesting for its record of a woman's involvement in 'seditious' publishing. Few women were ever brought to trial for the offence. In the case of Jane Curtis, the court proceedings were brief, and are here quoted in full:

> Mr. Holt. May it please Your Lordship, and Gentlemen of the Jury, here is an Information brought against *Jane Curtis*, and it sets forth, that the defendant did publish and put to sale a

seditious Libel against my Lord Chief Justice *Scrgogs* [sic], the Defendant pleads not Guilty, if we prove it upon her, you are to fine for the KING, and if not you are to say so, and no more.

Mr. *Williams* said (who was a Council for the Defendant) he would admit the Record, whereupon they proceeded no further to tryal, but the woman being called, she said,

Mrs. *Curtis*. I was ignorant in the matter, and knew no such thing, my Lord, my Husband, and please your Lordship was in the Country a hundred miles off of me, in *Lincolnshire*.

Mr. *Justice Jones*. You did it ignorantly, and simply, without any malice, and I suppose, you are heartily sorry for it. You see your Neighbour there Mrs *Smith*, hath shewed good discretion in the behalf of her Husband; she has ingeniously declared that he shall come and make submission, and if I find you as submissive, and as sorry for what you have done, I may do the like for you,

Mrs. *Curtis*. In any thing that I have done, I know not my self Guilty, and if I am, I beg your Lordships pardon with all my heart, my Lord, or any bodies else.

Mr. *Justice Jones*. I know you will find mercy from my Lord *Chief Justice*, and therefore go and make your submission.

Then the jury proceeded to give their verdict, and there Foreman said, Guilty.[3]

On first glance, this brief exchange between Jane Curtis and Justice Jones may be taken to confirm the stereotype of women's ignorance and submissiveness in the face of male authority. A closer inspection, however, might suggest something of the way in which women working to print, publish and distribute opposition pamphlets could negotiate some room for manoeuvre within the legal and social constraints of the time.

Submission or subversion?

Jane Curtis's words are few, but revealing. She offers two lines of defence in mitigation of her alleged crime: first, that she was ignorant ('I was ignorant in the matter, and knew no such thing') and, second, that her husband was away at the time ('my Husband, and please your Lordship was in the Country a hundred miles off of me, in Lincolnshire'). Simple ignorance and absent husbands are excuses which women in the book trade seem often to have claimed. A surviving letter from the bookseller

Elizabeth Calvert, for example, written during one of her frequent imprisonments in the 1660s and designed as an appeal for release, offers a similar explanation. She claims that, with her husband Giles absent from the shop, himself in prison for seditious publishing, she had innocently and unwittingly sold off as 'waste paper' some remaining sheets of the offensive pamphlet with whose publication he was charged. In fact, far from ignorantly selling off old paper, she had organised the reprinting and distribution of a whole new edition of the pamphlet, to replace Giles's copies which had been seized by the authorities.[4] The absence of a husband was also an excuse used by the husbands themselves. In 1668 a printer called Redman, when accused of printing *Queries about Ireland*, explained that while he himself was away from home (escaping pursuit for debt) his wife had accepted the book for printing without being aware of its content. In 1681 the printer Astwood said that he had been 'abroad' when his wife had taken in for printing the manuscript of *A Raree Show*. Braddyl, another printer, explained in 1683 that three sheets of the *Growth of Popery* had been printed by his wife in his absence.[5] The prevalence of absent husbands in investigations of illegal and seditious printing can be explained by the difference in legal status between man and woman.

In seventeenth-century English law, a wife was defined as a *feme covert*, under civil subjection to her husband, who was legally responsible for her actions. This principle of coverture meant that 'a married woman is not responsible for a crime committed by her in her husband's presence or in concert with him, and such a situation raises a presumption of coercion by her husband'.[6] Obtaining indictments against wives was therefore difficult, and even if a woman was clearly the instigator of the crime, it was usual for juries to be directed to acquit the wife and convict the husband as her legal 'head'. The usefulness of the absence of the husband as a defence was that it compromised this legal view of the husband's responsibility. In law, a husband was indeed technically responsible for his wife's actions, but no reasonable jury would be likely to indict a man when he was far enough away from his wife (and the crime) for the legal view to be seen to rest on a fiction. This legal framework which refused to married women any individual agency or responsibility for their actions necessarily positioned women as simple and ignorant. The speed with which Justice Jones accedes to Jane Curtis's offered view of herself as ignorant and unsupervised suggests that he was quick to interpret her words within the framework in which he had been trained.

Jane Curtis, then, is offering words which the law will understand, and ones which, emphasising her ignorance and her husband's absence, speak a formula familiar to men and women operating in the 'seditious' world of opposition publishing. Her second statement, where she apparently accepts her guilt, is however more ambiguous. Justice Jones refers to the previous trial – Francis Smith's – where Smith's wife, Eleanor, appeared on her husband's behalf. Jones's message to Jane Curtis is that if she demonstrates a similar submission, he will put in a good word for her with Scroggs, saying in effect 'You present yourself as an ignorant, simple woman; behave, then, with proper submission, and I'll see what I can do'. Interestingly, Jane both complies with Jones's request, making a public apology for her misdemeanour, and at the same time subverts it. She begins, in fact, with an affirmation of her innocence ('In any thing that I have done, I know not myself Guilty') and ends with a throwaway offer to apologise to *anybody* if that's what he wants: 'I beg your Lordships pardon with all my heart, my Lord, or any bodies else'. But while complying with the *form* of statement she is required to make if she is to obtain her freedom and escape a ruinous fine, she is stubbornly equivocal. She avoids saying 'I *knew* not my self Guilty', the past tense pointing to past ignorance and, by implication, a realisation of guilt in the present; in stating 'I *know* not my self Guilty' she affirms her present conviction that her action was right, even though not – legally – innocent. Nor does she qualify this assertion by a concessionary 'but' ('but if I am guilty'); rather, she makes her assertion and adds 'and (not 'but') if I am . . .', thereby juxtaposing two opposing views of her behaviour. Jones's view of her guilt is thus prevented from superseding her own assertion of innocence. Moreover, her offer of apology to the judge and to anybody else is conditional ('if I am'): the implication, unspoken, is 'but I am not'.

This report of the trial, with its brief transcript of a woman publisher's words, is a useful document in exploring the position and activities of women in opposition publishing. The words spoken by Jane Curtis constitute a public performance, directed at (at least) two audiences: Justice Jones as representative of the legal system, and opposition sympathisers inside and outside the courtroom. They allow readings of both guilt (which is how Jones hears them) and, as I have argued above, innocence. The performance is itself a site of conflict between woman offender and male authority, and exists within a specifically legal (as well as a wider social) construct of 'woman'. Reading it is like watching a ritual dance, where both Jones and Curtis observe forms and conventions; but, while complying with the forms to secure her freedom, Jane Curtis uses that legal/social construct of woman to mark out a resistance.

What more is known of Jane Curtis suggests that such negotiations of compliance and resistance were for her a way of life. She was the wife of Langley Curtis, well-known as publisher of Henry Care's paper *A Pacquet of Advice from Rome* and a number of anti-Stuart pamphlets. He was himself imprisoned and pilloried for such activities. As is usual, Jane's name occurs in trade and other records when Langley is absent because of imprisonment or flight to avoid arrest. When most of the opposition stationers collapsed in the summer of 1682, the Curtises kept going. Throughout the early 1680s both of them were frequently arrested, fined and harassed. What is know of Jane Curtis suggests that she was far from the quiet and submissive wife Justice Jones urged her to be. When Stephens, the notoriously brutal Messenger of the Press, arrived on one occasion to search her house, she refused him entry. She was taken before the Court of the Stationers' Company to explain her behaviour, and on that occasion her language to Stephens was so abusive that the Court 'were apprehensive he might be in danger of his life by doing his duty'.[7]

The point has been made that, given the legal status of married women, it was virtually impossible to prosecute a wife, yet Jane Curtis was nevertheless brought to trial. That she was tried at all is a measure of the authorities' growing frustration with the opposition press in the 1680s. Lord Chief Justice Scroggs, the subject of the libel published by Jane Curtis, was the chief crusader against opposition publishing, and Jane Curtis's libel must have increased his frustration at the inability of the law to stamp out what he saw as sedition. In effect, he engineered her trial, allowing two witnesses to swear that Langley Curtis was dead, in order that Jane could be prosecuted as a *feme sole* – that is, an independent woman responsible in law for her own actions. That the Lord Chief Justice connived at perjury in order to get around the difficulty of coverture indicates perhaps the extent of his exasperation. Her friends offered bail, but he refused, and 'he swore by the name of God she should go to prison, and he would shew her no more mercy, than they could expect from a wolf that came to devour them'.[8]

Jane Curtis was not the only woman involved in opposition publishing in the late 1670s and early 1680s, when the printing of propaganda, verse satire and topical pamphlets reached a peak. Francis Smith's wife and daughter (both called Eleanor) irritated the authorities in much the same way and were also the focus of repeated investigation. The fame (or notoriety) of Francis Smith has eclipsed the activities of many others, including the women, yet the women can be demonstrated to have played an important part, alongside their male partners. In doing so they were carrying on a tradition of resistance and evasion established by a previous generation of women. That women had a particular and effective role to play in the survival of opposition, republican and radical publishing in this period has hardly been noticed by literary critics and historians.[9] It will be my contention that, without the commitment of women to the 'good old cause' of parliamentary and sectarian politics, in particular during the early years of the Restoration, the vigour of opposition politics would have been significantly diminished. The resurgence of pamphleteering and printed satire characteristics of the 1680s had its roots in the underground and secret presses of the 1660s, when a small group of women booksellers, publishers and distributors persistently defied the government's attempts at control via legislation and harassment.

An earlier generation

Printing and bookselling were essentially domestic businesses, involving the whole household: the master craftsman himself, his wife, apprentices, servants and children. Although it was the male who was the member of the Stationer's Company, the body which regulated the book trade, and it is his name that usually appears in the trade records, it is clear that the wife often played a full part in the running of the business. The regulations of the Company recognised that a widow could carry on the business after her husband's death, and she was allowed to take apprentices and to enter books in the Stationers' Register in the usual way. In looking for records of women's activity within the trade, then, it is inevitable that widows, or women whose husbands are absent, are easier to investigate, and in what follows the activities of widows are particularly prominent.

In the 1660s, the early Restoration years, several women's names are persistently linked with seditious printing and bookselling, and to understand Jane Curtis's role in the trade we can look to the activities of these women. In turn, the record of Jane Curtis's words can illuminate their position, for, like her, they were arrested, imprisoned and questioned repeatedly. Like other stationers' widows, these women – Joan Dover, Anna Brewster and Elizabeth Calvert – were allowed, under the rules of the Stationers' Company, to carry on trading independently. Earlier in the century, it had been usual for stationers' widows to remarry within the trade, usually taking another stationer, or an apprentice, as new husband. The pattern of remarriage and transfer of business to the man became less common as the century wore on, and increasing numbers of widows remained single and traded under their own names.[10]

Joan Dover first becomes prominent during the trial of her husband in 1664 for seditious printing. During Simon Dover's imprisonment pending his trial, Joan had been allowed to visit him on condition 'that she neither deliver papers to him nor receive them for him'. A letter found during a raid on her house before the trial shows that such precautions were ineffective. In the note, Simon Dover wrote from prison:

> I would fain see my sister Mary; therefore sister Hobbs will not come, take her order, and instead of her name, put in sister Mary's: it will never be questioned here. However, do it as wisely and handsomely as you can . . . You must either get Tom Porter, or some very trusty friend, (possibly CD may help you) to get for you a safe and convenient room to dry books in, as soon as possibly you can . . . Let me know what you intend to do with the two sheets and half. I will have it published, when I am certain I shall be tried.[11]

Not only was Joan being asked to forge a name on a visitor's warrant; she was continuing to oversee the printing of material related to the case, and needed a safe place in which to dry the sheets that came, wet, from the press.[12] Publication (that is, distribution) of printed material was to be held back until the most effective moment, once a trial was certain. Clearly, Joan Dover was competent to carry on in Simon's absence. Like the other wives of imprisoned men, she also petitioned and lobbied on his behalf, requesting the release of their apprentice 'that he may continue an important piece of work' and asking 'liberty of the prison' for her husband.[13] When Simon died in prison, she was left with a small son to support as well as a printing house to run, and quickly remarried. Her second husband was the printer John Darby. Soon after Simon's death, she was again under suspicion of seditious printing. Her name appears in a list of printers of Fifth Monarchist and Quaker literature compiled by an informer: 'Widow Dover' is held responsible for printing *The Jury-man Charged* and *England's Warning* as well as books by the Quaker writer Rebeccah Travers.[14] Warrants were issued against Joan and John Darby in May 1664, only a few months after Simon's death.

Evidence from the investigation of a secret press in Blue Anchor Alley four years later, in 1668, suggests that Joan Darby and Anna Brewster were working together.[15] Anna Brewster's husband Thomas had been tried alongside Simon Dover in 1664 and, like him, had died in prison. Attempts to trace the trail of offending pamphlets back from the hawkers who sold them on the streets to the printer who produced them was frustrated by the pyramid distribution network headed by Joan. The hawkers were supplied by a carpenter, who was duly questioned. His information was that he received the copies from Anna Brewster. Anna Brewster refused to name her own source of supply, but her son admitted that he had received papers from Joan Darby. L'Estrange, the Surveyor of the Press, found that his attempt to prosecute John Darby as printer was frustrated by the refusal of the women to talk; as L'Estrange wrote to Williamson, the Secretary of State:

> I do not heare that Darbys wife has been examined, & beyond doubt she'll confesse nothing, for she and Brewster, are taken to be

a couple of the Craftyest & most obstinate . . . of the trade. Agt. Darby himselfe, I see nothing as yet. So that only Brewster stands answerable, & Printing does not concern her.[16]

In hunting the printer, L'Estrange was blocked by the women's silence. All the information about the chain of distribution was useless, since L'Estrange could find no direct evidence to convict John Darby of printing the papers in question – *The Poor Whore's Petition*: 'Mr Derby the Printer is in Custody, but no witness appears directly agt him.'[17] While Joan's role in distribution was clear, only the circumstantial evidence of her marriage to Darby pointed to him as printer. As long as she refused to talk, he was safe from prosecution. Eventually John Darby, like Anna Brewster who had been committed to the Gatehouse for dispersing seditious pamphlets, was released.[18]

Elizabeth Calvert's career in the 1660s followed a similar pattern of persistent involvement in 'offensive' publishing, harassment and arrests. She had been imprisoned along with the men at the time of the trials in 1664, and was not immediately released once the trials were over. Her son, Nathaniel, had himself been released and fell ill; surviving petitions from Elizabeth for her release document his decline. She offered a physician's testimony as proof that Nathaniel was 'all the tyme of her said imprisonment . . . dangerously sick' and begged for her release to look after her son who was 'the comfort and staffe of her life and age'. Her release came too late: a second petition states that Nathaniel was 'ever since fryday morning dead and is yett unburied and that small livelihood shee hath left is nowe like to be lost and your petitioner utterly ruined'.[19] On her release in April 1664, she was doubly bereaved – of husband and elder son – and had another son, Giles, of about ten years old, to support. The business may well have been damaged by the fines and expenses incurred by the family since the Restoration: between 1661 and 1664 she herself had been arrested four times, and had spent a total of seven months in prison, as well as three months on the run with her maid, Elizabeth Evans.

Imprisonment and fines on this scale were expensive, and Elizabeth Calvert had to borrow money from several sources. She was certainly in debt to the Stationers' Company, as was Anna Brewster, who appeared before the Court of the Company to describe her poverty, her dependent children, and her 'low Condicion'.[20] Two years after her release, much of Elizabeth Calvert's stock, as well as her shop, the Black Spread Eagle in St Paul's Churchyard, was destroyed in the Fire of London. Nevertheless, she continued in business, finding new premises and publishing a range of non-conformist literature, by such writers as William Dyer, Richard Steele, John Wilson, John Owen, Benjamin Agas, and the Quaker Francis Howgill. While some of these books (despite their technical illegality in being unlicensed) were apparently uncontentious and their open publication caused no trouble, others were the focus of repeated investigations by the authorities. It seems that alongside her apparently acceptable line in nonconformist texts, she developed an 'under the counter' trade which was to bring her, repeatedly, to L'Estrange's notice throughout the rest of the 1660s.

Calvert's career after 1664 is a catalogue of arrests and interrogations, and can be pieced together from records in the Public Record Office. In 1665 she was arrested, though the cause is unknown; in 1667, 1668, 1670 and 1671, when she was eventually brought to trial, she was again under investigation. Her activities as a distributor of 'offensive' pamphlets stretched well beyond London, and surviving notes link her with the Bristol bookseller Susanna Moone, whom she supplied with consignments of virulently anti-Catholic pamphlets about the Fire of London. In 1668, at the same time that Joan Darby and Anna Brewster were running the distribution network for the Blue Anchor Alley press, Elizabeth Calvert was running a secret press in Southwark, which was eventually raided by the Stationers' Company. Her indictment for publishing 'Directions to a Painter' and 'Clarendon's Housewarming', anti-government satires usually attributed to Marvell, relates to the same year, and the poems may have been among the offensive material seized from the Southwark press. The burden of fines and bail (which, on one occasion, she jumped), must have been considerable. Yet the catalogue of arrests and interrogations continues relentlessly until 1671, and she continued in business until her death three years later.[21]

The evidence for the persistent activities of these women is overwhelming, but has rarely been noticed, even by historians of the book trade. If remarked on at all, the women have been relegated to a footnote or parenthesis and seen as aberrant. Kitchin, for example, calls them 'obdurate Whig spouses whose services to the Cause, *ludicrous though it may seem*, were real and constant' (my italics).[22] Yet the women's importance as producers and distributors of anti-government polemic was certainly clear to their contemporaries, and Roger L'Estrange's notes of his investigations point to his frustration at their activities. Why these particular women were so successful and so persistent is a question which obviously arises, and is one which can only be answered by setting their activities in the context of the control of print in the early years of the Restoration.

Controlling the press at the Restoration

When in 1660 Charles II was restored to the throne of England the maintenance of order, and the suppression of dissent, were central issues. Rumours of armed opposition caused panic, and actual risings, however small-scale and ineffectual (like Venner's of 1661), were quickly answered by arrests and imprisonments. Charles's policy towards the defeated republicans was, arguably, a tolerant one. Apart from the trial and execution of the regicides, and occasional waves of arrests when riots were threatened, past actions were by and large left uninspected: many of Charles's new supporters had been implicated in republicanism by their active or tacit support of Cromwell and the Commonwealth. Triumphalism and revenge on Charles's part would not have been conducive to peace and stability. It was, however, a tense time. Too many changes had been experienced in the recent past, and especially in the turmoil of 1659, for the new government to be confident of maintaining power and civil order. Information about what was being said – in taverns, in meetings, from pulpits, in London, in the provinces – was sought via spies and informers, and taken seriously when received. One of the conduits of anti-monarchist ideas was the printing press, and the control of seditious printing was part of a wider attempt to strengthen the fragile order which had been restored.

The first piece of legislation passed by the Cavalier Parliament was a Treason Act whose provisions covered offences related to printing, writing and preaching.[23] Charles II also retained the royal proclamation as a means of regulating the press and in 1662 the so-called 'Licensing Act' and the office of Surveyor of the Press were added to the measures for control. The very multiplicity of agencies involved in attempts at regulation (the King and Council, the Secretary of State, the Surveyor of the Press and the Master and Wardens of the Stationers' Company) may have complicated, rather than helped, the task of regulation.[24] For, despite this battery of controlling mechanisms, pamphlets regarded as 'seditious' continued to circulate.

Those attempting to control the opposition press in the 1660s saw as dangerous and subversive a whole range of writings which cross the boundaries of form and genre. *Considerations and Proposals for the Regulation of the Press* (1663), by Roger L'Estrange, Surveyor of the Press, sets out his criteria for judging a work as treasonable or seditious, and offers a catalogue of the most offensive publications of the first three years of the Restoration. Among the publications which, according to L'Estrange's definitions, were 'libels' are sermons, books of prognostications, short accounts of topical events, and religious polemic. To their contemporaries all such writings, regardless of genre, were interconnected, political coherent in their propaganda programme, and regarded as equally powerful in the dissemination of radical and subversive ideas.

A few brief examples can best demonstrate how, in the early years of the Restoration, the publication of such writing alarmed the authorities. In 1661 appeared the first of a series of three pamphlets which became known collectively as the *Mirabilis annus* pamphlets or 'The Year of Prodigies'. The pamphlets offer a catalogue of strange events, wonders and coincidences which imply God's anger at individual persecutors and at the kingdom more generally. The first was a warning to those who oppressed non-conformists, its Biblical language designed to remind Charles II of his father's fate:

> the Mene Tekel on the Wall did signifie evil to Belshazzar, who thought he knew all that God had done to his Father, yet humbled not his heart, but lifted up himself against the Lord of Heaven . . .[25]

Elizabeth Calvert's husband, Giles, was arrested for publishing the pamphlet, and while he was in prison she organised its reprinting. The words of the warrant which was then issued for her arrest indicate the seriousness with which Secretary of State Nicholas viewed such a pamphlet:

> being a forgery of false and feigned prodigies, prognosticating mischievous events to the King, and instilling into the hearts of subjects a superstitious belief thereof, and a dislike and hatred of His Majesty's person and government, and preparing them to effect a damnable design for his destruction, and a change of government.[26]

The second pamphlet in the series was published to coincide with St Bartholomew's Day (24 August) 1662, when ministers unable to conform to the Act of Uniformity were to be ejected. The third pamphlet celebrates its own evasion of 'the watchful eye that is continually upon the Press', and announced its own delayed publication as itself a work of providence.

Copies of the *Speeches and prayers* of the regicides executed in 1660 were equally inflammatory. Such pamphlets did not need to speak critically of the King: their very existence, presenting the regicides as martyrs, was an affront to the newly restored monarchy and its Parliament.[27] Another pamphlet, *The Phoenix, or the Solemn League and Covenant*, responded to the order for the public burning of the Covenant by simply reprinting together the texts of the Covenant and the King's declaration acknowledging his father's sins, and of a sermon by Calamy from 1649 on the subject of the dangers of covenant-breaking. The very juxtaposition demonstrated, with no need for commentary, the King's duplicity and the likely fate of oath-breakers.

L'Estrange, zealous to prove his royalist credentials by the thoroughness of his suppression of seditious literature, grew more and more frustrated as republican pamphlets of this kind continued to circulate. What rankled was that he knew who was responsible: a group of stationers he named 'Confederates', most of whom had been leading radical sectarian and republican publishers in the 1650s, and who now continued to publish in support of the 'good old cause' while managing to evade the penalties of the law. In his *Considerations and Proposals* of 1663 L'Estrange published his own recommendations for action, giving an account both of the seditious pamphlets whose printers and publishers had gone unpunished, and of the tougher measures which would effectively silence the opposition press. In L'Estrange's view, the wives of the 'Confederates' were as much a threat to order as their husbands; imprisoning the men made little impact on the production and distribution of 'libels', since the wives carried on alone. One of the women was Hannah Allen, who in the 1640s and 1650s had specialised in publishing Baptist, Independent and Fifth Monarchist literature. After the Restoration she and her second husband, Livewell Chapman, carried on their trade in republican pamphlets. Provocatively, after the trial and execution of Sir Henry Vane in 1662 – a *cause célèbre* for republicans – they published Vane's works. Such activities led to Livewell Chapman's imprisonment on several occasions. His release in May 1664, after 14 months in prison, was conditional upon both his own and his wife's good behaviour: 'the condition is to be that neither he nor his wife, nor any by their order, print, publish, or disperse any book or paper contrary to law'.[28]

L'Estrange was equally aware of the activities of the Calverts, and notes in his *Considerations and Proposals* Elizabeth Calvert's audacity in persisting in the publication of the *Mirabilis annus* pamphlets 'whilest her husband was a Prisoner for that very book'. L'Estrange grew increasingly frustrated: despite his gathering of intelligence and arrest and questioning of those involved, he was unable to bring them to trial:

> Giles Calvert did not only come off for This, but during his Imprisonment, (which continued till the Adjournment of the Parliament) his wife went on with the Prodigies; upon Proof whereof, She was likewise Committed, and is come off too.[29]

A cat and mouse chase developed, and despite frequent arrests and periods on the run for all of those involved, they were never arrested all at the same time, and so someone was always free to carry on the trade in sedition. The Chapmans, the Calverts, the booksellers Thomas and Anna Brewster and the printers Simon and Joan Dover were L'Estrange's principal targets in his appeals for stronger powers for himself and stricter penalties under the law.

In the autumn of 1663 matters came to a head. In September

there were rumours of a planned rebellion in the north of England, and L'Estrange was suspicious of the Confederates' involvement in printed propaganda designed to support the uprising. Acting on information received, he mounted a series of raids and found Twyn printing *A Treatise of the Execution of Justice*.[30] L'Estrange brought in both Elizabeth Calvert and her son Nathaniel (Giles had died in August, probably as a result of his imprisonment) as well as their maid and apprentice. Many others were arrested, including Thomas Brewster and his apprentice, Simon Dover and his apprentice, and others involved in binding and distribution. A series of show trials, staged in 1664, was the result. The printer Twyn, found guilty of treason, was executed. The printer Simon Dover and bookseller Thomas Brewster remained in prison, where they died. A reported 3,000 people 'of the same [i.e. republican] stamp' attended Brewster's funeral 'in the Phanatiques burying place in Bedlam'. L'Estrange lamented only the stationers' stubbornness: if they had been willing to give him information about their associates, they need not have died in prison. L'Estrange, who had earlier called for 'the breaking of That Knot' of stationers, presumably congratulated himself on a job well done. If so, he reckoned without the stationers' widows.

It would have been understandable if these women had decided to cut their losses – to resume trading in legal and inoffensive books in order to support themselves and their children. The record of their activities throughout the rest of the decade and beyond, as outlined above, shows that, far from accepting defeat, all three persisted in the offences which had cost their husbands' lives. In doing so, they fed the rising discontent with Charles and his government, and developed methods of avoiding authority which had become, by Jane Curtis's time, traditional ways of working among opposition stationers.

In the margins

This discussion has focused on an area which is, in many ways, seen as marginal. From the point of view of English literature, the kinds of pamphlets, sermons and verse satires published by these women are at the margins of literary study. In a culture which, despite the challenges of critical theory, elevates the role of the author, these women are marginal in that they were the material producers and distributors of books, not writers. In their own time they were, by virtue of their sex, marginalised legally and socially. In this last section, it is the issues raised by this definition of their activities as in many ways 'marginal' that will be inspected.

First, the issue of the literary/historical status of the texts they produced and circulated. The anonymity (for obvious reasons) of much of this kind of political writing, its topical and ephemeral nature, and perhaps even its popularity, have all contributed to its relegation to the 'minor' arts of Restoration England. There are, for example, no cheap student editions of Restoration satirical verse, and what is available is not always easy to read: the sheer weight of footnotes needed to elucidate characters and events as obscure as today's 'Spitting Image' would be to a Martian can be offputting. Political satire (especially verse satire) maintains a presence in English literature only in relation to a few authors, notably Dryden and Marvell, and until recently in the case of Marvell it has been treated as marginal to a writer perceived primarily as a lyricist. Recent work has done much to reinstate politics into the work of the canonical writers, but that has had no immediate effect on the valuation of the thousands of anonymous satires. In the introduction to his collection of *Poems on Affairs of State*, G. de F. Lord points to the numbers of verse satires circulating in the period: his estimate is of 5,000 surviving either in print or in manuscript from the period 1660–1714, with approximately 1,200 being printed. Interestingly, though, relatively few of these were printed before 1688: 'The few satires that were printed before the Revolution came from unlicensed presses. The rest circulated only in manuscript.'[31] Elizabeth Calvert's publication of the 'Painter' poems and 'Clarendon's Housewarming', in 1668, took such 'seditious' verse out of the sphere of manuscript circulation, the usual mode of distribution for virulent attacks on court and government, and into wider circulation. That she was pursued for this, and indeed that this was the only 'seditious' pamphlet for which she was ever brought to trial (three years later, in 1671), perhaps suggests a particular sensitivity on the part of the authorities to this kind of witty attack.

Marvell's poems apart, however, none of the many other 'seditious' works associated with these women usually qualifies to be considered as 'literature' at all. This should alert us to the ways in which generic categorisation of writing – into satirical verse, sermon, polemic, 'signs and wonders' pamphlets and so on – has prevented us from identifying the mix of radical writing as it was employed and experienced at the time. A contemporary like Roger L'Estrange, as suggested above, made no distinction by genre. He saw sedition of the same kind in many different forms of writing, and pursued them all with equal vigour. Marvell's *Growth of Popery* was as offensive, and for broadly the same reasons, as were the verse satires.

Connected with the marginality of these forms of writing in modern literary studies is the marginality of the role of material producers of books. Most of these texts are, unsurprisingly, anonymous, in order to protect the author from prosecution. Given that measures of press control were centred specifically on printers, authors were the people in the chain of production who were most likely to avoid detection altogether, while the printers and distributors, easier to trace since their activities were more difficult to hide, could suffer arrest, imprisonment, trial and – in the case of the unfortunate Twyn – execution. The anonymity of the texts adds to their lack of interest for the literary critic; the 'Painter' poems and *Growth of Popery* are probably the only titles mentioned in this chapter which are likely to be familiar to students of literature, precisely because of their attribution to a named author: Marvell. Yet, in keeping alive the values of republicanism and spreading anti-monarchist ideas, it was precisely these kinds of 'ephemeral' texts which sustained and focused, however crudely and virulently, the discourse of the 'good old cause' and a scepticism about government policies. The members of the book trade who took the risk of printing and selling such texts, and persisted in their activities despite repeated arrests, imprisonments and harassment, deserve our attention. That women were particularly prominent in doing so during the early years of the Restoration, and again in the 1680s, needs explanation.

One factor in their ability to avoid suppression was probably the inefficacy of the attempts to control the press more generally in this period. Licensing regulations were disregarded widely in any case, and few of these women, even in the case of inoffensive publications, complied with the requirements of licensing and registering copies. The 'Licensing Act' of 1662 was in itself inadequate: L'Estrange's prosecution of the male 'Confederates' in 1664 relied not on that Act, but on the statute for treason and the common law. The obsession of the controlling agencies with pursuing printers as the prime offenders, which underlay most of the attempts at regulation throughout the century, including the Licensing Act itself, was by the 1660s out of step with the development of the trade, in which booksellers had now superseded printers as the principal financial backers of publications. These weaknesses in legislation and regulation, and the multiplicity of agencies involved in control, effectively reduced the chances of imposing consistent and widespread controls on seditious printing.

It is possible that some of the women had influential friends who could offer them some protection. Francis Smith, the young member of the 'Confederates' who was put out of business after the 1664 trials, only to re-emerge as a leading opposition publisher in the 1670s and 1680s, had a protector in Lord Anglesey, who occasionally intervened on his behalf. Elizabeth Calvert's release, on one occasion, came in response to a note from Lord Carlisle, Marvell's patron, and her link with both men may have continued for much of the 1660s. It is in the nature of their activities, though, that the evidence for such associations is thin; it was in everyone's interest that such relationships should be hidden.[32]

Obviously, the removal of the male 'Confederates' had left something of a vacuum. The deaths of Giles Calvert in 1663, and of Nathaniel Calvert, Simon Dover and Thomas Brewster in 1664, coupled with the financial ruin of Francis Smith (who did not resume business for some years) and the disappearance of Livewell Chapman and Hannah Allen from the 'seditious' trade at about the same time, meant that several of the most experienced figures, as well as younger recruits (like Dover and Smith), had been silenced. In carrying on despite such losses, women like Elizabeth Calvert, Joan Dover and Anna Brewster were drawing on the experience they had gained while working in partnership with their husbands. Silencing the male 'Confederates' had been difficult, and their widows proved equally evasive. But why were they allowed to continue? If L'Estrange had successfully silenced the men, why did he find it impossible to silence the women? Part of the answer may be the fact that they *were* women, whose identity in law constructed them as marginal.

From the discussion of Jane Curtis's speech we can see that women's status in law as marginal figures – creatures incapable, technically, of crimes – may have worked to protect them. Their almost total invulnerability to prosecution during their husband's lifetimes, when as *femes covertes* their own crimes were the legal responsibility of the men, gave wives a greater freedom to publish and disperse illegal material. Jane Curtis, it will be remembered, could only be brought to trial because of perjured evidence that her husband was dead. Joan Dover, remarried to John Darby, was to some extent protected by her legal status as a married woman; moreover, in the absence of information which would directly link her distribution of seditious literature with his work as a printer, her silence when questioned effectively protected her husband, too. Elizabeth Calvert, during her independent career as a widow, could in theory more easily have been prosecuted. That she avoided prosecution for so long, and that it took so long to bring her to trial (three years after the misdemeanour had taken place) may indicate that there was a tendency among the judiciary to extend the legal view of wives and daughters to all women, seeing them all as naive and misled rather than rational beings in control of their own actions.

It seems likely, then, that these women were exploiting the law's (and society's) view of them as 'inferior' and 'not responsible' by regularly offering ignorance as an excuse. By insisting on ignorance and innocence (as in Elizabeth Calvert's story that she sold offensive pamphlets unawares, thinking that they were 'waste paper') and by refusing to offer information which would incriminate anyone else, they could eventually gain release and continue their activities. Despite L'Estrange's knowledge of their complicity, short of catching them in the act he could do little more than harass them.

Whatever the mixture of factors which assisted their persistence – the general ineffectiveness of press controls, the occasional intervention of an influential politician and the peculiar legal status of women no doubt all played their part –

the fact of that persistence remains. For more than a decade these women continued to offend, despite all efforts at prevention. They learnt ways of coping not only with the necessary secrecy of production and distribution, but also with the frequent arrests, fines and imprisonments which resulted when they were suspected. Above all, they learnt the value of silence. Their refusal to speak infuriated their interrogators, and is commented on by L'Estrange and his associates. But at a time of growing discontent with Charles's policies and the actions of Parliament, and a period of intermittent persecution of non-conformists, it enabled them to continue to publish writing which voiced opposition and heartened the apparently defeated supporters of republicanism and religious toleration. The ploys they developed – the pose of ignorance, the refusal to inform, the practice of 'saving harmless' their associates by rewarding them for their silence in turn – were all practices with which Jane Curtis and her colleagues, years later, were familiar.[33] Jane Curtis's recorded speech at her trial may be unique, but the resistance it marks was a direct inheritance from the experience of the previous generation of 'seditious' wives and widows. Few words from this earlier generation of women remain, but their actions during the difficult days of the 1660s sustained a tradition of opposition publishing which would again flourish in the 1680s.

Notes

1. T.B. Howell, *A Complete Collection of State Trials and Proceedings for High Treason and other Crimes and Misdemeanors.* 34 vols (London, 1816–28). vol. 6 col. 521 (hereafter cited as *State Trials*). R.L. Greaves, *Deliver us from Evil: the Radical Underground in Britain, 1660–1663* (New York and Oxford, 1986) echoes this view. His ch. 7 on the radical press (p. 207) begins 'Radical literature was the handmaiden of political and religious dissent'.
2. *An Impartial Account of the Tryal of Francis Smith upon an Information brought against him* . . . (London, 1680).
3. Ibid., p. 6.
4. The letter, dated 23 November 1661, is in the Public Record Office (PRO SP29/44:93); it is printed in M. Bell, 'Elizabeth Calvert and the "Confederates"'. *Publishing History* XXXII (1992), pp. 5, 49.

5. Public Record Office, *Calendar of State Papers: Domestic Series, 1547–1704* (London, 1856–1972) (hereafter *CSPD*) documents several such cases, including those of Redman (*CSPD*, 1668/9, p. 110) and Braddyl (*CSPD* 1683, Jan–June, p. 272).
6. D. Rosenberg, 'Coverture in Criminal Law: ancient "defender" of married women', *University of California, Davis (UCD) Law Review*, 6 (1973), 83–101. See also Sir Matthew Hale's *Historia Placitorum Coronae* (1736), p. 45.
7. Stationers' Company, Liber F, entry for 6 March 1688/9. For more on the Curtises, see T. Crist, 'Francis Smith and the Opposition Press in England, 1660–1688', unpublished PhD. thesis (Cambridge, 1977).
8. *State Trials*, vol. 8, col. 191.
9. Distinguished exceptions to this are R.L. Greaves, *Deliver us from Evil* and N.H. Keeble, *The Literary Culture of Nonconformity in Seventeenth-Century England* (Leicester, 1987).
10. For a description of patterns of women's activity within the trade throughout the seventeenth century, see M. Bell, 'A Dictionary of Women in the London Book Trade, 1540–1730', unpublished MLS dissertation (Loughborough, 1983).
11. *CSPD* 1663/4, p. 315, 27 October and *State Trials*, vol. 6, col. 557.
12. A warrant was issued, 25 January 1664, for Catherine Hobbs to visit Dover (*CSPD*, 1663/4, p. 452).
13. *CSPD*, 1663/4, p. 366.
14. *CSPD*, 1664/5, p. 148, printed in N. Penney (ed.), *Extracts from State Papers relating to Friends, 1654–72* (London, 1913), pp. 229–30. A fuller discussion of Joan Darby and the other 'Confederate' women is given in Bell, 'Elizabeth Calvert', pp. 28–33.
15. The evidence for the women's involvement in the Blue Anchor Alley press, and a secret press run by Elizabeth Calvert in Southwark at the same time, is presented in M. Bell, ' "Her Usual Practices": the Later Career of Elizabeth Calvert, 1664–75', *Publishing History*, XXXV (1994), pp. 5–64.
16. PRO SP29/239:5, L'Estrange to Williamson, 26 April 1668.
17. PRO SP29/239:6.
18. Anna Brewster continued in opposition publishing for many years. Ten years later, in 1678, she was in hiding after a warrant was issued for her arrest in connection with the publication of several pamphlets, including *The Letter about the Test* and *The Growth of Popery*. The following year she was imprisoned with Mary Thompson and two letter office clerks for dispersing another pamphlet, and in 1680 Francis Smith was publishing in her name, promising to 'save her harmless' (Bell, 'Elizabeth Calvert', pp. 30–1).

19. PRO SP29/95:98, SP29/96:64.
20. Stationers' Company, Court Book D, 109v–110, 5 June 1665.
21. This paragraph is derived from the more detailed account of her career 1664–71 given in Bell, "Her Usual Practices".
22. G. Kitchin, *Sir Robert L'Estrange: a Contribution to the History of the Press in the Seventeenth Century* (London, 1913), p. 111.
23. G. de F. Lord (ed.), *Anthology of Poems on Affairs of State: Augustan satirical verse 1660–1714* (New Haven and London, 1975), p. xxvi.
24. See F.S. Siebert, *Freedom of the Press in England 1476–1776; the Rise and Decline of Government Control* (Urbana, 1965) for details of legislation and controlling agencies.
25. ΕΝΙΑΥΤΟΣ ΤΕΡΑΣΤΙΟΣ: *mirabilis annus, or the year of prodigies and wonders.* . . (1661), preface. (*Mene Tekel; Or the Downfal of Tyranny* was the title of the pamphlet for which Twyn was executed two years later.) The other two 'Mirabilis annus' pamphlets, issued in 1662, are *Mirabilis Annus Secundus; or the second year of prodigies* and *Mirabilis Annus Secundus: or, the second part of the second years prodigies.* The pamphlets' popular generic title was reversed by Dryden in his *Annus Mirabilis*, 1666.
26. CSPD, 1661/2, pp. 106.
27. *The Speeches and Prayers* . . . (1660) appeared in three more editions with different titles and additions: *Rebels no Saints* . . . (1661); *A Compleat Collection of the Lives, Speeches and Prayers* . . . (1661); and a French edition, *Les Iuges Iugez, se Iustifiants* (1663).
28. M. Bell, 'Hannah Allen and the Development of a Puritan publishing business', *Publishing History*, VIII (1989) 5–66.
29. R. L'Estrange, *Truth and Loyalty Vindicated* . . . (1662), p. 57.
30. The title, as printed on the title page, begins: *Mene Tekel; Or, The Downfal of Tyranny*.
31. G. de F. Lord (ed.), *Poems on Affairs of State: Augustan satirical verse, 1660–1714*, vol. 1 (New Haven, 1963), Introduction, pp. xxvi, xxxii.
32. For the relationship between Francis Smith and Lord Anglesey, see Crist, 'Francis Smith', ch. 1. The possibility of Carlisle as protector of Elizabeth Calvert is discussed in Bell, 'Elizabeth Calvert'.
33. 'Saving harmless' is the phrase used for indemnifying those imprisoned or fined. A hawker, for example, might have prison fees and fines paid for her by the bookseller/printer who supplied her. See n. 18 for an instance of this.

4 Two sansculotte poets: John Freeth and Joseph Mather

Charles Hobday

Most of the so-called Jacobin poets who in the 1790s drew inspiration from the French Revolution were middle-class by birth and education, but there were also working men among them. Socially and sometimes politically, the relationship between the middle-class poets and their plebeian contemporaries was not unlike that between the bourgeois members of the Jacobin Club and the Parisian sansculottes. Two of these sansculotte poets, John Freeth and Joseph Mather, stood apart from the rest because of their direct and intimate relationship with their audience. Both were ballad-writers, singing their songs in public and publishing them themselves, in broadsheet or in book form. They occupied the position of tribal bards, speaking for and to the local communities of which they were members, and their songs were the faithful expression of political and social attitudes which were widely shared. Freeth, the Birmingham publican, was for over forty years the spokesman of a petit-bourgeois radicalism which linked the populist Whiggism of the elder Pitt with the Jacobinism of the 1790s. Mather, the Sheffield file-cutter, spoke for a more proletarian brand of radicalism; his rapid transition from Methodism to industrial and thence to political militancy is typical of a class with little independent political experience which was beginning to assert itself as a force in its own right.

'John Freeth, Poet'

John Freeth was born in Birmingham in 1731, and in early life was apprenticed to a brassfounder. He had begun writing songs by 1761, and published his first collection, *The Political Songster*, in 1766. *The Birmingham Directory* in the following year listed him under 'Miscellaneous Tradesmen' as 'John Freeth, Poet'. In 1768 he took over the Leicester Arms tavern, popularly known as 'Freeth's Coffee House', which his family owned, and made it a centre for political activities. A historian has stated that 'the history of popular political consciousness in Birmingham, especially during the years of the American revolution, is in good part the history of the Leicester Arms'.[1] As Freeth recalled in 1790:

> My hobby-horse and practice for thirty years past has been to write songs upon the occurrence of remarkable events, and nature having supplied me with a voice somewhat suitable to my stile of composition, to sing them also, while their subjects were fresh upon every man's mind, and being a Publican, this faculty, or rather *knack* of singing my own songs, has been profitable to me; it has in an evening crowded my house with customers, and led me to friendships which I might not otherwise have experienced.[2]

New editions of *The Political Songster*, each containing many additions and omissions, appeared in 1771, 1784, 1786, 1790 and 1794. He also published several other collections. A list printed in some copies of the 1790 edition of *The Political Songster* contains the names of about 400 subscribers, most but by no means all of them living in the Birmingham area.

Freeth composed his ballads in haste, to be sung while their subjects were still topical, and not infrequently adapted an old song of his own to fit new circumstances. Most of them, as he pointed out on the title page of *New Ballads* (1805), were set to 'old familiar tunes', and if at times he strained metre or rhyme in fitting them to the music, on other occasions he showed considerable skill in handling a wide variety of metres and stanza forms. Those of his poems not intended for singing are usually less effective than his ballads, though he could handle the octosyllabic couplet skilfully, as in his comment on the younger Pitt's financial policy:

> As artful as a GERMAN JEW,
> He pays off one, and borrows two,
> And tells us by this state finesse,
> The public debt is getting less.[3]

He rarely used the heroic couplet, and his attempts at the ode often lapse into bathos; such a couplet as

> And sure that plan must be of noble use
> Which tends in price provisions to reduce[4]

is hardly in keeping with the dignity of an ode.

'John Free'

Freeth issued some of his collections under the pseudonym 'John Free', identifying himself with the popular conception of 'the freeborn Englishman', proud of his liberties and always prepared to defend them. It was because John Wilkes was seen as the champion of the Englishman's liberties that Freeth and thousands of others supported him throughout the 1760s. A copper token bearing Freeth's portrait has the inscription:

> Britons, behold the Bard of Freedom, plain and bold,
> Who sings as Druids sang of old.[5]

Here we have the patriotic myth of the Druids inspiring the Britons in their resistance to Roman aggression, found, for example, in Cowper's 'Boadicea'. Freeth had lived through the 1745 rebellion and two wars against France and Spain, and his radicalism was of a traditional Whig type, patriotic, even jingoistic, hostile to Jacobites, Papism, France and Spain, which he associated with absolute monarchy and religious persecution, and to the Scots, the mainstay of the Jacobite cause. His anti-Scottish prejudice was intensified in the early years of George III's reign by the influence exercised by the king's Scottish favourite the Earl of Bute. In 'The Pope's Address to his good Friends in England', an attack on the Quebec Act of 1774, he suggested that George was controlled by crypto-papists and Jacobites, and in 'The English Lion' (1779) he attributed British defeats in the American War to 'the *thistle* supplanting the fair English rose'.[6] This prejudice crops up in the most unexpected places; in a ballad in praise of canals he writes:

If the waters of Trent with the Severn have vent,
   What mortal can have an objection?
So they do not proceed to cut into the Tweed,
   With the Scots to have greater connection.[7]

His ideas on defence and foreign policy were those which Tories and Country Whigs had preached since William III's day: opposition to a standing army, foreign alliances and the use of British troops in Europe; reliance for defence on the Navy and a strong militia; and a policy of fighting wars at sea rather than on land. He favoured a vigorous foreign policy, however, to be enforced by using the Navy; he denounced as appeasement the agreement with Spain over the Falklands reached in 1771, and deplored the Government's failure to prevent the partition of Poland by sending a fleet to the Baltic.

His attitude towards most politicians was profoundly cynical. In 'The Ins and Outs', written in the 1760s, he reached the conclusion that

There is not a statesman among all the band, sir,
But tells you he acts for the good of the land, sir;
Yet plain it is seen, that these patriot pretenders,
Who call themselves, Englishmen's glorious defenders,
Do talk, and talk only; for faith, the main plan, sir,
Is to put in their pockets as much as they can, sir.[8]

In the years before 1782 the only politician, apart from Wilkes, for whom he showed any enthusiasm was William Pitt the elder, later Earl of Chatham, but even he did not escape criticism. When Freeth satirised all the prominent politicians from Walpole to Bute in 'The Statesman' (1762), he accused Pitt of inconsistency in sending British troops to defend Hanover and accepting a pension from George III.

His radicalism is most apparent in his earlier ballads in his disrespect for the monarchy, as in 'The Old King's Ghost' (1768), in which George II's ghost warns the king:

Be cautious! for fear you should split on that rock,
Which brought the unfortunate Charles to the –.
If fawning addresses the throne could secure,
James the second would never have fled from the shore.[9]

This song may have brought him in danger of prosecution; he announced in 1770 the forthcoming publication of 'Wilkes's Enlargement. An Ode By J. Freeth, With an occasional Song, in Lieu of the old K.'s Ghost, which is deemed unsafe.'[10] His Whiggism was of a type which was conscious of the precedent of 1649 as well as that of 1688, as is shown by his references to Cromwell. At a time when Cromwell was denounced by Tories as a regicide and by aristocratic Whigs as a dictator who dispersed Parliament by force, Freeth admired him as the scourge of both tyrannical kings and corrupt Parliaments. In 1768 he wrote:

> Yet methinks at St. James's, what's wanted the most,
> Is something resembling old Oliver's ghost,

and 'Clear the House' (1771?), which describes a debate in the Lords, concludes with a prayer

> For an *Oliver's broom*,
> Such as once made a general sweep,[11]

These passages support Christopher Hill's suggestion that while Tory and Whig historians condemned Cromwell 'some more positive aspects of Oliver and his revolution lived on in popular memory'.[12]

One important aspect of Freeth's political activity, for which he was probably well paid, was the writing of election songs. The Warwickshire election of 1774, for which he wrote six songs, was particularly significant. Although Birmingham was not represented in Parliament, qualified electors in the town could vote for the two county members. For many years candidates selected by the county aristocracy had generally been returned unopposed, but in 1774 Birmingham commercial interests secured the defeat of the aristocracy's candidate, John Mordaunt, whom Freeth denounced in a song as 'a tool to an infamous court'.[13]

Freeth made frequent use of the supernatural in his political songs. Satires in which ghosts returned to comment on contemporary events, as in 'The Old King's Ghost', had been popular since the 1670s; Richard Glover's 'Admiral Hosier's Ghost' (1739) is perhaps the best-known example. A variant on this form is Freeth's 'News from Elysium' (1770), in which

William Beckford, the Pittite Lord Mayor of London, on arriving in the next world reports on the political situation to George II and his ministers, who join him in drinking Chatham's health. The Devil figures prominently in several ballads. In 'Beelzebub's Trip to Warwick', written during the 1774 Warwickshire election, the Devil announces his support for Mordaunt, and in 'The Devil and the Pope' (1775) the Pope informs the Devil of his support for the candidate in a Leicestershire by-election to whom Freeth was opposed. 'The Diaboliad' (1779) tells how the devils seek a successor to Pluto, and after various candidates have been proposed Satan finally nominates Sir Hugh Palliser, the enemy of the popular opposition figure Admiral Keppel.

The American War

During the controversy over Parliament's right to tax the American colonies, Freeth whole-heartedly supported the colonists. In 'American Contest' (1774), his comment on the Boston Tea Party, he depicted the colonies as Mother England's daughter, 'a fine lusty grown lass', and described how

> Her high pamper'd matron, to luxury prone,
> In folly and fashion extravagant grown,
> Pretended she's got an old reck'ning to pay,
> And could wipe off the score, if her daughter drank tea.
>
> By the invoice the girl at an instant could see,
> If she took to the goods, a hard bargain 'twould be;
> So, as soon as the cargo was brought to the key,
> In a passionate air toss'd it into the sea.[14]

His sympathy with the Americans did not abate when the dispute developed into war. 'Bunker's Hill, or the Soldier's Lamentation' (1775) passionately protests against the bloodshed:

> Did they who bloody measures crave,
>   Our toil and danger share,
> Not one to face the Rifle-Men,
>   A second time would dare.
> Ye Britons who your country love,

> Be this your ardent pray'r:
> To Britain and her colonies,
> May peace be soon restor'd,
> And knaves of high and low degree,
> Be *destin'd to the cord*.[15]

Like other opposition propagandists, Freeth condemned the Government's use against the colonists of Red Indians and Hessian mercenaries, whom he described respectively as 'Savage Monsters' and 'German Butchers'.[16]

After France and Spain entered the war, while continuing to support the Americans, he called for resistance to these new enemies and wrote recruiting songs. In 1779 the combined French and Spanish fleets swept the Channel, threatening Britain or Ireland with invasion, and Volunteer corps raised in Ireland to meet this danger forced the government to lift restrictions on Irish trade. In this crisis outraged patriotism, hatred of Lord North's government and the example set by the Americans and Irish drove Freeth to adopt an openly revolutionary position. His song 'The Volunteer's Rouse', which begins as a call to resist foreign invaders, ends with a summons to rebellion:

> The SONS of HIBERNIA to danger awake,
>   Redress by such means did insure;
> Pursue the example, ye BRITONS, and make
>   Your liberties ever secure.[17]

In other songs of this period he bitterly contrasted British defeats with the victories won in the Seven Years War, and as the Navy regained control of the sea after 1780 he produced a series of songs exulting over French, Spanish and Dutch defeats. Meanwhile he kept up his attacks on the Government and the system of corruption of which he saw the personification in North, in ballads with such titles as 'The Stream of Corruption', 'The State Beggars' and 'Taxation: or, The Courtier's Creed'. On the general election of 1780 he commented:

> Bankers, and Brokers, leave London in haste,
>   A love for their country pretending;
> And greedy CONTRACTORS, of Boroughs in quest,
>   To Tinkers and Taylors are bending;

Fine words are display'd, fair promises made,
But when the grand work is effected,
Till six years are gone, out of twenty, scarce one,
See the PLACES for which they're elected.[18]

As the reference to contractors suggests, Freeth saw the war as part of the system of corruption, a point which he made again in 'The Trading War':

To get a snug penny, since fighting began,
The WAR to encourage, seems far the best plan;
For WAR is a TRADE, I'll uphold it, by which,
Though thousands grow poor, many hundreds get rich.[19]

Pitt the Younger

Freeth greeted North's resignation in March 1782 with a shout of triumph, and in 'Corruption Defeated: or The Premier Routed' hailed a new age of reform:

A generous flame diffuses round,
  And statesmen brightest powers employ;
Throughout the kingdom, hark! the sound,
  'Reform, reform, is all the cry.'[20]

In this euphoric mood he was prepared to forgive even George III. He produced a new version of 'The Old King's Ghost' from which the references to Charles I and James II were omitted, and which concluded:

Hope flatters each bosom – Peace flutters her wing –
Success to OLD ENGLAND, and long live the KING.[21]

But he also noted as an evil omen in another song, 'The State Pensioners', that North and the manager of his corruption fund, John Robinson, had been granted pensions. Very reluctantly, the king agreed to the formation of a Government headed by the Marquis of Rockingham and drawn from the two main opposition groups, Rockingham's followers and Chatham's former supporters. When on Rockingham's death in July the king appointed the Earl of Shelburne, leader of the Chathamites, to succeed him, however, most of the Rockingham group went into opposition. Freeth gave expression to his despair in a rewritten version of 'The Ins and Outs':

> At ROCKINGHAM's death, which the land much affected,
> Fresh scenes of confusion broke out unexpected;
> For soon as the Fates to the shades had decreed him,
> The bone of contention – was who should succeed him;
> And patriots, who cannot their jealousies smother,
> Their union dissolve, and abuse one another. . .
>
> In Freedom's fair cause, then, ye souls that are hearty,
> Away with the idle distinction of party;
> Redress to obtain, and on slavery to trample,
> Look, look at Hibernia, and catch the example:
> Rouze, rouze, then ye Britons, be bold and united,
> By arming alone can you get yourselves righted.[22]

But the British people ignored this new call to revolution. Instead, Rockingham's followers, now led by Charles James Fox, united with North's group in 1783 to vote down the Government, and the king was compelled to agree to the formation of a coalition Ministry by the two groups. 'When the *Coalition* took place,' Freeth later wrote, 'I went with the popular tide, and joined in sentiment with those who reprobated that extraordinary measure.'[23] His song on the coalition's India Bill, set to the tune of 'The Vicar of Bray', reached the cynical conclusion:

> And this is truth, I will maintain,
>   Tho' minds may be divided;
> That men in power, let who will reign,
>   By interest will be guided.[24]

He completely approved the king's dismissal of the Ministry after the defeat of the India Bill in the Lords and his appointment of a new one headed by the younger Pitt, then only twenty-four, and his songs on the subsequent elections were uniformly hostile to the coalition.

His high hopes of Pitt were speedily disappointed. His disapproval of the taxes on retail shops and maidservants introduced in 1785 was strong enough to cause him to invoke the shade of Wat Tyler. In 'Budget Day' he recalled that

> A poll-tax once, old hist'ry says,
>   Created bloody strife;
> By TYLER WAT, an insolent
>   Exciseman, lost his life,[25]

and another song, 'The Londoners' Petition against the Shop Tax', suggested that

> A paltry tax on servant maids
>   Of foes creates an host,
> And may when levied. . . from the shades,
>   Bring up Wat Tyler's GHOST.

These approving references to Tyler anticipate Paine's defence of him in *Rights of Man* by seven years. 'The Londoners' Petition' continues:

> The friends to commerce, justice says,
>   Have better cause to frown,
> With them no fav'rite ever was,
>   More suddenly let down;
> Then let us beg, since in the case,
>   The KING can do no wrong
> The reins in other hands you'll place,
>   For BILLY's quite too young.[26]

Although Freeth continued for the next five years to criticise Pitt's new taxes, he praised other aspects of his policy, such as the commercial treaty with France, and in 1788 he reversed his former opinion of the Premier in a song entitled 'The Coach Drivers: Or, Billy's not too Young'. He could still be caustic about members of the royal family; when the king's aunt, Princess Amelia, bequeathed most of her fortune to her German nephews, he commented that she had 'Left ENGLAND her BONES and HESSE CASSEL her GOLD'.[27] His references to George III, however, were almost all respectful; in 1786 he even called him 'the best of princes'[28] and in a poem on the centenary of the 1688 revolution he declared that

Britain her greatness is sure to maintain
While GEORGE in the hearts of his *subjects* shall reign.[29]

By 1788, in fact, he had apparently ceased to be a radical in any meaningful sense of the word.

In the 1780s radicals were particularly concerned with three issues: parliamentary reform and the extension of the franchise; the abolition of the slave trade; and the Dissenters' demand for the repeal of the Test and Corporation Acts. The campaign for parliamentary reform aroused little interest in Birmingham, perhaps because the 1774 elections had shown that its voters could influence the Warwickshire county members, and Freeth had nothing to say about it. The agitation against the slave trade, on the other hand, found many supporters there, and was conducted by a committee which included both Anglican and Dissenting ministers. Freeth's song on the subject, however, was completely unsympathetic, as its conclusion indicates:

> But so it to numbers appears,
>   If Commerce we aim to restrain,
> Britannia but very few years,
>   The Empress will be of the main;
> To lessen let's make it our care,
>   The burthens upon our own backs,
> For Britons too many there are,
>   More mis'rable souls than the BLACKS.[30]

Freeth, whose political associates included many Dissenters, might have been expected to back their campaign against the Test and Corporation Acts, but his ballad 'The Test' ridicules the Dissenters' claims. A probable explanation is his fundamental indifference to religion. He satirised all the Churches in 'An Hudibrastic Epistle'; 'State Game: or, The Road to Church Preferment' (1787) illustrated how ecclesiastical appointments were made for political reasons; and he denounced the church courts in 'The Spiritual Inquisition' (1786) as 'a stain on the land which makes FREEDOM her boast'.[31] His targets in other ballads were examples of superstition or fanaticism, from the Gordon Riots to John Wesley's prophecy that the world would end in 1836. In his references to religion he manifests both his strength and his weakness, a down-to-earth common sense combined with a coarseness of fibre which often reminds one of Cobbett.

Freeth and Society

Freeth's politics and his outlook on society can fairly be described as petit-bourgeois. Like Hogarth, he disapproved of both the idle poor and the idle rich. When the Overseers of the Poor in 1765 put forward proposals for the foundation of the Birmingham General Hospital, on the ground that 'more than half the Manufacturers [i.e. industrial workers] in the Town of Birmingham are not Parishioners of it, and cannot be entitled to any Relief from the present [workhouse] Infirmary',[32] he objected that it would attract beggars. He satirised the frivolous diversions of fashionable society and denounced gambling. He was not hostile to popular amusements, however; he wrote songs in praise of horse-racing, prizefighting, fox-hunting and other sports. He had little use for the cult of sensibility which influenced many middle-class reformers; he approved of cockfighting, and applauded Parliament's refusal to ban bull-baiting.

Freeth's outlook was that of a tradesman. Whatever promoted trade, and especially Birmingham's trade, whether a commercial treaty with France or the construction of canals, was desirable; whatever hindered it, whether high taxes or abolition of the slave trade, was not. Far from being an advocate of the new ideas of *laissez-faire* and a market economy, however, he strongly supported the traditional English policy of state intervention to protect popular living standards. During his lifetime there were seven periods of dearth serious enough to provoke widespread food riots, and he regarded it as axiomatic that the state should punish those who took advantage of a shortage to force up prices. In some stanzas written in 1770 he declared:

> Was a monarch like Prussia's to guard English ground,
> Where plenty's bestow'd mis'ry would not abound,
> For he'd hang those who dar'd to ask five-pence a pound
> For the glorious roast beef of old England,
> The glorious old English roast beef.[33]

In another song he attributed high food prices to 'ingrossers, forestallers, regrators', rackrenting landlords and high taxes.[34] The Tudor legislation against forestalling, engrossing and regrating[35] was repealed in 1772, but they remained offences at common law until 1843, and Freeth expected the law to be enforced. His view that the needs of the poor took priority over freedom of trade is implicit in the title of one of his songs: 'Written extempore, on hearing that Mr Skipwith, member for Warwickshire, was remarkably active in preventing the exportation of Wheat, by opposing the motion in the house of Commons' (1770). He supported Skipwith's re-election in 1774. 'The Colliers' March', his ballad on an incident in 1782 when a crowd of colliers marched into Birmingham, as they told the authorities, not 'with the intention of committing any Depredations, but to Regulate the Prices of Malt, Flour, Butter, Cheese, etc.'[36] and withdrew peaceably on receiving assurances that prices would be reduced, is completely sympathetic in tone. E.P. Thompson has written about such protests:

> It is the restraint, rather than the disorder, which is remarkable; and there can be no doubt that the actions were approved by an overwhelming popular consensus. There is a deeply felt conviction that prices *ought*, in times of dearth, to be regulated, and that the profiteer put himself outside of society.[37]

This was a conviction that Freeth certainly shared.

Although a townsman, he showed himself conscious of rural grievances, as in his ballad 'The Cottager's Complaint. On the intended Bill for enclosing Sutton Coldfield' (1778). More surprising is his attack on the game laws in a song of 1784:

> Reason's bounds are o'er-run,
>   When those wise laws we shun
> Which nature thought proper to frame;
>   For what greater right,
>   Has a Duke, Lord, or Knight,
> Than any one else to the Game?[38]

This appeal to reason, the law of nature and natural rights against the law of the land is profoundly radical in its implications, foreshadowing Freeth's transformation from a Pittite to a Jacobin.

Freeth the Jacobin

Apart from his annual grumble about the budget, in the later 1780s Freeth seemed to be moving steadily away from his earlier radicalism. It was the French Revolution which reversed the process. His earliest poem on the subject, 'The Troubles of France' (1789), whole-heartedly applauded the storming of the Bastille and especially the National Assembly's decision to nationalise Church property – a measure which, he suggests, Pitt might well imitate. He sees the revolution in an international perspective, as the successor to that in America and the inspiration of others to follow. Here in fact we have the old Freeth, libertarian, patriotic, anti-clerical, opposed to high taxation, disrespectful towards kings and nobles, hostile towards the Bourbons and the papacy. 'The Rights of Mankind all the World over' (1790) lays even greater stress on the revolution's international significance; the line 'May the TURK live in peace and the NEGRO be free'[39] suggests that he had changed his mind about slavery. Another indication of his reviving radicalism was the songs which he wrote during the 1790 elections in support of Thomas Thompson, the Foxite candidate for Evesham and an advocate of parliamentary reform.

When sympathisers with the revolution held a dinner in Birmingham on 14 July 1791, three local magistrates organised a 'Church and King' mob which attacked Dissenting meeting houses and prominent reformers' homes and ran riot for three days. Although Birmingham's middle-class reformers tended thereafter to lie low, Freeth and eleven friends who shared his views continued to meet nightly at the Leicester Arms, and were nicknamed 'the Twelve Apostles' by their political opponents. They included James Bissett, another local poet, who had acted as deputy chairman at the 1791 Bastille Day dinner, when he was beaten up by the mob, and in 1796 contributed a song to Coleridge's journal *The Watchman*.

In his songs of the 1790s Freeth opposed the war with revolutionary France for traditional 'Tory' reasons. It was being fought in the wrong place and in the wrong way, he maintained, by sending troops to Europe and subsidising foreign allies:

> Thus pro and con the farce goes on,
>   But what makes many frown,
> However large may be the charge,
>   JOHN BULL for all comes down.[40]

The same point is made in another song, significantly entitled 'Money and Men at Home' (1794?):

> All to no purpose, such is the case,
>   Many brave fellows abroad are sent;
> Always for fighting the ocean was,
>   And still is Britannia's element. . .
>
> Old DADDY BULL, as the story's told,
>   Lately in one of his random fits,
> To *Prussia* sent six score barrels of gold,
>   Who pockets the rhino and quiet sits.[41]

Freeth objected to the war for another reason. It was being fought to replace the Bourbons on the French throne, but what guarantee was there that, once back in power, they would not prove as great a nuisance to Europe as they had been in the past? In a song written in 1800 he declared:

> French kings to humble heretofore
>   European States were joining;
> Now down, to monarchy restore
>   They strongly are combining;
> But long, I trust, fight on we must
>   With vigour unabated,
> Before the Bourbon family
>   Gets firmly reinstated.[42]

Not that he had any great faith in the durability of the republic. As early as 1794 he made what proved to be an accurate prophecy of the advent of a Bonaparte:

> In fickle France, you'll see at last,
>   A monarch mount the throne;
> But rest assur'd, from what has pass'd,
>   The choice will be their own.[43]

He welcomed in songs written in 1801-2 the restoration of peace and two good harvests, after years in which food prices had reached unprecedented heights, and looked forward to the revival of trade with France. He supported the renewal of war in 1803, however, though with the prayer that 'A short and glorious war may it prove'.[44] He had changed his view of the war for the same reason as Wordsworth, Coleridge and Southey; he saw in Bonaparte an ambitious dictator who had betrayed the revolution, and whose career of aggression must be stopped. He ridiculed him in a number of poems which concentrated on his reconciliation with the Catholic Church, such as 'Bonaparte's Coronation' (1804), which is typical of Freeth in its mockery of monarchy and popery:

> At the scene let who would be allur'd,
>   From laughter some could not refrain,
> When the unction his HOLINESS pour'd
>   On the head of the new CHARLEMAGNE;
> At the mummery Gravity smil'd,
>   Whoever might feel disappointed,
> He's sure the most *promising* child
>   His HOLINESS ever anointed.[45]

Success in the war, he believed, depended on national unity, but this could be achieved only if the Government accepted a programme of reforms:

> To quell at once the hateful storm,
>   And stifle all confusion,
> Though cherish'd be the word *Reform*,
>   We'll have no *Revolution*.[46]

By his support for the war effort and his repudiation of revolution he belatedly achieved political respectability. When he died in 1808 an obituary in *Aris's Birmingham Gazette*, which was reprinted in the conservative *Gentleman's Magazine*, praised 'the harmless yet pointed sallies of his Muse',[47] without mentioning that he had once threatened George III with the fate of Charles I, summoned the English people to rebel, or lovingly recalled the precedent set by Wat Tyler.

Joseph Mather: from Methodist to Militant

Joseph Mather never achieved any sort of respectability, except perhaps during his short career as a Methodist. Born in 1737 at Chelmorton, Derbyshire, he was apprenticed in 1751 to the file trade in Sheffield, where he spent the rest of his life, working as a file-cutter or 'file-hewer'. With a wife and at least five children to support, he lived in poverty and was often imprisoned for debt. In Sheffield the cutlery trade was controlled by the thirty-three officers of the Cutlers' Company, while the administration of justice was in the hands of James Wilkinson, a wealthy fox-hunting squire-parson, and Colonel Robert Athorpe. Mather vented his hatred of this political and economic establishment, as well as augmenting his income, by writing songs and selling them in the streets and at race meetings and fairs. According to his editor, John Wilson, who drew on local tradition,

> in appearance he was low in stature, but his breadth
> fully compensated for any deficiency in height. . .
> Our author used to 'raise the wind' by vending his songs
> in the streets, seated on a grinder's donkey, or on
> the back of Ben Sharp's bull. Should it chance to begin
> raining, he would ride the animal into the nearest alehouse. . .
> He used to be seated . . . with his face to
> the animal's tail.[48]

The majority of Mather's songs are either descriptions of low life or satires on local characters and incidents, very few of which can be dated. The earliest that can are two on Sheffield races, written before races on Crookes Moor were discontinued in 1781, but some may have been written far earlier. Although his songs often lampooned the local magistrates ('justasses', he called them), they brought him into conflict with the authorities on only one occasion, when for singing a rude song about a local gentleman he was bound over to keep the peace for a year. After the year was up he wrote another song with the refrain 'I was muzzled a year', in which he satirised Colonel Athorpe ('beef-headed Bob') and the clergyman responsible for his arrest.[49]

In 1782, shortly after a murderer had been gibbeted on Loxley Edge, outside Sheffield, a Methodist preacher rebuked Mather for breaking the Sabbath, and told him that he was 'in the road to Loxley Edge'.[50] This warning so affected him that he became a Methodist, and for a few years produced verse which was as pious as it was dull. How long this period lasted is uncertain, but by 1785 he seems to have been straining at the leash. When in that year Wilkinson ordered some bodies to be removed from the churchyard so that the adjoining lane might be widened, Mather wrote 'The Black Resurrection', a poem curiously anticipatory of Hardy in theme and treatment, in which he denounced Wilkinson, in very un-Methodist language, as 'that black diabolical fiend'.[51] By 1787 he had certainly broken with Methodism. James Montgomery, the Dissenting editor of *The Sheffield Iris* and minor poet, asserted many years later that it occurred because Mather 'was tempted to the ale-house [and] fell into sin',[52] but there were other and more cogent reasons. In 'The File Hewer's Lamentation' or 'The Author's Petition to Fortune', with its refrain

> Wearied bones, despised and daunted,
>   Hungry guts and empty purse,
> Hung with rags, by bailiffs haunted,
>   Prove the times grow worse,[53]

he spoke, not only for himself, but for his fellow-workers. The Sheffield cutlers received no encouragement in their fight to defend their living standards from the Methodists, for official Methodism, as opposed to breakaway sects such as the Kilhamite New Connexion, then and for long after, was violently opposed to democracy and trade unionism. Mather rejected Methodism's egocentric obsession with individual salvation for a morality based on solidarity with his fellows. From his Methodist period he retained an intimate knowledge of the Bible, which provided him with a constant source of imagery. When he said 'Give, oh give me Agur's prayer'[54] he expected his hearers to recognize the text 'Give me neither poverty nor riches' (Proverbs 30:8). The Bible also supplied him with an appropriate vocabulary with which to denounce the cutlers' enemies. During the Industrial Revolution the working class, like the black slaves who composed the spirituals, identified their sufferings and struggles with those of the Israelites, and it was in this spirit that Mather dubbed obnoxious officials of the Cutlers' Company 'Pharaoh' and 'Haman', with the moral indignation and violence of language of an Old Testament prophet.

The most famous of his songs on industrial issues, 'Watkinson and his Thirteens', was written in 1787, after Jonathan Watkinson, the master cutler, had demanded that the journeymen, to compensate for their traditional claim to retain surplus material, should make thirteen knives for the price of twelve. Whenever Watkinson appeared in the theatre the cutlers in the gallery bawled it in chorus, and it continued to be sung long after his death. Wilson recorded in 1862:

> I can never forget the impression made on my mind when a boy on hearing it sung by an old cutler. . . . After the singer had 'wet his whistle' he requested his shopmates to assist in chorus, and then struck off in a manly voice, laying strong emphasis on the last two lines in each stanza, at the conclusion of which he struck his stithy with a hammer for a signal, when all present joined in chorus with such a hearty good will that would have convinced any person that *they felt* the odd knife would have been well employed in dissecting Watkinson's 'vile carcase'.[55]

When in 1790 the scissors-grinders went on strike the manufacturers, led by George Wood, senior warden of the Cutlers' Company, resolved to prosecute the leaders, five of whom were sent to prison. Mather's song 'Hallamshire Haman' applied the Biblical story of Haman to Wood, and in its last stanza turned the Methodists' threat of hellfire against the persecutor of trade unionists:

> So if his great master should send in the year,
> And cite him at his dreadful court to appear,
> In torments and flames he must certainly dwell,
> And discount resound from the corners of hell.[56]

When in 1792 Spence Broughton was hanged for robbing the mail, on the evidence of an accomplice thought to be more guilty than himself, Mather expressed the popular sentiment in verse:

> When the Lord shall come with fury,
>   Taking vengeance on his foes,
> There no bribed judge or jury
>   Will through interest then be chose.[57]

Here the religious imagery of the Last Judgment is again turned against the establishment. Blake was soon to do the same thing in his prophetic books.

Mather the Jacobin

There is no evidence that Mather was interested in politics before 1792; even so rebellious a song as 'Watkinson and his Thirteens' contains the loyal sentiment 'Success to our Sovereign who peaceably reigns'. In November 1791, however, a few workmen founded the Sheffield Constitutional Society to work for parliamentary reform, and by March 1792 it had 2,000 members, largely drawn from the cutlers. When Wood, now master cutler, convened a public meeting in June to adopt a resolution thanking the king for his recent proclamation against seditious writings, the local democrats took over the meeting and adopted an amendment reversing the sense of the resolution. Mather celebrated the occasion in a song, 'Britons Awake', in which he referred to Wood as 'Beelzebub' and gleefully recorded that 'Like Jericho's walls the address tumbled down',[58] and thereby identified himself with Sheffield's democratic movement. He would have found some of his former Methodist friends inside it, for the Kilhamite 'Tom Paine Methodists' were strong in Sheffield, and some of them advocated revolutionary action.

His next political song was even more significant. The publication of Burke's *Reflections on the Revolution in France* and Paine's reply, *Rights of Man*, had divided the nation into democrats and anti-Jacobins. When the latter revived the old anti-Jacobite song 'God Save great George our King' as their party anthem the democrats retaliated by producing parodies of it, among them Mather's 'God Save Great Thomas Paine' (1793). The political struggle is seen in terms of an apocalyptic battle between darkness and light; Paine, like Christ, 'makes the blind to see', and his opponents are identified with the forces of evil:

> Despots may howl and yell,
> Though they're in league with hell
>   They'll not reign long;
> Satan may lead the van,

And do the worst he can,
Paine and his 'Rights of Man'
　Shall be my song.⁵⁹

The song was adopted as their anthem by the Sheffield democrats, 10,000 of whom sang it after a mass meeting on Castle Hill in 1794.

Serious disturbances occurred in Norfolk Street on 4 August 1795 as a result of the conduct of Colonel Athorpe, acting as commander of the local Volunteers. When a crowd refused to disperse 'beef-headed Bob' rode among them with his sword drawn and wounded several people. The angry crowd began throwing stones, whereupon on Athorpe's order the Volunteers opened fire, killing two men and wounding others. Mather indignantly protested in his song 'Norfolk Street Riots':

The stones besmeared with blood and brains,
Was the result of Robin's pains,
Surviving friends wept o'er the stains,
　When dying victims bled;
As Abel's blood aloud did call
To Him whose power created all,
　Eternal vengeance sure must fall
　Upon his guilty head.⁶⁰

In addition to righteous anger, Mather had a second weapon: ridicule. In his ballad 'Raddle-neck'd Tups' he made full use of it, pouring scorn upon Athorpe, the Volunteers (who, he suggested, would be less ready to resist an invading French army than to shoot down their unarmed fellow townsmen) and the jury which at the inquest on the two men shot had brought in a verdict of justifiable homicide.

Mather's last years were embittered by sickness, poverty and imprisonment for debt, but he still had many admirers. A lady told a friend of Wilson's that her father 'used to send her when a girl to the old gaol, with a good Sunday dinner for Mather, *because he was a Jacobin*'. Although his death in 1804 went unrecorded in *The Gentleman's Magazine*, 'his remains were followed to the grave by many of the working classes of the town, who ever regarded him as their champion'.⁶¹

Notes

1. John Money, *Experience and Identity: Birmingham and the West Midlands 1760–1800* (Manchester, 1977), p. 103.
2. John Freeth, *The Political Songster or, A Touch on the Times* (Birmingham, 1790), p. iii.
3. Ibid., p. 202. This poem is not found in some copies of this edition.
4. John Freeth, *The Warwickshire Medley: or Convivial Songster* (Birmingham, 1780?), p. 131.
5. J.A. Langford, 'John Freeth: The Birmingham "Ballad-Maker" '. In *Mid-England*, No. 1 (Birmingham, 1880), p. 58.
6. John Freeth, *Modern Songs on Various Subjects* (Birmingham, 1782), p. 9.
7. Freeth, *The Warwickshire Medley*, p. 22.
8. Ibid., p. 4.
9. Ibid., p. 45.
10. John Alfred Langford, *A Century of Birmingham Life* (Birmingham, 1868), vol. I, pp. 125–6.
11. *The Warwickshire Medley*, pp. 40, 55.
12. Christopher Hill, *God's Englishman: Oliver Cromwell and the English Revolution* (London, 1970), p. 271.
13. *The Warwickshire Medley*, p. 71.
14. Ibid., pp. 1–2.
15. Ibid., p. 20.
16. Freeth, *Modern Songs*, p. 17.
17. Freeth, *The Political Songster* (1790), p. 68.
18. Freeth, *Modern Songs*, pp. 27–8.
19. Ibid., p. 58.
20. Freeth, *The Political Songster* (1790), pp. 54–5.
21. Ibid., p. 51.
22. Ibid., pp. 48–9.
23. Ibid., p. iv.
24. Ibid., p. 128.
25. Ibid., p. 39*. Pages 37*–40* are inserted in some copies after p. 48.
26. Ibid., pp. 104–5.
27. Ibid., p. 77.
28. Ibid., p. 169.
29. Ibid., p. 159.
30. Ibid., p. 183.
31. Ibid., p. 216. This song is not found in some copies.
32. Langford, *A Century of Birmingham Life*, vol. I, p. 154.
33. Freeth, *The Warwickshire Medley*, p. 10. Why did Freeth think of Frederick II as a benevolent paternalist? Was he influenced by the

glorification of him during the Seven Years War as a 'Protestant hero'?
34. Ibid., p. 24.
35. Engrossing: 'buying up large quantities of corn, etc., with intent to sell them again'; forestalling: 'raising the price of certain goods, by buying merchandise on its way to market, or dissuading persons from bringing their goods there'; regrating: 'buying corn, etc., in any market and selling it again in the same place, so as to raise the price'. *Jowitt's Dictionary of English Law*, 2nd edn (London, 1977), pp. 701, 815, 1529.
36. Roy Palmer (ed.), *A Touch on the Times. Songs of Social Change 1770–1914* (Harmondsworth, 1974), 275.
37. E.P. Thompson, *Customs in Common* (London, 1991), p. 229.
38. Freeth, *The Political Songster* (1790), p. 119.
39. Ibid., p. 174; Palmer, *A Touch on the Times*, p. 278.
40. John Freeth, *A Touch on the Times; Being a Collection of New Songs to Old Tunes* (Birmingham, 1803), p. 31.
41. Ibid., pp. 42–3.
42. Ibid., p. 8.
43. Ibid., p. 31.
44. Ibid., p. 1.
45. John Freeth, *New Ballads, to Old Familiar Tunes* (Birmingham, 1805), p. 6.
46. Freeth, *A Touch on the Times*, p. 28.
47. *The Gentleman's Magazine*, 78 (1808), 955.
48. John Wilson (ed.), *The Songs of Joseph Mather* (Sheffield, 1862), pp. vii–viii.
49. Ibid., p. 5.
50. Ibid., p. 20.
51. Ibid., p. 45.
52. John Holland and James Everett, *Memoirs of the Life and Writings of James Montgomery* (London, 1854–6), Vol. V, p. 274.
53. Wilson, *Songs of Joseph Mather*, p. 2.
54. Ibid., p. 3.
55. Ibid., pp. 63–4.
56. Ibid., p. 32.
57. Ibid., p. 7.
58. Ibid., p. 36.
59. Ibid., pp. 56–7.
60. Ibid., p. 41.
61. Ibid., pp. ix, x.

5 'Beware of reverence': writing and radicalism in the 1790s
Paul O'Flinn

Writers said some invigoratingly radical things in the early 1790s. Writers like Tom Paine who cheered his readers by noting in *Rights of Man* (1791): 'I do not believe that monarchy and aristocracy will continue seven years longer in any of the enlightened countries in Europe.' A year later, Mary Wollstonecraft, in *Vindication of the Rights of Woman*, berated a society in which it appeared that woman 'was born only to procreate and rot'. In the same year William Blake insisted in *The Marriage of Heaven and Hell*: 'Prisons are built with stones of Law, brothels with bricks of Religion.' Also in the same year Anna Barbauld, in her poem 'On the Expected General Rising of the French Nation in 1792', appealed to revolutionary France to 'Strike hordes of despots to the ground!' Still in 1792 Helen Maria Williams's poetic epistle 'To Dr Moore' tore into reactionary defenders of the status quo and scorned them as:

> Those reasoners who pretend that each abuse,
> Sanctioned by precedent, has some blest use!

In the following year, in which Britain went to war with France, William Godwin's *Enquiry Concerning Political Justice* asserted: 'Government in reality, as has abundantly appeared, is a question of force, not consent.' Three years into that war, the hero of Robert Bage's novel *Hermsprong* noted sourly: 'War is lunacy, and we call in all the powers of reason to prove it wisdom.'

And so I could go on, quoting more of the epigrams, couplets, slogans and prophecies illustrative of that extraordinary explosion of radical writing from the early 1790s, a period probably unmatched in British history for its intellectual daring and its moral courage. The conventional and surely correct explanation for this phenomenon is that it represents the cultural articulation of a unique conjuncture in Western history, the years that saw the American revolution of 1776, the French revolution of 1789 and, in Britain, the onslaught of the Industrial Revolution. In a couple of decades three giant revolutions whose consequences we are still negotiating transformed the ways people in the Western world were governed and the ways they earned a living and, following on from that, the ways they loved one another and fought one another, the ways they excelled and the ways they relaxed. What the seven quotations in the first paragraph represent are some of the ways the writers of the time tried to intervene in that chaos, tried to articulate the process, to check it, describe it, deflect it, expand it, celebrate it and think it through.

Two hundred years later, how do we as students of the period approach that complex, dizzying moment of cultural and political history? Surely the way to come nearest to the truth is to try to arrive at a sense of the cultural discourse as a whole with its interconnections and contradictions rather than settling for a specialised study of a single voice in that massive cacophony. By this I mean that to split the seven texts cited in the first paragraph into the literary (Blake, Barbauld, Williams and Bage) and the non-literary (Paine, Wollstonecraft and Godwin) and then to shunt the latter group off to the Politics Department is to impoverish any sense of the 1790s that might emerge at the end of a process of study. That impoverishment is of course only deepened if we then make a further split into major Romantic (Blake) and minor Romantic (the rest) authors, with Barbauld, Williams and Bage disappearing up a footnote or two and Blake foregrounded as a solitary genius.

Blake knew Paine, he dined with Godwin, he worked with Wollstonecraft. She was a welcome visitor to Williams's salon in Paris where she renewed acquaintance with Paine. Later she married Godwin. Like Paine, she had been part of the circle of writers around the radical London publisher Joseph Johnson, as had Blake and Godwin. When the latter visited Bage in 1797, he sent an account of the visit to Wollstonecraft, who had reviewed *Hermsprong* the previous year. The hero of that novel is put on trial at the climax of the story for, among other things, distributing Paine's *Rights of Man*. The point I am making is that these writers' lives and ideas are a productive tangle. To unpick that tangle is first to simplify and then falsify.

To extend the same argument another way – Mary Wollstonecraft is not simply a feminist any more than she is simply a novelist or a mother or a failed suicide or a teacher. She is all of those things and much besides. You cannot separate *Vindication of the Rights of Woman* from her novel *Wrongs of Woman*. They are rather two attempts by the same woman to come at the same problem in varied ways at specific moments of her experience. To pull the two texts apart into different academic disciplines is to lose hold of their interdependence and to lose sight of entire dimensions of both. Like the rest of us, Wollstonecraft is a multi-layered human being and our study should work with that fact. To look at her simply as a novelist or simply as a feminist is to look at her through half an eye. Seen whole, she can move a reader to fresh ways of seeing and thinking as she demands a whole response. Seen through traditional subject blinkers, she is reduced to a figure that mediates between Burney and Austen or Locke and Mill or Astell and the Pankhursts.

The problem with writers at the end of the eighteenth century is that they refuse to stay within the tight boundaries that were constructed later on for academic convenience. Driven by the intense pressure of events at the start of the 1790s, Mary Wollstonecraft wrote her extended political pamphlet *Vindication of the Rights of Woman* in six weeks. Godwin followed in the next year, 1793, with his philosophical treatise *Enquiry Concerning Political Justice*. But in 1794 he recast and developed some of those ideas as fiction in *Things as They Are* and Mary Wollstonecraft made a similar tactical switch to the novel with *Wrongs of Woman* that she was working on when she died in 1797.

If we are to understand the work of these writers we must follow the course of their development rather than wave farewell to them as they pass beyond an arbitrary frontier marked 'literature'. If we are to grasp why a writer previously as prolific as Blake lapsed into a silent decade in the mid-1790s, during which he completed no major work, then we will search in vain for an answer if we search for one exclusively within those literary confines. The same is true of another contemporary working-class writer, Ann Yearsley, who produced a mass of poetry, prose and drama between 1784 and 1796 but then there is nothing and in 1806 she died. The reasons for those bursts of creativity and those years of frustration lie in the rhythms of the politics and the history and the culture of the times. Our task then is to try to listen to those rhythms and work with them rather than shut them out as irrelevant distractions to the study of literary texts.

In attempting to work in this way I would like to suggest that the term 'Romantic', traditionally used to describe late eighteenth-century and early nineteenth-century literature, is increasingly more of a hindrance than a help. Tom Paine, read by millions in the 1790s and the most influential writer of his generation, is often not much more than an aside in literary studies of the age because his bold rationalism means that he does not fit with most of the conventional connotations of Romanticism, which allegedly gets off the ground at this moment. A recent persuasive study by Jon Mee has demonstrated at length the kind of violence that has been done in the past to Blake's work to make it fit in with Romantic paradigms.[1] Feminist scholars like Janet Todd and Anne Mellor have revealed the ways in which definitions of Romantic poetry based on the work of the so-called big six (the male poets Blake, Wordsworth, Coleridge, Byron, Shelley and Keats) have been used to delete or marginalise the work of women poets, most of them unavailable in any form until the recent anthologies edited by Roger Lonsdale and by Jennifer Breen.[2] In short, it is clear that when we use a loaded term like 'Romantic' we are dealing more in the prejudices and enthusiasms of the present than with the facts and complexity of the past.

Blake makes my point rather more sharply:

> If the doors of perception were cleansed everything would
> appear to man as it is – infinite.
> For man has closed himself up, till he sees all things
> through narrow chinks of his cavern.[3]

This is why the concept of 'writing' that stands at the centre of the present volume particularly commends itself. It gets us out of the cavern of 'Romantic literature' and allows us to look freely around at the infinite variety of cultural production in the 1790s, without being anxiously concerned about the status and acceptability of specific texts. It is my experience too that students, working thus uninhibitedly on the period, begin to be excited producers of their own meanings rather than passive consumers of the rows of received wisdom along the shelves labelled 'Romantics' in the library.

If we look in this way, one of the first things that must strike us about some of the writing of the 1790s is its enormous courage and originality. Government anxiety to repress dissent in the wake of the French Revolution culminated in the treason trials of 1794 when the writers John Thelwall, Horne Tooke and Thomas Holcroft faced the death penalty. They were acquitted but the warning to fellow writers was clear enough. 'Terror was the order of the day; and it was feared that even the humble novelist might be shown to be constructively a traitor' wrote Godwin in the 1795 Preface to *Things as They Are*, explaining the decision to withdraw the Preface to the 1794 edition. The earlier Preface had described the text accurately enough as 'a general review of the modes of domestic and unrecorded despotism by which man becomes the destroyer of man'. Booksellers, perhaps guessing that the average judge was too indolent to read a three-volume novel but might well glance through a one-page Preface, persuaded Godwin to drop it.

The story of the missing Preface to *Things as They Are* is worth centring because it reminds us of the threats that circled every writer's desk at the time. The radical Joseph Priestley, author and discoverer of oxygen, had his home, library and laboratory wrecked by 'Church and King' rioters in 1791. Tom Paine fled to France in 1792 and was outlawed in his absence. Thomas Spence, expelled from the Philosophical Society in Newcastle for a lecture he gave them entitled 'The Rights of Man', was imprisoned in 1794 and again in 1798, and so too in the latter year was Joseph Johnson, the major radical publisher of the decade. Richard Brothers, seer of visions in the same mode as Blake, was put in an asylum in 1795 while Blake himself was tried for sedition in 1804. In the hard light of these facts it is possible to see that the seven statements I quoted in the first paragraph of this chapter were not easy appeals to fashionable applause but rather the brave stances of men and women made more and more aware as the decade progressed that they risked everything for their views.

Seen from that angle, much of the writing of the 1790s takes its origin not in the 'spontaneous overflow of powerful feelings' hailed by Wordsworth's famous remark about poetry but instead in the chronically stressed calculations of men and women about how much they could say without ending up in gaol. Christopher Hill has insisted that we should not accept most texts from the past at face value because to do so is to collude with the censors who shaped them, and this is particularly true of those who wrote in the frightened years following the French Revolution.[4]

The wonder is that so much intransigent work got written if not always published. Blake's *The French Revolution* survives in only one proof copy because at that late stage even a courageous publisher like Johnson seems to have had second thoughts and spiked it. In that poem, written in 1791, Blake imaginatively confronts, in the same way that Paine was shortly to do in *Rights of Man*, the argument that lies at the heart of the conservative case as articulated by Burke in *Reflections on the Revolution in France* (1790). This is the insistence that an aristocratic order bases its claim to rule on the massive authority supplied by precedent or, as the poem's King calls it, 'The nerves of five thousand years' ancestry' (l.70). An unfocused narrator at the start of the poem prefers to call it the 'slumbers of five thousand years' (l.8) and subsequently the aristocratic order is always associated with images of repression, stagnation, age and decay. By contrast, it is only as the common people move towards the exercise of power that the poem is able to conclude with 'morning's beam' (l.306).

In short, *The French Revolution*, like the French Revolution, is a sustained attack on the power of precedent, and again and again in the writing of the 1790s you can see that attack being extended. Paine's *Rights of Man* incorporates a translation of the 1789 Declaration of the Rights of Man and of Citizens by the French National Assembly, and hence places a copy of this subversive document in the hands and the minds of his multitude of British readers. There they might see that 'Men are born, and always continue, free, and equal in the respect of their rights. Civil distinctions, therefore, can be founded only on public utility.' Or: 'The unrestrained communication of thoughts and opinions being one of the most precious rights of man, every citizen may speak, write, and publish freely . . .'[5]

Impelled by that spirit, writers are possessed of an intense curiosity, a need to explore and to challenge. It is curiosity that drives Mary Wollstonecraft not merely to theorise comfortably about a society 'very differently organised'[6] but actually to go and live in one: she was in Paris from December 1792 until April 1795, through the first years of the war with Britain, the execution of Louis XVI and Marie Antoinette and the whole of the Reign of Terror. It is curiosity, a pioneering desire to go where too few women before had been allowed, that tempts a host of women to risk ridicule and plunge into print for the first time in these years.[7] It is a similar, obsessive curiosity that Godwin places at the centre of consideration in *Things as They Are*.

It is worth pausing for a moment over the last example. *Things as They Are* presents us with an ordinary hero, Caleb Williams (after whom the novel is titled in later editions), who suspects that his employer, the aristocratic Falkland, has committed a murder and allowed a couple of innocent working men to hang for it. Caleb tracks Falkland's guilty secret down to a locked chest, whereupon Falkland turns upon Caleb, pursuing and persecuting him till the end of the novel. Reading the novel in the terms supplied by classical tragedy, recent critics have suggested that curiosity is Caleb's tragic flaw.[8] But this seems to me to miss the novel's point, which is rather to suggest that curiosity is man's original virtue and not some sort of psychological inadequacy; it only becomes acutely problematic in a society that has dirty little secrets locked away in chests to preserve power and privilege. The text is thus a single-minded investigation of the nature of human curiosity and its contradictory social construction, a paramount issue for writers faced with the persecutions of the 1790s as we have seen. (Put that way, it is easier to understand why, when the novel was serialised for ITV in the Autumn of 1983, it was found necessary to invent a servant named Jane, whose task is to love Caleb devotedly and marry him at the end. This dislocation of the novel's prime concern and its replacement with a piece of romantic tripe is evidence of the extent to which the text breaks with the traditional concerns of the form and needed to be brutally rewritten in order to meeet conventional expectations.)

An intense, exercised curiosity is an inevitable result of the industrial and political revolutions sweeping the West at that time. 'Beware of reverence' Godwin urged readers in *Political Justice*. If nothing any longer was sacred, if everything about the world was open to change, if the laws of culture, economics and government were being rapidly rewritten, then human curiosity was encouraged to surge across human institutions, noting perhaps for the first time an absurdity here, an inconsistency there, intolerable blocks everywhere. What I would therefore like to do in the rest of this chapter is to glance at how, in the light of that curiosity, a small but I think representative sample of radical texts scrutinised three aspects of life – namely, religion, class and gender/sexuality – that must be addressed in the construction and reconstruction of any conceivable form of human society.

Religion

Atheist arguments began to be heard in late eighteenth-century Britain – for example, in Matthew Turner's *Answer to Dr Priestley*, written in 1782[9] – but the two radical writers from the 1790s that I would like to look at in this section both believed in their own god. What they did not believe in was the authority of the Bible as the Word of God. If the Bible is the transcendent Book, if it is a unique text because of its divine inspiration, it at once renders all other books to some extent irrelevant and unnecessary. It follows that what humanity needs to know for its happiness and salvation is in the Old and New Testaments and everything else is superfluous, a distraction; our response to the Book should be silence and humble study rather than the production of competing books. What I am driving at is one of the convictions that seems to me to be at the foundation of the work of Wollstonecraft and Paine: the conviction that the supreme and final authority of the Bible and its traditional interpretations have to be overthrown if writers are to have space to breathe and to work.

An obvious example of what I mean can be found if we look at the Biblical account of the origin of women:

> And Adam called all the beasts by their names, and all the fowls of the air, and all the cattle of the field: but for Adam there was not found a helper like himself.
> Then the Lord God cast a deep sleep upon Adam: and when he was fast asleep, he took one of his ribs, and filled up flesh for it.
> And the Lord God built the rib which he took from Adam into a woman: and brought her to Adam.
> And Adam said: This now is bone of my bones, and flesh of my flesh; she shall be called woman, because she was taken out of man.
> (Genesis 2: 20–23)

The message here is clear enough. Prelapsarian man made language, which predates the existence of woman. Woman was made out of man's spare rib in order to be a helper to him. Man uses his language to name woman and to define her as an extension of himself.

Any feminist writing on feminist politics has to break with that account if it is not to curl up and die under a sense of its own pathetic redundancy. It is for this reason that Mary Wollstonecraft argues in her *Vindication*:

> Probably the prevailing opinion that woman was created for man, may have taken its rise from Moses' poetical story; yet as very few, it is presumed, who have bestowed any serious thought on the subject ever supposed that Eve was, literally speaking, one of Adam's ribs, the deductions must be allowed to fall to the ground, or only be so far admitted as it proves that man, from the remotest antiquity, found it convenient to exert his strength to subjugate his companion, and his invention to show that she ought to have her neck bent under the yoke, because the whole creation was only created for his convenience or pleasure. (p. 109)

Two significant things are going on in this magnificently scandalous sentence. Wollstonecraft refers not to Genesis but rather to Moses. At once she stands opposite not God, with whom there is clearly no arguing, but rather a named male author who would say that sort of thing, wouldn't he. Secondly, what Moses offers is not literal truth, much less the word of God, but rather a 'poetical story' – what she later on calls 'Moses' beautiful poetical cosmogony' (p. 175). Behind the admiration conveyed by that epithet 'beautiful' lies a massive repositioning of the Bible, a cancelling of its claim to absolute authority and its redefinition as imaginative literature.

There is a parallel move being made in Tom Paine's *The Age of Reason*, Part I, written in Parisian exile and published there in 1794. Like Wollstonecraft, Paine is not an atheist. Right at the start, he insists: 'I believe in one God.'[10] Again like Wollstonecraft, he regards, the Bible as literature rather than the exclusive word of God which leads him to suggest: 'In many things, however, the writings of the Jewish poets deserve a better fate than that of being bound up, as they now are with the trash that accompanies them, under the abused name of the Word of God' (pp. 413–4).

I would like to quote Paine at some length, both to supply a fuller sense of the man and his ideas and because I find his words after two hundred years are a mix of sharp sanity and melancholy consolation in a week in which, as I type, five Catholics have been murdered by their fellow countrymen in Ulster ostensibly because they interpreted the Bible unacceptably:

> I do not believe in the creed professed by the Jewish Church, by the Roman Church, by the Greek Church, by the Turkish Church, by the Protestant Church, nor by any church that I know of. My own mind is my own church.
>
> All national institutions of churches, whether Jewish, Christian or Turkish, appear to me no other than human inventions, set up to terrify and enslave mankind, and monopolize power and profit . . .
>
> Every national church or religion has established itself by pretending some special mission from God, communicated to certain individuals. The Jews have their Moses; the Christians their Jesus Christ, their apostles and saints; and the Turks their Mahomet, as if the way to God was not open to every man alike.
>
> Each of those churches show certain books, which they call *revelation*, or the Word of God. The Jews say that their Word of God was given by God to Moses, face to face; the Christians say that their Word of God came by divine inspiration; and the Turks say that their Word of God (the Koran) was brought by an angel from heaven. Each of those churches accuses the other of unbelief; and for my own part I disbelieve them all. (pp. 400–01)

For the sake of clarity and reasonable brevity I have quoted a series of flat assertions without the sustaining argument that surrounds them, but nevertheless I think the flavour of the man and his ideas is here. There is, for example, the instinctive internationalism, which allows him to see the exclusive claims of local belief systems in absurdly deflating perspective. There is the heroic individualism, inspirationally confident of its own powers and so mordantly suspicious of the pretensions of any institution and the demands that it makes on the subject. But above all there is the implicit realisation that for writers to function freely, to produce their words, the Word has to be displaced, its claim to overarching truth challenged. Once that task is accomplished then writers are free to speak without inhibition, free to interrogate their own experience without being shackled by the 'mind-forg'd manacles' that Blake's 'London' links to the institutional power of the 'Palace' and the 'blackening Church'. Once writers start to do that they are faced with another solid wall, another barrier in the way of liberated articulation – the fact of class and its determining control of cultural life in the 1790s.

Class

In the space of a short chapter there is time only to point to one or two of the many ways in which the class nature of British society constructed the writing of the 1790s. The best place to start is to remember Raymond Williams's insistence that late eighteenth-century authors constitute a much wider cross-section of British society than is the case in any previous generation.[11] The stereotypical but not inaccurate image of the average Augustan author as an Oxbridge graduate with a comfortable living in an undemanding rural parish is replaced at the end of the century by an ex-corset maker (Tom Paine) and a former actress (Elizabeth Inchbald), by a servant (Elizabeth Hands) and an engraver (William Blake), by a milkmaid like Ann Yearsley or a one-time seamstress like Mary Wollstonecraft.

The fact that they come from outside the elite gives all of these writers a productively contradictory attitude to an inevitably elite, written culture. They strive to enter that culture but they seek to change it, so that simultaneously they extend and destroy, reinforce and dismantle the dominant network of ideas and values within which they create and in which they are entangled. Those at the end of the eighteenth century with the education to read books, the spare cash to buy them and the leisure time to consume them were by definition a class living well in that society and therefore unlikely to entertain the dreams of something different, the desires for radical change of a corset-maker or a milkmaid. What all of these writers face therefore is a constant struggle to adjust their ideas to their public, to write in ways that express their hopes but will prove tolerable to their readers, that explore new ranges of hope and fantasy but remain within the orbit of a largely conservative market.

These facts help us to understand matters as diverse as William Blake's fight to produce and distribute his work outside the conventional structures of publishing or Tom Paine's successful breakthrough to an entirely different, popular readership with the use of cheap editions or Ann Yearsley's complex relationship with her patronising patron Hannah More.[12] They also help us to get inside the battery of tensions that are the making of a text like *Vindication of the Rights of Woman* in which Mary Wollstonecraft on the one hand addresses herself very specifically 'to those in the middle class, because they appear to be in the most natural state' (p. 81) and yet on the other hand spends an invigorating proportion of her text describing those in that state as superstitious, cunning, irrational, sentimental and ignorant. There is a parallel, bewildering ambivalence in Elizabeth Inchbald's novel *A Simple Story*, published in 1791 a year before *Vindication*. Here there is a tale whose happy ending appears to endorse a dominant class and its power that the preceding four volumes reveal as arbitrary, tyrannical, emotionally frozen and quite mad.

We are talking about an era of immense social upheaval, one which witnessed, in E.P. Thompson's phrase, the making of the English working class. In response to that, the new writers strove to express themselves in new ways, to mark their difference from the old dominant culture by breaking with its formal conventions and stylistic habits. Mary Robinson started earning a living, like Elizabeth Inchbald, as an actress and then led a life of tumbling variety during which she was at various times and among many other things in a debtors' prison, mistress of the Prince of Wales, partially paralysed and a good friend of Godwin and Wollstonecraft. She could and did write as conventionally as anyone but there are moments when her experience drives her into startling freshness. Her poem 'January, 1795' is such a moment, a wonderfully direct poem of forty-four lines with scarcely a main verb; instead, a dense pack of nouns, participles and bitter epithets gives us the sort of realistic sketch of a class-divided city and its wildly diverse people that is normally thought to be unavailable until the following century.[13]

It is in the work of Blake that the formal articulation of the facts and the tensions of class is most evidently to be found in the early 1790s. In the 125 lines of *The Book of Thel* there are at least twenty-one questions and in the 218 lines of *Visions of the Daughters of Albion* there are no fewer than forty-seven. Many of these questions are rhetorical and unanswered, spun out in apparently self-generating strings. *The French Revolution* is substantially built around ten speeches by eight different speakers but there is no dialectical, Bakhtinian dialogue here, rather a sense of men shouting to make themselves heard over the rumblings of revolution, each anxious to mark out his own space and no one with the time or the flexibility to listen to or be persuaded by anyone else. And then there is *The Marriage of Heaven and Hell*, a whirling mixture of fantasy and slogan, poetry and prose, theological speculation and radical graffiti, words and pictures, literary criticism and world history. The stylistic features of all of these four texts speak of a man no longer content to see the world and write it out in those acceptable ways that inevitably encode acceptable values. Instead, the rules of writing are thrown aside, text is mixed with image and readers/beholders are forced to work at the object in front of them, slowly producing in alliance with Blake the new meanings, the new angles of vision, the new questions that are essential if the new society with its new geography of class power and tension is to be apprehended. As Blake himself puts it in a typical burst of challenging interrogation and exclamation that captures the irreconcilable differences of experience in class society:

> Does he who contemns poverty, and he who turns with abhorrence

> From usury, feel the same passion – or are they moved alike?
> How can the giver of gifts experience the delights of the merchant,
> How the industrious citizen the pains of the husbandman?
> How different far the fat-fed hireling with hollow drum,
> Who buys whole cornfields into wastes and sings upon the heath!
> How different their eye and ear! How different the world to them!
> With what sense does the parson claim the labour of the farmer?
> What are his nets and gins and traps, and how does he surround him
> With cold floods of abstraction and with forests of solitude,
> To build him castles and high spires, where kings and priests may dwell,
> Till she who burns with youth and knows no fixed lot, is bound
> In spells of law to one she loathes. And must she drag the chain
> Of life in weary lust?
>
> (*Visions of the Daughters of Albion*, ll. 121–34)

These lines are spoken by the poem's raped heroine, Oothoon, and what she draws from her trauma here is an intuitive sense of the modes in which the class oppression of 'kings and priests' is not separable from sexual oppression, the oppression of the chained woman with whom the passage closes. It is to that issue that I would now like to turn.

Gender and sexuality

I take 'sex' to mean the basic biological difference between men and women, 'gender' to mean the massive weight of social conditioning with which society surrounds that difference and 'sexuality' to mean the way that men and women, on the basis of sex and gender, express themselves sensuously and seek sensual fulfilment.

Any engagement with these terms in the 1790s has to start with Mary Wollstonecraft's *Vindication of the Rights of Woman* because of that text's courageous and extensive analysis of the processes of gendering. There are two aspects of that analysis that I would like to draw attention to. First is the way that Wollstonecraft presents a materialist account of the way that gendering happens. She writes of young girls: 'Taught from their infancy that beauty is woman's sceptre, the mind shapes itself to the body, and roaming round its gilt cage, only seeks to adore its prison' (p. 131). Later she adds: 'Men order their clothes to be made, and have done with the subject; women make their own clothes . . . and are continually talking about them; and their thoughts follow their hands' (p. 170). Behind two key phrases here – 'the mind shapes itself to the body' and 'their thoughts follow their hands' – lies a central insistence that women are the way they are not because of their souls, their star signs or their biology but because of the concrete details of their repeated physical experience, in particular the confined and patronised experience that eighteenth-century society imposes on them. But, having established that, Wollstonecraft is no mechanical materialist, and the second thing that strikes me about *Vindication* is the fact that by far the longest section of the work, Chapter 5, is a detailed piece of feminist literary criticism, concerned to show the part that culture and the texts out of which it is made has to play in the distorted and demeaning construction of her contemporaries.

At a time when Wollstonecraft was making ideas of this sort a part of the intellectual currency of the age, the rethinking of sexuality and its constitution would inevitably become an issue both for herself and for her contemporaries. In some texts this investigation is implicit, indirect, even unconscious. For example, it is my experience in teaching Godwin's *Things as They Are* over the years that many readers find this a powerfully homoerotic novel. An intense mutual affection is repeatedly acknowledged by the two male protagonists and it is then simultaneously repressed and tortuously sublimated into an obsessive and destructive mutual pursuit/persecution. To reject that reading is to be unable to find any convincing explanation for the muddled anguish and distraught passion that tears the pages of the two tragic endings that Godwin provided for the novel.

Other texts explore sexuality and its expression much more directly. Ann Yearsley's 'The Indifferent Shepherdess to Colin', first published in 1796, is not so much about indifference as about liberty, a word that is repeated with growing insistence at the end of each of the poem's seven stanzas. The pastoral form that Yearsley employs here is a conventional mode for describing conventional sexual desire. But Yearsley's twist is to see that desire as a trap for women, so that every stanza is packed with terms that reinforce that sense: 'snare . . . Dominion . . . servile . . . confine . . . Bereft . . . Slave . . . fettered'. The poet writes out a mood in which a kind of calm chastity is the only way for a woman to preserve her freedom in 1796:

> For my eternal plan
>   Is to be calm and free.
> Estranged from tyrant man
>   I'll keep my liberty.[14]

Chastity is not the subject of Elizabeth Inchbald's *A Simple Story* (1791). Rather, the text is concerned to explore forbidden areas of sexuality. The novel has at its centre the adolescent Miss Milner (she is never given a first name) who falls in love with her guardian, a Catholic priest named Dorriforth. As guardian and as priest he is thus doubly her father, doubly barred from sexual availability by the taboo of incest and a vow of celibacy. At one level the novel is a daring romantic story about the way these barriers are removed but at another it investigates the fearsome psychological price that has to be paid as a result in terms of displaced violence, irrational tyranny, bloody duels and decades of neurotically inarticulate anger.

Conclusion

Wherein nothing is concluded. But as I stop there are a few points I would like to make about what I have tried to do in this chapter. J.R. de J. Jackson's *Romantic Poetry by Women: A Bibliography 1770–1835* (Oxford, 1993) lists the works of over 900 women poets from that period. It would probably be fair to say that most twentieth-century literary critics, myself included, have not read the work of most of those women and yet that has not stopped us in the past from generalising confidently about the literature of the period and its characteristics. We must learn to stop doing this, particularly as more determined research aided by more sophisticated information technology is constantly expanding and changing our sense of the past and its writing. All anyone can do, all I have tried to do in the preceding pages, is speak about the apparent archaeology of the small area of the vast field in which excavation has occurred. If Romantic critics in the past have offered Coleridge's 'Christabel' or Keats's 'La Belle Dame Sans Merci' as culturally representative women all I can say is that in the particular part of the site where I have been digging better candidates look to be, say, Ann Yearsley's forlornly aware shepherdess or perhaps the magnificent Maria Fluart, waving a threatening pistol and adroitly saving the heroine of *Hermsprong* from a forced marriage.

As the world caught in a triple spiral of revolutions appeared to spin out of control, Blake was to insist that 'I must create a system, or be enslaved by another man's' (*Jerusalem*, Plate 10, l.20.) What we have in the writing of the 1790s is a glimpse of men and women, impelled by brave curiosity, involved in precisely that kind of system-making and system-breaking, inspiring examples of Marx's dictum that in transforming the world we transform ourselves.

The result was a massive expansion in human aspiration and human self-knowledge, as Wollstonecraft's extension of feminist thinking took its place beside, say, the pioneering anarchism of Godwin and the proto-socialism of Paine. It is now more than two centuries since the cold February day when the latter set about writing the last paragraph of *Rights of Man*. But he was able to turn the dank gloom outside into a message of political optimism for the future and to conclude: 'It is, however, not difficult to perceive that spring is begun. Thus wishing, as I sincerely do, freedom and happiness to all nations, I close the Second Part.' Paine knew that there are more things in heaven and earth than are dreamt of by either eighteenth-century complacency or twentieth-century cynicism. Contact with that sort of awareness is still the best reason for reading the writing of the radicals of the 1790s.

Notes

1. Jon Mee, *Dangerous Enthusiasm: William Blake and the Culture of Radicalism in the 1790s* (Oxford, 1992).
2. Janet Todd, *Feminist Literary History: A Defence* (Oxford, 1988); Anne K. Mellor (ed.), *Romanticism and Feminism* (Bloomington, 1988); Roger Lonsdale (ed.), *Eighteenth-Century Women Poets* (Oxford, 1990); Jennifer Breen (ed.), *Women Romantic Poets 1785–1832: An Anthology* (London, 1992).
3. 'The Marriage of Heaven and Hell', *The Poems of William Blake*, ed. W.H. Stevenson (London, 1971), p. 114.
4. Christopher Hill, 'Literature and History', lecture delivered at the Ruskin History Workshop 'The Future of English' Conference, June 1991.
5. Thomas Paine, *Rights of Man* (Harmondsworth, 1969), pp. 132, 133–4.
6. Mary Wollstonecraft, *Vindication of the Rights of Woman* (Harmondsworth, 1975), p. 197.
7. Stuart Curran, 'Women Readers, Women Writers', in Stuart Curran (ed.), *The Cambridge Companion to British Romanticism* (Cambridge, 1993) persuasively estimates the number of published women authors in the late eighteenth and early nineteenth century as 'actually thousands'.
8. See, for example, Don Locke, *A Fantasy of Reason: The Life and Thought of William Godwin* (London, 1980) and Peter H. Marshall, *William Godwin* (Yale, 1984).
9. On this subject, see David Berman, *A History of Atheism in Britain* (London, 1988).
10. *The Thomas Paine Reader*, eds Michael Foot and Isaac Kramnick (Harmondsworth, 1987), p. 400.
11. See the statistics in Part Two, chapter 5 of Raymond Williams, *The Long Revolution* (Harmondsworth, 1965).
12. For an informed recent account of this relationship, see Chapter 4 of Donna Landry, *The Muses of Resistance: Laboring-Class Women's Poetry in Britain 1739–1796* (Cambridge, 1990).
13. Breen, *Women Romantic Poets*, pp. 72–3.
14. Ibid., pp. 102–3.

6 Four Jacobin women novelists
Loraine Fletcher

I

Such a carpetbagging title may seem to elide individuality. To group four women novelists – Mary Wollstonecraft, Mary Hays, Elizabeth Inchbald and Charlotte Smith – under one heading threatens to perpetuate the disesteem in which academic criticism has held them. Though Wollstonecraft is now established on women's writing courses, and all have been reprinted, they are still less well-known than they should be. But they have enough in common to justify considering them together, and the uniqueness of each novel should emerge sufficiently, however brief the account, to encourage further reading.

All four were in their late twenties or older when the French Revolution began in 1789. They had already discovered that the 'normal' woman's life of marriage and motherhood was either impossible to achieve or did not bring the fulfilment promised by conduct books for young women, by mainstream novels of courtship, and indeed by much of their culture. They were defining for themselves feminist attitudes which were just starting to be called 'radical', a new word for a new complex of beliefs. They inevitably attracted hostility: these are the hyenas in petticoats[1] of contemporary male myth, asserting the right to polemicise, to connect the domestic with the public life and so politicise sex and the family. Their novels are critical of marriage, especially arranged or ill-considered marriage but sometimes of marriage in principle, critical too of the unequal distribution of wealth and power between upper and lower classes and between men and women. They often represent institutionalised religion and the law as elaborate devices to keep the poor and women in their places. Typically, they image society as a prison: their novels are full of prisons or of houses which, even if comfortable, become prisons, confining and marginalising women in turrets or remote rooms.

The Revolution in France secured the abolition of titles, an end to the Church's power, the promise of wider electoral representation and of divorce with equitable settlements for women. The first two years brought change with relatively little violence, and in 1790 and 1791 similar change seemed imminent in England. Ending the second part of *The Rights of Man* in February 1792, Tom Paine wrote: 'what pace the political summer may keep with the natural, no human foresight can determine. It is however not difficult to perceive that the spring is begun.'[2] This was an alarming thought to the majority of the English middle class, but inspiriting to the reformist Jacobins, a word with a complicated derivation. Dominican monks were known as Jacobins in France because their first monastery in Paris was in the Rue St Jacques, Jacobus in Latin. So the members of a political club who rented a Dominican refectory for its meetings during the 1780s also became known as Jacobins – satirically, as they weren't like monks – and they adopted the name themselves. The Jacobin club formed the nucleus of the most extreme revolutionary group in the new government, which had seats on the left side of the Convention chamber, while more moderate groups who wanted change by legal and non-violent means occupied the centre and right, giving us the concepts of left and right that have dominated European political thinking for the last two hundred years. During the first three years of the Revolution the Jacobins gained power over their rivals. English sympathisers with the early ideals of the Revolution, however moderate, also became known as Jacobins, a term of abuse which was used loosely during the 1790s and well into the next century for almost any reformist writer. Among the male novelists to whom the term was applied are Robert Bage, William Godwin and Thomas Holcroft.

The English Jacobins authors, then, had a political purpose, and Wollstonecraft, Hays, Inchbald and Smith used the novel, that most important arena for ideological debate in the 1790s, to attack social injustice, to women especially. For the mainly male academics who have formed the canons of English literature, they are altogether too earnest, their work too heavily loaded with a sense of their wrongs, too awkwardly autobiographical, to be considered artistic in the Austen manner. There's some truth in this. They simply are not as witty as Austen, though Smith and Inchbald come close. They have no firm Anglican base as Frances Burney and Austen had, no model feudal order or paradigm of love and marriage. They knew what they didn't like – things as they were[3] – but felt less sure of what they did like, and what social and sexual relationships should be. Yet even because of their uncertainties many readers can respond to them more directly than to Burney or Austen, and value the jagged and desperate tone in their fiction. Their ideas remain as controversial and their techniques as demanding now as for their first readers.

An important technique they share is the formation of close links between narrator, heroine and reader through the narrative methods they choose. The narrator often addresses the reader directly in preface or text, and uses autobiographical material, intended to be recognised as such, in her heroine's distresses. Heroines are usually readers themselves, and often writers, who therefore share a narrator's and reader's task of discriminating between outdated literary stereotype and fresh authentic expression. We are encouraged to see the novels as commentaries on the institutional tyranny of which author, heroine and reader are all assumed to be victims. First person confessional narrative draws listeners inside or outside the novel into a character's subjective account of oppression. Sometimes an apparently omniscient narrator will leave lacunae in the story, or get it wrong, encouraging the reader to construct the heroine's experience from her own imagination. Stereotypical novelistic situations like the heroine's rescue are rewritten in ways that disturb old assumptions about gender. They are very literary writers, and their narrators work partly through contrast with competing texts.

II

Of the four, Mary Wollstonecraft (1759–97) was perhaps the most influential, in her own time and afterwards, and the one all the others knew, though they didn't all know each other. Her upbringing by a violent father and a beaten, passive mother made her a passionate advocate of women's rights when she was hardly old enough to articulate such concepts. As we construct women's lives in history, we do so out of our sense of a feminist continuous present. In her imaginative biography of Wollstonecraft, *Vindication* (1993), Frances Sherwood asserts a community of experience from one generation to another, and the heroine's sensibility feels very modern. This is inevitable, from our perspective two hundred years on, and a useful corrective to the common prejudice when we first approach pre-twentieth-century writers and their work, that 'in those days' women's feelings and problems were quite different from our own, and somehow simpler. Nothing could be less true. But it is well to remember also that Wollstonecraft is probably more remote, in her response to religion or natural landscape, than we might like to think. She fictionalised her own life twice, inventively and passionately, in *Mary, A Fiction* (1788) and *The Wrongs of Woman, or Maria* (1798, posthumously). The titles of these novels root them firmly in an eponymous author's experience, but suggest also that subjective experience may be distanced through the imagination into a text to be passed around and shared.

Jean-Jacques Rousseau for Wollstonecraft as for them all was the strongest philosophic influence. Rousseau, followed by the Jacobin writers, holds that the heart and mind, naturally benevolent at birth, are debased by the false standards of society, and childhood innocence is compromised or lost. Like the heroines of the other women radicals, the heroine in *Mary, A Fiction* is an exemplar of sensibility or sentiment (near synonyms in the 1790s). Though heroines of sensibility differ, some characteristics remain constant: they are imaginative, and impulsive in their loves and friendships; they are literary or musical, lovers of solitude and natural landscape, depressive, with a tendency to illness or mental disturbance; at odds with their society, they are its natural victims. As John Mullan says in *Sentiment and Sociability*, where he identifies the discourse common to doctors and novelists to describe the conditions that afflict the exceptional mind, 'the best people become ill, their sensitivities visceral and privatised'.[4] The Jacobin writers directly blame a corrupt and claustrophobic England for their heroines' illnesses. In their loneliness and unease with traditional social forms and in their love of natural landscape, Jacobin heroes and heroines anticipate the alienated personae of the *Lyrical Ballads* and the isolated speaker of *The Prelude*.

Wollstonecraft claims in her Preface to *Mary*:

> Those compositions only have power to delight and carry us willing captives, where the soul of the author is exhibited, and animates the hidden springs. Lost in a pleasing enthusiasm, they live in the scenes they represent, and do not measure their steps in a beaten track, solicitous to gather expected flowers, and bind them in a wreath, according to the prescribed rules of art.[5]

More than ten years before Wordsworth's Preface to the *Lyrical Ballads*, she writes a manifesto for the woman's novel, claiming to break with the past and find a more subjective, autobiographical and 'romantic' narrative. The metaphors are similar: the enthusiasm of Wollstonecraft's author animates the hidden springs of creation, a gynocentric variant of Wordsworth's spontaneous overflow of powerful feelings. *Mary* does indeed exhibit the soul of the author, and breaks established courtship-novel patterns, which frequently ended in the happy marriage of the heroine to a more rational and more powerful lover-mentor.[6] Though this is a third person narrative, everything is seen through the heroine's consciousness, and the novel follows the growth of Mary's mind, learning about the demoralisation of wives and the devaluing of daughters in her own family. Her friend Ann dies at Lisbon where Mary had taken her in an attempt to save her life, an episode based on Wollstonecraft's accompanying her friend Fanny Blood to Lisbon. Mary has been married off by her dying father early in the narrative, and though her husband is absent his shadowy presence dominates the novel, making it harder for her to carry out her philanthropic aims. He is not intentionally a villain, and no individual is to blame for the waste of Mary's life, only the social ethic which assumes there are no other choices for women than dependence on father or husband. When Charles returns, Mary conforms to what society considers her duty, but

> when her husband would take her hand, or mention anything like love, she would instantly feel a sickness, a faintness at her heart, and wish, involuntarily, that the earth would open and swallow her.[7]

The only rescue the heroine can hope for is the peace of death:

> Her delicate state of health did not promise long life. In moments of solitary sadness, a gleam of joy would dart across her mind – she thought she was hastening to that world *where there is neither marrying*, nor giving in marriage.[8]

In the twelve years between the beginning of *Mary* and the unfinished *The Wrongs of Woman*, Wollstonecraft's life became still more adventurous and painful. She went to Ireland as a governess, but her employers, Lord and Lady Kingsborough, dismissed her when their daughter became, they thought, too attached to her, and indeed this daughter retained all her life the unconventional political and religious ideas she absorbed as Wollstonecraft's pupil. Wollstonecraft returned to London where she met the radical publisher Joseph Johnson, the placid centre of a turbulent circle of writers and artists, who printed work by Blake, Godwin and Paine, among others, during the 1790s. He published *Mary* and gave Wollstonecraft some financial independence at last as a reviewer for his magazine, *The Analytical*. She found through his circle a greater confidence and happiness, if briefly.

In November 1790, Edmund Burke published his reactionary *Reflections on the Revolution in France*. Since the Civil War political feeling had never been so violent, for the aristocracy and middle class had everything to lose by the spread of reformist opinion. Events in France were reported in detail and much discussed. Wollstonecraft's *A Vindication of the Rights of Men* was published before the end of the month, the first of over one hundred replies to Burke. In January 1792 she produced after a few weeks' hurried writing her most influential work, *A Vindication of the Rights of Woman*, in which she attacks contemporary systems of education designed merely to make young girls sexually attractive and marriageable, advocates physical and mental exertion in their education, and stresses their potential as useful, rational partners for their husbands and as educators for their children. Her tone is persuasive, and the moderation of her arguments appealed almost as much to a conservative as to a radical readership. Later in the same year, she went to Paris to observe the Revolution, by then deteriorating into violence with the September massacres, and no longer a possible model for change in England. There she met Gilbert Imlay, an American by whom she had a child, Fanny, but Imlay deserted her, which led to her first suicide attempt by poison in 1795. She was persuaded to travel to Norway and Sweden with Fanny and a maid to look after Imlay's business interests there, and in her *Letters from Sweden* (1796) she feelingly conveys the bleak Northern landscape as appropriate setting for her thoughts. She returned to London to find Imlay living with a mistress, and in despair made a second attempt at suicide, throwing herself off Putney Bridge, though she was saved by fishermen. But early in the following year, 1796, Mary Hays reintroduced Godwin to her. They became lovers, and lived in separate houses in the same street while she was writing *The Wrongs of Woman*.

This is a darker novel even than *Mary*, and the archetypal text of all women's confinement. The story begins in the middle, and the opening paragraph finds Maria in an old castle haphazardly renovated as a lunatic asylum. Her husband has arranged to have her confined there, partly because she has run away from him, partly so that he can claim her money. It is a dramatic opening that offers to break free from the conventions of contemporary Gothic texts:

> Abodes of horror have frequently been described, and castles, filled with spectres and chimeras, conjured up by the magic spell of genius to harrow the soul, and absorb the wondering mind. But, formed of such stuff as dreams are made of, what were they to the mansion of despair, in one corner of which Maria sat, endeavouring to recal her scattered thoughts![9]

The self-conscious narrator differentiates between the novel of horror created from fantasy and read for thrills, and Maria's authentic experience of entrapment. The reference to Prospero in *The Tempest* is typically iconoclastic. An authoritarian patriarch viewed in the eighteenth century as Shakespeare's fictional self, he too seems consigned to irrelevance in Wollstonecraft's new myth of women's broken lives. As Gary Kelly says,

> Maria herself is as much Mary Wollstonecraft as she is Mary Queen of Scots, prisoner of sex in the age of Reformation, and

Marie Roland and Marie Antoinette, victims of a ruined Revolution. In the heroine's fate – and the work now gains force from history and necessitarian philosophy rather than sentimental fiction – is exemplified the accumulated wrongs of woman throughout modern European history.[10]

Wollstonecraft's object, she says in her Preface, is

> the desire of exhibiting the misery and oppression, peculiar to women, that arise out of the partial laws and customs of society ... the history ought rather to be considered as of woman, than of an individual.[11]

She admits no exceptions. Yet though the subplot of the prison wardress Jemima, raped and brutalised young, emphasises the novel's pessimism, it also emphasises the idealism, for Jemima finds a loving self lost since childhood through sympathy for her prisoner. Maria's husband, married after a slight acquaintance, is more than usually misogynistic:

> His intimacy with profligate women, and his habits of thinking, gave him a contempt for female endowments; and he would repeat, when wine had loosed his tongue, most of the common-place sarcasms levelled at them, by men who do not allow them to have minds, because mind would be an impediment to gross enjoyment. Men who are inferior to their fellowmen are always most anxious to establish their superiority over women.[12]

'Most' is double-edged here. It means 'very', but implies also that all men are anxious to some degree.

By this time Smith, Inchbald and Ann Radcliffe had established the gothic castle or old house as a metaphor for the legal subordination and social confinement of women. Radcliffe, however, sets her novels in the past and abroad, and avoids overt political comment. Maria has been separated from her baby daughter, and is desperate to escape. In the mainstream novel of courtship, in *Tom Jones* (1749), *Sir Charles Grandison* (1753–4) or *Evelina* (1778), and many other eighteenth-century novels that accept the conventions of gender, narrative interest often turns on the rescue of heroine by hero. This is also true of many modern Mills and Boon-type novelettes. It is characteristic of writers of the 1790s that they use stereotypical plot situations and gender constructions in fresh ways, and Wollstonecraft was grimly ingenious in her plan for the heroine's fellow prisoner Henry Darnford, with whom she falls in love and who rescues her from the isolation her husband has planned. (All four Jacobin novelists create heroines who form extramarital attachments.) But though ostensibly the lover and hero, Henry was to prove another villain, Wollstonecraft's notes show, confirming the novel's anti-male bias.

The bonding of author, heroine and reader is particularly intimate here. In prison Maria soon reads all the books Jemima can bring her, and

> writing was then the only alternative, and she wrote some rhapsodies descriptive of the state of her mind; but the events of her past life pressing on her, she resolved circumstantially to relate them, with the sentiments that experience, and more matured reason, would naturally suggest. They might perhaps instruct her daughter, and shield her from the misery, the tyranny, her mother knew not how to avoid.[13]

The book the reader holds, then, encapsulates both the author's and the heroine's experience, and the reader herself, a surrogate daughter to both, is offered the polemical text as warning against inconsiderate or perhaps against any marriage. In *Women in Romanticism* Meena Alexander discusses Maria's impulse to transmit her experience to her lost daughter, linking this with Wollstonecraft's own impulse to write for women. Of the final scene before *The Wrongs of Woman* breaks off, she writes:

> To instruct others, particularly other women, presupposes a bond of experience, a veracity of knowledge that can be passed on, a sense that the intimate self however betrayed by the state of the social world is part and parcel of a finer order, a world that must be brought into being through mental labour. To be a mother, however fraught with anguish, is to be part of the future.[14]

But Wollstonecraft didn't live long enough to finish the novel. After legally marrying Godwin in March 1797, she had a second daughter, another Mary, in September, and died of septicaemia a week later. Godwin's *Memoirs of the Author of A Vindication of the Rights of Woman*, published in January of the following year with the unfinished novel, revealed her affair with Imlay, her illegitimate daughter, suicide attempts and premarital relationship with himself. It is a splendid tribute to her courage, but it was not well received, and effectively silenced the voice of radical feminism for another two generations. Readers who admired the rationality of *A Vindication of the Rights of Woman* were shocked by the *Memoirs* and the extremism of the novel, and little was heard of Wollstonecraft through the nineteenth century, since her reputation might compromise more respectable proponents of women's rights.

III

Like Wollstonecraft in *Mary*, her friend Mary Hays (1760–1843) also incorporates overtly autobiographical episodes in *The Memoirs of Emma Courtney* (1796), fictionalising Godwin and William Frend and reproducing their letters verbatim. Hays' talent is the slightest of the four, and her autobiographical material is less controlled than Wollstonecraft's, but her self-conscious techniques for engaging the reader are effective. When the heroine goes to meet her father, who has given her up at birth to an aunt, he is scornful of the women's reading that has formed her ideas. His books are locked away out of Emma's reach.

> He soon discovered that my imagination had been left to wander unrestrained in the fairy fields of fiction, but that, of historical facts and the science of the world, I was entirely ignorant.
>
> 'It is as I apprehended,' said he: – 'your fancy requires a *rein*, rather than a *spur*. Your studies, for the future, must be of a soberer nature, or I shall have you mistake my valet for a prince in disguise, my house for a haunted castle, and my rational care for your future welfare for barbarous tyranny.'
>
> I felt a poignant and suffocating sensation, too complicated to bear analyzing, and followed Mr Courtney in silence to the library. My heart bounded when, on entering a spacious room, I perceived on either side a large and elegant assortment of books, regularly arranged in glass cases, and I longed to be left alone, to expatiate freely in these treasures of entertainment. But I soon discovered, to

my inexpressible mortification, that the cases were locked, and that in this intellectual feast I was not to be my own purveyor. My father, after putting into my hands the *Lives* of Plutarch, left me to my meditations; informing me, that he should probably dine at home with a few friends, at five o'clock, when he should expect my attendance at the table.[15]

Emma's poignant and suffocating sensation derives from her father's easy use of anti-Gothic or anti-Sentimental satiric fiction to justify himself and make her look foolish. He has in mind the many imitations of Charlotte Lennox's *The Female Quixote* (1752), in which an absurd, romance-reading heroine is made to see the error of her ways. If not barbarously tyrannic, he has been cruel and neglectful, but even the all-important discourse of novels seems to be on the patriarchal side, so no wonder a novel-heroine feels suffocated. The book is closing on her. The reader, who holds a first person narrative by and about a woman, is aligned with Emma in her discomfiture as her father trivialises women's experience together with the romances that afford an escape from it.

But though Emma is barred from choosing among the omnisicient male texts, she seizes what she can, and despite the apparent incongruity of the choice of Plutarch's *Lives*, she absorbs her book well enough to listen to the men's dinner-table politics in a patriotic and republican mood, and to hold her own in the argument. Her talk gains her the sympathy of Mr Francis, who has written books on constitutional reform, and with 'figure slender and delicate, his eye piercing and his manner impressive',[16] as in Lawrence's drawing of Godwin with Holcroft at the latter's trial for treason in 1794, is clearly to be identified with Godwin. The contemporary reader also sees the possibility of deploying 'male' knowledge, and gaining access to the 'male' world of history and philosophy, without compromising her own sensibility.

IV

Elizabeth Inchbald (1753–1821) fictionalises autobiography too, and involves her reader through the ideological contrast of competing texts. She left home in Suffolk at eighteen, longing to become an actress. In London on her own and looking for work she was alarmed by men's advances and women's suspicions, and married an actor whom she might not perhaps have accepted in other circumstances. They worked hard, though without much success, in touring companies, reduced at one point to eating raw turnips in a field, but later they acted with Mrs Siddons and her brother John Kemble. Inchbald drew on her relationship with Kemble for the teasing erotic struggle in *A Simple Story* (1791) between the overbearing Dorriforth and the heroine, Miss Milner, translating it from the theatrical world to an aristocratic setting more familiar to novel readers. The structure of *A Simple Story* exemplifies the classic double narrative, the plots of the bad and good heroine, here mother and daughter. In such narratives, one woman asserts herself, is disobedient to patriarchal authority and comes to a miserable end, while the other suppresses her 'selfish' individuality, adopts the standards of her older male mentor, and marries happily.

But the title of *A Simple Story* is ironic, and the narrative constantly undermines the defence of patriarchy overtly offered, through the distance between what we are told and what we are shown. Miss Milner, whose Christian name it never occurs to the narrator to mention, is an orphaned heiress left the ward of her father's friend Dorriforth, a wealthy Catholic priest who dresses like a layman and conducts religious offices in private, as was customary in the late eighteenth century. At first a marriage between them appears impossible, and as Jane Spencer points out, 'it is Miss Milner who, Lovelace-like, is attracted by the very quality which debars the fulfillment of desire, the beloved's purity'.[17] Miss Milner is generous, affectionate and forgiving. Her only initial faults are her wit and an occasional desire to go out in the evening, though caprice and extravagance assert themselves later in the absence of other power or pleasure. Dorriforth like his Jesuit friend Sandford is overbearing and inconsistent. He nourishes feuds and resentments, refusing to see his orphaned nephew because his sister made a marriage he did not consent to. A battle for dominance begins between him and his ward which lasts until their marriage. The constant failure of men and women to understand each other is irremediable and ever-present, as Inchbald implies by her occasional shifts into the present tense. Miss Milner

> is wounded to the heart by the cold and unkind manners of her guardian but dares not take one method to retrieve his opinion. – Alone, and to Miss Woodley, she sighs and weeps; he discovers her sorrow and is doubtful whether the departure of Lord Frederick from that part of the country, is not the cause.[18]

The attraction between the two is vividly suggested through gestures of repression and embarrassment. The narrator deeply disapproves of the heroine's high spirits, and straightfacedly makes a Burneyan assumption that she is in need of moral education, which Dorriforth can provide. When his titled cousin dies and he receives a dispensation of his vows from the Pope, he asks her to marry him, though with the reservation that 'I am no longer engaged to Miss Milner than she shall deserve I should.'[19] The unreliable narrator loads the dice against the heroine until the reader longs to make common cause with her, to enter the novel by force and point out that she does not deserve Dorriforth's and Sandford's bullying. After Miss Milner's and Dorriforth's marriage they live together happily until his prolonged absence abroad incites her to run away with a former suitor. She dies soon afterwards. Miss Milner's dysphoric plot, the story of gender struggle and defeat, subverts the second, euphoric story of passive obedience ending in her daughter Matilda's happy marriage. It is probable, though, that Inchbald intended *A Simple Story* to end with the marriage of Dorriforth and Miss Milner, and that she added the heroine's adultery, her death and Matilda's story because her publisher did not think the first half long enough for a novel. And certainly, in spite of the violent passions on both sides, the tone of the first half is comic, and the enemies' need of each other and their reconciliation is entirely convincing. Nothing in Miss Milner's portrayal prepares us for her adultery.

However this may be, Miss Milner is a major creation: even when dead, she dominates the second half of the narrative. Matilda is very dull, and the sense of Miss Milner's loss predominates to the end. Terry Castle says in *Masquerade and Civilization*, that here

> is the same freedom – the exquisite extremism – one associates with Emily Brontë. *Wuthering Heights* may be the work *A Simple Story* most anticipates, not only because of the similar double

narrative structure (each fiction takes place over two generations), but because of the way Inchbald succeeds in communicating, with startling economy, reserves of the most intense feeling.[20]

Castle's account emphasises Miss Milner's free, transgressive personality. Yet the novel's atmosphere is predominantly one of claustrophobia. The heroine is boxed-in by custom, the church, and the judgement of a none-too-sympathetic narrator, with whom the reader constantly wants to quarrel. To express her feelings Miss Milner must put her head out of the sash-window or escape the house altogether in masquerade costume, half-Diana and half-whore.

A *Simple Story* is, as Castle says, Inchbald's masterpiece, elegant and ambiguous. *Nature and Art* (1796) is more schematic, witty in the Voltairean manner while dramatising Rousseau's perceptions of daily life as a humiliating struggle for money and position. He argued that the complex hierarchies of European society contravene the laws of nature. All the Jacobins were in some degree primitivists, suspicious of prevailing modes of education and privileging a 'native' community, often American Indian, over European society. Inchbald's Henry is brought up in an African tribe while his cousin William, the son of an ambitious Anglican dean, grows up in England; they are brought together when Henry returns to England in his teens. Henry's problem in reconciling Christian morality with 'things as they are' is reminiscent of Candide's:

> 'The world to come,' returned the Dean, 'is where we shall go after death; and there, no distinction will be made between rich and poor – all persons there will be equal.'
>
> 'Ay, now I see what makes it a better world than this. But cannot this world try to be as good as that?'
>
> 'In respect to placing all persons on a level, it is utterly impossible: God has ordained it otherwise.'
>
> 'How! has God ordained a distinction to be made, and will not make any himself?'
>
> The Dean did not proceed in his instructions.[21]

Inchbold links national and sexual politics. Agnes the heroine, the daughter of poor villagers in the dean's parish, is seduced by

William, who leaves her pregnant, so forcing her eventually into prostitution, while he becomes a lawyer in London. One of Inchbald's sisters became a prostitute, and the most powerful passages of *Nature and Art* describe the heroine's betrayal and descent into London's underworld. Few eighteenth-century fictional scenes are as disturbing as the birth of her baby. The third person narrative is mediated through Henry's consciousness as he wanders in a foggy wood, hearing a woman's cries and stumbling over a baby with a string round its neck:

> When the Dean's family had been at Anfield about a month, one misty morning, such as portends a sultry day, as Henry was walking through a thick wood, on the skirts of the parish, he suddenly started on hearing a distant groan expressive, as he thought, both of bodily and mental pain. He stopped to hear it repeated, that he might pursue the sound. He heard it again; and though now but in murmurs, yet, as the tone implied excessive grief, he directed his course to that part of the wood from which it came.
>
> As he advanced, in spite of the thick fog, he discerned the appearance of a female stealing away on his approach. His eye was fixed on this object, and, regardless where he placed his feet, he soon shrunk back with horror on perceiving they had nearly trod on a new born infant, lying on the ground.[22]

Like the narrator, the reader does not see Agnes clearly and can only guess at the social terrors that have almost caused her to strangle the child; these tragedies were frequent, and Inchbald excels in the Gothic of the ordinary. Such extremity of experience can never be fully shared by an outsider, much less judged by the law. Inchbald develops the narrative to a programmatic but very effective climax. Many years later, Agnes is tried and condemned to death by William, now a famous judge. He does not recognise her after years of stealing and prostitution undertaken to support herself and their son. Inchbald like Wollstonecraft forges thematic links between private oppression and public tyranny.

V

Charlotte Smith (1749–1806) considered herself primarily as a poet rather than a novelist; her first publication was *Elegiac Sonnets* in 1784. This was published at Smith's expense, though it was unexpectedly successful: the many reprintings and later additions show how she hit the taste of her time. The sentiment that she sees as the proper subject for a sonnet surrounds a melancholy figure in a sympathetic landscape. The harmony between central figure and landscape setting is new to the sonnet, and is developed with interesting political overtones in her novels. As Stella Brooks points out, there are a number of beautiful and fragile figures in the sonnets representing youth, happiness, love, security or hopefulness. These personifications are Augustan in their brevity. They 'are painted with the lightest touch, but then allowed to fade as their inadequacy, like that of their creator in the face of intractable social and economic problems, is acknowledged'.[23] Smith was beginning to establish a public persona, to involve a wide readership in her sorrows. She turned to fiction, which paid better than poetry, when she separated from her husband and took on full financial responsibility for their nine surviving children.

In the ten long novels she wrote between 1788 and 1798, she combines political analysis and social satire with the broadest range of self-conscious techniques. In her preface, she confides in the reader the financial difficulties consequent on the separation, and the lawyers' corruption in failing to secure for her and her children the money she believed due from the Trust her father-in-law had set up for them in his will. She creates a public persona in her novels and children's books by introducing author-representative characters, and including recognisable versions of her friends, enemies, husband and children. In print she could castigate her enemies and defend her separation from her husband or her 'unwomanly' political views. As feminist critics have recognised, to tell one's story is an affirmation of power, even when the story contains crushing defeats. Her novels are highly self-conscious: we are encouraged to see her heroines as heroines, and so they often see themselves, while false heroines claiming to be authentic attempt to usurp their position. She uses conspicuously novelistic devices such as the rescue for complex effects. Techniques of marked parallelism or contrast, like the schematic doubling of Mrs Stafford in *Emmeline*, Geraldine in *Desmond*, all the principal characters of *Montalbert*, and Medora in *The Young Philosopher*, keep us aware of a manipulative and polemical author.

Smith's metafictional devices are so various that only a few can be touched on here. Sophie Elphinstone in *Celestina* (1791) is an author-representative character with a feckless husband who has grown up in the West Indies, as did Benjamin Smith. She prepares to tell her long inset story in a way that reminds us, and also reminds her, of early French romances:

> 'It is something like the personages with whom we are presented in old romances, and who meet in forests and among rocks and recount their adventures; but do you know, my dear Miss de Mornay, that I feel very much disposed to enact such a personage, and though it is but a painful subject, to relate to you my past life?'
>
> 'And do you know, dear Madam,' replied Celestina, 'that no wandering lady in romance had ever more inclination to lose her own reflections in listening to the history of some friend who had by chance met her, lost in the thorny labyrinth of uneasy thoughts, than I have to listen to you.'[24]

By reference to an earlier form of fiction, Smith keeps us conscious that this too is story, and that women's lives which are the subject of such stories change little from one generation to another. By making Sophie's marriage and distress similar to her own well-known history, Smith keeps us aware that she and the reader have a story to listen to and a story to tell, which may be as painful as Sophie's or Celestina's.

In *The Old Manor House* (1793), Smith's use of Gothic symbolism, an emblem of the female body as well as an emblem of the state, contradicts her narrator's account. On the level of narrative, the hero Orlando's visits to Monimia's room are innocent. The lovers' innocence is maintained by the narrator against the slander of a dissolute aristocracy. But Smith's treatment of the Gothic turret and locked, isolated room makes the confined heroine a symbol of sexuality, clandestine but powerful, opposing conventions by which the old can control or forbid marriage. The fourteen steps up the Gothic turret's stairway correspond to Monimia's age, usually the age of puberty, when Orlando first finds his way there. His breaking the rusty lock on the hidden door, and her cutting the 'old-fashioned glazed linen'[25] that lines her room symbolise loss of virginity. The secret way leads up to the head of her bed. The marked absence of linkage between narrative and emblematic direction makes decoding a matter of choice for the reader. The meetings both are and are not 'innocent', depending on whether we follow the surface narrative or the implications of the Gothic symbolism. By such means, Smith encourages her reader to question and redefine the concept of innocence. Later the villain, Sir John Belgrave, learns the secret of Orlando's access to Monimia's room and determines to go the same way himself, but she is willing to leave Rayland Hall for ever rather than risk this. Smith conveys emblematically through her Gothic rooms and passageways her response to the common contemporary assumption that an unmarried woman who has lost her virginity is fair game, that where one man has secretly gone, anyone may follow. Whether we accept the reading of Orlando and Monimia as lovers almost from the start, or see the narrative ambiguities as indicators of the sexuality in a still unconsummated relationship, the implication is the same: erotic love is not controllable by the manor's autocratic owner Mrs Rayland, that is, by the regulations of the state; and marriage is a private not an institutional matter.

Rayland Hall's inhabitants and visitors form a microcosm of England's hierarchy, an idea that Smith took from Burke's metaphor of the crumbling castle in need of renovation as an image of the state in *Reflections on the Revolution in France*. All her houses need new ownership, or demolition. *The Old Manor House* has merely a sense of novelistic closure in its hero's and heroine's final prosperity, but their story has a more appropriate, imaginative ending when the two meet in Hampshire beside the ruins of an old castle, its foundations almost obscured by snow and ivy. Love for Smith is anarchic, capable of overturning the authority represented in her houses.

Smith takes for granted that young women among her fictional characters, and her readers, will see their lives in imaginative, novelistic terms. S.R. Martin notes that 'Lady Mary's maid [in *The Young Philosopher*] seems to be a prototype of Catherine Morland of *Northanger Abbey*, albeit of a different social class, in her comparison of reality with the world of Gothic novels'.[26] But Lady Mary's maid is only one of numerous readers from every class in Smith's novels who try to shape their lives in accordance with their favourite fictions. The novel of courtship ended in marriage and it was assumed that a young woman's goal was marriage. The relationship between text and reader of this genre was therefore peculiarly personal and intense, with each text offering a more or less sophisticated code of conduct for what might be the one significant choice of a woman's life. The texts Smith's heroines and anti-heroines read are of course always less abrasively realistic than the ones they appear in. While the anti-heroines are misled, the heroines never are. Smith always provides a formally happy ending, but in *Montalbert* (1795) and *The Young Philosopher* (1798) an older woman in a difficult or unhappy marriage is central to her story; Smith is increasingly inclined to imply that refusal to marry might be the best choice after all.

She wrote of the death of her favourite child, Augusta, in the preface to *Marchmont* (1796), blaming the Trust lawyers for their refusal to advance money when it was most needed. Probably she wanted to take Augusta abroad to a better climate. Some acquaintances dismissed her as mad in the following year, though she was then writing *The Young Philosopher*, her last and one of her most demanding novels. In a sense she was mad, as one can see from her correspondence, obsessive about the will, absorbed by the belief that she had been cheated for years. She was not so much paranoid as genuinely victimised by her husband's family as well as by lawyers, and she never recovered from Augusta's death. Her last novel is particularly interesting in its self-conscious use of this autobiographical material and its subversion of literary stereotypes.

In the preface Smith claims that as lawyers are

> such men as in the present state of society stand in place of the giants, and necromancers, and ogers [sic] of ancient romance, men whose profession empowers them to perpetrate, and whose inclination generally prompts them to the perpetration of wickedness, I have made these drawings a *little* like people of that sort whom I *have seen*, certain that nothing I could *imagine* would be so correct, when legal collusion and professional oppression were to be represented.[27]

Sir Appulby Gorges, Mr Solicitor Cancer and their colleagues amply fulfil her promise of ogres. Smith herself becomes a presence in the novel through the account of Laura's lawsuit, the loss of her daughter and her approach to insanity. Laura's attempts to have her father's will settled, her disgust with lawyers and preoccupation with business matters would make her recognisable as a version of Smith to anyone who had read the earlier novels and their prefaces, or the children's books. There is no evidence that she was treated for mental illness like her heroine Laura, but many indications in the letters that she was a source of anxiety to her friends. In *The Young Philosopher*, Laura's daughter, abducted by a lawyer, eventually returns to her, but this is scarcely represented in the novel, and Laura does not fully recover. We are meant to understand that one daughter will never come back.

Twice in the novel Laura sits on a rocky shore, watching the tide come in, as the speaker sits in number twelve of Smith's *Elegiac Sonnets*, 'On Some Rude Fragment of the Rocky Shore', placed opposite the most striking of the illustrations. Five illustrations were added to the fifth edition, and two of these, by far the best, were drawn by Thomas Stodhard. Blake, John Flaxman and Stodhard were friends and drew together in the evenings in the early 1780s. In one of his bitter epigrams Blake wrote:

> I found them blind, I taught them how to see
> And now they know neither themselves nor me.[28]

Whether or not Blake taught Stodhart to see, there is a resemblance to Blake's style in the drapery of Stodhard's illustration. An elegantly dressed young woman, clearly a heroine, sits on the seashore. Behind her a ship is being driven onto the rocks by a storm. She holds a book open in her hand, as does the reader of the *Elegiac Sonnets*. Her gaze is on neither the threatened ship nor her book, but turned inward on her own sadness. The picture admirably illustrates the sonnet's and indeed the whole volume's definition of sensibility. The book held in the hand links reader with pictured heroine, overtly the projection of Smith inside her volume.

This intimacy of reader, writer and heroine, together with Stodhard's picture and the continued reprinting of these very popular sonnets through the 1790s, allows Smith to superimpose her own image on the image of the despairing Laura. Early in

Laura's story her baby dies, the predatory laird Kilbrodie is hunting her, and she sits on a rock waiting for the tide to drown her. As if directing the reader's attention back to Smith's sonnet, Laura says,

> 'I saw myself destitute of everything, and cast like a shipwrecked wretch on the shore, from whence, if I attempted to return, greater horrors awaited me than those I was sure, by staying, to encounter from famine.'[29]

Near the close of the novel she has lost Medora, and has gone mad. We see her sitting on the Sussex seashore, and Sussex is the background for much of Smith's poetry. Although Laura holds no book in her hand, the scene is again reminiscent of 'On Some Rude Fragment of the Rocky Shore':

> It was on an heap of the fallen cliff, and where other fragments beetled fearfully overhead, that the poor mourner sat; her eyes were concealed by her hands, her arms resting on her knees. She seemed listening to the burst of waters on the shore, and to be quite regardless of our approach.[30]

It is no accident that Laura is twice placed in a pose so characteristic of the 'I' of the sonnets. We are intended to identify the two. As the cruelty and corruption of lawyers took Medora from Laura, the author implies, so Augusta was taken from her, and as Laura has been driven mad, so has she. Sometimes Smith's intertextual games remind one of Philip Roth, but they are not funny. With admirable tenacity she projects her personal grief and mental disturbance into her novel, and remains in control of her material. She makes herself in both senses heroic.

There are many self-conscious variants of novelistic stereotype in *The Young Philosopher*, including the multiplication of the heroines and a female rescuer. Smith also reworks Sade's St Mary-in-the-Woods episode from *Justine* (1791) into her creation of Arnly Park, a beautifully restored Gothic Manor with chalets in its grounds arranged like settings in a pornographic novel, housing a kidnapped harem of women for the entertainment of the owner Sir Harry Challoner and his guests. In her description of the layout of the estate, Smith shows the respectable side of

Arnly Park in close contiguity with the Sadeian world of women's imprisonment and rape. In *Justine*, one of the imprisoned women is 'retired', that is murdered, each time a new recruit is brought to St Mary-in-the-Woods, but Sir Harry's women once their first youth is gone become domestic servants. Smith's vision is less nightmarish and apocalyptic than Sade's, but she makes her own bitter comment on her society's uses for women. Arnly Park suggests in its male domination and frightened hierarchy the final triumph of political reaction in England in the year after Wollstonecraft's death. Smith refers to Wollstonecraft in the preface to *The Young Philosopher* as a writer 'whose talents I greatly honoured, and whose untimely death I deeply regret',[31] while towards the end of the novel Laura repeats a precept from Mrs Mason, the governess in Wollstonecraft's *Original Stories*, 'first, to avoid hurting anything; and then, to continue to give as much pleasure as you can'.[32] Smith wrote her preface in the June of 1798, following the January when Godwin published the Memoirs of Wollstonecraft, and it is characteristic of her that she was eager to pay her own tribute to the younger woman and place herself in the radical feminist camp, by then in disarray.

VI

The Jacobin novelists profoundly influenced Austen and of course Mary Shelley. They helped Austen to define by contrast her own more conservative attitudes as she grew up in the 1790s. She inherited from them a self-conscious and politically sophisticated tradition, and made the most of it, though as a devout Anglican she rejected Jacobin ideology altogether, and it has only a shadowy presence in her novels. The Crawfords are never allowed to argue a sceptical point of view on religion or politics, though to speak and act as they do they would have to have one: Mary's comments about the clergy, for instance, are ascribed to frivolity, not agnosticism. But the radical voice in *Mansfield Park* is implicit in Inchbald's translation from Kotzebue, the disruptive *Lovers Vows*, which defends female sexuality and the 'fallen' woman. It is implicit, too, in elements of plot and setting derived from Jacobin fiction in general and from *The Old Manor House* in particular: the political house as microcosm of England, which in Austen's novel needs no change or new ownership; the feckless elder brother who dies in *The Old Manor House* but who is allowed in *Mansfield Park* to reform and keep his rights of primogeniture; the heroine's progression from upper room to moral centre of her community. But though Austen rejects the 'old-fashioned' radical politics of the 1790s, some social change and renewal are celebrated in *Mansfield Park*. From the cramped Portsmouth house, where a room looks like a passageway to somewhere better, come William, Fanny and Susan to contribute to England's safety and comfort.

In *Emma*, a gentrified radicalism besets the heroine, and forms her greatest threat. Critics have discussed Emma as imaginist and failed novelist, but nobody has noted how political is her fiction-making. Emma's mind has been tainted by the dangerous though appealing culture of the Jacobins, and her 'stories' like theirs are essentially opposed to Christian patriarchy. Like Smith, Emma imagines that birth and education don't matter in marriage, and that social boundaries are easily crossed; like Inchbald and Hays that even heroines may form extramarital relationships; like Wollstonecraft that intelligent responsible women may be happier unmarried. Whether or not Emma actually reads Jacobin novelists is immaterial; their ideas are in the air by now, and part of even provincial culture. But her attempts as shadow novelist to organise the Highbury material into radical patterns can only impede, not change, the narrator's conservative ending. This conservatism is beautifully focused in Knightley's great estate and the Martins' prosperous farm. At the strawberry-picking Emma's consciousness is moving closer to the narrator's. She sees Donwell Abbey in the foreground and behind it, in perspective, the Abbey Mill Farm, the picturesque vista held in the curve of hill and river:

> The considerable slope, at nearly the foot of which the abbey stood, gradually acquired a steeper form beyond its grounds; and at half a mile distant was a bank of considerable abruptness and grandeur, well clothed with wood; – and at the bottom of the bank, favourably placed and sheltered, rose the Abbey Mill Farm, with meadows in front, and the river making a close and handsome curve around it.[33]

The image rebukes the Jacobins' grim symbolic Gothic and their Rousseauvian conviction that Nature is hostile to hierarchy. The sheltering lines of Austen's landscape lock together Donwell Abbey and the Martins' farm. This is an England that by 1815 Austen found herself powerful enough to define and shape. Her construction of the good society has probably been a greater force for conservatism than that of any other English writer. In these two houses Emma and Harriet will settle, distanced half a mile from each other now, and through their children ensure the perpetuation of England's hierarchy into the future.

A few months after *Emma*, Wollstonecraft's and Godwin's daughter was creating in *Frankenstein* a novel which, Gary Kelly claims, draws formally and thematically on *The Wrongs of Woman* and *Caleb Williams* (1794).[34] It is true that Shelley works in a tradition of confessional first person narrative, though her protagonist is deeply unreliable, true also that the women in *Frankenstein* are almost entirely powerless. Frankenstein, archetypal European male and victor in the struggle fought and lost by women of the previous generation, expresses his desire to control and repress the female principle by the manipulation and rape of nature. He wants to 'penetrate into the recesses of nature, and show how she works in her hiding places'.[35] He fears female sexuality yet needs, like Clerval and Walton, to leave something behind, 'a new species',[36] and so seeks a way to bypass women and reproduce asexually. The process of making the monster is described in terms of pregnancy. Frankenstein begins with a conception, and after confinement and painful labour arrives at the 'most gratifying consummation of my toils',[37] a consummation followed by what we would call post-natal depression. He is horrified at the result of his labours, and yet the task of creating a female monster would be still more repugnant, for she might become ten thousand times more malignant than her mate, or worse, might turn in disgust from the male monster to the superior beauty of man, and rape *him*. Frankenstein usurps woman as well as God when he presumes to create. Shelley's feminism is guarded and deeply encoded, her signs more ambiguous and harder to read than the old 1790s Gothic signs of imprisonment, and she offers no friendly, polemical intimacy of author with heroine and reader.

But the Jacobin writers have too often been treated merely as precursors of Austen and Shelley, when they are well worth reading for their own sakes. They blur the line between life and fiction. The author projects her own experience into her novel in a bid for the reader's recognition and sympathy. But her experience also gives her the authority to rewrite her world, and she manipulates fictional conventions to surprise her reader and differentiate her ideology from that of patriarchal novelists. The links she forms between author, heroine and reader suggest that real solutions are needed for women's problems outside the novels, beyond the metafictional happy endings that may be found for problems within them.

Notes

1. Horace Walpole wrote to Mrs Hannah More on 24 January 1795, 'Thou excellent woman! Thou reverse of that hyena in petticoats Mrs Wolstencroft, who to this day discharges her ink and gall on Marie Antoinette.' '*Correspondence*, eds W.S. Lewes *et al.*, vol. 3, p. 397.
2. Thomas Paine, *The Rights of Man*, ed. Henry Collins. (Penguin, 1969), p. 295.
3. William Godwin's *The Adventures of Caleb Williams* (1794), alternatively titled *Things As They Are*, may be seen as the private working out of an essentially political conflict, and in that sense the novel is about the condition of England, and the Terror in France.
4. John Mullan, *Sentiment and Sociability: the Language of Feeling in the Eighteenth Century Novel* (Oxford, 1988) p. 2.
5. Mary Wollstonecraft, Advertisement to *Mary, A Fiction*. In '*Mary*' and '*The Wrongs of Woman*', ed. with an introduction by Gary Kelly (Oxford, 1976).
6. See Jane Spencer's *The Rise of the Woman Novelist: from Aphra Behn to Jane Austen*, (Oxford, 1986), esp. pp. 140–67.
7. '*Mary*' and '*The Wrongs of Woman*', ed. Kelly, p. 67.
8. Ibid., p. 68.
9. Ibid., p. 75.
10. Kelly, introduction to '*Mary*' and '*The Wrongs of Woman*', p. xvii.
11. Wollstonecraft, Author's Preface to *The Wrongs of Woman*, ed. Gary Kelly, p. 73.
12. Wollstonecraft, *The Wrongs of Woman*, p. 146–7.
13. Ibid., p. 82.
14. Meena Alexander, *Women in Romanticism: Mary Wollstonecraft, Dorothy Wordsworth and Mary Shelley*, (London, 1989), p. 146.

15. Mary Hays, *The Memoirs of Emma Courtney*, ed. with an introduction by Sally Cline (London, 1987), p. 20.
16. Ibid., p. 34.
17. Introduction to Elizabeth Inchbald '*A Simple Story*' and '*Nature and Art*', ed. by J.M.S. Tompkins with an introduction by Jane Spencer, (Oxford, 1988), p. xix.
18. Ibid., p. 91.
19. Ibid., p. 142.
20. Terry Castle, *Masquerade and Civilization*, (London, 1986), p. 291.
21. Inchbald, '*A Simple Story*' and '*Nature and Art*', with a portrait and introductory memoir by William Bell Scott (London, 1880), pp. 410–11.
22. Ibid., p. 460.
23. Stella Brooks, 'The Sonnets of Charlotte Smith', *Critical Survey*, 4, 1, (1992), 15.
24. Charlotte Smith, *Celestina: A Novel* (4 vols), ed. T. Cadell, 1791, vol. 2, pp. 247–8.
25. Smith, *The Old Manor House: A Novel*, ed. with an introduction by Anne Henry Ehrenpreis (Oxford, 1969), p. 31.
26. S.R. Martin, 'Charlotte Smith, 1749–1806, A Critical Survey of her Works and Place in English Literary History'. PhD Thesis, University of Sheffield, 1980, p, 105, note 22.
27. Charlotte Smith, *The Young Philosopher: A Novel* (4 vols), ed. by Cadell and Davies, 1798, preface, p. vii.
28. Cited by Mona Wilson, *The Life of William Blake* (1927), p. 13.
29. Smith, *The Young Philosopher*, vol. 2, p. 139.
30. Ibid., vol. 4, p. 343.
31. Ibid., preface, p. v.
32. Ibid., vol. 4, p. 228.
33. Jane Austen, *Emma*, (Harmondsworth), p. 355.
34. Gary Kelly, 'Jane Austen and the English Novel of the 1790s'. In *Fetter'd or Free? British Women Novelists 1670–1815*, ed. Mary Anne Schofield and Cecilia Macheski (Ohio, 1986), p. 291.
35. Mary Shelley, *Frankenstein*, ed. Johanna M. Smith (Boston, 1992), p. 51.
36. Ibid., p. 55.
37. Ibid., p. 54.

7 Chartism and popular fiction
Steve Devereux

I

If the period from about 1780 to the 1840s is viewed as one of an intense radicalisation of literature, then the attempt by several prominent Chartists to write serialised popular fiction provides an ironic and salutary postscript to that era. Such a project is improbable enough but seems even more unlikely given the hostility to popular publishing and the cultural sophistication displayed by Chartist journals before their 'conversion' to popularism (1847–8).

Chartist criticism was often surprisingly good and maintained the partisan tradition of the Romantic critics. As might be expected, Chartist journals (over a hundred titles[1]) lionised Burns, Shelley and Byron[2] while vilifying apostates such as Wordsworth and Southey[3] and promoting the work of lesser figures who might be regarded as 'fellow travellers' (such as Ebenezer Elliott the 'Corn Law Rhymer'). But alongside these partisan reviews were far more analytical articles such as those debating the relationship between politics and poetry[4] and those intended to introduce American and European writers.

Given the Anglo-centrism of Victorian culture, the broad vistas surveyed by some Chartist critics is as unexpected as it is refreshing. A detailed obituary to Edgar Allan Poe assesses his contribution to the development of American literature. An article on Pushkin predicts the influence of his work on the development of Russian literature.[5]

Chartist reviewers showed a strong preference for poetry over prose fiction and most periodicals published poetry generated by the movement itself – much of it anonymous and conventional, some provided by the movement's better known personalities such as Jones, Massey, Harney, Linton and Sankey. Poetry could be used far more readily to promote Chartism than could prose fiction.[6]

Popular fiction was denigrated at every opportunity and the anonymous *Northern Star* reviewer of the *Illustrated Penny Novelist* makes Chartism's objections to the popular perfectly clear:

> We think novel reading, at the best, only an indifferent substitute for a worse occupation of time. But we are not ignorant of the fact that however we may moralise, many hundreds of new-born intellects of modern improvement and enlightenment look out for novels with avidity.[7]

Yet most Chartist periodicals were publishing serialised novels by the late 1840s. How had such a *volte-face* come about? Before an explanation can be offered, it will be necessary to define 'popular' as accurately as possible. Any attempt at a definition, however, inevitably invokes an area of contention between schools of cultural studies.

Although those critics most closely associated with the Communist Party have frequently had to make rapid adjustments to accommodate policy changes (most notably between the Third Period and Popular Front cultural policies during the mid-1930s), it is generally true that 'conventional' Marxists postulate a cultural struggle between the working class and the bourgeoisie that parallels political and economic class conflict.[8] An oppositional working-class culture exists which is the embryonic culture of a socialist future. Those writers whose work is in 'the historic interests of the working class'[9] contribute to and develop this culture. For critics such as Gustav Klaus, Martha Vicinus and Jack Mitchell, Chartist fiction constitutes an early contribution to this development which would be completed by the 'general maturing of the international proletariat'.[10]

This version of working-class culture remained more or less intact until structuralist ideas began to penetrate Communist intellectual circles, notably as a result of the writings of Louis Althusser. Popular culture was increasingly seen as an 'ideological machine which dictated the thoughts of the people'.[11]

Popular culture was no longer to be analysed in order to assess its oppositional potential, but in order 'to reveal the ways in which textual structures might be said to organise reading or spectating practices'.[12] Popular culture was yet another instrument through which the dominant class exerted its control. This and similar definitions of 'popular' largely replaced oppositional or 'culturalist' versions in Britain during the 1970s, particularly where the influence of the Centre for Contemporary Cultural Studies was felt.

By the 1980s, however, a far more 'pluralist' approach to popular culture had emerged, largely through an application of concepts originating in the thought of the Italian Communist, Antonio Gramsci. Popular culture is the possession of neither class, but should be 'viewed as a force field of relations shaped, precisely, by . . . contradictory pressures and tendencies'.[13]

> Whereas, according to the dominant ideology thesis, bourgeois culture and ideology seek to take the place of working-class culture and ideology and thus to become directly operative in framing working class experience, Gramsci argues that the bourgeoisie can become a hegemonic, leading class only to the degree that bourgeois ideology is able to accommodate, to find some space for opposing class cultures and values. A bourgeois hegemony is secured not via the obliteration of working-class culture, but via its *articulation to* bourgeois culture and ideology so that, in being associated with and expressed in the forms of the latter, its political affiliations are altered in the process.[14]

Such a definition clearly reaffirms the importance of the conditions under which popular texts are created and therefore the need for a historical approach. This 'turn to Gramsci', however, does not necessarily avoid the structuralist assumption that the presence of a given cultural phenomenon can be explained by its observable function.

Stuart Hall, for example, suggests that,

> The problem was essentially this: how to contain the popular classes within the orbit and authority of the dominant culture, while allowing them the formal right to express opinions. To do this, a press was created that *reflected* popular interests, tastes, preoccupations, concerns, levels of education (sufficient, that is, to win popular identification and consent); but which *did not become* an authentic 'voice' of the popular interest, which might then be tempted to voice its opinions independently, and thus forge a unity as a social and political force (as the Chartist press had attempted

to do). The new 'popular' press was a press *about* and *bought by* but not *produced by*, or *committed to the cause of*, the popular classes. The formula for this type of cultural incorporation was generated out of a synthesis between two earlier models: the Sunday press and the popular miscellanies.[15]

Clearly, the popular press did (and does?) perform the functions that Hall assigns to it – but can we assume that this is why it was created? And by whom? How did those 'tastes' and 'interests' that it reflected arise? As Eileen and Stephen Yeo point out, 'No . . . cultural form can be seen as natural, or spontaneous, or as the simple product of popular demand.'[16] Class conflict may be regarded as a 'force field' shaped by 'contradictory pressures' without assuming that this was the intended or expected outcome for any of the participants. The Trades Union Congress (TUC), for example, is a working-class organisation 'articulated' to the employers' leadership of society, conveying the CBI's imperatives to its members. But this function does not explain the existence of the TUC nor can it account for the allegiance and motivation of its members.

As successive definitions of 'popular' are considered, it becomes increasingly clear that each depends upon the critic's view of the relationship between class and culture. In order to identify the popular elements of Chartist fiction, however, it will be necessary to define 'popular' in terms of its origins, forms and archetypes.

II

It is self-evident that the growth of a popular *literary* culture depends upon the existence of a literate working class. Although arguments continue over figures, R.K. Webb estimates, using contemporaneous reports and surveys, that about three-quarters of the working class could read by the 1830s.[17] Although early attempts at mass education are largely responsible for this growth, an appetite for literature was clearly being cultivated by the increasing tendency for political conflicts to be aired through the medium of print.

Early nineteenth-century governments were clearly not advocates of a popular press and attempted to use legislation against its development. In 1817 a stamp duty of sixpence (6d) was levied on all periodicals in the hope that this would make radical papers too expensive for working class readers. Actually, the stamp duty and further legislation in 1819, accelerated the growth of illegal, 'underground' publications, known as the unstamped press.[18] Although these papers cannot be regarded as a working class press, their proliferation, alongside similar attempts by conservatives to gain the attention of a growing working class readership, was clearly shaping and reinforcing certain tastes and expectations.

Just as Hannah More's religious tracts reflected the form and distribution patterns of secular broadsheets, so the magazines published by the Society for the Diffusion of Useful Knowedge and the SPCK often mirrored radical and popular publications. As popular publishing became big business, fortunes could be made out of satisfying newly acquired tastes and reading habits which were deepened and extended through mass production and widespread distribution.

The degree to which popular literature altered during this period is revealed through a comparison with eighteenth-century popular publishing, which consisted largely of broadsides (single sheets printed on one side), broadsheets (printed both sides) and chapbooks (single sheets folded to make a sixteen-page booklet). These were distributed by itinerant 'chaunters' who performed the ballads that they sold.[19] Myths, legends, almanacs, riddles, crime stories, scandals, complaints against harsh employers, gallows speeches and so on sustained this popular press which was essentially a printed expression of an oral culture. The popular literature that had all but replaced it by the 1840s was far more consciously a printed medium[20] designed to meet the expectations of an anonymous readership rather than the appetites of a performer's audience.[21]

Serialised popular fiction developed expectations, conventions and archetypes that rapidly solidified into a repeatable format. Some of the earliest examples are reprints or imitations of Gothic and picaresque novels from the eighteenth century. Later, Dickens was massively plagiarised and plundered for such titles as Edward Lloyd's *Sketches by Bos* and G.W.M. Reynolds's *Pickwick Abroad*.

Serial writers soon discovered how to adapt middle-class models for a working-class readership. Their version of the

Gothic, for instance, retained its stylistic conventions, archetypes and supernatural elements, but used them to tell a much wider range of stories. Even in its adapted form, though, the Gothic novel was probably too exotic and archaic for working-class readers for whom the 'domestic novel' was more resonant. Originally based upon the experiences of a family, the vicarious pleasures offered by lurid descriptions of an innocent heroines's travails made the 'wronged maiden' an increasingly dominant archetype as in J.M. Rymer's *Ada the Betrayed*. Although this genre clearly owes much to eighteenth-century sentimental novels, the depths of sorrow plumbed were never so deep that recovery was not possible, most ending happily with virtue rewarded.

As Louis James points out, both the Gothic and domestic versions of the popular novel retained a rigid moral framework, but merely as a structuring and legitimising device rather than as evidence of a morality shared by writer and reader.[22]

During the 1840s French popular fiction flooded the English market and, like earlier influences, was rapidly imitated and assimilated. These imported *feuilletons* resembled the home-grown variety but were far more exuberant and used more 'exotic' urban settings such as the worlds of slum-dwellers, of vice and criminality. This influence helped popular fiction to cater to those appetites that the broadsides and crime gazettes had cultivated. The French influence also reinforced the serialists' penchant for melodrama that

> provided fiction with an approach to the story in which the aim is emotion, emotion for its own sake rather than as an effect incidental to human situations. Characters become reduced to easily recognisable stock figures, very good or very bad, and the plot only serves to lead up to the 'strong' scene where, in stylised ritual, the hero confronts the villain, or the villain confronts the hero.[23]

One of the most effective transmitters of the French style into English was the ubiquitous G.W.M. Reynolds, whose *Mysteries of the Court of London* was directly culled from Eugene Sue's *Mysteries of Paris*. Reynolds helped to create a truly urban popular fiction in which the horrors and delights of the city were entertainment enough without recourse to the pastoral, the

Gothic or the sentimental genres *per se*. Reynolds was in turn imitated and the dozens of 'Mysteries' that followed the original 'tried to show city life, with all its activities and classes of society, as an organic whole. The picture is held together by a central character moving among all classes'.[24]

To summarise, it is clear that the popular printed culture of the early nineteenth century developed out of a complex relationship between product, appetites and expectations, a relationship which drove writers to experiment and to adapt their texts to meet a demand that had been awakened by the political, social and technological developments of previous decades. Such a culture has little potential of becoming the 'oppositional' culture of the unreconstructed Marxists. But neither does it look much like the hegemonic model in which 'working-class culture is articulated to bourgeois culture and ideology'. As the conventions and archetypes of a popular printed culture coalesce into a stable form, the ideological and moral impact of its various elements is reduced to a set of codes that can be activated at any time, that are ceaselessly reiterated to meet working-class expectations.

The persistence of such a culture meant that popular radicalism, of the kind that was possible up to 1836 (when stamp duty was drastically reduced) was no longer feasible, while the efforts of conservatives to reach a mass audience by direct appeals were equally thwarted. Chartism was the first mass political movement to find itself in competition with this 'new' popular culture, the growth of which coincides with the movement's decline. It is perhaps not so surprising after all that those Chartists who were seeking to revive the movement should attempt to do so, in part, by writing radical popular fiction.

III

The earliest examples of Chartist fiction were invariably a combination of moral tract and reportage. Thomas Cooper's stories, for example, superimposed an increasingly moralistic framework upon descriptions of working-class life.[25] When Feargus O'Connor began his campaign for land reform, he turned to writing short stories to illustrate the superiority of small-scale farming. An anonymous allegory, *Political Pilgrim's Progress* (now attributed to Thomas Doubleday) was one of the earliest attempts by a Chartist to use fiction to discuss political issues.[26] *The Pioneers, or a Tale of the Radical Rising at Stratheven in 1820* was probably the first Chartist serialised novel to use the events of the recent past as its setting.[27]

Chartist journals also serialised a large number of reprinted stories of national struggles from Europe, such as *William Tell, or Switzerland Delivered*.[28] Some of Ernest Jones's earliest work was clearly a follow-on from this kind of writing, his *Romance of the People* being a fictionalised account of Poland's struggle for independence.[29]

Several Chartist writers appear to have made a conscious decision to move away from such heroic writing and towards a more recognisably popular form of fiction. Each of the texts discussed below begins with an exordial justification for writing what their readers would clearly recognise as popular:

> The romance of fiction cannot equal the romance of truth.
> Well then – such I pourtray. To reflect in simple language, the domestic wrongs and sorrows of society – such as they are at present – in a plain, simple, and unvarnished tale.[30]

> But in order that those wounds that afflict society may be healed, it is necessary that they first be probed by the pens of those who advocate the cause of famished poverty against bloated wealth.[31]

> The fiction department of literature has hitherto been neglected by the scribes of our body, and the opponents of our principles have been allowed to wield the power of imagination over the youth of our party, without any effort on our part to occupy this wide and fruitful plain.[32]

Apologia of this kind were common rhetorical devices in the opening pages of much popular fiction, usually in the form of a moral justification for telling a sordid story. The writer thereby remained respectable in the reader's eyes and a pretext was provided for an interest in the morbid and the prurient. An apologia was also a means of whetting readers' appetites. Thus Ernest Jones, at the beginning of *Woman's Wrongs*, shrugs his shoulders, so to speak, and promises his readers a sordid tale: 'If I draw pictures at which you shudder – if I reveal that, at which your heart revolts – I cannot help it.'[33]

In the texts which follow these openings (Ernest Jones, *Woman's Wrongs*, 1851; Thomas Martin Wheeler, *Sunshine and Shadow*, 1849; Thomas Frost, *The Secret*, 1850), there is much that might be regarded as successful political writing. But, more importantly, in each the political element is crucially weakened by the demands made by the conventions of the popular. There are several points at which the tensions thus created severely deform the texts. There is space here, however, to consider only two related aspects of the popular in relation to Chartist fiction – the use of a conventionalised moral framework and of the archetype of the wronged maiden.

In *Woman's Wrongs*, Jones sets out to show not only how women are the ultimate victims of social evils such as poverty and unemployment, but also how women are victims 'through all the social grades'.[34] The first of four related stories follows the fortunes of a working-man's wife, Margaret Haspen, and opens with her giving birth in the most squalid of conditions. Because she is experiencing difficulties, her neighbours call for Doctor Cutter, a grotesque creation closely modelled on the brutal doctors of broadside ballads:

> When Cutter entered, Margaret was uttering fainter cries of exhaustion.
>
> "Well, well my girl! What's the matter? They tell me you've a starling that won't come out of his cage! Ha, Ha! that's all. We must open the door. What's the lock broken, and the key lost? Ha, ha! Well, let's see! Children are like a bottle of wine? the beginning's more pleasant than the end, Ha, ha, ha!"
>
> He set about his task.
>
> "Never mind! Patience! A little steel medicine – ha, ha! – and all will be right."
>
> The sight of his preparations terrified poor Margaret.
>
> "No, no!" she shrieked, writhing at the bottom of her bed.
>
> "You'll kill me – I won't – let me alone!"
>
> "Ha, ha!" giggled Mr Cutter; 'never mind – all done in a minute. No, no! eh? You didn't always say no, my dear! so it's too late to say it now. Ha, ha!"
>
> "What a witty man he is!" tittered the gossips at the door.[35]

No doubt Jones intended to make readers pity Margaret. But, as a recognisable popular fiction figure, is not Cutter also intended to be a source of entertainment? And the two authorial intrusions maximise the macabre aspects of the scene rather than creating sympathy for Margaret. Add to this the conventional features of villainy (the numerous 'ha, ha!' interjections, for instance, and the melodramatic punctuation) and the success of this scene as a 'set piece' clearly militates against its didacticism.

Unemployment, victimisation and drunkenness eventually compel Margaret's husband to a life of crime, his degradation culminating in the slaughter of his former employer. The police catch Margaret literally red-handed, cleaning blood from the floor and walls, and she is finally executed. Haspen has revenged himself upon the cause of his misery, but only at the cost of his life. Margaret must die an innocent victim betrayed accidentally by the daughter she had once saved from Haspen's drunken rage. In this bloody and exciting crime story there is very little to bear out Jones's exordial claim to be changing his readers' outlook.

At the climax of the story, Haspen, Latchman his accomplice and, finally, Margaret, are hanged in public. A few minutes before her death 'despite years of hardship and hunger – despite grief and age – she looked beautiful – very beautiful – that moment!'[36] As she faces death, Margaret is serene: ' "God bless you! He knows I don't deserve to die. Hush! Mary! – Don't cry so, Mary!" and the soft cajoling tenderness of the mother turned her choking tones into an angelic music. Another moment, and her lifeless corpse was dangling in the air before the myriad of spectators.'[37]

The sacrificial figure of Margaret Haspen is undoubtedly a powerful symbol within the text, but the success of Jones's writing here once again weakens it as propaganda. Executions were a common subject for broadsides and in crime stories such as the Newgate tales.[38] In Jones's version, however, it could be argued that, by including spectators who relish the scene, he discourages his readers from regarding the hanging as entertainment (because they would not identify themselves with such an overtly ghoulish group). Why then does Jones leave the last word to this grim chorus?:

'Is that the child of the woman that has just been hung?' one of them asked the girl who carried Mary.

'Yes, sir!'

'Poor thing! What will become of it?' said another.
'Lucky for her, she's pretty!' rejoined the first. Both smiled knowingly, twirled their clouded canes – and entered a shop.[39]

The reader is almost invited to join in the sniggering at Mary's implied fate – prostitution – and we are given a static view of society that precludes any possibility of the change of heart Jones ostensibly recommends.

In Book Two Anna, a young milliner, catches the eye of a medical student. After being tormented by her lascivious landlord (thereby having her virtue tested and proven), she is thrown onto the street. When the medical student finds her she refuses, on pain of death, to take refuge in his lodgings but obligingly collapses in his arms only to wake by his fireside:

> A light flame began to leap upward in the grate, like the pulse of hidden life . . . her hair's brown luxuriance fell in a ravishing shower over her white shoulders – her symmetrical beauty lay in listless helplessness . . . The heating draught, the nourishing viands, roused the dormant pulse of animal life, while the love in every look and tone, the strange magnetic influence of affection, lulled and charmed alike the higher faculties of heart and brain . . . Oh! nature! why did you make them human? Oh Fate! why did you bring them thus together?
> World! judge not harshly of them. She fell? let her who would have stood under the same circumstances, throw the first stone! He sinned – he did sin – but, by temptation and the danger, weigh the crime.
> That was a night of ecstacy.[40]

How similar is Jones's presentation of Anna's seduction to Margaret's execution. In each the effect is voyeuristic. Jones's refusal to condemn the couple might be regarded as a strident blast against Victorian sexual hypocrisy, but it also gives the reader licence to enjoy the scene which, as it develops, reveals other aspects of Anna's identity:

> She was his? she felt it – yes, she felt instinctively the full force of that union: hesitation and fear had flown – and she gave herself up, after a passing coyness – the last faint stand of retiring innocence before its foe – to the full torrent of her generous, ardent enthusiastic love. She tried to drown reflection in continued ecstacy.[41]

Anna has become the innocent who, once initiated, loses all restraint, a common enough type in the more salacious forms of popular fiction.

After a brief period of domestic bliss, Anna finds herself abandoned, heart-broken and pregnant. She dies soon after having Trelawny's (the medical student's) child and her body finds its way onto the slab at an anatomy class:

> All the students turned towards the dissecting table.
> Weldon *raised the head of the body.*
> Suddenly a piercing cry came from the backmost seat, and Charles Trelawny fell senseless to the ground.
> *He had recognised the face of Anna!*
> 'What's the matter? – what is it?' asked the professor.
> 'Nothing, sir,' said Weldon coldly; 'it's only Mr. Trelawny, who has found out that this is the body of his mistress, – and that it is he who has killed her.'
> 'Ah! I understand,' said the professor; 'take away the body.'
> 'Yes!' observed the young man in an undertone. 'Daughter of the people! you have worked – you have suffered – now your fate's accomplished: your body has administered to the *amusement* and to the *instruction* of the favoured few: now to the pit society gives you in the common graveyard: and SLEEP! DAUGHTER OF THE PEOPLE!'[42]

Trelawny is confronted with the physical evidence of his crimes in a manner that places the relationship between the classes in a direct and grim light. The contrast between Weldon's public and private voices is also effective, as is that between this scene and Anna's 'giving of her body' to Trelawny earlier. The potential for class retribution is weakened, however, by Trelawny's loss of consciousness and the reader's attention is drawn, through Weldon, to the dissected corpse, his threnody serving Anna up as another sacrificial lamb to class society. The ostensible moral content of the scene provides the framework and the pretext for another set-piece that owes much to the popularity of stories about Burke and Hare and Sweeney Todd.[43]

Thomas Frost's *The Secret* is the most conventionally popular of the texts analysed in this chapter. It makes use of the *deus ex machina* of unexpected inheritance and the device of mixed identity – both frowned upon, Vicinus tells us, by serious Chartist novelists.[44] Chartism figures largely in the text but is gradually subsumed to the love and inheritance plot. Frost's novel has a happy ending which involves class conciliation and a hefty dollop of the pastoral. Yet, despite the text's conventionality, Frost's use of the wronged maiden archetype is far more restrained than is Jones's.

In *The Secret*, Lizzie Vincent is the obligatory poor but honest servant girl who is seduced and abandoned by her employer's son. She gives birth to a still-born child in the workhouse, walks the streets and is arrested as a vagrant. In prison she is protected by the Chartist hero of the novel, Ernest Rodwell, a compositor. He declares his love for her, they are married and eventually, live happy ever after. What Lizzie and Ernest do not know, however, is that she is in fact the legitimate daughter of the Duke of Belgrave. At about the time she was born (it is revealed), the Duke's servant girl (Lizzie Vincent senior) gives birth to his illegitimate daughter, dying shortly afterwards. Mark Vincent, the child's grandfather swaps babies so that the Duke's bastard is raised as Lady Alicia, and his rightful heir as the servant, Lizzie Vincent.

The connection between 'Lizzie' and the Duke is hinted at from the beginning of the text, but the denouement does not come until Mark Vincent, arrested during a Chartist uprising, uses his knowledge of the secret to procure his release from prison. The revelation of 'Lizzie's' true identity is made to the reader during the nadir of her misfortunes.

The birth of 'Lizzie's' child in the workhouse is described delicately when compared with Jones's treatment of Margaret Haspen's confinement:

> In the lying-in ward of St Giles's workhouse, did the hapless child of Elizabeth Vincent see the light, but survived its birth only a few hours. Charles Ducape had heard nothing of his victim since she had written to him, imploring his assistance for the sake of the unborn child – *his* child – for he made no inquiries concerning her, though he must have known how wretched must have been her position, dependent in such a trying moment upon law enforced charity.[45]

Frost exploits the scene not through the grim and bawdy humour of Jones's Doctor Cutter, but by a general peroration against the social evils of the time that compel honest working girls to choose starvation and misery or prostitution:

> For industry and virtue there is nothing possible under the present system of society, but poverty and misery. Observe the seamstresses, the milliners, the straw-bonnet makers, the book-folders or any other class of females, and it will invariably be found, that those who dress the best, and fare the best, are those who, when they have left off work, add to their slender earnings the wages of prostitution. But the attentuated form, the sunken eyes, the pallid cheeks, the transparent fingers – these are the marks of the virtuous![46]

While this is an effective piece of propaganda in which the Victorian work ethic is undermined (and is further ironised by 'Lizzie's' true status as an aristocrat), it confirms for Frost's male readers the popular myth that all well-turned-out working girls were available.

The restraint in Frost's treatment of his wronged maiden, together with his broad hints about 'Lizzie's' connections with Lord Belgrave, make possible a wealth of ironies, wish-fulfilment and vicarious class revenge for those readers who guess 'Lizzie's' true class identity. When Charles Ducape, for instance, rejects the pregnant 'Lizzie', he is throwing away a rich and beautiful heiress whose child would have made him the father of a Duke.

In contrast to the bourgeois Ducape, Ernest Rodwell's proposal to 'Lizzie' is couched in the most honourable terms including an extraordinary diatribe on the distinction between profane and holy love. Add to this the circumstances (they are both in prison) and the fact that Ernest falls for 'Lizzie' when she is at her most desolate, and the reader is left in no doubt that it is his proletarian worthiness that enables him to divine her natural nobility.

The text also includes descriptions of the graces of the *apparent* Lady Alicia (the real Lizzie Vincent). When an Earl proposes to her, it is on the night of a splendid ball in the most exotic setting possible:

> Exotics of the choicest and most beautiful description were on every side of the youthful pair – the camelia with its dark glossy leaves and crimson blossoms . . . and the warm atmosphere was

perfumed with the fragrance exhaled from the orange and the myrtle . . . 'You will permit me then, to ask your father for his sanction to our union,' said the Earl of Castledale: and his voice fell upon the ear of the patrician maiden like the low soft notes of a dove heard from some dusky wood on a still evening in summer.[47]

The pastoral element, developed further at the end of the novel, is characteristically used by Frost to suggest moral virtue, but such an idyll from aristocratic life seems curiously out of place in a Chartist text. Its very inclusion, however, provides another clue to 'Lady Alicia's' true identity which, if guessed at, makes the scene a luscious fantasy for Frost's working-class readers. In this sense, the mixed identity plot is one of the text's strengths in that it enables readers to identify with *both* women as proletarian heroines: Lady Alicia is noble and virtuous in the role of a wronged servant; Lizzie displays grace and beauty when she is cast as Lady Alicia.

When 'Lizzie' is finally reinstated as Belgrave's daughter, readers continue to identify with her as a former servant and can delight, with her, at the beautiful clothes, riches and admiration that are bestowed upon her. But because she is noble in spirit (is this because of her experiences as a servant?), her love for the equally noble Ernest is unabated, despite her father's threats to disinherit her. Not only is proletarian morality revealed to be superior to both bourgeois and aristocratic values, Frost's readers are flattered by the lovely heiress's preference for an artisan. Such purity is finally rewarded, however, as the Duke relents and bestows a handsome settlement upon the couple.

Ernest Rodwell, the proletarian hero who had spent the first half of the text plotting an insurrection, wins nobility, beauty and wealth. Virtue is rewarded. Alicia's marriage to Ernest also means that she cannot resume her status as the Duke's heiress, leaving Lizzie Vincent in that role so that Belgrave is compelled to recognise his illegitimate 'back-stairs' offspring, providing further gratification for Frost's working-class readers.

Frost's treatment of the theme of the wronged maiden, then, despite his conventional plotting and his deft side-stepping of the issues raised by the inclusion of the Chartist movement in the text, provides a far greater scope for commenting on the relationship between the classes than does Jones's treatment of very similar themes. Whereas Jones's extreme and habitual use of melodrama suppresses the reader's capacity to identify with victimised women, Frost's skilful plotting and happy ending encourage the reader to identify with both working-class characters and others who display proletarian virtues. Bourgeois and aristocratic characters are defeated, not by a working-class uprising, but because of their own moral decrepitude.

In creating such a closed text, however, Frost resolves class conflicts *within the text* by creating extraordinary situations and by ensuring that virtue is always rewarded. The text becomes, ultimately, an entertainment, a comedy of manners tailored for a working-class audience. Frost, like Jones, was compelled to activate the established codes of popular fiction and to meet his readers' expectations rather than radicalising them.

If *Woman's Wrongs* is a melodrama and *The Secret* is a comedy of manners, then Thomas Martin Wheeler's *Sunshine and Shadow* is essentially a *bildungsroman*. It follows the fortunes of one Arthur Morton, his early life and education, his development as a Chartist activist, his escape from the law to the Americas where he meets, once again, his first love, Julia North. It traces his unemployment and destitution on returning to England, his descent into crime and his continual rededication to Chartism. Resembling the activitist's autobiographies of the later years of the century (Samual Bamford, Joseph Arch and Thomas Cooper for example) and sharing many characteristics with twentieth-century working-class novels, it has long been a favourite of critics of the genre.

Wheeler's wronged maiden is quite different from the victims found in the other Chartist texts. Julia North is the sister of Arthur's well-off schoolfriend. The Norths are wine merchants whose star is rising as Arthur's is falling. As an artisan, he confines his affections to a fervent correspondence with the fair Julia who, in keeping with the conventions of the sentimental novel, is offered by her family to the inevitably repugnant Sir Jasper.[48]

When Arthur is wrongly arrested as an arsonist during the Chartist Convention in Birmingham, he escapes and sets sail for America, but is shipwrecked halfway. On board the ship that rescues him is the lovely Julia, bound for the West Indies where Sir Jasper is Governor. There follows a shipboard romance that is introduced to the reader by the familiar device of an apologia:

> Let not the censorious or prudish blame my heroine. Love in her was no crime, albeit she was the bride of another, – it was the result of feelings as pure as nature ever implanted in human breast: the treachery of her relatives, and the baseness of Sir Jasper, were the circumstances which caused it to verge upon crime – or rather, should we say, retributive justice. Let the saint and the hypocrite rail on – we write not for their perusal, we heed not their censure; we picture nature as it is – veritable flesh and blood – glowing with warm and ardent feelings – feelings which are apt to overpower the senses; but far better is it so than us to fall into the Dead Sea waters of apathy, or wallow in the mire of cold and frigid selfishness.[49]

This throbbing precursor – strikingly similar to Jones's exoneration of Anna's and Trelawny's 'night of ecstacy' – is followed by Arthur's wooing of Julia by a lengthy and pained explanation of his political views (just as Rodwell had overwhelmed 'Lizzie' by a lecture on profane and holy love). Relationships between proletarian males and upper-class women are always handled with the utmost decorum in Chartist fiction, both Morton and Rodwell embarking on their most moralistic speeches when alone with upper-class women. Within the conventions of popular fiction, high-born women could no longer be portrayed as virtuous if they showed sexual interest in working-class men.

Once in the West Indies, Julia becomes an exotic figure, pining to death for love of Arthur. She must die of course, for any other course of action would weaken her presentation as an object of sentiment. In the depiction of this love affair there is no trace of the realism that some critics have claimed to find in Wheeler's portrayal of human relationships. Arthur, on hearing of Julia's imminent demise, must see her for the last time:

> "Kiss me, Arthur, – it is our first and last kiss of love; may you be happy and prosperous as you deserve to be, and when sadness shall cloud your soul sometimes think of me. And if the spirits of the departed can again visit this earthly sphere I will, in those moments, hover round and console you. Adieu! Adieu!"
>
> Wildly, passionately, did Arthur press his heated lips to the icy cold ones of his beloved, and with eyes blinded with tears, and frame trembling with emotion, he gazed his last on his first love – the beauteous and lamented Julia North.[50]

Jack Mitchell makes the point that Julia is a 'same woman yardstick',[51] a device for contrasting the treatment of one woman by the upper class (Sir Jasper), the bourgeoisie (her family) and the working class (Arthur Morton). This is undoubtedly the case and the contrast contributes to the reader's appreciation of Arthur's inestimable decency (just as Rodwell's treatment of 'Lizzie' compares favourably with the Duke's and Ducape's). What is true of the overall structure of the text is less true of single episodes, however (particularly in serialised fiction), where, as we have seen in Jones's text, scenes are presented in a manner that undermines the novel's didactic purposes.

Louis James' view of the plot of a popular novel as a moral framework that exists in order to facilitate the presentation of 'strong' scenes (see above, page 133) seems particularly apt in regard to Julia North's death scene, for instance, which must be drained of all its potential social and political significance if it is to be effective as the climax of a popular romance. She dies, as wronged maidens must, not bewailing the social evils and mores that have sealed her fate, but as a pale, beneficent and beautiful sacrificial lamb.

Whereas Jones sanctifies the carnage in *Woman's Wrongs* with an epicedium, usually delivered by a choric figure who *is* aware of the social implications of the death scene, Wheeler is less concerned with indicting Sir Jasper and the Norths for the evil they have done than with exonerating Arthur from any criticism that might be levelled at him for having played a love scene with a married woman:

> True, his love was unhallowed; neither religion nor custom would have sanctioned its indulgence; but when did love succumb to earthly ties – opposition but rivets its chain – it needs not the world's approbation to fan it into flame – it lives on its own elements, and burns the fiercer the more it is frowned upon.[52]

IV

It can be seen, then, that the forms, archetypes and conventionalised didacticism of popular fiction made it exceedingly difficult for the Chartists to adapt the genre for the advocacy of their political cause, in contrast to the ease with which they were able to write radical poetry (and, in the case of Ernest Jones and Thomas Frost, in contrast to the comparative success of their non-political fiction).

In order to write popular fiction (and no other form of fiction could reach the intended audience), they had little choice but to rehearse an established set of codes, to fulfil a contract to meet their readers' expectations (and with serialised fiction, this contract had to be renewed with each instalment). But must this always be the case? Given the persistence of a virtually static popular literary culture (today's television soap operas are the unmistakable expression of this culture's tenacity), can a genuinely radical novel ever reach a mass audience? Can those difficulties first illuminated for us by the Chartists ever be resolved?

Some left critics would answer yes to all these questions. They would point to the social problem novels of the 1880s (notably those by Margaret Harkness, John Overton and W.E. Tirebuck); to the politically motivated fiction of the 1920s and 1930s; to the 'angry young man' novels of the 1950s; and above all to Robert Tressell's *The Ragged Trousered Philanthropists*. But because these texts have received so little critical attention, much of the criticism that has been written has been of a descriptive and defensive nature. This is a pity for a more analytical approach to some of these texts would certainly add to our understanding of the relationship between class, literature and radicalism, and would lessen the impact of the often arbitrary shifts in theoretical positions in this field, as outlined at the beginning of this chapter.

Notes

1. For a complete list, see J.F.C. Harrison and D. Thompson, *Bibliography of the Chartist Movement* (Brighton, 1978).
2. For a close study of the influence of Byron on Thomas Cooper, for example, see Philip Collins, *Thomas Cooper, The Chartist: Byron and the Poets of the Poor* (Nottingham, 1969). Burns seems to have occupied a special position in the movement's hagioscope, one reviewer describing him as 'the friend of humanity, the brother of man, the scourge of the oppressor, the soother of the oppressed – a republican, a democrat: in principle and practice, an honest Chartist' *The Chartist Circular* (20.2.41). Burns died forty-two years before the word 'Chartist' was coined.

3. 'Unlike those great spirits [Burns, Byron and Shelley], WORDSWORTH passes from amongst us unregretted by the great body of his countrymen, who have no tears for the salaried slave of Aristocracy and pensioned parasite of Monarchy.' Obituary from *The Democratic Review* (May, 1850), p. 473.
4. 'The Politics of Poets', *The Chartist Circular* (11 July 1840 to 29 August 1840).
5. *The Labourer*, III, p. 130. This article includes a translation of some lines of Pushkin's verse thirteen years before they were published in *Russian*.
6. See Martha Vicinus, *The Industrial Muse* (London, 1974), chapter 3, part I.
7. *The Northern Star* (28 January 1843), p. 3.
8. This is not to say that this is Marx's view. He regarded the economic struggle between classes as the base upon which arose the superstructure which included culture. The notion of parallel struggles probably originates in Bogdanov's Proletcult movement in post-Revolutionary USSR. It does not become Communist orthodoxy until the advent of the Popular Front in 1934 to 1935.
9. Gustav Klaus (ed.), *The Socialist Novel in Britain* (Brighton, 1982), p. viii.
10. Jack Mitchell, 'Aesthetic Problems of the Development of the Proletarian Novel in Nineteenth Century Britain'. In David Craig (ed.), *Marxists on Literature* (Harmondsworth, 1975), p. 250.
11. Tony Bennett, 'Introduction: Popular Culture and the "Turn to Gramsci" '. In Tony Bennett, Colin Mercer and Janet Woollacott (eds) *Popular Culture and Social Relations* (Milton Keynes, 1986), p. xii.
12. Ibid.
13. Ibid., p. xiii.
14. Ibid., pp. xiv–xv.
15. Stuart Hall, 'Popular Culture and the State'. In Bennett, *et al.* (eds), *Popular Culture*, p. 36.
16. Eileen Yeo and Stephen Yeo (eds), *Popular Culture and Class Conflict 1590–1914* (Brighton, 1981), p. 137.
17. R.K. Webb, *The British Working Class Reader, 1790–1848* (London, 1955).
18. Louis James cites a figure of 560 illegal publications in 1836. Louis James, *Fiction for the Working Man, 1830–50* (Harmondsworth, 1963), p. 36.
19. See Martha Vicinus, *Broadsides of the Industrial North* (Newcastle, 1975).

20. This was as much the result of technical innovation as it was of social and political factors. Rotary presses and improved paper making from the 1820s allowed for far more sophisticated products that were often effectively illustrated. See Patricia Anderson, *The Printed Image and the Transformation of Popular Culture 1790–1860* (Oxford, 1991).
21. See E.P. Thompson, *Customs in Common* (London, 1991), p. 8.
22. James, *Fiction for the Working Man*, p. 89.
23. Ibid., p. 172.
24. Ibid., p. 193.
25. See, for instance, Thomas Cooper, *Seth Thompson, Stockinger* (1842) and *Wise Saws and Modern Instances* (London, 1845).
26. Thomas Doubleday, *Political Pilgrim's Progress, The Northern Liberator* (19 January 1839 to 30 March 1839).
27. *The Pioneers* was serialised in the *Scottish Chartist Circular*. The periodical folded, however, after the fourth instalment, leaving only a fragment of the planned serial. Its fate provides a graphic illustration of the extent to which Chartist fiction was dependent upon the success of Chartist journalism.
28. *English Chartist Circular* (1842).
29. Ernest Jones, *Romance of the People, The Labourer*, vol. II (1847–1848). This text was later published as a three-volume novel, *The Maid of Warsaw* (London, 1855).
30. Ernest Jones, *Woman's Wrongs, Notes to the People*, vol. II (1851–1852) p. 515.
31. Thomas Frost, *The Secret, The National Instructor* (25 May 1850 to 19 October 1850), p. 2.
32. Thomas Martin Wheeler, *Sunshine and Shadow, The Northern Star* (31 March 1849 to 5 January 1850), 31 March 1849, p. 3.
33. Jones, *Woman's Wrongs*, p. 515.
34. Ibid.
35. Ibid., p. 517.
36. Ibid., p. 612.
37. Ibid.
38. See, for instance, the broadside 'The Gibbeting of William Jobling at Jarrow Slake' (Newcastle, 1832), Vicinus, *Broadsides*, pp. 40–41.
39. Jones, *Woman's Wrongs*, p. 612.
40. Ibid., p. 671.
41. Ibid.
42. Ibid., p. 712.
43. The story of Sweeney Todd first appears in Thomas Peckett Prest's 'The String of Pearls', *The People's Periodical* (London, 1846). The story is based on a French crime recorded in *Les Rues de Paris*,

though the belief that some butchers sold human flesh seems to have been part of popular culture long before this date, James Catnach (the publisher) actually being imprisoned in 1818 for making such a claim against a Drury Lane butcher.
44. Martha Vicinus, 'Chartist Fiction and the Development of a Class-Based Literature'. In Gustav Klaus (ed.), *The Socialist Novel in Britain* (Brighton, 1982), p. 11.
45. Frost, *The Secret*, p. 166.
46. Ibid., p. 165.
47. Ibid., p. 20.
48. A typical popular fictional version of the theme is *Prest's Viceroy; or the Horrors of Zindorf Castle* (London, 1844), pp. 239–45.
49. Wheeler, *Sunshine and Shadow*, (23 June 1849), p. 3.
50. Ibid., (4 August 1849), p. 3.
51. Mitchell, Jack, 'Aesthetic Problems . . . '. In David Craig (ed.), *Marxists on Literature*, p. 262.
52. Wheeler, *Sunshine and Shadow* (4 August 1849), p. 3.

8 Collaboration and co-operation: a contextured-political reading of Edith Simcox's Autobiography of a Shirtmaker

Pauline Polkey

> There are times when the story of one life is so interwoven with the story of its time, when the thought and conduct of one individual soul is so typical of the life of its generation, that to tell the story of one, is to tell the story of the other.
>
> (Helen Blackburn, *Women's Suffrage*)[1]

The original motive for my work for this volume was inspired by research I had undertaken on Edith Simcox's *Autobiography of a Shirtmaker*: a handwritten journal, of some 130,000 words, held at the Bodleian library, Oxford; the first date of entry is 10 May 1877, and the last is 29 January 1900.[2] What rapidly became clear to me was the extent to which the *Autobiography* provided a record not only of Simcox's life, but also of other women's lives with whom she was personally and/or politically involved, and the numerous friendships, networks, organisations and campaigns of which those women were a part. It is a text that has been greatly misrepresented and misconstrued by commentators, who have focused almost exclusively on Simcox's description of her 'love-passion' for George Eliot. While the *Autobiography* undoubtedly *is* a passionate account of that relationship, this chapter offers a contextured reading of the journal, drawing in its aproach on some observations of the Personal Narratives Group:

[Contexts play] an essential role in grounding and validating the interpretation of women's personal narratives. They show the importance of the interpersonal relationships within which the life story emerges; they illuminate the significance of the intersection of individual life and historical moment; they address the importance of the frameworks of meaning through which women orient themselves in the world; and they allow us to explore the ways in which the interpreter's own context shapes both the formation and interpretation of a personal narrative.[3]

The chapter is divided into two parts. Part One begins with a general consideration of recent feminist theoretical debates on autobiography. I then offer a 'theory in practice' demonstration of how specific approaches can be utilised in reading Simcox's *Autobiography*. Part Two outlines the methodological practices that I applied in my work on the other women whom Simcox mentions in her *Autobiography*. Here, my principal aims are to allow readers access to the bibliographic material that I collated – which, given the limited length of this chapter, are more usually referred to than examined – and to offer possible investigative route/s for those who work on autobiographical texts. I argue that to properly understand these writings we need to recognise the co-operative and collaborative practices deployed by their politically active authors. I conclude – with an 'inconclusive' section – by mapping the 'personal narrative' of my investigation onto one particular woman, 'Miss Williams,', whom Simcox describes as having 'professed a feeling for me different from what she had ever had for anyone, it might make her happiness if I could return it; & then she said "Imagine what it is to have that feeling & to be obliged to go away from you" ' (23 July 1881).

Throughout this discussion, my aim is to show the ways in which feminist collaborative writings and organisations were fuelled by political activism; and to argue that, on the one hand, this reflected a political motivation to 'make public' that activism, and, on the other hand, can be seen to reveal an interpersonal construction of subjectivity, as well as a highly individualised articulation of a 'sense of self'.

Part One: Theorising the auto/biographical I/'eye'

> Historically, psychologically, intellectually – & it may be admitted from pure carnal curiosity too – I should like to know how many women there are who have honestly no story to tell, how many have some other story than the one which alone is supposed to count & how many of those who think it worthwhile to dissect themselves are in a position to tell all they know of the result.
>
> (Edith Simcox, *Autobiography of a Shirtmaker*, 17 October 1887)

Throughout much of the 1980s and, to date, the 1990s, feminists have rightly attempted to re-define autobiography within a system that opens it up to self-writings produced by women. Included within this category of intellectual endeavour are a range of critical editions and case studies such as Estelle Jelinek (ed.) (1980); Domna C. Stanton (ed.) (1984); Sidonie Smith (1987); Shari Benstock (ed.) (1988); Bella Brodzki and Celeste Schenck (eds) (1988); Carolyn Heilbrun (1989); Personal Narratives Group (eds) (1989); Valerie Sanders (1989); Mary Corbett (1992); and Liz Stanley (1992).[4] A substantial body of feminist work has been occupied with a revisionist process, resulting in an archaeological groundwork much valued by those academics who are no longer required to sift through seemingly endless critical texts that promote the notion of autobiography as being first, a singularly male prerogative; secondly, a white, European product historically rooted in the early modern period; and thirdly, the exclusive property of a particular social elite.

In some feminist-based studies, priority is given to theoretically countering the various critical models upon which male-based texts are formulated, and/or to retracing women's importance within the development of autobiography. Others, most notably Stanton's *The Female Autograph*, take a deconstructivist approach – and one which has provoked considerable debate among feminists over recent years – in which she attempts to 'excise' the *bio* from autobiography, aiming to 'bracket the traditional emphasis on the narration of "a life," and that notion's facile presumption of referentiality' (p. vii).

Arguably one of the best ways of approaching the numerous case studies and editorial collectives that are mentioned above, is to utilise Stanley's adaptation of Ann Jefferson's (1990) terminology of their forming a 'metanarrative', 'in which successive editorial texts act as commentaries on those that came before'.⁵ This approach allows for a vital engagement, and recognition of strong referential links, with other works, as well as providing a framework within which discursive commentaries can be made in formulating disagreements and forging new directions. Within this perspective, feminist commentaries and works form part of a 'polyphony' of voices (Stanley's term) – albeit 'editorially enshrined' – in which ideas, theories and practices are viewed not so much as a singular, individualistic concern, but rather as a collective one. Another feature of feminist-metanarratives is that they can be seen to provide discussion, argument, and counter-argument, and thus the ideal atmosphere – however hot the temperature might sometimes become! – in which to formulate new growth in feminist discourses. Such a view is perhaps best summed up by Shari Benstock in her Introduction to *The Private Self*, where she writes that:

> My sense of the collective work now underway on women's autobiographical writings – and there is an immense amount of work in progress – is that no-one is taking the old definitions of genre and gender, theory and practice for granted. No one adopts a theoretical stance without a close look at the implications of that stance. Often, various theories are brought into play with each other (and this has been a defining feature of feminist theory all along) so as to measure the usefulness and truthfulness of these theories in relation to each other, with special attention to questions at hand: gender, race, social class, religious affiliation, sexual preference, historical and cultural contexts. (p. 4)

In response to Stanton's insistence upon an excision of the 'life' – and her exclusive emphasis upon *textual* constructions of autobiography – a wide range of feminist-metanarratives have been produced. Brodzki and Schenck, for example – who themselves work within a poststructuralist framework – while concurring with Stanton's 'sense of strong theoretical scholarship on women's autobiography and the need for revising "existing discursive and ideological boundaries"' (p. 12), argue their intention to

> restore the *bio* Stanton excised from autobiography. We strongly believe that the duplicitous and complicitous relationship of 'life'

and 'art' in autobiographical modes is precisely the point. To elide it in the name of eliminating the 'facile assumption of referentiality' is dangerously to ignore the crucial referentiality of class, race, and sexual orientation; it is to beg serious political questions. (pp. 12–13)

Mary Corbett argues along similar lines in stating that

> The poststructuralist desire to celebrate what Paul de Man called the 'de-facement' of the autobiographical subject proceeds from an imperative that makes very little sense to those of us – e.g., women, sexual and ethnic minorities – whose histories and subjectivities have always been effaced. (p. 6)

In problematizing the 'de-facement' model for women, Nicole Ward Jouve argues that 'we have been asked to go along with Deconstruction while we had not even got to the Construction stage. You must have a self before you can deconstruct it'.[6] Likewise, Treva Broughton's review article 'Signs of Life', suggests that there is a current desire among feminists to 'find ways of reclaiming the "bios" – the historical and hence socio-political resonance of autobiography – from the tyranny of post-structuralist obsession with textuality and post-romantic idealizations of the self'.[7]

But it is in Stanley's *The Auto/biographical I* that the most fully worked-out, feminist (published) response to the deconstruction of women's autobiographies has been made. Stanley deals with what she considers to be the symbiotic relationship between autobiography and biography, hence: auto/biography. This approach represents a dynamic move towards embracing the 'primacy of everyday life and its concrete material events, persons, conversations', and demands that 'At some point, surely, we have to accept that material reality does exist, that it impinges upon all of us all the time, that texts are not the only things' (p. 246). Stanley's point is crucial, raising questions about the extent to which academics in pursuit of theoretical enquiries, and failing to embrace social materiality within that pursuit, are in danger of deserving the kind of indictment made by Jane Haggis in her discussion of 'The Feminist Research Process – Defining a Topic':

> As someone from a working-class environment and culture, my encounter with university 'knowledge' brought the discovery that working-class people were not 'there' within the academy as participants or subjects but as 'others', as 'ordinary people' to be studied and observed. . . . An implicit judgemental attitude of 'we know' ensured that 'the working class' remained a category for study and not participants in the making of socialist knowledge. Little space was accorded the commonsense knowledge and logic which I knew operated sensibly to inform ways in which people conducted their lives. Even less space or recognition was given to the distinct presences and realities of working class women.[8]

There are two specific aspects of Stanley's work that I wish to focus on here, and which I regard as having potentially liberating implications for feminist interpretative practices of auto/biography: first her expansion of (canonical) boundaries around which women can be seen to construct a life; and secondly, her critique of what she terms the 'limelight'/'spotlight' approach of conventional biographers. I shall deal with each of these points in turn, showing how they can be applied to Simcox's *Autobiography of a Shirtmaker*.

Writing a life: expanding the boundaries

Stanley argues for a relational understanding of autobiography and biography, and does not section off the written from the oral. Nor does she privilege those texts that are canonised as 'classic' over those that are deemed 'popular'. For Stanley, auto/biography might include, for example, curricula vitae, plays and films, autobiographical poems, and spoken autobiographies, as well as published works; to which list I would add self/portraits, letters, diaries, notebooks and historical chronologies. (See also Carolyn Helibrun's discussion of this in her book *Writing a Woman's Life*.)

How, then, can such an 'open' approach be applied to Simcox's *Autobiography*, without falling into the danger of forcing a 1990s feminist-political reading on a text that was written over one hundred years ago? First, as I have already indicated – and will go on to discuss in more detail in Part Two – the journal refers to numerous women (and men) with whom

Simcox was personally and/or politically involved. As such, it becomes quite straightforwardly an auto/biographical record within the definition Stanley offers; that is to say, in constructing her own life, Simcox also engages in the process of constructing the lives of others. An example of this can be seen in Simcox's account of the effect that political activism had upon a number of women's lives. One politically active woman with whom Simcox worked very closely was Emma Paterson (1848–86): founder of the Women's Protective and Provident League (WPPL), and campaigner for women's trades unions. (She and Simcox were the first women delegates to attend the Trades Union Congress in 1875). Paterson died at the age of thirty-eight, after suffering from diabetes, a year after Simcox took her to see Dr Elizabeth Garrett Anderson for a diagnosis, a visit which Simcox records as follows:

> "She is dying," was the verdict, though there is a gleam of hope till proper treatment has been tried & failed & Mrs Anderson does not expect it to succeed; thinks she will not live 6 months – or three, my business is to get her at least to try. Mrs Anderson is very good – offers to attend her constantly as is needed if she takes lodgings near enough, since she [Paterson] will not entertain the idea of a hospital. (8 November 1885)

After Paterson's death, Simcox wrote that 'Mrs Paterson had little more than a twelve month after Mrs Anderson's verdict. The shock came to me then; her temper & character were suffering from the struggle with the world & illness together & for her sake it was as well. We are to see if it is possible to build her a monument' (31 January 1887). As to the strains from which she suffered, Simcox describes a particularly unpleasant series of illnesses she experienced, in the midst of work for the WPPL, as follows:

> . . . busy about Pimlico women; a deputation of them here one evening, a Tuesday, to tea & talk (for the substance of wh. see W.[omen's] U.[nion] J.[ournal) was curiously associated with a sick headache; the next Thursday after a long afternoon Comttee & delayed dinner, same phenomenon recurred, with a slight development of "shingles" next morning. Mrs Anderson advised quinine "nervous exhaustion", but either that remedy or a common cause a week or two later led to a mild cold (aggravated

by 20 minutes in the garden on a damp cold day) turning into spasmodic asthma – a fit wh. the doctors insisted on taking seriously, tho' I did not feel bad myself. Came up to London with difficulty & went to bed again here, wriggled through the League business & Pimlico controversy without material hindrance. Asthma followed by "psoriasis gultata" about elbows & ancles wh. disappears in two or three weeks to be succeeded by affection of the calf of the legs; & that, on my next visit to Harlaxton, by slight eczema about the back of the hands & fingers. Harrogate recommended; also assiduous Turkish baths. (17 May 1886)

Clearly, what these auto/biographical entries reveal is the extent to which some women came to terms (individually and/or collectively) with both understanding, and curing, what Elizabeth Garrett Anderson termed the 'half-starved slave-driven maids of all work' (*Autobiography*, 4 October 1880),[9] and also the extent to which politically active women such as Simcox, Paterson and Garrett Anderson, built up self-supportive networks and friendships so as to cope with the inevitable strain of that activism.

Secondly, the *Autobiography* is often shaped, and informed, by a range of auto/biographical material and discourses, inasmuch as Simcox can be seen to situate her sense or self/sense of others, through inclusion of such things as records of conversation between people, letters, reviews of (autobiographical/ biographical) publications, drafts of public speeches, descriptions of political meetings, newspaper articles, and so on. After Eliot's death in 1880, for instance, Simcox developed a network of friendships and alliances with a number of other women, including Elizabeth Garrett Anderson, Bessie Belloc, Barbara Bodichon, Maria Congreve, Eleanor, Elizabeth and Mary Cross, Sara Hennell, Gertrude Lewes, Maria Lewis, and Elma Stuart: each of whom shared with her 'auto/biographical' information about Eliot in the form of letters, conversations, anecdotes and portraits. While some of these connections were not entirely amicable – Simcox frequently records feelings of irritation with Elma Stuart, for example – what held these women together was a reciprocal desire to gain knowledge and share information about Eliot, offered on a somewhat *quid pro quo* basis.

Spotlighting the subject in view of the reader

Stanley characterises what she refers to as the 'limelight'/ 'spotlight' approach to conventional biography as

> a cast of one under the limelight supported by a few bit-part players who come and then typically go in the relative darkness around the star . . . The 'spotlight' approach to 'modern biography' emphasises the uniqueness of a particular subject, seen in individualised terms rather than as a social self lodged within a network of others. It casts these other people known and liked or disliked throughout the subject's life into the shadows; and doing so has interpretative importance for the way we understand 'a life', not only as textually related but also as interactionally understood. It essentialises the self, rather than focusing on the role of social processes in producing – and changing – what 'a self' consists of. And it enshrines an entirely de-politicised notion of 'greatness', presenting this as a characteristic of individuals rather than the product of political processes and constructions. (pp. 131–214)

In my work on Edith Simcox, I came across numerous examples of such a tradition. Marghanita Laski's *George Eliot and Her World*,[10] is a case in point. Laski frames Simcox as a 'tragic admirer [of Eliot] . . . and an undoubtedly emotional lesbian (p. 102), and despite offering an (albeit brief) outline of Simcox's political activism, Laski's 'spotlighting' approach is clear. Taking the confidential air of one conveying her subject's 'real' feelings, Laski's verdict on Simcox is as follows:

> Unfortunately for her [Simcox], in 1872 she fell in love with Marian who, though often impatient of Edith's devotion and obviously less drawn to her than to her other admirers, never gave her a final *congé*. Admittedly, Edith's adoration could be tiresome. (p. 102)

Here, Simcox is posited as a 'bit-part player', with the 'spotlight' on 'Marian'. While Lillian Faderman's approach in *Surpassing the Love of Men* is more theoretically focused than Laski's, she picks her way through the *Autobiography* in order to construct Simcox as a figure bestowing unrequited 'romantic friendship' upon Eliot, taking her as her 'muse and model'.[11] As can be seen from the following extract, Faderman's analysis forms another example of the 'spotlight' approach, with Eliot as the central subject, and Simcox as a peripheral, quasi-tragedean figure. Faderman is like Laski in that, listing Simcox's immense involvement in a variety of political, social and literary fields, she finally focuses her discussion exclusively on the effect that Eliot is presumed to have had upon Simcox. Her description is as follows:

> Edith Simcox founded a cooperative shirtmaking factory, served on the London School Board, started a lodgers' league, organised trade unions for women and men, and lectured extensively on topics such as socialism, women's work, suffrage, and conditions in China. She wrote for intellectual journals and political newspapers, and she published several books. *Such Herculean efforts by a woman born in the mid-nineteenth century were possible because she took Eliot for her muse and model.* In a patriarchal culture like Victorian England, the worship which a romantic friend bestowed upon the object of her love, and her desire to be worthy of that love, may have been one of the few stimuli which motivated achievement in a woman's life. (p. 163; emphasis mine)

This concern with the Simcox–Eliot relationship is not entirely misplaced, but the structures of that relationship were far more complex than Faderman so condescendingly allows, and are not reducible to an individualistic-based stimulus created through a desire for 'romantic friendship' on Simcox's part. Most significantly, what Faderman ignores is the collaborative and co-operative nature of Simcox's political activism, in which she can be seen to have worked with (numerous) *others*.

What I find most inexplicable about the numerous versions of the Simcox–Eliot relationship, as I shall go on to show, is their failure to consider the fact that Simcox was herself amorously pursued by a 'Miss Williams'. No critic or biographer – feminist or otherwise – has made reference to Williams, despite the record of her obvious demonstrations of passion for Simcox in the *Autobiography*. Why the astonishing silence? In part, such an omission can be explained through the main source whereby most critics come to read the *Autobiography*, via McKenzie's *Edith Simcox and George Eliot*.[12] This partial transcription of the *Autobiography*, while providing the source for an undoubtedly sustained interest in the journal over the past thirty years – the original manuscript is kept in the Bodleian, and is, in parts, extremely difficult to decipher – represents a skewed version, framed as it is by a particularly insidious and homophobic introduction by Gordon Haight, who writes:

> The Victorians' conception of love between those of the same sex cannot be fairly understood in an age steeped in Freud. Where they only saw beautiful friendship, the modern reader suspects perversion. The relations beteen Verena Tarrant and Olive Chancellor in *The Bostonians* James described as 'one of those friendships between women which are so common in New England', and he dissects the twisted psychological strands without apparent horror of what the schoolgirl today labels Lesbianism . . . In these cases as well as with Miss Simcox's account of her wild passion for George Eliot we must avoid reading back interpretations that could never have been suspected when they were written.[13]

Although different in tone and perspective, Haight's sexological account is comparable to Faderman's hypothesis of 'romantic friendship' between women, which she defines as being: 'love relationships in every sense except perhaps the genital, since women in centuries other than ours often internalised the view of females as having little sexual passion' (p. 16). In my conclusion to this chapter, I give an account of my discovery of who 'Miss Williams' was, the political organisations/women's networks she worked within, and her publications. In examining Simcox's auto/biographical account of her relationship with Williams, I utilise a *contextured* approach, which I shall now outline.

In antithesis to the skewed interpretation of Faderman's 'muse and model' thesis, I specifically locate the *Autobiography* within a contextured examination of numerous woman-based networks and friendships of which Simcox was a part, and situate it within the social, political and cultural climate in which it was written. Arguably one of the most important contributions of recent feminist work on auto/biography is our insistence on contextured understandings of auto/biographies. The word 'context' is defined by the Personal Narratives Group as meaning: 'to weave together, to twine, to connect. This interrelatedness creates the webs of meaning within which humans act. . . Context is not a script.

Rather it is a dynamic process through which the individual simultaneously shapes and is shaped by her environment' (p. 19).

It would be a mistake, however, to view the 'webs of meaning within which humans act' as necessarily seamless; or to take for granted a 'female tradition' within auto/biography that is continuous, unified and teleological, and to ignore the very differences, gaps and contradictions, within which the structuring of gender can best be understood. Gender – in the conflated form of 'femininity'/women's experience – is not to be 'really' found in literary and/or non-literary texts, however much they might be seen to be representational. Rather, gender is an identity that exists in *relationship* to other things: race, sexuality, class, culture, politics, and so on; it is also itself a relationship: feminine means non-masculine.'[14] As Linda Anderson argues in 'At the Threshold of the Self':

> It would be wrong to see the production of autobiographical narratives as having no ideological significance – no basis within nor reference to history or culture . . . It is necessary to take into account the fact that the woman who attempts to write herself is engaged by the nature of the activity itself in re-writing the stories that already exist about her since by seeking to publicise herself she is violating an important cultural construction of feminity as passive or hidden. She is resisting or changing what is known about her. Her place within culture, the place from which she writes, is produced by difference and produces difference.[15]

Part Two: The personal narrative of a feminist research student . . .

> The effort to bring political liberty to the daily lives of women is not an isolated movement, nor a mere sudden outgrowth; it forms part of the continuity of history and must be treated as such; it is part of the continuous action and reaction between law and custom out of which human institutions are moulded and by which public conscience is modified.
>
> (Helen Blackburn, *Woman's Suffrage*, p. v)

My work on the *Autobiography* has necessarily involved a degree of 'detective' work,[16] with the aim of locating the identity of a number of little known – and seemingly elusive – women, and placing them within the particular feminist, social, political and intellectual contexts and networks in which they and Simcox were a part. Some women, like Barbara Bodichon, Bessie Belloc, Annie Besant, Emilia Dilke, George Eliot, Elizabeth Garrett Anderson, Violet Paget/Vernon Lee, Emma Paterson, and others, were not difficult to locate, given that a range of biographies, social and political histories, academic theses, dissertations and feminist publications, are already in existence about them. Other women whom Simcox refers to, however, like Kit Anstruther-Thomson, 'Rhoda [Garrett]' (whom I initially assumed to be Rhoda Broughton, with all the consequences of a misinformed – and over-zealous! – reading), Mary Hamilton, 'Miss [Lucy] Harrison', 'Miss [Eliza] Orme', the seemingly elusive 'Miss [Caroline] Williams', and numerous others, were more difficult to trace. Because these women's biographies have yet to be written, we lack any evaluation of their political involvement and activism in such organisations as the WPPL (later the Women's Trade Union League), the women's suffrage movement, the London School Board and workers' co-operatives. (Mary Hamilton, for instance, ran a co-operative shirtmaking firm ('Hamilton & Co.') with Simcox, based initially at 68 Dean Street, Soho (1875–8), and later at 27 Mortimer Street, Cavendish Square.)

The process of 'detective' research is often quite mechanical – evaluating and re-evaluating sources, historical texts and cross-referencing biographies; it is occasionally dead-end, and sometimes motivated by the merest hunch. More often than not, I have started simply with a list of names given by Simcox: 'Miss Williams', 'Miss Orme', 'Mrs Paterson', and have then proceeded to connect those names through such contexts as the political movements that they were involved in; examining minutes taken from meetings they attended; the periodicals and journals they each wrote for; biographies written about them (despite the inaccuracies I sometimes discovered within those texts); and even by geographically locating them through details of their private addresses in, for example, the *Englishwoman's Review*, and in private papers held in such places as Girton College. (See, for instance, minutes of meetings of the London Association of Schoolmistresses (Emily Davies Collection IX/LSM 2), which includes addresses of all its members (1860–88), some of whom Simcox refers to in her *Autobiography*.)

Places to go in search of . . .

In compiling an index drawn from the *Autobiography*, I made a record of any written work that the women had published, and, where possible, gathered autobiographical and biographical information from a number of archives and sources held in such places as the Fawcett Library, Girton College, the London Library and the British Library. See especially, Barrow (1981)[17] for a detailed, comprehensive (and not particularly dated) outline of material kept in these places; and also Doughan (1992)[18] for a review of the archival treasures to be found in the Fawcett library, alongside an acerbic insight into the limited funding policy given to such a worthy institution: 'If some substantial appropriate investment is not made soon,' writes Doughan, 'documents will start rotting away – and (I suspect to the secret delight of many in the academic establishment) so will women's history. Those of us to whom it is important should be looking at ways of preventing this happening' (p. 137). Doughan also includes an extensive list of addresses of resource centres that are extremely useful for those interested in women's studies/gender studies. Such places can be extremely rewarding, not only for the material that they hold, but for the help – and encouragement – that can be offered by archivists and other researchers.

Discourses in print

In this subsection, I list a number of publications that I found particularly useful, and which are available either in the 'places' cited above, or else through inter-library loan. Most of the material are 'primary sources', and I draw attention to the problematic nature of such sources below. One reason for my inclusion of a (brief) bibliographic list here is because, as a postgraduate research student, I came across many students, both undergraduate and postgraduate, who simply had no knowledge about the range of material available, or even about the existence of such resource centres as the Fawcett Library. The list I offer is therefore meant as a 'signpost', pointing to texts that might be of use to those interested in women's studies/gender studies; some excellent reference books containing guides to printed and archival material are also included.

Journals, periodicals

English Woman's Journals (1858–1864), Englishwoman's Review (1866–1910), Victoria Magazine (1863–80), Shafts: A Paper for Women and the Working Classes (1892–9). Women's Suffrage Journal (1870–90) and Women's Union Journal (1876–90).

Chronicles, records, histories

Countess of Aberdeen, ed., (1900); Helen Blackburn (f. p. 1902/1972; 1895); A. Amy Bulley and Margaret Whitley (1894); Frances Hays (1885); Ray Strachey (1928).[19]

Reference books

Margaret Barrow (1981); Virginia Blain, Patricia Clements and Isobel Grundy, eds, (1990); Patricia Hollis (1979); Barbara Kanner (1980; 1988); Jane Leggett (1988); Philippa Levine (1987); Dale Spender (1982).[20]

Given that much of my analysis is informed by woman-based historical chronologies, records and commentaries, there is a need to be aware of the potential limitations of utilising such discourses as a means of making claims to 'truth', and also of the danger of essentialising 'women's lives'. As June Purvis points out in her article on 'Using Primary Sources',

> Even when using women's journals as sources, the feminist researcher has to be aware that the content of such publications, like other journals, is shaped by the preferences of the editors, drawn presumably from the middle classes. Working-class women were less well schooled than their middle-class sisters, and would, in addition, have had less time and opportunity to write, edit or publish articles in the press. As a result, the various issues affecting their daily lives may still have been under-represented in women's journals, and issues affecting middle-class women over-represented.[21]

Unhappily, Purvis's caveats are all too justifiable in terms of the lack of details about working-class women's lives in some of the discourses I referred to; gaps and fissures are striking, and my scrutiny of those discourses is suitably cautious. Such sources do, however, provide vital information, and the records – partial as they might be – have allowed me access to a political scene that existed during the late nineteenth century. I discovered that there are immense rewards to be gained from this kind of exploratory/ fact-finding groundwork, and I was greatly impressed by the results of that work on two counts. First, by evidence of the co-operative and collaborative nature of women's political activism; and secondly, by the sheer volume of writings that the women had produced.

Co-operation and collaboration

It is important to clarify my use of two key terms – 'co-operation' and 'collaboration' – and the feminist bases upon which I utilise them. The *Shorter Oxford English Dictionary* defines 'co-operation' as 'working together or with others to the same end; pertaining to co-operation'. Alongside such a definition, my utilisation of the term is informed by an added historical-political dimension in respect of the nineteenth-century Co-operative movement wherein the Co-operative Society acted as a 'union of persons for the production or distribution of goods, in which the profits [were] shared by all the contributing members' (*Shorter OED*). Co-operative Stores became places where 'goods [were] sold at a moderate price, the profits, if any, being distributed among the members and customers' (ibid.).

One example, of such a Co-operative/co-operative venture was the shirtmaking firm, Hamilton & Co. (briefly referred to above), which Simcox co-ran with Mary Hamilton. In her article 'Eight Years of Co-operative Shirtmaking',[22] Simcox offers an auto/ biography of the firm, in which she does not 'spotlight' any single 'heroine' of the firm's success, preferring instead to construct the project under the aegis of a collective, self-supporting unit, run for and by women. The article is striking, not only for its detailed account of the system of sweated labour (Simcox was an active member of the Anti-Sweating League), but also for the sense in which Simcox's use of the collective terms 'we' and 'our', reflect a desire to show that both the Shirt and Collar Makers' Union and Hamilton and Co. were collectively and co-operatively set up and organised, rather than individually based. In recounting the 1875 public meeting at which the Shirt and Collar Makers' Union was formed, and principles upon which Hamilton & Co. were based, Simcox writes:

> Our suggestion of a co-operative workshop, where the shirtmakers should be their own employers, and divide amongst themselves the whole price paid by the hosier to the contractor, was not allowed to drop [by the women shirtmakers]. We were pressed to say how it was to be carried out: one and another said she would like to join if it *could* be carried out; and as each discussion left the ladies of the trade more hopefully interested in the project, it left the rash reformers, who were *not* (yet) of the trade more nearly pledged to realise the hopes they had helped to raise. (p. 1039; emphasis original)

There is a clear indication in 'Eight Years of Co-operative Shirtmaking' that women's political networks and co-operative organisations form a veritable *tour de force*. Highlighting the collective nature of the firm's establishment, Simcox outlines the project as follows:

> It should be explained that our ignorance of the nature of 'business' in general and manufacture of shirts in particular was absolute and complete. We endeavored to improve our minds by taking in the *Warehouseman and Draper's Journal*; we studied the *Sewing Machine Gazette*; we were filled with envy of the educational advantages enjoyed by tailors, who have classes where the scientific mysteries of their craft are unveiled to students; we gazed at every shop window decorated with the garment on which our minds were set; we purchased for private contemplation and analysis a selection of, so to speak, 'representative shirts' of all distinction. . . Much midnight oil was burnt as the shirtmakers, after their day's work, met to confer with us as to the time and place of beginning operations, the manufacture of a specimen, and the composition of our original staff; and as our first sewing-machine drove cumbrously to our meeting-place on the top of a 'four-wheeler', the historically-minded amongst us wondered whether, in days to come, the cabload would rank in the annals of co-operation with the wheelbarrow in which the Rochdale pioneers trundled their stock-in-trade down Toad Lane in 1844. (p. 1040)

The gently self-amused, and yet wonderfully purposeful, confident and celebratory (auto)biography of the firm clearly reflects the sense of pleasure that the work must have created.[23] Simcox explains that 'many members of the House of Commons'' bought from Hamilton & Co., and that 'The bench of bishops, of course, were represented on our books, and that the last precocious scholar of Balliol[24] should be unable to "go up" without our assistance seemed the most natural thing in the world' (p. 1047). Thus, Hamilton & Co. had, in Simcox's account, successfully infiltrated the very heart of the British establishment.

My application of the term 'co-operation' is therefore both gender-specific and politically-specific: in referring to political movements and organisations it denotes a principled, collective way of women working together. It is important to make clear, however, that my use of 'co-operation' does not carry with it an unqualified assumption that the 'co-operative' *nature* of women's political ventures and organisations was at all unproblematic or without discord/s, difference/s or disagreement/s. Rather, my approach recognises that while the aims of political movements and organisations might have been ostensibly clear-cut in terms of their founding principles – as in, for instance, the WPPL/WTUL and the London Women's Suffrage Societies – they were also comprised of individuals drawn from a range of different social and cultural backgrounds, each with her own personal/experiential and ideological agenda. As any historical chronology of women's political activism shows, many political organisations – particularly the Women's Suffrage Societies – frequently underwent internal splits, modifications, transitions and reconstitutions throughout the late nineteenth and early twentieth centuries. My interest lies in charting the numerous sea-changes that took place within the late nineteenth-century women's movement, and in locating the ways in which women's political activism functioned co-operatively and collectively: however problematic and factional that activism might have been.

The *Shorter Oxford English Dictionary* defines 'collaborator' as 'one who works in conjunction with another or others . . . *esp.* in literary, artistic or scientific work'. Having consulted numerous feminist periodicals, journals and other published material during the period 1870–1900, what I found striking was the extent to which so many of the women I was researching had collaboratively published their writings. Not only had they – collectively – produced literally hundreds of polemical articles on such contentious issues of the day as women and education, work, union affiliation and sexuality, many of them also compiled all-important documentary records of political events (suffrage meetings, and so on), as well as feminist-based discourses, on such topics as women's history, economics, culture, politics, literature, law, medicine and philosophy. Often written in celebratory fashion – characteristically brandishing facts, figures and statistics and didactic flamboyance – such publications were often achieved as a result of cross-referencing between journals and periodicals, and between authors, adding to an ever-growing body of information that women controlled. An overwhelming feature of such information is a clear propagandist message to the reader: women's history is in the making.[25]

I shall now conclude this chapter by returning once more to Simcox's *Autobiography*, in which I show how a contextured reading, drawing on primary texts, led me in search of 'Miss Williams', and my discovery of her identity.

Conclusion: in search of Miss Williams . . .

My attempt to trace the identity of 'Miss Williams' became a compelling task. I began the process of locating who Williams was on the basis of a political connection between Eliza Orme, Williams and Simcox: both Williams and Orme are described in the *Autobiography* as having had breakfast at Simcox's home 'both very happy in eager "discourse"' (3 November 1881). Orme also had political connections with Emma Paterson. In her entry of 9 November 1879, for instance, Simcox describes how Orme and Paterson combined in a successful attempt to get Simcox elected to the London School Board: 'Miss Orme single-handed converted James Beal the Liberal agent into a sense of my overwhelming merits and power, Mrs Paterson, I imagine, "set on" the Westminster Club and Nettleton'. The political network between Simcox, Orme and Paterson also included, among others, Williams. In item four of the first publication of the Women's Protective and Provident committee, for instance, 'Miss Williams' is listed as being a member of that committee:

> 4. The committee consist of Miss Williams, Miss Downing, Miss Sims, Miss A. Davies, Mr Hodgson Pratt, Miss Faithful, Miss Wade, Mr and Mrs Reed, Miss Sutherland, Mr S.S. Taylor, Mr Gale, Mr Allerdale Grainger, Miss Browne and Mr and Mrs Paterson.[26]

I then began to search through archives held at the Fawcett Library, in the hope that Williams might have been involved in the women's suffrage movement, but to no avail. Quite by chance, however, I came across references to articles written by 'C. Williams', one of which was entitled: 'Union Among Women',[27] in Barbara Kanner's *Women in English Social History 1880–1914*. Given the proof I already had of Williams's connection to the WPPL, I ordered copies of the articles from Girton College, where a set of *Englishwoman's Review (EWR)* (1870–1903) is kept (Blackburn Collection). The results were extremely rewarding. I discovered that the author's name was Caroline Williams, and that she had written on women's suffrage; women's history, organisations and networks; women's writing, newspapers, education and public speaking; as well as women in local government, school boards; and men's views on women's duties. Two articles, in particular – in Volumes IX and X – proved invaluable in enabling me to locate the addresses not only of Williams herself, but also many other politically active women to whom Simcox refers in her *Autobiography*.[28] They also provided substantial – as opposed to merely circumstantial – evidence as to the connection between Williams and Simcox. In the 'Record of Events', Williams includes a section entitled 'Political Club for Women', and writes that

> Many women interested in political and social questions have felt the want of some central place of meeting, where opportunity would be afforded for serious discussion and interchange of opinion and information. Persons usually living in the country, and those who, by their surrounding circumstances, have hitherto been prevented from joining any of the movements of the day, would find in the new club the best means of becoming acquainted with the work of others and of discovering where they could render useful help. A Provisional Committee was appointed, consisting of the following ladies:-
> Mrs Chaplin Ayrton, 98, Palace Gardens Terrace, W.
> Miss Browne, 58, Porchester Terrace, W.
> Miss Gibson, 21, Endsleigh Street, Tavistock Square, W.C.
> Miss Hamilton, 68, Dean Street, Soho.
> Miss Lucy Harrison, 80 Gower Street, W.C.
> Mrs Stewart Headlam, 19, Collingham Place. S.W.
> Miss Orme, 38, Chancery Lane, W.C.

Mrs Paterson, 2, Brunswick Row, Queen Square, W.C.
Miss Simcox, 1, Douro Place, Victoria Road, Kensington.
Miss Ward, 19, Dorchester Place, W.
Miss Williams, 9, Porchester Square, W.
Hon Sec. *pro tem.*, Miss Raisin, 154, Camden Street N.W.
(Vol. IX, pp. 569–70)

Williams states that annual subscription would be five shillings, and that 'The premises of the club will be in a central part of London, convenient to members living in the environs. They will consist of rooms for reading and writing and for conversation, discussion and lectures, and will open on Sundays and week-day evenings' (pp. 569–70). The aim of the club was to 'secure the co-operation of all classes. . . The only qualification of membership being interest in social and political questions' (p. 570). The second article, in Volume X, records that on the 8 April 1879 a public meeting was held in St George's Hall, Langham Place, with the aim of establishing the club. Williams writes that 'Mr. Leonard Courtney[29] occupied the chair; there was a large attendance. Miss Edith Simcox explained the objects and constitution of the proposed club' (pp. 180–81). Clearly, given the evidence, Simcox and Williams were active members of radical and progressive political movements, with a shared interest in developing the personal and political aspects of women's lives.

There are two particular entries in the *Autobiography* which make explicit the extent of Williams's attraction towards, and desire for, Simcox. The first, written on the 22 July 1881, states:

> Just after I had come in Miss Williams called. My mother betrayed the fact that we were just going to dinner & asked her to wait for me. We began conversation & were just started when she came again to fetch me. I was put out at the discourtesy & interference & bolted half a dinner, fidgetted [sic] for an interval & returned. I *hope* I was not to blame – of course I was in some way – the poor creature professed a feeling for me different from what she had ever had for any one, it might make her happiness if I could return it; & then she said 'Imagine what it is to have that feeling & to be obliged to go away from you.' I did not feel any unkind dread – What would it be for her *not* to go away – but I thought of my like love & urged upon her that *I* did not deserve such love as I

had given to Her [Eliot], it pained me like a blasphemy – I suppose I was wrong to say this – it hurt her & she had not the readiness to seize the confidence as a proof of kindness. She said I was very philosophical & a little cold . . . she went away a little hurt, though I rather wooed her at last. The only thing that checks my impulses of tenderness is the fear lest there is some flightiness & want of moral balance in her nature – a want of the fixed points, to which one needs to appeal.

A number of points emerge in my reading of this extract. First, there is the evidence that Simcox was not at all isolated in her same-sex desire for Eliot, since Williams was clearly a woman with whom she talked about, and shared, the sexual nature of that passion. Secondly, it seems that Simcox positions herself as identifying with Williams, not only in terms of the intensity of the same-sex erotic passion, but also the pattern of unrequited love: 'I thought of my like love & urged upon her that *I* did not deserve such love as I had given to Her [Eliot], it pained me like a blasphemy.' Likewise, there is a similar sense of flirtatious gesturing that Eliot often demonstrated towards Simcox in the lines: 'she went away a little hurt, though I rather wooed her at last'.

There is, however, a crucial difference between Simcox and Williams, which relates to Martha Vicinus's discussion of girls' boarding school training in the nineteenth century, and the development of same-sex relationships.[30] Vicinus argues that the school's ideology demanded that 'Bodily self-control became a means of knowing oneself; self-realization subsumed the fulfillment of physical desire. Love itself was not displaced, but focused on a distant object, while nonfulfillment – sacrifice – became the source of personal satisfaction' (p. 215). On the evidence of her *Autobiography*, Simcox was able to meet up to such rigorous self-control, discipline, and sacrifice – although it was fraught with immense difficulties – in her relationship with Eliot. Despite her occasional emotional remonstrations towards Eliot, she always constructed herself as able to maintain self-control: to outward appearances, at any rate. In Williams, however, she recognises, and fears, a different type of character altogether: 'the fear lest there is some flightiness & want of moral balance in her nature'. Alongside her (potential) 'fear' of being discovered by her family, there is also the possible class distinction – or a difference in background – to be made between Williams and Simcox. Williams's sense of impatience, and her disregard for social conventions, as instanced through her interrupting the family meal, makes Simcox feel 'put out at the discourtesy & interference'.

In the second entry, made some nine months later, Simcox writes that 'Poor Miss Williams is not to be helped', and goes on to say that

> I do not know that it is my fault, when physical sanity is wanting one cannot count on establishing a fundamentally wholesome relation, & it was not wholesome as we were. If I made any mistakes I was not unpunished, for it was not pleasant to me to have quoted to anyone those most sacred words of Her to me – still less to have made the sacrifice in vain. Poor thing! I am not very fortunate in my efforts to 'play with souls' & have 'matter enough to save my own'. (6 March 1882)

The phrase 'to "play with souls" ' – taken presumably from Robert Browning's poem, 'A Light Woman'[31] – is very *à propos*, given the poem's themes of 'tangled' love, infidelity and the inability to 'master one's passions'. Simcox does not offer further details about why she considers the relationship not to be 'wholesome', although her description of Williams lacking in 'physical sanity' – presumably equating same-sex desire with physical illness – suggests that her worst fears were realised, and that Williams became, in some way or other, 'out' of control, and unable to manage the 'sacrifice' expected of her. There is also another dimension to the relationship, as revealed through a further entry, in which her feelings of responsibility, if not 'guilt', for Williams, are made clear. She writes:

> Miss Williams's soul lays heavy on my conscience: have been glancing at St Ignatious's Life – I wish I had the power of constraining souls. (14 September 1881)

The search goes on

My analysis of Simcox's references to Caroline Williams is inconclusive, fraught with conjecture, and based upon *textual* 'evidence'. I have recently discovered evidence that suggests

Williams was also a member of the London Association of Schoolmistresses, along with numerous others, whose names I recognise from the *Autobiography*: Lucy Harrison, Miss Lanchester, Miss Raisin, to list only a few. Clearly, there is still a great deal more research to be done on these women's lives, the networks of which they were a part, and the friendships they formed.

I have discussed the Simcox–Williams relationship with many other people, and what most of us find astonishing is the fact that Williams has been ignored (obliterated?) in every critical discussion published, to date.[32] I find that 'omission' not merely an oversight, but evidence of the way in which most academic readers of the *Autobiography* have focused upon, and spotlighted, the central figures of 'Eliot–Simcox'. My position is to argue that Simcox was, indeed, part of a wider network of politically active women, and was also connected to women whose identity and orientation was lesbian: she records, for instance, Violet Paget and Kit Anstruther-Thomson staying at her home (7 August 1894) – although whether it was her connection with the Pioneer Club that brought her into contact with them, or her acquaintance with them that led her to join the club is never made clear; she also refers to a 'lovers' quarrel' between Mary Hamilton, 'Rhoda [Garrett]' and 'Miss Richardson' (5 January 1879), and of Hamilton's 'escape' with Richardson to Montrose (28 January 1879). As the journal reveals, these women found ways of demonstrating and communicating their identity to one another, however problematic that might have been because of constraints imposed upon them by cultural, social and political conventions.

There are many connected strands to this chapter, in which I demonstrate how particular theoretical approaches to Simcox's *Autobiography* allow for a contextured-political appreciation of it. Through utilising a range of feminist and woman-based texts, I have shown how the process of detective research – in search of names, places, texts – reveals a fascinating and intricate record of women's political activism, sexual orientation, friendships and networks during the late nineteenth century. My understanding of what I term the 'co-operative' and 'collaborative' nature of some of that activism stems, in part, from Helen Blackburn's insight into the contiguity of women's lives and her argument that 'the story of one life is so interwoven with the story of its time . . . that to tell the story of one, is to tell the story of the other'. This is not to assume a position of generality, wherein 'women's lives' are essentialised without considering the importance of difference; or to concede that texts – including autobiographies, chronologies, records, polemical articles – can reveal 'the truth' about those lives. Rather, it is to urge upon the reader that we fail politically, theoretically and factually if we ignore questions of co-operation and collaboration in favour of a spotlighting history of women's lives.

Notes

Please note that that all references to Edith Simcox's *Autobiography of a Shirtmaker* (Bodleian Library (MS, Eng. Misc. d. 494)), are based on my transcriptions. I am grateful to the Keeper of Western Manuscripts at the Bodleian, who has given me permission to publish a full transcript of the *Autobiography*. (All references are made to date of entries, not page numbers.)

1. H. Blackburn, *Women's Suffrage. A Record of the Women's Suffrage Movement in the British Isles, With Biographical Sketches of Miss Becker* (first published, Oxford, 1902; New York, 1971), p. 23.
2. All references to the *Autobiography of a Shirtmaker* (Bodleian Library, MS. Eng. Misc. d. 494) are based on my transcriptions, to be published, in full, by Oxford University Press (forthcoming).
3. Personal Narratives Group (eds), *Interpreting Women's Lives: Feminist Theory and Personal Narratives* (Bloomington and Indianapolis, 1989), p. 23.
4. E. Jelinek (ed.), *Women's Autobiography* (Bloomington and London, 1980); D.C. Stanton (ed.), *The Female Autograph* (Chicago and London, 1984); S. Smith, *A Poetics of Women's Autobiography: Marginality and the Fictions of Self-Representation* (Bloomington and Indianapolis, 1987); S. Benstock, *The Private Self: Theory and Practice of Women's Autobiographical Writings* (London, 1988); B. Brodzki and C. Schenck (eds), *Life/ Lines: Theorizing Women's Autobiography* (Ithaca and London, 1988); C. Heilbrun, *Writing a Woman's Life* (London, 1988); Personal Narratives Group (eds), *Interpreting Women's Lives: Feminist Theory and Personal*

Narratives (Bloomington and Indianapolis, 1989); V. Sanders, *The Private Lives of Victorian Women: Autobiography in the Nineteenth-Century* (London, 1989); M.J. Corbett, *Representing Femininity: Middle-Class Subjectivity in Victorian and Edwardian Women's Autobiographies* (Oxford, 1992); L. Stanley, *The Auto/Biographical I: The Theory and Practice of Feminist Auto/Biography* (Manchester, 1992).
5. A. Jefferson, 'Autobiography as Intertext: Barthes Sarrante, Robbe-Grillet'. In M. Worton and J. Still (eds), *Intertextuality: Theories and Practices* (Manchester, 1990); cited in L. Stanley *The Auto/Biographical I: The Theory and Practice of Feminist Auto/Biography* (Manchester, 1992), p. 98.
6. N. Ward Jouve, *White Woman Speaks with Forked Tongue: Criticism as Autobiography* (London, 1991), p. 7.
7. T. Broughton, 'Signs of Life', *Journal of Gender Studies*, 1, 2, (1991), 193.
8. J. Haggis, 'The Feminist Research Process – Defining a Topic'. In L. Stanley (ed.), *Feminist Praxis: Research, Theory and Epistemology in Feminist Sociology* (London, 1990), p. 68.
9. See John Sutherland's biography of Mrs (Mary) Humphrey Ward (Oxford, 1990) for his discussion of how she suffered under male (Harley Street) doctors, who offered various nostrums for her eczema. Humphrey Ward was, of course, a contemporary of Simcox's.
10. M. Laski, *George Eliot and Her World* (London, 1973).
11. L. Faderman, *Surpassing the Love of Men: Romantic Friendship and Love Between Women from the Renaissance to the Present* (London, 1985), p. 163.
12. K.A. McKenzie, *Edith Simcox and George Eliot* (Oxford, 1961).
13. G. Haight in K.A. McKenzie, *Edith Simcox and George Eliot* (Oxford, 1961), p. xv.
14. My thanks to Elaine Hobby for suggesting this to me.
15. L. Anderson, 'At the Threshold of the Self'. In M. Monteith (ed.), *Women's Writing: A Challenge to Theory* (Sussex, 1986), p. 59.
16. See also, M. Ferguson (ed.), *The History of Mary Prince, A West Indian Slave, Related by Herself* (London, 1987), E. Hobby, *Virtue of Necessity: English Women's Writing 1649–88* (London, 1988), L. Stanley with A. Morley, *The Life and Death of Emily Wilding Davison: A Biographical Detective Story* (London, 1988), and T. Thompson (ed.), *Dear Girl: The Diaries and Letters of Two working Women 1897–1917* (London, 1987), for their discussions on the 'detective' process of researching archives, historical chronologies and original manuscripts.

17. M. Barrow, *Women 1870–1928: A Select Guide to Printed and Archival Sources in the United Kingdom* (London, 1981).
18. D. Doughan,'The End of Women's History? A View from the Fawcett Library', *Women's History Review*, 1, 1, (1992), 131–9.
19. Countess of Aberdeen (ed.), *Women in Social Life: The Transactions of the International Congress of Women of 1899* (London, 1900); H. Blackburn, *Women's Suffrage, A Record of Women's Suffrage Movement in the British Isles, With Biographical Sketches of Miss Becker* (first published, Oxford, 1902; New York 1971); (ed.), *A Handbook for Women Engaged in Social and Political Work* (Bristol and London, 1895); A.A.Bulley and M. Whitley, *Women's Work* (London, 1894); F. Hays, *Women of the Day: A Biographical Dictionary of Notable Contemporaries* (London, 1885); R. Strachey, *The Cause: A Short History of the Women's Movement in Great Britain* (London, 1928).
20. M. Barrow, *Women 1870–1928: A Select Guide to Printed and Archival Sources in the United Kingdom* (London, 1981); V. Blain, P. Clements and I. Grundy (eds), *The Feminist Companion to Literature in English*, (London, 1990); P. Hollis, *Women in Public: The Women's Movement 1850–1900* (London, 1979); B. Kanner, *Women in English Social History, 1800–1914*, vol. 2 (New York and London, 1988); *The Women of England, From Anglo-Saxon Times to the Present, Interpretive Bibliographical Essays*, (London, 1980); J. Leggett, *Local Heroines: A Women's History Gazetteer of England, Scotland and Wales* (London, 1988); P. Levine, *Victorian Feminism, 1850–1900* (London, 1987); D. Spender, *Women of Ideas and What Men Have Done to Them, From Aphra Behn to Adrienne Rich* (London, 1982).
21. J. Purvis, 'Using Primary Sources when Researching Women's History from Feminist Perspective', *Women's History Review*, 1, 2, (1992), 289.
22. E.J. Simcox, 'Eight Years of Co-operative Shirtmaking', *Nineteenth Century*, June 1884, 1037–54.
23. My thanks to Elaine Hobby for expressing this to me.
24. Balliol was the Oxford College especially involved with 'East-End Settlements', and regularly sent students as 'missionaries' – philanthropists to help in working-class areas.
25. After writing this, I came across Antoinette Burton's article ' "History" is Now: Feminist Theory and the Production of Historical Feminisms', *Women's History Review*, 1, 1, (1992), 25–38, in which she argues that 'For feminists, 'history' is and must be NOW' (p. 26). I am struck by the similarity between current feminist sense of immediacy, with that of feminists writing in the late nineteenth and early twentieth centuries.

26. Cited in H. Goldman, *Emma Paterson: She Led Women into a Man's World* (London, 1974).
27. C. Williams, 'Union Among Women', *Englishwoman's Review*, VI, (1875), 55–7.
28. C. Williams, 'Political Club for Women', *Englishwoman's Review*, IX, (14 December 1878), 569–70; 'Political Club for Women', *Englishwoman's Review*, vol. X, (15 April 1879), pp. 180–81.
29. Leonard Courtney was married to Kate Courtney, one of Beatrice Webb's sisters. Both Courtneys were pacifists, and received death threats during the Boer War for their active and public opposition to the War; Kate Courtney assisted in Emily Hobhouse's exposure of the treatment of Boers in British concentration camps. Kate Courtney's unpublished *Diary* is held in the London School of Economics Library, and her *War Diary* privately published, is held in the Fawcett Library. See Sybil Oldfield's *Women Against the Iron Fist: Alternatives to Militarism 1900–1989* (Oxford, 1989), for an extremely useful discussion of Kate Courtney's political work.
30. M. Vicinus, 'Distance and Desire: English Boarding School Friendships, 1870–1920'. In M.B. Duberman, M. Vicinus and G. Chauncey, (eds), *Hidden from History: Reclaiming the Gay and Lesbian Past*, (England, 1989), pp. 212–29.
31. My thanks to John Lucas for referring me to Browning's poem.
32. Many, many thanks to the Feminist Research Group, Department of English, Loughborough, for having provided me with an opportunity to discuss my work, and for their comments, 1991–1994.

9 The 1920s: radicals to the right and to the left

John Lucas

I

On 7 April 1921 T.S. Eliot wrote to Richard Aldington to tell him that

> Having only contempt for every existing political party and profound hatred for democracy, I feel the blackest gloom. Whatever happens will be another step towards the destruction of Europe. The whole of contemporary politics oppresses me with a continuous physical horror like the feeling of growing madness in one's brain. It is rather a horror to be sane in the midst of this, it is too dreadful, too huge for one to have the comfortable feeling of superiority. It goes too far for rage.[1]

We now know that when Eliot wrote that letter he was suffering from a deep, personal crisis. But that strikes me as of less significance than his apocalyptic sense of the impending 'destruction of Europe'. It has been said that in his letters Eliot has the uncanny knack of taking on the manner of voice he thought would be acceptable to his correspondent: and as Donald Davie astutely notes, Eliot here sounds very like D.H. Lawrence, the writer Aldington at this time admired above all others. In addition, Eliot is saying very much the kind of thing that Lawrence had recently been saying.

In *D.H. Lawrence's Nightmare: The Writer and his circle in the years of the Great War*, Paul Delaney quotes David Garnet's report of an outburst which Lawrence directed at a group of Bloomsburyites who had gathered at a London apartment on the afternoon of 11 November 1918, to celebrate the armistice. With 'sombre joy', according to Garnet, Lawrence told his captive audience that they were wrong to think the war was over:

> The hate and evil is greater now than ever. Very soon war will break out again and overwhelm you. . . The crowd outside thinks that Germany is crushed forever. But the Germans will soon rise again. Europe is done for: England most of all the countries. This war isn't over. Even if the fighting should stop, the evil will be worse because the hate will be dammed up in men's hearts and will show itself in all sorts of ways which will be worse than war. Whatever happens there can be no Peace on Earth.[2]

Delaney does not report Eliot to have been present on that occasion: but as a close friend of the leading figures of Bloomsbury it seems reasonable to suppose that an account of Lawrence's words would have been passed on to him. And between then and his own letter enough had happened across Europe for him to feel that Lawrence's dire prophecy had been amply fulfilled. To the October 1917 revolution in Russia we can add the Troubles and then civil war in Ireland, the political and social chaos in Germany, and, nearer to home, the setting up of soviets in post-war Glasgow, major strikes of 1920, especially those of miners and dockers (the dockers refused to load weapons intended to help Polish and White Russian troops push back the Red Army), the founding in 1920 of the Communist Party of Great Britain, and much else besides.

Will Dyson's cartoon in the *Daily Herald*, which was carried shortly after the treaty of Versailles, is at one with Lawrence's forebodings. It shows the world's elder statesmen emerging from the railway carriage, their smug smiles challenged by the words of one of them. 'Somewhere I hear a child crying', he says. In the bottom left-hand corner of the cartoon a new-born baby howls its eyes out, and draped across its belly a sash bears the legend *Class of '39*.

There is, then, good reason to believe that in the aftermath of 'The War to end all Wars' large numbers of people soon realised it had done nothing of the sort. Some like Lawrence said so. Others felt it deep in their bones. Still others had anticipated 'the destruction of Europe' before a shot had been fired. There isn't the space to go into that here, but we have only to recall Henry James's grieving over a 'lost' England to realise how powerful the sense of an ending was in the summer and autumn of 1914. And to James's lament for the suddenly vulnerable 'record of the long safe centuries' we can add Edward Thomas's brooding apprehension of loss as it is felt for and spoken at the close of his great poem, 'As the Teams' Head-Brass': 'and for the last time/I watched the clods crumble and topple over/After the plough share and the stumbling team.'

That poem was written in May 1916, before the Somme and before Thomas's brief and fatal journey to the trenches. Like several other of his poems, it is a deep elegy for an England which is already becoming mythic: an England identified with pastoral values and all that they imply of rootedness. It is therefore significant that in this poem Thomas sits 'among the boughs of the fallen elm' to talk to an aged ploughman. As I have noted elsewhere, the elm had become during the late nineteenth-century a kind of unofficial symbol of England. You can find it in any amount of writing of the period, from William Morris's 'Thoughts Under an Elm Tree' to *Howards End*, where the elm stands over the house itself and is meant to operate as a symbol of continuity – cultural, social, even political. That in Thomas's poem the elm should be 'fallen' hints therefore at the loss of such continuity: and this sense of loss swells as the ploughman remarks that the very night the tree was felled by a blizzard one of his mates was killed. 'The second day In France they killed him.'[3]

In her comment on 'As the Team's Head-Brass', Edna Longley suggests that 'the main stress is on an essential continuity: human progress is like that of 'the stumbling team'.[4] This is to forget the sombre note struck by the phrase 'for the last time' and the freighted meaning of the fallen elm. What haunts Thomas is the sense of something going, for ever. Because he hugely admired William Morris – 'Except William Morris there is no other man whom I would sometimes like to have been', he wrote to Gordon Bottomly in 1908 – we can read into Thomas's passionate feelings about rural England a recognition that it ought to be held in common, not be the emptily magic place of 'Adlestrop', where for a 'minute' birdsong evokes an Edenic garden no sooner registered than lost. Stan Smith has importantly noted how

Thomas's socialist convictions issue in his concern for 'the actual, troublous life of every day and toil of the hands and the brain together' and, therefore, in his 'Tolstoyan poems about digging and sowing and cutting wood'.[5] And it is then relevant to note that at the outbreak of war Lawrence was considering setting up a kind of Tolstoyan commune. In January 1915 he wrote to his old Nottingham friend, Willie Hopkin, who had introduced Lawrence to socialist ideas and who was himself a passionately committed socialist, to ask Willie to come to the cottage in Bucks where he and Frieda were staying. There 'we will . . . talk of my pet scheme. I want to gather together about twenty souls and sail away from this world of war and squalor and found a little colony where there shall be no money but a sort of communism as far as necessaries of life go, and some real decency.'[6]

But when two weeks later he wrote to Lady Ottoline Morrell about his plan, he put it rather differently.

> After the war, the soul of the people will be so maimed and so injured that it is horrible to think of. And this shall be the new hope: that there shall be a life wherein the struggle shall not be for money or for power, but for individual freedom and common effort towards good . . . It is no good plastering and tinkering with this community. Every strong soul must put off its connection with this society, its vanity and chiefly its fear, and go naked with its fellows. . . Not self-sacrifice, but fulfilment, the flesh and the spirit in league together, not in arms against one another. And each man shall know that he is part of the greater body, each man shall submit that his own soul is not supreme even to himself. To be or not to be is no longer the question. The question now, is how shall we fulfil our declaration 'God is'.

Goodness only knows what Lady Ottoline thought Lawrence was on about: he seems to be offering her a mixture of Tolstoyan socialism and nostrums taken from alternative communities of free love, dance and sun-and-nature worship to which he'd been introduced by Freida and whose histories have been excellently studied by Martin Green. But perhaps she would have heard alarm bells ringing when he goes on to tell her that the community he has in mind 'is commonly based, not on poverty, but on riches, not on humility, but on pride, not on sacrifice but complete fulfilment in the flesh of all strong desire, not on forfeiture but upon inheritance, not on heaven but on earth. We will be Sons of God who walk her.' In addition, 'We will be aristocrats, and as wise as the serpent in dealing with the mob. For the mob shall not crush us nor starve us nor cry us to death. We will deal cunningly with the mob, the greedy soul, we will gradually bring it to subjection.'[8] From socialism to fascism in the space of two paragraphs.

Yet although it is easy to accuse Lawrence of woolly-headedness, it is more important to note his letters suggest that like many at the time he sensed the possibility of huge changes and wanted to try to tap into them, to discover what they were. Hence his story *England, My England*, with its prophetically imaginative exploration of the lost will-power of Egbert, the super-civilised, charming, Bloomsbury-like character, his energies sapped away, his sophistication draining him of all robustness. This sense of an ending, of the destruction of Europe, while it anticipates works like Oswald Spengler's *Decline of the West*, is also close to Yeat's view of history, according to which two thousand years of one form of civilisation is about to pass into its opposite. And like Yeats, Lawrence yearns for an aristocratic community which can set itself against and rise above 'the mob'. In this, as has often enough been noted, they are close to those other reactionary modernists, Eliot, Pound and Wyndham Lewis, for all of whom the war brought about the final toppling of the values on which Western European civilisation had been built. Pound's friends had died, he snarls in 'Hugh Selwyn Mauberley', 'For an old bitch gone in the teeth/For a botched civilisation.' The high beauty of such a civilisation has been lowered to the level of a street woman ravaged by syphilis (the lost teeth) because she has prostituted herself, has become available to anyone, has laid herself open to the mob.

There is a possible echo of this in *The Wasteland*, where in the talk between the pub women one reminds the other of how Albert will 'want to know what you done with that money he gave you/To get yourself some teeth. He did. I was there./You have them all out, Lil, and get a nice set,/He said, I swear, I can't bear to look at you.' It's true that working-class people often lost their teeth early. At the outbreak of war many would-be volunteers were rejected because they couldn't cope with army food. Their teeth had been rotted by a diet in which sugar, poor quality margarine and condensed milk played a large part. But the focus on women's lost teeth hints at a male disgust which includes the imputation of syphilis: and this makes more sense when we realise that in post-war England men had good reason to be aware of women's increased sexual freedom and activity, a matter to which I shall return.

For the moment though, I want to pursue a rather different matter: fear and/or hatred of 'the mob'. Among the writers I have so far mentioned this was a common response. Lawrence came to it as a direct result of the war, when he and Frieda were hounded by 'patriots'. This prompts a stream of virtually insane letters in which Lawrence again and again tells his correspondents that he wants to wipe people out. But even here, threaded through the ravings, are notes to which it is possible to react more sympathetically, as when, writing from Littlehampton, he says that

> It is this mass of unclean world we have super-imposed on the clean world that we cannot bear. When I looked back, out of the clearness of the open evening, at this Littlehampton dark and amorphous like a bad eruption on the edge of the land, I was so sick I felt I could not come back: all these little, amorphous houses, like an eruption, a disease on the clean earth: and all of them full of such a diseased spirit, every landlady harping on her money, her furniture, every visitor harping on his latitude of escape from money and furniture. The whole thing like an active disease, fighting out the health. . . . It is too horrible. One can no longer live with people: it is too hideous and nauseating. . . . One feels a sort of madness come over one, as if the world had become hell. But . . . . it can be cleaned away.[9]

There is no denying the Nietzschean hatred of what has been called 'bungalow culture' here. But equally there is an echo of that Morrison utopian socialism which Lawrence had picked up in his early days and which he never entirely dropped. People ought *not* to have to live such pinched lives.

II

As soon as Lawrence could leave post-war England he did so. Hell could not perhaps be cleaned up but he at least could clear off. The protagonist of *Kangaroo* (1922) looks back from the ship's rail as he and his wife sail away from Folkestone and watches England 'slipping like a grey coffin into the sea'. 'The mob', it seemed, had triumphed after all, and its success spelt the death of England. To repeat, this extreme right-wing fear of democracy was widespread in the post-war years and is to be found in some of the most celebrated writing of the time. Everybody knows that Yeats' 'The Second Coming' broods over the possible violent movement from one civilisation to another. Hence, the power of its famous closing lines: 'And what rough beast, its hour come round at last./Slouches towards Bethlehem to be born.' This anti-Christ undoubtedly finds its starting point in the much-invoked beast of chapter 17 of the Revelations of St John the Divine. But 'slouches'? The word is surely meant to call to mind the habitual working-class gait (at all events as it was perceived through the eyes of those who had been brought up to worry about the 'health' of the race and eugenecists' warnings of impure stock.) Yeats' rough beast is Demos. We know that when he was at work on his poem he re-read the books of the *Prelude* in which Wordsworth describes his growing disillusionment with the French Revolution. He even incorporated certain of Wordsworth's key phrases into 'The Second Coming'.[10]

Given the chaotic brutality of the Irish troubles Yeats' dark reading of history's 'blood-dimmed tide' is scarcely surprising. But although the rough beast is symbolic of the clashes between the Black and Tans and the Irish Irregulars and, then, the IRA and the Free Staters, it also evokes the October Revolution of 1917 as well as events in post-war Germany and, for that matter, Britain. As I have already noted, new signs of democratic strength gleamed out from the grey muddle of those years. To those I have previously mentioned can be added 'The Coupon Election' of 1918 with, as consequence, an increased number of Labour MPs; the successful campaign to give women the vote; protests, hunger marches, the possibility of the first Labour Government (to be realised in 1924). The times were also making for the General Strike, which duly arrived in 1926. Even the Spanish influenza pandemic which raged across the world in 1919 and killed some million and a half people – a far higher figure is sometimes quoted – could be seen as symptomatic or symbolic of the dangerous times in which people lived. Such times seemed positively to be welcomed by soldier-writers who had survived the war. By Siegfried Sassoon, for example, announcing that he had become a socialist and by his writing for the *Daily Herald*. By Ivor Gurney, several of whose poems are shot through with a hatred of war-mongers and profiteers and of the aristocrats and gentry, the class enemy identified and ridiculed in 'The Silent One', identified elsewhere as 'The Prussians of England', and threatened in a sonnet of that title which ends with the poet warning the masters that England's children, as yet slaves, will 'forge a knife [To] cut the cancer threatens England's life.'[11] Judging from the insubordinations and acts of virtual or genuine mutiny among ranks that followed the armistice, Gurney was not speaking for himself.

Most of this is well known, even if official denials of army unrest were for too many years taken on trust: and the emergence of reactionary modernism as a form of resistance to mass culture – to 'the mob' – is also often-enough documented. Eliot's phantasmagoric vision of falling towers – 'Jerusalem Athens Alexandria/Vienna London/Unreal' – is intimately connected to his equally phantasmagoric vision of 'hooded hordes swarming Over endless plains'. These are the barbarians whose arrival Cavafy had predicted with awful fascination in one of the great poems of modern times. But whereas at the end of Cavafy's poem their arrival and the 'sort of solution' they promise is deferred, by the time Lawrence, Yeats and Eliot were writing, the barbarians – 'The mob' – had arrived, bringing with them not so much the promise of solution as the certainty of dissolution. Now the towers are falling or have fallen.

Or have they? For while we must inevitably be struck by the powerful note of impending disaster carried in much writing of the early 1920s, and by the writers' determination to save civilisation or at least shore up fragments for a future, we can hardly avoid recognising that many people thought civilisation was still safe or, less optimistically if more radically, felt it would be a long time a-dying. The Labour government of 1924 was a minority one and soon replaced; the General Strike ended in defeat for the workers (because of the betrayal of the unions by their leaders); and after all only women over the age of thirty had the vote. Perhaps civilisation wasn't going to sink after all. It certainly seems the case that if we are to understand the fury of much radical writing of the decade – whether left or right – we shall have to take note of the paradox that values seen as not merely out of date but thoroughly discredited nevertheless refused to die. We have, in a word, to understand key antagonisms of the decade as most powerfully focused on the oppositions, even hatreds, of sons for fathers and, perhaps, daughters for fathers too. Hence, Owen's 'The Parable of the Old Man and the Young'. (The father–daughter tensions most often get into literature via autobiographies and memoirs in which women insist on leaving home – especially for the life of an art student and thus entry into bohemian society). And, more rarely, though just as interestingly, we need to note the hatred of some sons for some mothers. (Julian Grenfell and Auden are cases in point.)

I am deliberately using the term 'civilisation' in a way that plays fast and loose with definitions. The point is that for those on the right 'civilisation' meant traditional values, or ones expressed through whatever opposed and preceded mass commodity culture and democratic politics; for those on the left it was more liable to signify worn-out liberal values. For others, civilization was the past, whatever that might be, brought into the present. The disagreements were as endemic as the hopes and fears: a world lost for some was for others a world to be gained. What nobody could quite grasp was the determination of capitalism to survive, nor could radicals credit the strength with which it fought. *That* was the 'civilisation' they had to contend against. It would eventually lead them to organise a fight back. Hence the move into the Communist Party for many of them.

This is why Arnold Bennett's novel for 1922, *Mr Prohack*, is so interesting. A few years earlier, Bennett had published a most remarkable wartime novel, *The Pretty Lady* (1918). In that novel London is repeatedly seen by night: it is a city of darkness, terror, random killings. At one point the novel's central character, a middle-class entrepreneurial business man, G.J. Hoape, finds himself 'in solitude, and surrounded by London. He stood still, and the vast sea of war seemed to be closing in over him. The war was growing, or the sense of its measureless scope was growing. It had sprung, not out of this crime, or that, but out of the secret invisible roots of humanity. . .' Bennett very finely establishes his ironically named protagonist's sense of being in a world he cannot understand, in which he has lost his bearings.

Gone are all the middle-class certainties of pre-1914 England, those complacencies which had oozed from, say, Forster's Henry Wilcox or Bennett's own Edwin Clayhanger. Now there are only solitude and death. (There were indeed zeppelin attacks on London in the First World War, and people were killed in bombing raids, but Bennett deliberately intensifies fears of such raids in order to give us Hoape at the end of his tether, adrift in darkness.)[12]

Yet a few years later in *Mr Prohack* this feeling of radical insecurity is exchanged for a glibly formulaic presentation of misunderstandings between a father and son in which Bennett aims for geniality and instead hits a note of intolerable smugness.

> Charlie had gone to war from Cambridge at the age of nineteen. He went a boy, and returned a grave man. He went thoughtless and light-hearted, and returned full of magnificent and austere ideals. Six months of England had destroyed those ideals in him. He had expected to share in the common task of making heaven in about a fortnight. In the war he had learnt much about the possibilities of human nature, but scarcely anything about its limitations. His father tried to warn him, but of course failed. Charlie grew resentful, then cynical. He saw in England nothing but futility, injustice and ingratitude. He refused to resume Cambridge, and was bitterly sarcastic about the generosity of a nation which, through its War Office, was ready to pay to studious warriors anxious to make up University terms lost in a holy war decidedly less than it paid to its street-sweepers. Having escaped from death, the aforesaid warriors were granted the right to starve their bodies while improving their minds. He might have had sure situations in vast corporations. He declined them. He spat on them. He called them 'graves'. What he wanted was an opportunity to fulfil himself. He could not get it, and his father could not get it for him. While searching for it, he frequently met warriors covered with ribbons but lacking food and shelter not only for themselves but for their women and children. All this, human nature being what it is, was inevitable, but his father could not tell him so. All that Mr Prohack could effectively do, Mr Prohack did – namely, provide the saviour of Britain with food and shelter. Charlie was restlessly and dangerously waiting his opportunity. But he had not developed into a revolutionist, nor a communist, nor anything of the sort. Oh, no! Quite the

reverse. He meditated a different revenge on society (ch v, 'Charlie': section II).

Charlie plans to become a mechanic. Some revenge! The tone of this preposterous passage is plainly intended to deflect any serious consideration about the condition of post-war Britain. Ex-soldiers starve because of human nature, not because of governmental indifference. We might compare the bitter anger of Gurney's lines about returned war heroes: 'Where are they now, on state-doles or showing shop-patterns./Or walking town to town sore in borrowed tatters./Or begged. Some civic routine one never learns./The heart burns – but has to keep out of face how heart burns' ('Strange Hells'). And we might then note that Mr Prohack and his wife are driving through Hyde Park when they come upon a procession of unemployed, accompanied by 'guardian policemen, a band consisting chiefly of drums, and a number of collarless powerful young men who shook white boxes of coppers menacingly in the faces of passers-by. 'Instead of encouraging them, the police ought to forbid these processions of the unemployed' said [Mrs Prohack] gravely. 'They're becoming a perfect nuisance.' 'Why!' said Mr Prohack, 'this car of yours is a procession of unemployed!' (ch. XIII, 'Further Idleness': section II). If evidence were needed to explain the intensity of hatred the young often expressed for the old at this time, *Mr Prohack* would be a good place to look.

III

1922 was, of course, the year not only of *Mr Prohack* but of *The Waste Land*. The works confront each other across an unbridgeable gulf. Bennett's novel breathes an air of unruffled contentment. 'Well,' it says, 'we've had the war and it didn't amount to very much. And now it's back to business as usual.' Eliot's great poem, on the other hand, throbs with a sense of catastrophe. Is either work more 'right', more sensitively attuned to the historical moment than the other? Here, it may help to note that also in 1922 C.F.G. Masterman produced a follow-up to his famous *The Condition of England* of 1909. *England After the War* has much to say about the damage inflicted on the middle and upper classes of English society, which Masterman thinks is severe and will prove lasting. Paraphrasing Masterman's contention in his study *The Nineteen Twenties*, Douglas Goldring says that Masterman concluded that

> The best of the younger generation of the privileged had been killed, maimed or ruined. Tens of thousands of families, formerly in comfortable circumstances, had been bereaved of their sons and heirs, while high taxation and financial loss forced a large number of owners of stately homes to sell their estates, their pictures and their furniture to Canadian, American or native profiteers.[13]

No doubt these losses fed into the fears of Yeats, Eliot, and others, that a 'new commonness' was threatening the civilisation with which they identified. But money changing hands simply meant that others now had it – like Mr Prohack. And as Goldring acutely remarks, Masterman's diagnosis of the upper-class's lost influence erred on the side of defeatism.

> In view of the resumption of political power by members of the 'old' aristocracy, which took place during the years in which the ex-cavalry officer, Viscount Margesson, was patronage secretary and Chief Whip, it is curious to note that in 1922 Masterman believed that the aristocracy had 'vanished'. Even the hated 'cavalry generals' – whose blunders the official historians could not wholly conceal – were not, as a caste, either much diminished in numbers of deprived of their control of the military machine.[14]

Change, that is, was either happening in some subterranean, hidden way, the extent and nature of which had to be guessed at from occasional surface shifts, most of which turned out to cause merely temporary displacements (strikes, the election of a Labour government); or it wasn't really happening at all. In other words, reading disaster – or of course, infinite promise – into isolated incidents might be well in excess of probability. Events in Russia had undoubtedly brought with them new hopes, bright visions, but elsewhere the falling towers were perhaps all in the mind. The old order, corrupt and senile as it undoubtedly was, simply refused to die. It is this perception, I think, which explains the curious sense of impotent loathing about some writing of the 1920s, the feeling that there is nothing to be done. Evelyn Waugh in fact says as much in his diary entry for 1 February 1925: 'On

Friday morning I received a letter from Richard Greene telling me he is become definitely engaged to Elizabeth. It makes me sad for them because any sort of happiness or permanence seems so infinitely remote from any one of us.'[15] And going with this is the equally desperate feeling that even if the old order were eventually to collapse, nothing worthwhile would take its place. This radicalism of the right can often be located in the satire of the time. We are told that most satire is reactionary: on behalf of stability, even rootedness, it speaks out against the new. But Evelyn Waugh is opposed to both new and old. Right and left radicals at least have this in common: contempt for a way of life that ought to be over but which, to borrow a phrase of Robert Graves, 'still goes on'. Where they differ is that left radicals want the overthrow of the old because they have a vision of a better society in the making – one which is in many ways modelled on the new communist society of Soviet Russia. Radicals of the right, on the other hand, either fear a total collapse into the barbarism of the rough beast's new Jerusalem or hope for a regeneration of society through religion or the emergence of a truly strong man. (The connections between the two are close: Mussolini, who came to power in 1922, is the Nietzschean strong-man as risen God. And if that seems ridiculous, I need only to point to some of the things Lawrence was saying during the decade and which Pound, Yeats and Eliot would be saying a bit later. And yes, I know the left made the same mistake with Stalin.)

Impotent loathing. The old order should be dead but will not lie down. This is the feeling generated by Graves's play *But it Still Goes On*, which is perhaps best thought of as a footnote to a major theme running through *Goodbye to all that*: detestation for his father. In a postscript to his autobiography Graves adds a footnote dealing with the objections of Graves senior to the way his son had written about him. My father is, Graves tells his readers,

> apparently grieved that I am not a good Graves – in spite of characteristic talents obviously, to him, inherited from the male line . . . he has been forced to excuse my behaviour by blaming it on injuries I incurred while gallantly serving family, God and King in the trenches – and on subsequent enrichments, outside the radius of the decently happy family circle . . .[16]

As for the play itself, the key speech comes when Graves's hero, Dick, says

> Well, perhaps one way of describing the catastrophe is to say that it was the moment when the last straw broke the back of reality, when the one unnecessary person too many was born, when population finally became unmanageable, when the proper people were finally swamped. Once they counted: now they no longer count. So it's impossible to feel the world as a necessary world – an intelligible world in which there's more hope or fear for the future – a world worth bothering about – or, if he happens to be a poet, a world worth writing for – a world in which there's any morality left to bother about, but his own morality: *that* gets more and more strict, of course.[17]

But there's no 'of course' about it. Graves's mixture of despair and Nietzschean scorn for the world of mass democracy, widely shared during the 1920s and linked to the sins of the fathers (they had failed to keep order), sanctioned the kind of amorality in which the Bright Young Things indulged and which they glorified as a form of contemptuous resistance to the older generation which had led the world to war and ruin.

Hence, the drink, the drugs, the jazz and the sex.[18] Waugh's diaries, for example, provide endless reports of joyless drunkenness, as here, in an entry for 30 June 1924:

> At about 6.30 we got a drink and went to an Indian theatre. We saw some singularly incompetent Tibetan dancers and a man with a beard who did a few of the simplest tricks . . . when I arrived at Baldhead's dinner they were all quite drunk. I soon drank all I could find and was well contented. A ghastly hulloing outside the windows announced the arrival of Tony Bushell, indescribably drunken, waving a bowler in one hand and an umbrella in the other and carolling his desire to rape Lady Calthorpe. He was unsuccessful in this but stripped himself naked in preparation for the act. Alastair put him to bed on some chairs. We came back very drunk and slept.[19]

Shift the class register and a passage such as this remarkably echoes the cancelled opening of *The Waste Land*, where Eliot ventriloquizes the boozy reminiscences of a would-be man-about-town, whose idea of a good time is to put his foot through a drum, sop up some gin and make a girl squeal.[20]

This is only *not* radicalised behaviour because its self-destructive implications deny the possibility of social transformation. The age of Eliot's anonymous speaker isn't given, but he sounds rather older than Waugh, or than Nicky the drug-taking son in Coward's play, *The Vortex*, or than Dick of *But it Still Goes On*. It might, however, be said that for all of them a nihilistic blackness underlies and licenses their behaviour.

Yet we need to recognise that much of this nihilism was the stuff of fashion, as the light-weight novels of Aldous Huxley both recognise and betray. *Crome Yellow* (1921) and *Antic Hay* (1923) were at the time hailed as caustic accounts of the world of contemporary ideas. To me they read as exercises that collude with what they pretend to attack. They are knowing, gossipy, jokey *romans-à-clef*: fictional versions of the world of 'William Hickey' (and of course that famous gossip column was a regular feature in *The Daily Express* during the 1920s). They belong to the demi-world of metropolitan fashion well written about by Martin Green in *Children of the Sun* and less reliably by Hugh David in *The Fitzrovians*, a book which, while it is far less important than Green's, does usefully trace the movements of café society during the 1920s.[21] Huxley takes nothing seriously. In an early chapter of *Antic Hay* the hero, Gumbril, discusses with a Mr Bojanus the possibility of revolution coming to England. Bojanus proclaims himself a great admirer of Lenin:

> 'So am I,' said Gumbril, 'theoretically. But then I have little to lose to Lenin. I can afford to admire him. But you, Mr Bojanus, you the prosperous bourgeoisie – oh, purely in the economic sense of the word, Mr Bojanus . . .'
>
> Mr Bojanus accepted the explanation with one of his old world bows.
>
> '. . . you would be among the first to suffer if an English Lenin were to start activities here.'
>
> 'There, Mr Gumbril, if I may be allowed to say so, you are wrong.' (ch. III)

Mr Bojanus then explains that he believes in revolution because it brings liberty only to a few, like himself, and would make a nice change. I would not call this radical fiction.

Nor is there really any radical impulse in the way Huxley writes about sex in *Crome Yellow*. Two young women talk about the danger of repressing what one of them calls

> one's instincts. I'm beginning to detect in myself mysterious symptoms like the ones you read about in books. I constantly dream that I'm falling down wells: I even dream that I'm climbing up ladders. It's most disquieting. The symptoms are only too clear . . . One may become a nymphomaniac if one's not careful. (ch VII)

Yet Huxley's flirty way with Freudian ideas does at least hint at the sexual revolution that was then undoubtedly taking place and which may legitimately be called radical. There's no space here to follow through the radicalising of relationships in the 1920s: the *ménages-à-trois* for example, the openly acknowledged lesbian affairs, the campy homosexuality of Oxford aesthetes. The success of Ronald Firbank's *Valmouth* (1919), *Prancing Nigger* (1924) and the wonderfully louche *Concerning the Eccentricities of Cardinal Pirelli* (1926) are a clue to the new licence as are such memoirs as Nina Hamnett's *Laughing Torso* and Kathleen Hale's *A Slender Reputation*. This radicalism will go some way towards explaining the outcry that accompanied the publication of *Ulysses* in, yes, 1922. I am here thinking less of public guardians of morality than of the responses of such otherwise very different people as Virginia Woolf, with her famous sneer at the 'pimples on the face of the bootboy at Claridge's', and D.H. Lawrence's accusation that Joyce was 'doing dirt on life'. (An accusation Lawrence's most ardent academic follower, F.R. Leavis, was for ever to echo.)

It is sometimes said that Woolf is merely covering up. *Ulysses* anticipates what she wants to do in *Mrs Dalloway*. But it's also just possible that she resented Leonard Bloom as an uxorious but loving man and husband. Nearly all the men she knew were 'buggahs' or ruthless philanderers. That's what men *were*. As for Lawrence, by the 1920s he was well into his theorising about women having to deny their own sexual pleasure in order to guarantee men theirs. Hence, of course, *The Plumed Serpent* (1926), and *The Woman who Rode Away* (1928). Leavis thinks this tale 'an astonishing feat of imagination', possessing a unique poetic power which lies 'in its earnestness and profundity of response to the problems of modern civilisation',[22] although I have more recently and more reasonably heard it described as a 'snuff story'.

In contrast, and as Declan Kibberd has brilliantly argued:

> it is clear that Leopold Bloom – intended by his creator to speak as an ordinary man outraged by the injustices of the world – had outraged the world by his very ordinariness. In all likelihood, the stay-at-home English had cannily sensed that Joyce, despite his castigations of Irish nationalism, was even more scathing of the 'brutish empire', which emerges from the book as a compendium of 'beer, beef, business, bibles, bulldogs, battleships, buggery and bishops.' It is even more probable that, in their zeal to defend the great novelistic tradition of Austen, Dickens and Eliot, they were as baffled as many other readers by a 'plotless' book which had become synonymous with modern chaos and disorder.[23]

Kibberd importantly sees Bloom as 'the androgynous anti-hero [who acts] as the embodiment of Joyce's utopian hopes'. Here, then, 'ordinariness' becomes a decisive rebuke to that reactionary modernism of Lawrence, for whom 'the problems of modern civilisation' can be resolved only by great men. It also does devastating damage to the self-inspired myth of Bloomsbury as the epitome of civilised values. (How a coterie of such obvious second-raters are still allowed to get away with their self-promotion would beggar belief were it not for the amount of money and numbers of reputations at stake.) And this is why the response of Edgell Rickword to *Ulysses* is so important.

Rickword wasn't at all outraged by Joyce's great novel. Quite the contrary. He praises its 'plebeian hero', speaks with passionate approval of Joyce's achievement as a master of prose, and although he doesn't himself write at length about the novel, he presumably sympathises with the views of his cousin who, in 'A Note on Fiction', identifies a profound irony at work in *Ulysses*:

> that within the subject, the contrast between actual impulse and appearance which that, too, assumes in consciousness. From this profoundly critical standpoint he is able to exteriorise and objectify vast psychological tracts that as a rule lurk shapelessly outside the

action of the novel . . . And regarding with an equal eye the response both to external and internal stresses, attributing no more value to the one than to the other, he is able to compel both into the same perspective and so set in motion events that, occurring simultaneously on both planes, are in themselves adequate and self sufficient.[24]

True, the article concludes by calling Dedalus and Bloom 'symbols of disintegration', which is not likely nowadays to compel wide assent; but the general tenor of the piece is as intelligent and perceptive as it is warm in its praise for Joyce's achievement.

By the time 'A Note of Fiction' appeared in *The Calendar of Modern Letters* in 1926 its author, C.H. Rickword, was dead, victim of a car accident. Printing it was not merely Edgell Rickword's act of homage to a cousin he was close to and much admired, but, whether he intended it or not, signalled the beginning of the end of his friendship with Wyndham Lewis. When Rickword and Douglas Garman began the *Calendar* in 1925 Rickword had written to Lewis asking him for contributions, and his review of Lewis's *The Art of Being Ruled* (1926) concluded that the book was 'a marvellous piece of navigation or charting of our position'. As Rickword's biographer Charles Hobday notes, 'Lewis's writings occupy 97 pages in the *Calendar* – more space than any other contributor except Rickword himself – and another nine are devoted to reviews of his books'.[25] Hobday thinks that Lewis would have been in sympathy with Rickword's denunication of 'the amorphous, inhuman, *valueless* mess in which liberal-egalitarian-scientifico-humanitarianism has landed us'. (This mess and more besides is touched on in Rickword's poem 'Luxury', written in 1924, with its vision of how 'The churches' sun-dried clay crumbles at last,/the Courts of Justice wither like a stink/and honourable statues melt as fast/as greasy garbage down a kitchen-sink'.)

Yet sympathy between the two men was bound to be short-lived. Lewis quarrelled with everyone, of course, and usually over artistic matters. But his quarrel with Rickword was over politics. Rickword's radicalism was leading him to the left, whereas Lewis was increasingly and fanatically attracted to fascism. Hence, his hostility to *Ulysses*. This first surfaces in *The Art of Being Ruled*, where Lewis criticises the wordiness of Joyce's stream of consciousness. But the major attack comes in February, 1927, in Lewis's own magazine, *The Enemy*. Here Lewis distinguishes between the novel's form and its content. The latter is 'simply the material of a fairly conventionally imagined (clichéd, indeed) naturalism . . . The shabby-genteel pride and intellectualism of lower middle-class Dublin in 1904, however real they remain for Joyce, can retain no significant reality in Europe after the 1914–18 war.' As for stream of consciousness: it apparently collapses the distinctions of space and time into a space-time substance which robs the human mind of 'the independent shaping power through which it imagines (in art, most particularly) possible futures'.[26]

IV

Although Lewis's criticisms of *Ulysses* are misguided, two things need to be said in his defence. First, while he is wrong to identify Joyce with naturalism, he is not wrong to see in naturalism a form of art that is in all senses reactionary. Secondly, it is clear that he took art seriously. In this he is essentially part of that modernist movement which believed passionately in the value of artistic creation and therefore its possibilities and responsibilities. It is this which gives such an edge to critical writing of the decade, whether of the right – as in the essays of Eliot and of his journal *The Criterion* – or of the left, for example the essays and opinions of Rickword and *The Calendar of Modern Letters*. Both kinds of modernism are modes of resistance to what their upholders see as the decade's prevailing ethos, its decadent exhaustion: of a world gone smash.

Even those determined to take a less apocalyptic view of the 1920s were liable to feel tremors that might be presaging disaster. Bennett's very interesting novel of 1927, *Accident*, uses a train journey in order to feel towards the articulation of a deep apprehension about contemporary society and the forces lying beneath its surface. As Bennett's protagonist Alan Frith-Walter boards the boat train at Victoria, he thinks of the taxi-driver who had delivered him to the station and of the porters who had handled his luggage: 'Something wrong somewhere: something wrong! . . . Society was sick.' On his journey towards the continent and holiday his conscience goads him about the money he is going to squander 'on inexcusable self-indulgence. Were his heart and brain in such a state that he could find no better use for riches?' Bennett very persuasively builds an atmosphere of suspense and impending disaster, and in due course the express does indeed crash. But then he lapses from symbolic potentiality into his naturalistic mode, and the novel shrinks to become a jokey tale of lovers reconciled.

The date of *Accident* is therefore significant. It was started in the immediate aftermath of the General Strike. That strike was the first (and last) of its kind. It promised (or threatened) much and it achieved very little. It ended in defeat for the strikers, especially and most bitterly for the miners, and the defeat of working-class interests could be taken to mean that despite a momentary hitch, 'society' or 'civilisation' was safe. Bennett's novel might almost be a concealed commentary on the strike's outcome from the standpoint of those opulent ones who, briefly alarmed by working-class militancy, were soon able to relax. The world wasn't going to be turned upside down after all.

Yet the strike was an extraordinary moment and it *might* have succeeded. According to Samuel Hynes, writing of *The Auden Generation*:

> at that point in their lives they had no political awareness, no sense of social realities, no sense of the moment in which they lived as a point in history. The change in consciousness had begun, and the brightest of the young were beginning to see their situation as different from the past, and requiring new solutions. But it was only a beginning, a window that had been opened onto the Waste Land.[27]

Leaving aside Hynes's comfortable notion that the brightest of the young must have been those with public school and Oxbridge educations (the young miners who went on strike obviously didn't know what they were doing or why), it has still to be said that he is almost certainly wrong to confuse the campy way Auden reported himself as having worked for the strikers – as though it was all a great joke – with the fact that he nevertheless chose that side rather than the side of the bosses, which was after all the side he came from.

On the other hand, it is probably dangerous to isolate the strike as a *decisive* moment. It undoubtedly dramatised the contrast between those with power and riches and those without either and whose lives were subject to and often wrecked by the powerful ones who still owned the state. Yet while its outcome seemed yet another confirmation that the war had changed the basic rottenness of a society, which before 1914 had been divided between ostentatious opulence and terrible deprivation, it also provided an instance of what might happen at some future date. Nobody in 1926 or 1927 could know that there wouldn't be another, more successful General Strike; and as the decade moved to its close there were good reasons to suppose that radical or violent or even apocalyptic change was waiting to happen, whether by accident or design. Hence, the gleefully dystopic vision of Auden's 'Get There If You Can' with its re-run of the trochaic octameters of Tennyson's 'Locksley Hall', that hymn to mid-nineteenth-century visions of expanding empires and the 'federation of the world'. In Auden's land 'you once were proud to own' there are now 'Smokeless chimneys, damaged bridges, rotting wharves and choked canals/Tramlines buckled, smashed trucks lying on their sides across the rails'. A wrecked industrial landscape is symbolic of a society doomed to imminent death: 'If we really want to live, we'd better start at once to try/If we don't it doesn't matter, but we'd better start to die.'

Auden's poem was written in April 1930. A few months earlier Evelyn Waugh had concluded his second novel, *Vile Bodies*, with his main character, Adam Fewick-Symes, sitting 'on a splintered tree stump in the biggest battlefield in the history of the world'. In an author's note Waugh explains that 'The action of the book is laid in the near future, when existing social tendencies have become more marked', and the tendencies he must have had in mind are those which in the novel are associated with the Bright Young Things: their moribund world of drunken, joyless promiscuity, a way of 'starting to die' – which, in the course of the novel, some in fact do. It has been said that the explanation for Waugh's novel beginning as a slight satire on metropolitan socialites and ending on an altogether deeper note has to do with the break-up of his marriage, which occurred as he was at work on the novel. I don't believe it. Or rather, I think his rancorous loathing of the people about whom he writes becomes clearer to himself as he writes, compelling him to identify them in dystopic terms: all those parties, all those vile bodies. And the smash, when it comes, is imaginatively proper. Waugh's novel is yet another example of how, in the 1920s, radicals of the right shared a diagnostic sense with the radicals of the left of the deep malaise of the society in which they lived. It couldn't still go on, could it?

Notes

1. Quoted by Donald Davie in " 'The Dry Salvages': a Reconsideration." *Poetry Nation Review* May/June, 1991, p. 24.
2. Paul Delaney, *D.H. Lawrence's Nightmare* (Hassocks, 1979), p. 385.
3. I have dealt at some length with this in my *Modern English Poetry: From Hardy to Hughes* (London, 1986), esp. pp. 53–5.
4. Edna Longley (ed.), *Edward Thomas: Poems and Last Poems* (London, 1973), p. 353.
5. Stan Smith, *Edward Thomas* (London, 1986), p. 181.
6. D.H. Lawrence, *Letters: Vol. II, 1913–16*, eds G.J. Zytaruk and J.T. Boulton (London, 1981), p. 259.
7. See his *The Mountain of Truth: The Counter Culture Begins. Ascona 1900–1920* (London, 1986), esp. pp. 29–34 and *passim*.
8. D.H. Lawrence, *Letters: Vol. II*. pp. 272–3.
9. Ibid. pp. 375–6.
10. For this see the article by Patrick J. Keane, "Burke, Wordsworth and the Genesis of 'The Second Coming' ", *Bulletin of Research in Humanities*, Spring, 1979, pp. 76–94.
11. In this context it is worth noting a crucial letter Gurney sent to his friend Marion Scott in October, 1917, in which he speaks of liberties kept alive by ordinary people who fought "the fathers of the present 'Prussians of England' ". R.K.R. Thornton (ed.), *The Letters of Ivor Gurney* (Manchester, 1991), p. 354.
12. A fuller discussion of this novel can be found in my *Arnold Bennett: A Study of his Fiction* (London, 1974), pp. 180–6. Darkness in the post-war years can become for radicals on the right an expression of that negritude which itself signals a retreat to the "jungle" of barbarism. Hence, the fear of jazz. For this, see David Craig and Michael Egan, 'Decadence and Crack-Up'. In Stephen Knight and Michael Wilding (eds), *The Radical Reader* (Marrickville, New South Wales, 1977), pp. 11–35.
13. Douglas Goldring, *The Nineteen Twenties* (London, 1945), p. 19.

14. Ibid. p. 21. This conflicts with David Cannadine's contention in his massive *The Decline and Fall of the British Aristocracy* (London, 1990) that the Great War dealt the aristocracy a body blow from which it never recovered. Would that it had.
15. M. Davie (ed.), *The Diaries of Evelyn Waugh* (Harmondsworth, 1979), p. 202.
16. Robert Graves, *But it Still Goes On: An Accumulation* (London, 1980), p. 23.
17. Ibid., p. 293.
18. There is an excellent study of the post-war drug scene by Marek Hohn, *Dope Girls: The Birth of The British Drug Underground* (London, 1992). As for jazz and its presumed decadence, Kathy J. Ogren's *The Jazz Revolution: Twenties America and The Meaning of Jazz* (London, 1989) has much of relevance to say for the English context.
19. Davie, *The Diaries of Evelyn Waugh*, p. 164.
20. T.S. Eliot: *'The Waste Land': A Facsimile and Transcript*, ed. Valerie Eliot (London, 1971), p. 4.
21. Martin Green, *Children of the Sun: A Narrative of 'Decadence' in England After 1918* (New York, 1976) and Hugh David, *Three Fitzrovians: A Portrait of Bohemian Society, 1900–1955* (London, 1988).
22. F.R. Leavis, *D.H. Lawrence, Novelist* (Harmondsworth, 1964), p. 287.
23. Declan Kibberd, 'Bloom the Liberator', *The Times Literary Supplement*, 8 January 1992, p. 4.
24. Alan Young (ed.), *Edgell Rickword: Essays and Opinions, 1921–1931* (Manchester, 1974), p. 241.
25. C. Hobday, *Edgell Rickword: A Poet at War* (Manchester, 1989), p. 98.
26. For this I am indebted to an essay by Paul Edwards, 'Wyndham Lewis versus James Joyce: Shaun versus Shem?', *Irish Studies Review*, 7, Summer, 1994, p. 12.
27. S. Hynes, *The Auden Generation: Literature and Politics in England in the 1930s* (London 1979), p. 34.

10 Literature, lying and sober truth: attitudes to the work of Patrick Hamilton and Sylvia Townsend Warner

Arnold Rattenbury

(NOTE: Much of the work of both authors is currently available, and readers of this chapter may seek it out if they don't already know it. Largely for this reason, quotations in what follows are chiefly from out of print, or very obscure, or the more neglected or not yet published sources.)

'I have left most of my works in Lancashire under the management of Methodists, and they serve me excellently well', wrote Robert Peel in 1787. An odd departure-point for excursions into recent literature perhaps, yet Edward Thompson found, in Peel's obvious approval of a newly docile workforce, evidence that Methodism had begun to fulfil 'the desiderata of capitalism' long before capitalism itself had even perceived the need.[1] Could it be that more history works this way than we have been used to reckon, that Thatcherism for instance could only succeed in Britain because its desiderata, too, had been fulfilled long before 1979?

By that year personal success was already measured in acquisitions; consumerism – 'property-owning democracy', an earlier Tory prime minister had called it – was on a roll; religion might be failing, but from that domestic shrine, the television set, another opium already pervaded the home; Art must entertain and its intellectual content – a sense of Art as 'Intellect raised to the level of Passion'[2] – was now so much derided that Orwell's poor prose, for instance, could be levelled up, A-levelled indeed, to seem artistic; people might *feel* but must not *think*. If the comforts of thought were called for, send not for Art but a therapist, a philosopher, a steamroller, an Iris or a Rupert Murdoch, for anything but practitioners of Art. At any rate, something had happened in the State by 1979 for its hard-won Welfare to be dismantled as might be a theatrical set. This cannot be blamed, I think, on politicians playing politics – unless one is prepared to consider all trendsetters, whether in academia or studio, politicians themselves.

Some such longer view seems best to explain the curious reputations of Patrick Hamilton and Sylvia Townsend Warner, dead in 1962 and 1978 respectively: alive that is, before Thatcherdom. Parts of the work of both – not always the most important parts – have remained obstinately in print continuously until now, when some at least of the best is available again.[3] Yet neither has achieved the bestsellerdom beloved of market economies, nor that proper sanctity for the dead but objectionable, which markets allow, full critical approval.

Patrick was biographised by his brother in 1972, discussed by a number of us (friends and others) at dead of night on television in 1989, biographised again by Nigel Jones in 1991 and again by Sean French in 1993.[4] His reprints have been introduced by J.B. Priestley (twice), Michael Holroyd, Claud Cockburn[5] and acclaim has come from Graham Greene, John Betjeman, Anthony Powell, Osbert Sitwell, Doris Lessing, Keith Waterhouse, Philip Hensher – a bewildering company.[6] And yet, and yet. Sylvia meanwhile was remembered by twelve of us in a journal 'celebration' of 1981, again by Bea Howe in 1988, shared with her lover Valentine Ackland a joint study by Wendy Mulford that same year, was biographised on her own by Claire Harman in 1989, and one might have thought self-portrayed in her *Letters* of 1982 and her *Diaries* of 1994 were the selection and editing involved not, as will be seen, questionable at least.[7] And yet, and yet – again. Though all these occasions have supplied details from life and related them to passages in the work of both my friends, none has asked of the work what proves to be so obstinately printable about it, what must surely be increasingly dated claims upon us in a world so readily farewelling Welfare. Indeed, though all this attention clearly responds to some sense of need, a certain air of condescension, if not actual belittlement characterises both main biographies – Sean French's of Patrick, Claire Harman's of Sylvia. Apart from Michael Holroyd's introduction to *Twenty Thousand Streets Under the Sky*, for common sense about Patrick one has to go half a century back to an obscure article by the stage director Eric Capon[8] or into remainder shops for P.J. Widdowson's essay about the novels;[9] for love of Sylvia, across the Atlantic to articles by Eleanor Perenyi and Simon Watney.[10] And that is a good deal odder than starting from Robert Peel.

Patrick Hamilton's work consists of twelve novels (six of them grouped as trilogies), five stage plays and three radio plays, written between 1925 when he was 20 and 1954.[11] Eight years later, at the age of 58 he died – partly of drink, partly from the permanent after-effects of a severe car accident in 1932, partly due no doubt to a massive course of seven electric shock treatments for depression in 1956, partly – surely – of inanition. For that last eight years, four chapters of a discontinued novel and two fragmentary versions of the non-fictional *Memoirs of a Heavy Drinking Man* are all there is to show. Booze, a wrecked racked body and electro-convulsive therapy aside, it is at least likely that this block on imaginative creativity is a simple admission that he had nothing more to say. And so it seems. The last novel, *Unknown Assailant*, published in 1955 to round off *The Gorse Trilogy*, written in what are (for him) short staccato sentences, perfunctory, rounds off everything else as well. From those twenty-year-old beginnings onward, looking back, his direction had been single, his view consistent though deepening in perspective – softer or more scathing as growing wisdom required. To make such judgements requires of course that Patrick had 'something to say', that there was not simply craftmanship but intellectual content to his work – hard, it seems, for biographers to believe.

From the beginning almost everything Hamilton wrote required intense restriction in the space allowed for action. Even the long train journey of his juvenile first novel *Monday Morning* seems to work well only because its characters are encapsulated, trapped as his characters always will be. Action is to be crammed into boarding house, saloon bar, the space behind the bar, bedroom, car seat, prison cell. Characters travel beyond these limits, it is true, but always return (by enclosed journey), and action *between* characters must also be confined. Moreover the characters themselves are increasingly liable to further restriction by those other sealed-in qualities of drunkenness, schizophrenia, silence between classes, somnambulism, blindness,[12] but chiefly – and from the start – by a strangle-held version of English language. They can only express themselves codedly, by clutching at single phrases which may once have expressed a thought but are now become mantras, catch-phrases, slogans only *thought* to express a thought or belief. They are not telling us or each other tales, they are telling beads. Though he later used the habit more sparingly, at first Hamilton capitalised the initial letters of words in such phrases – Priestley, unnecessarily, scathing, since he was to adopt the habit himself, called the habit Komik Kaps – so that looking down a page of Hamilton's dialogue can make you feel enthicketted yourself. Or characters will wall themselves in behind stockades of phrase so as to be entirely impenetrable, as in the terrible courtship of Ella by Mr Eccles in *The Midnight Bell*, when Ella's small commonsenses simply collapse and shiver like misdirected arrows against the plank-like clichés of Mr Eccles's impregnable certainty. By 1939 and the eve of the war, in *Impromptu in Moribundia*, speech, even of so limited a sort, has become unnecessary: instead of conversation, balloons rise up from the tops of characters' heads encapsulating what they mean in 'thinks' slogans of the kind used in advertisement or comic-strip. But far earlier than this, newly introduced characters will fetch forth their own particular versions of the code. In his second novel (and the first uniquely Hamiltonian), the wonderful *Craven House* of 1926, Mrs Hoare out-Hamiltons his own capitalisation of initial letters by being, in crisis, able to communicate *only* by capital letters.

This was all the result of serious research, if you like – except that its laboratory was simply the way that Patrick lived. Later, during the war, when everyone was a transient and pubs perpetually crowded as a consequence, groups who went drinking together were necessarily parted by the pressure. Speaking to Patrick in such a situation you would see his eyes glaze over, despite your best efforts, take on a particular stare, and know suddenly that he was listening sideways to someone else's conversation, ears almost flapping, gathering clichés from the talk of strangers. Even more disconcerting was it when your party split another way and you and he were in different conversations. You noticed the same glaze come over his eyes, knew again what was happening and wondered in alarm if he were collecting clichés now from *you*. Drinking his raw materials in. Solitary drinking which, as a general condition, came later was another matter: even in *Hangover Square*, that drunken odyssey in progress at the time I recall, his concerns were far beyond the three isolated characters and the confines he describes. He was in a real world enough, reducing it in place and number.

What he found in reality and the quite different reality he made of it were of course very funny. Everyone remarks this who values him. He is everyone's comic genius, mine too. But he is also not in the least funny. Hamilton is dealing with a language at the end of its tether to *any* reality. *These* characters in *this* (fictional) reality are coming to an end themselves. A frayed language becomes them. Of the 250 pages which make up my edition of *Craven House*, Book II, a mere fourteen pages, covers the whole of the First World War. That sort of reality, carefully proportioned, is irrelevant to Hamilton's purpose. What matters is only this craven boarding house which you cannot or will not leave, this microcosm of the world you are stuck with, a world where class is in conflict with class: here, only, can you control that conflict. Those who go out – the office-working Mr Spicer (briefly a soldier), the schoolboy Master Wildman, very occasionally for the purpose of shopping the owner Miss Hatt – do so only to bring back further confirmations, more and more frayed in language as they are, that *this* reality perfectly matches *that*. There is one exception, and it shapes the novel. The maid-of-all-work and the cook, who actually run the place, go out to a party of their working-class kind. Audrey the Maid, returning after the party, Answers Back.

'She Answered Back', says Miss Hatt.
'She Answered Back', whispers Mrs Hoare, and there is a pause.
'Keep your Hair on', quotes Mrs Hoare, and gives a quick fearful glance at the womanly glory thus insulted. Which rather upsets Miss Hatt, who feels she rather wants to look at herself before replying. 'Well. She must go. That's all. She must be Dismissed'.

'Dee – Eye – *Ess* —', began Mrs Hoare, measuredly, but Miss Hatt cuts in with 'I'm not going to be insulted in my own house, you know'.

'I should think not', says Mrs Hoare. 'Dee, Eye, Ess —'

'It's too much of a good thing', says Miss Hatt. 'I've got to show that young girl that I'm not such a fool –'

'As you look', says Mrs Hoare, fully alive to the seriousness of the situation . . .

'Did you hear that part about the Aitch?' whispers Mrs Hoare, who plainly regards that as the principal crime.

'The Aitch?' queries Mrs Spicer.

'Well never mind about the *Aitch*', says Miss Hatt, a little curtly (and very natural, too). 'The point is she Answered Back'.

'Yes', says Mrs Spicer. 'I gathered that'.

'And she must Go', says Miss Hatt.

'Jee, Oh', interjects Mrs Hoare, decisively, and Miss Hatt is seen raising her eyes to heaven, as though calling upon God.

'Spells Go', says Mrs Spicer, aptly.[13]

Good comic stuff for sure, but it sets off disaster. I don't believe the *machinery* of a Hamilton novel was ever so crude again, but it is hard-working Audrey after her working-class party that sets it off. She is replaced by working-class Bertha, who cannot suppress what seems to be laughter at everyone else, though this is generally interpreted as a curious way of breathing. Mrs Nixon, who has terrorised her daughter Elsie well into adulthood, holding over her the threat of a splendid son Mr Jock Nixon, finally flips her lid and cuts up Elsie's only evening gown to prevent her attending a dance. Master Wildman frustrates her by taking Elsie out to buy another. Mr Spicer is discovered in a marital infidelity. A totally incomprehensible and uncomprehending Russian becomes a part of the household where she has to battle her way not only between languages but through thickets of code, tsarism, a revolution, and the forest of Mrs Hoare's capital letters. And then arrives Mr Jock Nixon, the great and splendid threat, to announce himself, with glee and pride as a fascist thug. Here is the character from outside upon whom the characters have learned to depend. 'Expect he deserved it', says Mr Spicer, of the victim of one of Mr Jock Nixon's proudly described atrocities.[14] Miss Hatt succumbs to hysterics and decides to close her Craven House. And so the book too closes, with the escape of Elsie and Master Wildman to Love and – a last cough from the book's machinery – the unequivocal working-class kindness towards them of the removals men carting *Craven House* away.

Three years later, in his first play *Rope*, Hamilton's concern is with that last Jock Nixon-ish violence of action only. The space is even more restricted now – down to a single room containing a chest, in turn containing a corpse. This last fact is known only to the murderers, two privileged wealthy youths, and to ourselves the audience and co-conspirators therefore. It is a brilliant stroke. The other characters, friends and relatives of the corpse, and the poet chosen by Hamilton to express revulsion, are not culpable: only the villains and ourselves as accessories. The society in which this happens is *ours*.

This is of course a merciless way to tear the bones from the flesh of novel or play, but forced upon us by the determination of almost every critic or biographer not to see that novels and plays are flesh, bone, blood, mind of authors, that writing about 'comic genius' or 'masterly stagecraft' won't do. Hamilton's work itself becomes as much a corpse as anything in *Rope* unless one attempts to discover *why* comedian/craftsman employs himself as he does.

Making a special point about Theatre, Richard Eyre has written:

> Each art form . . . thrives on metaphor: things stand *for* things rather than being the thing itself, a room can become a world, a group of characters a whole society. It involves the astonishment of the unreal, the strange, magnified proportions that occur naturally in childhood.[15]

This aspect of Hamilton's art – in novel as much as drama – could hardly be better put. But there is another aspect: his knowledge, and his ability to astonish us with it, of how that 'whole society', that 'world from a room' actually works. 1926 is very early for a young English author to be perceiving and naming fascism as the ultimate protection of boarding house bigotry – fascists are again in the background of his third novel *Twopence Coloured* of 1928 – or then to see fascism as immediately murderous. Knowledge went further than that, however. The skivvying basement working class of *Craven House* may have been crudely conceived but was deliberate; and the novels of 1931, 1932 and 1934 which together make up the trilogy *Twenty Thousand Streets Under the Sky*, look back to Audrey who 'Answered Back about the Aitch' and also – coolly – at that Love to which Elsie and Master Wildman had been helped to escape. The central characters, one for each book – Jenny, a prostitute, Bob, a would-be author barman, Ella, a barmaid – are not precisely the industrial proletariat as defined by Marx but are, for all that, workpeople within Hamilton's understanding – within his tender understanding indeed, considering the savagery with which he could write and, in this trilogy, did.

After *The Siege of Pleasure*, the second book in the sequence, Hamilton suffered the appalling road accident which left him with a partially withered arm, a painful limp and a disfigured face for life. Laid up and unable to write, he read prodigiously, chiefly Marxist works. Too much has been made of the suddenness of this preoccupation, and there is another obstacle of misrepresentation to overcome.

What has to be called the Hamilton Archive consists mainly of papers which Patrick's brother Bruce, a very poor novelist, was able or chose to keep, a large part of them letters to each other. Family memories, ambitions, relationships are endlessly anatomised; but, as is the case with that other sibling record – of Harold, a failed painter, about his brother, the poet Wilfred Owen[16] – this is a sick, inverted, sometimes jealous, often taunting correspondence, filled with palpable dishonesties on both sides – a matter dealt with supremely well in French's biography. (As French points out, it is some 'brotherly love', for example, that has Bruce writing a thriller in which he Bruce, actually murders Patrick).[17] Still, there the Archive is, and the possibility exists of tracing almost every fictional incident in the novels back to some event in reality – though of course the reality recorded in such a claustrophobic situation may itself be fictional invention. This piggybacking fiction upon fact has two curious effects. First, the written work can seem a reflection, *not* a creation. And secondly, the claustrophobia acts in much the same way as Jane Austen's celebrated 'little bit (two inches square) of ivory', which for so long allowed scholars to deny that her novels also contain the immensities of Enclosure, Napoleonic War, religious and social revolution, even feminism. In the end we still don't know *why* a particular 'real' event fulfilled its fictive purpose and, since we cannot know so long as we proceed this way, don't ask. Slam goes the door on Eyre's 'world from a room'. Bang goes not only the whole necessity called Art but even common-or-garden reasonableness.

The notion that Hamilton suddenly became Marxist because of hospitalised reading in 1932 is clearly preposterous. The journey from *Craven House* through *Twopence Coloured* and *Rope* to the first two trilogy volumes, *The Midnight Bell* and *The Siege of Pleasure* was from a clear perception that class-warring capitalism would self-destruct after some final fling with a specifically fascist violence, to an increasing concern with the behaviours and humanities possible to working people who would be active in this process. His attitude to Love as being commoditised through *all* classes leaps, it would seem, from the *Communist Manifesto* – before he had read it? There is nothing sudden or less than doggedly consequential about an arrival at Marxism. No doubt the end of the trilogy, *The Plains of Cement*, written after the accident, is the best of the three books, may even have benefited from crash-course reading. It is also the trilogy's logical, not newly intrusive, end in 1934.

The almost identical suggestion of suddenness and irrelevance to her previous writing is made about Sylvia Townsend Warner's joining the Communist Party in 1935. In fact, as unsudden as Patrick, Sylvia had been writing poems about Rosa Luxemburg in 1924 and 1925, excoriating investment capital and male chauvinism in the first half of her novel, *Lolly Willowes* in 1926, ridiculing missionary imperialism throughout *Mr Fortune's Maggot* of 1927, spreading before us what Simon Watney has called 'an allegory of class relations in all their grim absurdity' in *The True Heart* of 1929, aghast at the horrors of a 'peace' produced by the First World War in her riotous narrative poem *Opus 7* of 1931 and, since 1932, working on her great novel of middle-class desertion towards revolutionary engagement, *Summer Will Show*. Her *Diaries*, though no political record, have pawky radical asides even at their most flibbertigibbet in the 1920s – as do *The Letters*, despite clear evidence of editorial excision of political views (q.v.). And then, in the quietness of that unusual declaration of mutual love, the shared volume of poems by herself and Valentine Ackland, *Whether a Dove or a Seagull* of 1933, there echoes beyond this 'room' that 'world' in one poem of Sylvia's, a world so set with 'traps... springs and pitfalls' that she, who has always been wary, is 'caught, now, perhaps'.[18]

As in so many of her poems, then and later, 'caught' might be of politics or love: common sense says both – for no-one apart from her literary executors yet does – what caused the rejection of the evidently satirical 'light' novel of 1934. (We need to know: at the time Sylvia herself noted, 'It is a nice piece of work. I am glad I persevered with it').[19]

Joining the Communist Party may have been, as some assert, by shove from Valentine – despite her famous shyness, quite pushy enough when I knew her – but Sylvia's journey to that point, like Patrick's to Marxism, had been steady and intellectually informed beginning probably far sooner than 1924 (while Valentine was still, and for some time to come, a society Deb). You don't proceed from Rosa Luxemburg to 'the grim absurdities of class' by sortilege. And anyone who could write in 1931, about her war-disillusioned, peace-disillusioned, green-fingered, flower-selling, gin-swigging Rebecca of *Opus 7*:

> ... markets matched themselves to her supply
> as in political economy

or that Rebecca's neighbours

> ... village Hampdens, gathered in the tap
> forsook their themes of bawdry and mishap
> to curse a government that could so fleece
> on spirits under proof, and call it peace

was not going to need much pushing into further political analysis or commitment four years later. Neither can a journey begun so early have been made in the wake of lesbianism (though the somewhat dubious feminism sometimes claimed for *Lolly Willowes*[20] might have been part of it), since Valentine and she became lovers only in 1930, until when Sylvia had been actively heterosexual. Quite evidently very different by nature, despite

Valentine's beautiful phrase that their lives 'joined up imperceptibly all along their lengths',[21] they joined themselves up to the Communist Party, as perhaps they did most things, for entirely different reasons – Sylvia carefully, with great deliberation and, like most I ever knew, some reservations; Valentine on the lam, unreservedly, a-burst with compassionate feeling, much as she had fallen into marriage and out of the Catholic Church, into and out of love affairs before and throughout her marriage to Sylvia, into and out of the Communist Party, into and out of the Catholic Church again, eventually into the Society of Friends.[22] It is too simple to write of one as intellectual, the other as emotional; but in that amalgam which is each person, reason or feeling can seem to dominate, one lead the other. Valentine plunged regardless, Sylvia must have the consent of reason. The pell-mell-ery of Valentine's communism is very clear in a series of unpublished letters, some by her, some by Sylvia, to their friends the Liptons (q.v.); Sylvia's more stately Pall Mall progress, in *Summer Will Show*.

This astounding novel, published in 1936, has two heroines and one unheroic man as central protagonists: Minna who ends up dead on the Paris barricades of 1848, Sophia who ends up reading the *Communist Manifesto* published that same year, and Frederick to whom Minna is mistress and Sophia wife. Other characters gather around these three, and indeed Frederick is virtually displaced from the book by those about him. Though he got it by marriage, Frederick represents property, stability, the *status quo*; Minna a rag-tag-and-bobtail Europe of dissatisfaction and incipient rebellion. Sophia travels away from one towards the other, betraying Class, espousing Cause, and carefully analysing Cause in the persons of its other adherents. In the spareness of this three-sided configuration, but in no other way, Sylvia resembles Patrick: that is, in paring perception down to a minimum not of place, but of pivotal character. And the perception is of course of her *own* times, as it was for Patrick, whatever period he might pretend to occupy. To say that any historical novel must be contemporary with its author rather than its subject should be so much a commonplace as to be unworthy of remark – though when one reads such a phrase as 'goes far beyond the scope of historical accuracy to a sense of historical actuality'[23] one must begin to wonder. Certainly, setting the book as she did, much research went into it, but she was writing *Now*: of course it was 'actual'. *Summer Will Show* can even (if needs must) be read as allegorical autobiography with Sophia (for Sylvia) dry-eyed, thoughtful, calm despite death of children, break-up of marriage, loss of fortune, faith, status, change of country, discovery of love, political involvement; Minna (for Valentine) all passion and abandon. (To do so would be wilful, if only because Sylvia always regarded herself, even in her eventually anguished love, as forever fortunate.)

Nonetheless here, in this duality, intellect and emotion, we come to the hub of that great wheel across Time where the Art of Sylvia and Patrick found itself until Time ended for each of them. Many spokes led to it, connected it to the hard travelling rim of experience, each spoke carrying back for absorption distinguishable shocks from every change in surface, every jolt in the track of England. There were as many ways as there were jolts and surfaces to join oneself to communists, and only one of them was the intellectual adoption of analysis or philosophy – however much the hub might muddle all the shocks together.

Lionel Trilling, by fluke (it must be), seeming to announce Mrs Thatcher's assumption of power in 1979, would remove all spokes but one:

> I speak of the commitment that a large number of the intelligentsia of the West gave to the degraded version of Marxism known as Stalinism. . . . At its centre was the belief that the Soviet Union had resolved all social and political contradictions and was well on the way to realizing the highest possibilities of human life. . . . The Stalinists of the West were not commonly revolutionaries, they were what used to be called fellow-travellers but they cherished the idea of revolution as the final, all-embracing act of will which would forever end the assertion of our individual wills. . . . Their animus against individual will expressed itself in moral and cultural attitudes which devalued all the gratuitous manifestations of feeling, of thought, and of art, of all such energies of the human spirit as are marked by spontaneity, complexity, and variety.[24]

Not surprisingly a one-spoked wheel won't turn, and buckles.

Three concerns – not one central belief – appear in every account of people joining the 1930s Communist Party in Britain: mass unemployment, peace, and the rise of fascism foreign or home-grown. The great campaigning, recruiting issues were the Hunger Marches, the National Unemployed Workers Movement's 'black coffin',[25] Mosley swash-battering his way about London's East End, the prevention of war by support for Spain; more gradually, steady redefinition as militant anti-fascism of what had been a primarily pacifist peace movement born of the First World War. There was much to *feel* about all this: guilt at empire, shame at profit, despair like Auden's at the desolation of his beloved industrial midlands landscape, rage like Valentine's at the condition of Dorset labourers tied to foul farm cottages.[26] You have often to work some way down such individual lists before you come to the seventh heaven of Soviet Russia – though come to it you will. Left-wing concerns, in a Britain with no policies (then too) against unemployment or nascent fascisms, increasingly approved of the one country which appeared to differ in this respect – and not just to communists either. Approval tipped over into idolatrous mawkishness sometimes, and communist leadership was, in this sense, deeply religious, Stalinist fanatics as bibliomantic about Marxist texts as Ernie Bevin about the Bible itself. It is worth noting that Sylvia has her Sophia attack the bigotries of communists in her 1848 Paris, loyal and active communist as she was in 1936: bigotry was not universal, I mean. But, as recusants never tire of saying, plenty were hoodwinked into a totally uncritical Russophilia. None of this, however, gainsays how and why an active and various membership gathered.

As to that other part of Trilling's equally religious demonology supposing a clone-like attitude to Literature, both Patrick and Sylvia had, by 1934 and 1935 respectively, been long established as artists of notable individuality. Far from being less 'spontaneous' or 'complex', these individualities in fact increased. From *Craven House* (1926) to *Unknown Assailant* (1955) Patrick's progress is die-straight, more idiosyncratically his at every pause for publication. Along the route are better or worse books no doubt, and methods alter, but no book points another way. Sylvia is in the same case. From the almost single-voiced early novels to the crowds of character in the later, she is increasingly unlike anyone else in attitude. There is no side-tracking because of Patrick's sudden taste (if in fact it was so sudden) for Little Lenin Library titles, or because of Sylvia's occasional boilersuit poem, her falling for Stalin, or even because of that short spell of abasing herself before supposedly heroic working people:

> The reviews of *Summer Will Show* are all very spotless so far, so that my pinafore is still quite presentable – just another bourgeois stylist.[27]

Indeed it was precisely the 'spontaneity, complexity and variety' of artists *inside* the Communist Party, the difference of each to each that, moving among them as a youngster, became for me the hallmark of membership, my capture. Rex Warner wrote sharp allegory, Montagu Slater a mix of cinematic documentary with Greek Chorus, Edgell Rickword a dry highflown Drydenesque line to deal with Appeasement's filth, O'Casey magicked Irish speech into universal poetry, Hugh Sykes Davies embraced surrealism, in one book Pamela Hansford Johnson made the front and back legs of a pantomime horse act for a whole society.[28] It was hard then – it is hard now – to discover a greater variety *outside*. Among Communist Party members actually doing the creative writing, one can go so far as to claim this love of difference as policy: *every* form, style, angle, approach, quirk, oddity was to be pursued.[29] This was by no means true of course of a pontificating leadership which did *not* do the creative writing, but one needs to remember the considerable autonomies existing within what is so often (later) called a monolithic party – the sometimes more than geographical separateness of its Districts, the often conflicting interests of Industrial branches differently trade-based, or between as well as within Professional Groups. Neither *Left Review* in the 1930s nor *Our Time* in the 1940s, journals around which communist authors, artists and musicians gathered in both decades (and for both of which Sylvia wrote) accepted cultural priorities laid down by others – about the super-importance of worker-writing, for instance.

In 1948 the Central Committee wanted everyone, writers specifically included, to celebrate the centenary of the *Communist Manifesto*; the Historians' Group, by then deep into English, Welsh and Scottish studies in the wake of work by A.L. Morton and Christopher Hill, and supported by the Welsh District and several Industrial branches, wanted to celebrate the centenary of Chartism; in what was then a fairly influential editorial position at *Our Time*, my own (communist) decision was to edit and introduce and force through a centenary edition of *Wuthering Heights*. To have a sense of the period you have to feel the presence of all these diversities, all of which involved loyal and active members. What held us, held them, held British communism together was not Stalinist idolatry, not Trilling's suppositional bigotries, not even some important hand-holding with other progressives on a Popular Front against fascism, but total agreement about the necessity for a working-class revolution in England. (That extraordinarily irrevolutionary paper doll of a document, *The British Road to Socialism*, in all its many frocks, belongs to the 1950s and after.) The great uniting word was 'Change'.

Michael Holroyd comes near, but not quite near enough, to hitting the mark when writing about Patrick's *Twenty Thousand Streets*:

> His Marxism became a method of distinguishing between the avoidable and the unavoidable suffering of people, and, in so far as literature can change social conditions, such a vivid facsimile in fiction may have helped to do so. . .[30]

Patrick himself was more precise when, in 1939, he came to excoriate England as *Moribundia* and gave the Moribundian establishment the single political slogan 'Unchange!' But for writers the word 'Change' had a far more immediate professional meaning even than that. I see that much later, in 1974, both of us by then long outside the Communist Party, I wrote to Sylvia after reading a batch of poems she had recently sent me:

> Forget all the political desiderata, the difference between what we would and what we can, and the function of all Art is Change. People aren't to be the same after reading us as before. We know more about revolution than all the politicians because, in this sense, it's a permanent part of conduct . . . as I am startled all over again by hearing some Mozart quartet I know perfectly well already. . . . So changed, yet so prepared for change do you leave us that had it been in your charge only, we must long since have achieved that other Revolution the politicians make such a meal of.

To this she replied – more concerned, it is true, with whether the cyclamen she had planted in front of my home had yet appeared, and the importance of good works to parsonage daughters, and the difficulties of my getting to her by rail *via* Chichester and Yeovil – no, it was the letter before which had observed 'all poems are oysters' – and how she had been 'knocked flat as a fish' by *La Clemenza di Tito* at a Prom:

> I pride myself on being a moral writer, a Mr. Fairchild in taffeta petticoats. Voltaire is my great-grandfather. I am the niece of Diderot. I plant little traps and hope the quickness of the hand deceives the eye. But why describe my method? Yours is much the same. I shall cherish your analysis of the nature of Art. It is as well fitting as a snake's skin. The joke is that while we are doing it, we are both perfectly unconscious of what we are up to. It is our native wood-note.[31]

Nor is there anything exceptional in this as an exchange for that date or earlier (not even in the double fun of snakeskins shed to be grown again, or of wood-notes that are *not* wild). Auden was of much the same mind, if not commitment:

> In our age the mere making of a work of art is a political act. So long as artists exist, making what they please and think they ought to make, even if it's not terribly good, even if it only appeals to a handful of people, they remind the management of something managers ought to be reminded of, namely, that the managed are people with faces, not anonymous numbers, that *Homo laborens* is also *Homo ludens*.[32]

He could have gone further to remark that, in any situation of managing and managed, the latter resent the former, and that management's neglect of Art may seem sensible therefore, for Art, like Sylvia's 'planted traps', is also dangerous.

Alas, Progress perpetually offers hostages to Misfortune; and Trilling had one thing going for him.

There was another, wholly undangerous kind of writing within the compass of communism than those of Sylvia, Patrick and such Change-directed, distinctive, revolutionary fellows as O'Casey. A long tradition of self-tuition in the British labour movement, gathered during the 1930s around the Workers Education and Music Associations and in *ad hoc* Left Book Club groups, but also continuing in solitary, produced much *experiential* writing – writing, that is, descriptive of working-class experience. In 1936, reporting the South Wales miners' sit-in strikes of the previous year, Montagu Slater described reading a striker's 'manuscript novel, some short stories, his poems, and an account . . . of the strike'.[33] Introducing Julius Lipton's *Poems of Strife*, also of 1936, Cecil Day Lewis quoted, with evident excitement, Lipton's letter of introduction to him:

> I find it very difficult and inconvenient to write, owing to the fact that my time is spent most of the year in seeking employment, and when I am successful, . . . I work for fifteen hours each day, in a 'sweat–shop' wielding a heavy press iron.[34]

Poems of Strife was published by the communist Lawrence Wishart press, as were the novels of coalminer Lewis Jones, East End garmentworker Simon Blumenfeld and others; but the movement – for such it has to be called – went further and wider than that: Walter Brierley's *Means Test Man* to Methuen, Harold Heslop's coalmining novels to Boardman (and elsewhere), James Hanley to Chatto's and Lane, Leslie Halward to Michael Joseph, and so on. The whole phenomenon of the sheer bulk of experiential writing (including the fake proletarian writing it excited) is beginning to be studied with a pride it deserves, notably in Andy Croft's *Red Letter Days*.[35] But there is a danger in reaching back – perhaps from a sense of divisions *now* – towards a mythic version of the days of the Popular Front as they never were, in which everyone went in the same direction believing the same thing. Writers, like other people in agreement about one issue only, were going in many directions and believing different things. Experiential writing of the sort I am recalling is not concerned *as writing* with Change but with Confirmation. Like hymns in chapel, some of which were its literal precursors, it was for the converted. The fact that Brierley's *Means Test Man* and *Sandwich Man* are deeply depressing doesn't matter so long as the reader's response is, 'Thank God, someone understands my life!'

Fake or genuine, all work of this kind issued from a single standpoint: that the expression of working-class experience, preferably industrial, must inevitably be valuable *as literature*: and of course only rarely was it. Historically valuable maybe, but that's another matter. Over that part of it avowedly communist, experience naturally included propagandist agitators within the confines of plot; but the limits of recording actual experience must remain here too, limiting response and the possibilities of Change even further. That's to say: characters might advocate political change, but were constrained within the rules of accurate reporting from actually changing the reader's response to reality in the ways that Art attempts – by imagery, ridicule, gobbledygook, exaggerations *beyond* experience, symbol, prose rhythm, verse rhythm, rhyme, and the rest. The best of the experiential partisans (to me) was John Summerfield, his *May Day* and, in particular, the very short *Trouble in Porter Street*.[36] It so happens that Sylvia read *May Day* and wrote about it – with obvious diffidence, in the stilted language of her first days as party member, and with marked qualifications – to that same Julius Lipton:

> I think it is very good. I hope he will be as fertile as Zola, to whom with his large canvas and his lively characters he has a certain resemblance. Altogether I think we may congratulate ourselves on this book. I don't at all mind it being sectarian, myself. . . . A certain sectarian stiffening is all to the good. There will be a danger as long as workers are under capitalism that they will read for . . . a relaxation and release from their conditions. We have found that very objective books, though they enjoy them, don't remain in the memory as much more than a circus. A sectarian novel like this may stay in the mind as a circus with a message, a relevant circus.[37]

Clearly dressed-up 'objective' policy was not her kind of writing: she had, after all, just published *Summer Will Show* – to change, not to confirm us. Nonetheless Sylvia was well aware that experiential writing could outreach itself and live in imaginative air. Perhaps her favourite poet of all was Clare,[38] and the novels of James Hanley, the poems of Idris Davies, let alone the plays and *The Rainbow* of D.H. Lawrence, the poems of Hardy, had lately taken that magically transforming journey. But by and large this had now become a way of writing to change nothing, a series of books more like each other than anything of hers or

Patrick's resembled anything else, a seemingly clone-like category to be called, at best, 'sectarian'. And it was to seem more so by 1979 when Trilling took it as exemplifying all the blessedly, dangerously other. By that date, anything claiming communism, or even disclaiming it from nearby, could be huddled behind the one Aunt Sally, then pelted.

In his Hamilton biography French cites the passage by Trilling already quoted as being 'both right and inadequate'. Going for greater adequacy no doubt, he then refines upon soviet aesthetics, particularly upon its predilection for novels with worker-heroes, and with the influence of such ideas on British authors. But what authors? John Summerfield perhaps, as a professional among the experiential. Harold Heslop certainly, since he had been elevated, by communists (and by Russian communists too) from among the experientialists. But Hamilton, the writer under discussion? Even to pose the question of an author disbarred, by the very nature of being middle-class, from this particular 'communist' literature, is to declare for daftness. Then why go on this soviet mystery tour? The answer, when it appears, has nothing to do with aesthetics, soviet or other, but with political prejudice. The answer is *Impromptu in Moribundia* which French describes as Hamilton's 'only political novel . . . so misconceived, in general and in detail, as to be almost beyond criticism'.[39] Yet French himself has admitted that, in a sense, the *whole* of Hamilton's work is political. In the end all the palaver about aesthetics has been only a long trek out round Uncle Joe and back to poor Aunt Sally. French doesn't like the politics expressed by *Impromptu*: its analysis of Moribundian England is Marxist, how awful!

There is indeed an aesthetic to discuss – to do with the actuality of how authors are to write when politically committed, as Hamilton was. By avoiding this, and by describing *Impromptu* as his 'only political novel', French slides in an unwritten undertext. A Life of Hamilton is worth writing because, except in one case, he was not political (although on pages so-and-so and so-and-so I shall of course admit that he was). This is a nice descant on Trilling's tune: that writers in the 1930s were 'not commonly revolutionaries' because, if they had been, they would have been incapable of 'art, of all such energies of the human spirit as are marked by spontaneity, complexity and variety'. If you have to remark such characteristics in someone's work, as

French is compelled to do of Hamilton's, then he cannot have been a revolutionary. The music now becomes complicated. If, with luck, you can find a book the revolutionary content of which is undeniable, then it must be a bad book and (fortunately) 'beyond criticism' so that you need not go into it, and it is perfectly safe to continue with your Life of Hamilton because, to put it bluntly, he is not what he was.

The actual music of that time was simpler.

In 1937 Sylvia and Valentine, Edgell Rickword and Stephen Spender went to Spain as delegates to a conference of the International Association of Writers for the Defence of Culture. (How those old titles resound!) There are several fluffy accounts of the episode by Spender,[40] and plainer ones by others.[41] Not surprisingly there is considerable confusion about what happened – I see, for instance, that Frank Kermode, reviewing *The Diaries of Sylvia Townsend Warner* for the *London Review of Books* is muddled by conflicts of evidence. What happened is far plainer than so much contradiction suggests.

A larger and more imposing delegation (including Auden) had been blocked by the Foreign Office refusing visas to all but accredited journalists. This smaller party, each of whom had press contracts, was the result. Once in Spain it was strengthened by the addition of the novelist Ralph Bates, then with the International Brigades and, in Madrid, by Nancy Cunard, then operating an outpost of her Paris-based Hours Press there. The conference 'rolled' from Valencia, to Madrid, to Valencia again, to Barcelona, eventually to Paris where, it was hoped, some of the visa-less original delegates might join it. (Some did. Spender later rounded on others for not doing so.)[42] But the small delegation had been uneasy throughout. Through all the travelling and conferring its duties had been partly fact-finding, partly supportive (especially of fellow intellectuals), partly pre-planning with other nationals future supportive action beyond Spain. Spender however had another, in the end governing, agenda: to find and 'rescue' from the Brigades, which had jailed him for desertion, his ex-lover and one-time Welsh guardsman, Tony Hyndman (a nice fellow: I later knew him briefly). Coolness inside the delegation, given the sexualities composing it, cannot have stemmed from homophobia;[43] but Sylvia and Valentine like Spender accompanied on that occasion by his close friend Cuthbert Worsley, had been in Spain as an independent couple the year before.[44] Such journeys were easy enough to make (Spender had been commissioned by the communist *Daily Worker*), and what you did with your own time was your own business. But as delegates, especially as delegates acting for others balked by the Foreign Office, your time was *not* your own. Sylvia was outraged; Spender, rather nastily, wrote her off as missish.[45] Charles Hobday's account in his *Life* of Edgell Rickword[46] is good about the delegation's work and movements, discreet about Spender. Spender's own doings alone are recorded with sympathy and without fluff, in Cuthbert Worsley's *Fellow Travellers*,[47] a book which is precisely evocative and immensely valuable, in the light of hindsights to come, for other reasons.

'Not novel . . . but memoir . . . fictionalising the names' is how Worsley describes it, recalling a largely gay community not in, but near the Communist Party. Apart from romantic and sexual attachments, these people too are concerned about unemployment, peace, Spain, home-grown fascism, go demonstrating with communists, read – some of them write – the same kinds of book or poem as other left-wing artists. They also possess a very definite idea of what life inside a Communist Party, to which they do *not* belong, entails. There is much talk about its discipline, its obliterations of self, a kind of cloning which Trilling will fix upon later – although in fact when Harry (Hyndman) and, quite separately, Martin (Spender) join, and a more amalgam character, Lady Nellie, draws close, none of the threatened immolations occur. Harry, it is assumed, enjoys discipline anyway because of his guardsman past, Martin is granted the right to make his own rules so is not self-obliterated, Lady Nellie is content to be 'used' so is no clone. The first perception persists however. More and more in this peculiarly honest and moving book, as in some few other, does it seem the case that the Communist Party you dreamed before you got into it was the one you remembered when you got out, whatever being inside was actually like – almost as if it betrayed you by *not* being what is wasn't. And this emotional recollection is entirely in line with characters presented throughout as wholly driven by emotional need and emotional response to events. That, too, seems right: nowhere that I know of has Spender's *Forward from Liberalism* which appeared that same year, 1937, been accused of a rational approach to communism. As Valentine had done, it lurches toward embrace. And here again Sylvia differs from her lover. After the delegation's return to England, she wrote to Edgell Rickword thus:

> In case the question of SS crops up, I would like to tell you what I feel . . . First consideration, that it must be admitted that since he was with us his poetry has definitely fallen off. This may be for internal reasons, it may be a process that would have happened anyhow; but we should not ignore the possibility that this is due to some mismanagement in our treatment . . . SS may not matter very much, but it does matter if our methods are such as to damage imaginative workers, because in that case, whether they leave or stay, we lose them for the best they were worth. . . . This will make him a considerable danger if he chooses to write a Backward from Communism.[48]

Prescient lady: one way and another he was to write several. Nor did his poems ever again attain that glittering late-adolescent sparkle of 1929 and 1933. Nor does Sylvia's communist concern with the quality of poems, which in fact, suit Trilling's fancy.

When I first met Hamilton it was as messenger, returning to him the proofs of *Hangover Square* and a typescript of *The Duke in Darkness*,[49] and as very much the junior in groups of pub-goers including such people as Randall Swingler, Claud Cockburn, Reggie Smith.[50] *Gaslight* was a recent stage hit, *Impromptu in Moribundia* recently published, and *To the Public Danger* had just been broadcast. After Swingler's disappearance into the army and my own re-emergence from it in 1943, and while Hamilton, I now realise, must have been writing *The Slaves of Solitude* and *The Governess* I saw him now and then in necessarily changed company – John Davenport, Arthur Calder Marshall, Jim Phelan, Maurice Richardson, I would have thought Julian Maclaren Ross, though he says not.[51] (When social meeting-places for writers in the wartime blackout were three or four contiguous Soho pubs and another pair off the Strand, many more than Dylan Thomas and Patrick Hamilton drank solidly and long: Orwell, more often considered a sobersides, for one.) However that may be, the list of titles in this paragraph alone is enough to stagger me now, and not a drink in sight.

What is amazing about that list is its sheer inventiveness. French perceives a major switch in Hamilton's direction after the accident, after the crash-course in Marxist reading, after *The Plains of Cement*. This muffles, I think, one truth in another and so disguises a more important continuity. In one sense *each* work represents a major switch in direction – to a Victorian setting, to Swiftian satire, to the new medium of radio, to hotel bedrooms and bars and schizophrenia, to a fairyland dukedom of elegant well-spoken prose, to the boarding house again but this time with characters who also move beyond it, to the Victorians again but this time further entrapped in somnambulism and the biblical rhythms of religious mania. Beside such variety, Hamilton's contemporaries Graham Greene and Christopher Isherwood can sometimes seem formulaic, and a general tendency from Priestley onwards to describe him as Dickensian because of his habit of hitting off character by catch-phrase, quite inadequate to describe what else he does, what he *invents*. But Hamilton's horror of capitalism holds constant through *all* forms, in *every* work, only deepening in disgust and determination for Change as they succeed each other. This constancy was aptly caught by Eric Capon in his discussion of the two Victorian plays in that distant article of 1947:

> this very Victorian middle-class . . . was able, once it had reached the height of its economic power, to establish modes of conduct that were to affect generations to come. This is indicated (in the play) as pointedly as should be necessary. . . . But the main concern, as always with Hamilton, is the steady withering-up of humanity, which is alarming in these Victorian settings because we know that from Manningham (in *Gaslight*) is descended Jock Nixon of *Craven House*, Wyndham Brandon of *Rope* and, most terrifying of all, Netta of *Hangover Square*. . . . Hamilton has charged the thriller-form with a content it is not usually asked to carry. Nor are audiences or critics ready to accept it.[52]

Perhaps it is the case that, having tried excoriation one way, he must follow *Gaslight* by trying another, for the first way on its own has achieved no Change. So *Impromptu in Moribundia* will switch again, to accept the images and phrases of contemporary society – 'the stereotypes and myths of English middle-class culture and consciousness' as Widdowson puts it[53] – quite literally: think-balloons, catch-phrases, noses that *are* dripping taps, queasy stomachs that light up to be *visible* battlegrounds, drunks that are *always* in evening dress and *always* attached to lamp-posts, a working class that can *only* light fires by smashing up grand pianos and storing coal in the bath, a perpetual bosky cricket match in the background. And *Hangover Square* will, in turn, proceed quite differently, restricting the world to a triangle of characters, one a fascist, reducing the triangle further to drunkenness and, within drunkenness, binding things even more tightly by schizophrenia. This last, described by Sean French as the novel's central flaw, is rather its most stupendous invention, for the book thereby *becomes* the Phoney War during which it was written. Within that tiny scope, that micro-scope it allows itself, is the national, perhaps supra-national schizophrenia of persons both engaged in anti-fascist war and actively *not* engaged. It was a schizophrenic *time*.

Then another huge invention, *The Duke in Darkness*, adventuring into fabular history – approximately sixteenth-century but it doesn't matter, for the drives are all contemporary. History has captured the Duke and his servant Gribaud, shoving them into parenthesis – the 'darkness' of the title, Hamilton's typically repetitive use of the word 'night', the Duke's feigned blindness, actual blindness, the blindness of political perception. All revolutionary aspiration, all possibility of progress, has been side-lined by outside cataclysm, by War – yet History *must* continue. The play was written, as far as one can tell, virtually turn and turn about with *Hangover Square*, so is the other side of Phoney War. Michael Redgrave, who both produced and played the part of Gribaud, delighted Hamilton by 'actually understanding the intentions of the author' and 'for being a Bolshie of just about my weight'.[54] Hamilton also pointed out to me, presumably to Redgrave also, that the Duke at one point paraphrases Lenin's *One Step Forward, Two Steps Back*:

> I can see these things. I have had time in my long, long darkness behind these walls, to see these things. . . . And at the end the game belongs to the people. You can work them into every kind of rage – you can suppress and dominate and torture them, as you

do, in their hundreds and hundreds of thousands – for years. And after you . . . there will be those dark or darker than you, to carry on your work. But still, this will not destroy the people. This will make them learn and live the more. You are condemned, however long and cruelly the battle is waged. And then the people will be all the world, and the world all the people – and the world will be its fair self, not the wild arena of slaughter, devilry, and misery it now is.

This is rather to paraphrase the William Morris of *A Dream of John Ball* than any Lenin pamphlet, but what's a source between four comrades (five, if you include the Duke)? French, who had dismissed *Impromptu* as Hamilton in 'sociological mode' dismisses *The Duke* as 'in his perfunctory, public-spirited ENSA mode'. Choice is hard: can French not read a play of images? Or does he believe that ENSA (Entertainment for the National Services Association) promoted calls for revolution?

In 1944 came *The Governess*, never published nor granted the imprimatur of West End production, and indeed apparently now lost save, in what seems to someone like myself shaken to the roots by stage performance, an emasculated radio version.[56] It was I thought at the time, Hamilton's masterpiece – as it is also his first apparent return to something tried before. The character of Inspector Rough and a prosperous Victorian setting are continued from *Gaslight*; but the earlier play had once more implicated the audience in guilt, much as had *Rope*. (Mrs Manningham, the central character, is palpably deluded until a flickering light which we can *see*, so far thought her chief delusion, turns us and the play on our heads.) In *The Governess* something altogether more complicated happens. There is a crime, to understand which we are drawn down and down through levels of catch-phrase, mantra, commonplace, the code, religious mania – at any one of which we may be implicated (overheard, as it were, in the pub) – to the eventual level of a child so terrified by induction, education into this bank-managed world that she walks and talks asleep. Here only, in this subconscious, is Truth to be found. We are at War – in Hamilton's view, at necessary War – and only a whimpering sleeping child retains humanity for us.

Nor is *The Slaves of Solitude* quite the simple return to a boarding house setting it may seem, for now we are at the end of that War, the victorious end of anti-fascism. What is to become of us, Hamilton asks, when here in the character of Mr Thwaites is home-grown fascism still?[57] Clear descendant of that line of bullies from Mrs Nixon who beat Elsie, threatening her with Jock Nixon in *Craven House* twenty years earlier, to Mr Eccles who terrified Elsa at *The Midnight Bell*, to Manningham who tried to madden his wife in *Gaslight*, to the terrible *Governess*, Mr Thwaites becomes, at least in Miss Roach's eyes, synonymous with that Hitler whom 'all the fuss has been about'. The tyrant is not a foreigner but part of the system here, so he must die; and Hamilton allows Miss Roach to kill him and get away with it. *The Slaves of Solitude* was written in 1945 and 1946, when was also the Labour landslide that set in train the Welfare State. Like light under the closed door of a room beyond, there was a sliver of hope: I even remember overhearing the innocent remark, 'My god, we've *voted* the revolution in!' Of all the terrifying characters Patrick ever created, Thwaites is possibly the most imperturbably evil; but still Miss Roach must be allowed to get away with it. They were heady days, those of 1947, when the book came out.

Clearly I have little time for French's attitude to Hamilton's politics, nor for his inability to imagine a time and mind-sets not his own; but French's book does not cheat. The available data is there. Even the synopses of plays and novels are accurate, though totally uninquisitive as to why they develop as they do. The basic problem remains: the habit of piggybacking fiction upon life, at least upon life as represented in the Hamilton Archive. He drank, therefore the drinking in *Hangover Square* is okay, but he was not schizoid, therefore the schizophrenia is a flaw. Or we are in wartime England with an established and popular playwright, popular entertainment was the province of ENSA, therefore *The Duke in Darkness* is ENSA-driven. Put like this the attitude seems silly: it is. Piggybacking is almost a fiction itself. In a very funny and enraged article, Sebastian Faulks complains of the de-magicking effect of the same process in Victoria Glendinning's *Life* of the magical Elizabeth Bowen:

> The novel marketplace is so crowded that many writers have decided that more money and as much creative satisfaction can be found in writing biographies or as the union of biographers has it,

in 'doing someone'. . . . The trouble with all these literary lives is that they lead onward and inward into shrinking and maddening circles.[58]

Faulks might have added 'away' to 'onward and inward', for the further 'in' biography of this sort goes, the more it 'proves' that the created character is 'actually' old so-and-so and the invented place merely that room over there, the further 'off' it scuttles from assessment, criticism, or just plain understanding of drive and purpose in Art. And the hell of it is that the wretched things are accepted. How about this, for instance, on the cover of *The London Review of Books* announcing its review of French's work?

EVERYBODY'S FAVOURITE SAD STALINIST DRUNK[59]

The review itself, called 'First-Class Fellow Traveller', is by that ubiquitous professor Terry Eagleton. He worries about Patrick's lady friends always having an M-sound to their names (Maraja Mackahenie? Martha Smith?), at the monstrosity of his female characters (none as monstrous as Mr Spicer or Mr Thwaites), and at the monstrosity of his men (should you prefer the other form of analysis). Late in the review, it's true the professor washes himself clean of all this stinking fish, ticks French off for dismissing Hamilton's politics 'as a quirk', and begins to consider the possibility that those great howls of Patrick's out of the 1930s and 1940s are such a cry for Humanity as is unvoiced in any of these latter nowadays: not even by Pinter, the ultimate inheritor of Patrick's attitudes to English speech. By now, however, it is too late. Eagleton, the layout man, the journal both of them work for – Media and Academe – have connived at Hamilton's trivialisation and belittlement. We should perhaps ask why, especially since Sylvia's case, though different in form, is another of Faulks's fictions, and to the same effect.

In 1994 were published *The Diaries of Sylvia Townsend Warner* despite a specific request to one of her executors, Susanna Pinney, that they remain unpublished.[60] The book falls into halves, the first of which is a generally happy, chattering record of freelance heterosexual intellectual life in late-1920s London, the second an often painful record of isolated life in Dorset with an increasingly undependable lesbian lover, Valentine Ackland. The story of this second half, we have often been told,[61] also exists in Sylvia's preferred form of letters she and Valentine exchanged and which it was the last great work of her life to edit for publication. No plausible explanation is given for publishing one way what Sylvia had wished another, but one is perhaps implicit in the *Diaries* themselves.

The halving of them is emphasised by a huge gap. A sequence presented as if continuous virtually omits the years 1932 to 1949. Accepting an editorial assurance that, in reducing the total, proportion has been carefully preserved, the average numbers of entries, as published, are between 50 and 100 a year. For the 1932–49 gap however entries are: 12 for 1932, 3 for 1933, 5 for 1934, 4 for 1935, none for 1936, 8 for 1937, none for 1938, none for 1939, 8 for 1940, 8 for 1941, 52 for 1942, none for 1943, none for 1944, 8 for 1945, none for 1946, 1947, 1948. In a journal the end entries of which suggest a span of fifty years, the central seventeen years are missing! There is editorial information suggesting that some of this is the result of Sylvia destroying material, presumably about Valentine, she found too painful to keep, but that cannot apply to the early heydays up to 1938 nor to the war years. Essential to remark therefore that those seventeen years include her most intense political activity (other, that is, than writing, which was always political) and particularly the years of those two staggering mistresspieces, *Summer Will Show* and *The Corner That Held Them*.

Make no mistake. There is not a sentence of Sylvia's I would rather not have read than read. The images gurgle up, even through pain, perpetually; the clauses glide and part, dancing with elegance; a word, a hint at quotation flings open windows on worlds beyond. There's magic in *The Diaries* as in everything else she wrote. But there also are her executors, Susanna Pinney and William Maxwell (her one-time *New Yorker* editor), and their amanuensis, Claire Harman, introducer of reprints of the novels, biographer, editor of *The Collected Poems*, *The Selected Poems* and now *The Diaries* – 'a one-woman Warner factory' indeed, as D.J. Taylor has called her in a review.[62] One needs to be careful, however, of what the factory is tooled to produce. Long ago Eleanor Perenyi drew attention to the peculiarity of the executors' procedure – the oddity of starting to biographise Sylvia by digging out of the *New Yorker* some unremarkable stories as *Scenes of Childhood* (1981), Susanna Pinney's strange decision to collect rejected or otherwise unpublished stories into *One Thing Leading to Another* (1985), the bizarre publication of the awful (and largely incredible) *For Sylvia* (1985), Valentine Ackland's confession of secret drinking.[63] Nor is that all.

In 1979 William Maxwell, the other executor, wrote to me thus of Sylvia:

> Towards the end of her life something she said made me suspect that she would like me to collect and edit a volume of her selected correspondence. I asked her if this was so and she said yes, and later gave me a list of half a dozen people who might have saved her letters. Your name is on it.[64]

There followed a long and increasingly amicable correspondence between Maxwell and myself. I sent him forty to fifty letters from Sylvia and was able to discover others – to Edgell Rickword, for instance. Particularly since Maxwell's experience was American and Sylvia's plainly English and the two so different, at Maxwell's request my letters began to turn more and more on the nature and permanence of Sylvia's political commitment. This seemed helpful and Sylvia on the way to not too great misrepresentation of the Hamilton sort. For instance, Maxwell wrote:

> I feel at last that I am not moving around in a mist. Everything that you say makes sense and if I can just translate it into the impersonal language of a footnote. . . . It seems ludicrous that some future biographer should have to go through the work of reassembling them (the letters). Would you have any objection to my sending the photocopies you provided me with to the museum [at Dorchester, where Sylvia's archive is housed]? And also your letters about her political beliefs, which I think any biographer would be as grateful for as I was. . . .[65]

So much for hope. *Letters*, edited by Maxwell, duly appeared in 1982, containing half of one letter to me, the joke only from one to Rickword, the politics excised from the almost wholly political correspondence with Julius and Queenie Lipton, and all but the safely feminist from the letters to Nancy Cunard, a firm introductory statement by Maxwell that Sylvia's political commitments appear not to have outlasted the War – were almost, it seems, a passing fad – and ninety-four letters to Maxwell and his wife. It is, in a way, a lovely book. Wit flows through it like the River Frome flowing past Sylvia's window. But no letter to Valentine either (to whom, reputedly, she wrote each day) is included – perhaps with better reason.[66] The red, loving heart of the woman is missing.

Trivialisation goes much further however. Once, when I asked her why there had been no novels after *The Flint Anchor* of 1954, she said 'Nothing big enough was left to say. We had fought, we had retreated, we were betrayed, and are now misrepresented. So I melted into the background as best I could, to continue sniping. You can pick odd enemies off, you know, by aiming a short story well'. (To this I had better add, since not everyone understood the words when first printed, that the fight/retreat/betrayal/misrepresentation sequence referred specifically to revolutionary aspiration, hers and mine, in a witch-hunting anti-communist time.) But there is ample support in *The Diaries* for this view of the novels as principal, the stories as secondary work. Frequently novels peter out on her, to her distress, and there are innumerable references to the stories as 'potboilers . . . breadwinners . . .' to be finished 'in order to pay the bills'. This makes the prior concern to publish stories, the lack of any information about the rejected novel or any of those that were never completed, so odd and so many of the references to available novels so fatuous. In by far the most thoughtful of her so-to-speak critical pieces, for instance, Claire Harman writes:

> This is part of what makes *Summer Will Show* a really remarkable historical novel. The ordinariness of historical events, even revolutions, is conveyed intact; there is not a breath of quaintness or 'period feel' to the writing. As in Sylvia Townsend Warner's later novels, *After the Death of Don Juan*, *The Flint Anchor* and, especially, *The Corner That Held Them*, there is a complete identification with the period, a contemporary feel which goes far beyond the scope of historical accuracy to a sense of historical actuality.[67]

Precisely so, and precisely because in essence they are *not* historical but contemporary novels. Sylvia is deeply engaged with her *own* times, is only and always political, and *that* is why whatever the ostensible period, setting and concerns may *seem* to be, however carefully researched for detail, and then however accurately described, the actuality is *now*. (Quite incidentally, because it is a quite different allegorical type of book, not re-living the present as past but mirroring the past, *After the Death of Don Juan*, unlike all the others, reeks of 'quaintness' and 'period feel'.) Again, Claire Harman writes, of *The Corner That Held Them*, in a bibble-babble sixth-form essay of an introduction:

> The main action of the book takes place between the years 1345 and 1382, dates as arbitrary as everything else in the novel.[68]

In fact Sylvia pitched the book very deliberately between the birth of Chaucer ('Well, his first or second birthday', she said: 'I want him on his feet')[69] and the dispersal of the Peasant's Revolt of 1381 ('It's no use leading to an event if it fails. Go for the failure'). The book looks long and coolly from the sidelines of an age when Literature was re-inventing itself from *court* to *English* – as writing by anyone contemplating revolution seriously must presently be about the re-invention of twentieth-century Literature. At the same time the long cool look is at a Black Death raging like fascism and popular risings defeated. Clues abound. When she sends her awful solitary male, Sir Ralph, to read her proto-Chaucer's 'Lay of Mamilion' it is to ask how useful it might be, for example. Without knowing what she was about I had, as it happens, published an article in 1944 about Chaucer and his relationship to the Peasant's Revolt (if any). Sylvia had seen this, and responded in part:

> I wish more writers about writers would remember to put in the circumstances of their economics. It might even help to dissipate this notion that we sing like birds and pick up a few worms.[70]

The book is at that level of practicalness, practical about what Sylvia knew best: women devoting themselves to an ideal even when palpably it was not working ('perhaps especially when it isn't working') and even when, for long passages of time, the cause seems false ('The thing, dear Arnold, is about all kinds of war, in fact'); and it is also feminist in that large sense of the word implied in writing to her well-beloved Nancy Cunard during 1944:

> I have a notice on my table telling me to attend at the Labour Exchange with a view to taking up employment of national importance – which means they will try to put me into a laundry. If I had taken to myself a husband, lived on him and made his life a misery (as undoubtedly I should have done, as no man has ever been able to bear me as a continuity) I should not be troubled with any of this. Being kept by a husband is of national importance enough. But to be feme sole, and self supporting, that hands you over, no more claim to consideration than a biscuit. The great civil war, Nancy, that will come and must come before the world can begin to grow up, will be fought out on this terrain of man and woman, and we must storm and hold Cape Turk before we talk of social justice. . . . How strangely we have met at last! How pell-mell, and how inevitably . . .[71]

That letter frames the mind of the whole book, its depths and ironies and revolt. Oby, the nunnery where almost all the action occurs, is founded because of a man's guilt, and for much of its time is held together by another man, Sir Ralph, whose priesthood is fraudulent.

There is none of Patrick's paring away the settings to single room or cell, no boiling down to irreducible bones of language. Rather, everything imagination can light upon is plucked, picked over, trimmed, chucked in the pot and seethed gently, on and on, spiced, peppered, salted and spiced again with wit. (Her cooking, French sorrel often dominant, was of this order.) Her stories and novels only *seem* to wander, meander, sit where they are and dawdle, be lackadaisical. There is always the meat of the thing, around which all this happens. Though Oby starts as small as anything Patrick might have devised, it extends, comes to administer farmlands, estates, sends itself out on missions beyond. What is constant throughout – though even friendly critics say it is the detailed state of the Abbey – is the state of Sylvia's mind, her purpose. This may appear to dart about, does dart about in a sense, but only to return. Every foray brings back something she seeks, to flavour the meat of the thing: whatever it is that Sylvia discovers to have happened in fourteenth or twentieth centuries, whenever host of assumptions around one central structure begins to crumble under pressure of events outside and within.

Though there's a sense of the whole Abbey, what happens may remain quite private to a single character, or be shared, because that is modern truth as Sylvia knows it. Degrees of faith differ: not all Nuns have any. There is long-standing anti-fascism – what the Americans will shortly be calling 'premature' anti-fascism – there is new-fangled anti-fascism, there is lip-service anti-fascism, there are adherents of Christianity not apparently Christian at all. Faith is not at issue in the book, only its forms and the structures about it. The Home Front in wartime was peopled by women, and Sylvia, particularly in her task of trying to billet evacuees, moved widely among them. The book is populated by women. There has been unfought (Phoney) war, fought war, belated victory, landslid Labour, and now there is Labour's incipient self-betrayal. There is a Nun with visions, a river on which the whole of the Abbey's economy depends which suddenly changes course and alters ownership as drastically as does nationalisation, an Abbess who would build, and plans, a steeple, the steeple's collapse, faith, different versions of faith, loss of faith, structure, destruction. Your perception of the whole of Life *now* is to change because the book astonishes you into seeing how Life *actually* operates.

Trivialising all this into some notion that so huge a writer falls upon dates for her fiction by happenstance begins, in time, to worry one about the probity of what is being done more generally. The emergent pattern is of Sylvia as wit, short story writer, stumblebum, and heroine of a tragic lesbian marriage. (The novels, when mentioned, are treated merely as longer short stories.) I do not mean to imply a conspiracy – unless there are conspiracies of innocence – and am as sure that Pinney and Maxwell loved the lady as that Harman never knew her; but wonder how such people can possibly reveal a genius they do not recognise. One knows, for instance, that many of the stories in *Scenes of Childhood* and *One Thing Leading to Another* are unworthily chosen, that the *Letters* selection is lopsided, that Claire Harman's rejection of what she calls Sylvia's more 'raucous' political poems in *The Collected Poems* (so-called) is odd because so many are in fact included – because the politics is not recognised as political? One knows – at least I know because she told me so – that Claire Harman treated the (then unpublished) *Diaries* as her guide in writing the *Biography*, without realising that a source without its heart can provide little more than a portrait's picture-frame. Now one is compelled to wonder how well or ill edited are *The Diaries* themselves. In his review of them, John Carey noted that they are 'packed with quotations from English, French and German poetry, slipped unmarked into the text, and often adapted to fit the context. Harman's notes never identify these, yet to miss them is to misunderstand that this is a world apprehended through literature as much as through the senses'.[72] In fact the scholarship amounts to little more than the insertion of '*sic*' after usually careless and hurried misspellings which might have been better corrected silently, especially since by no means all the misspellings have been picked up, and a word like 'marrow' stands more awkwardly still without its '*sic*'. As well as textual sources, people too are often unidentified, and not only those noted as 'unidentifiable'. Especially with the huge central omission here and in the Biography alike, the importance of which goes virtually unremarked, one does not feel *safe*, I mean.

> I was sent for to Sissinghurst once. *And* went! The Lady had asked, and civility suggested Yes, and there was an air of 'all us girls together' about myself, Valentine, Vita and whoever her lover then was. She tried me in the White Garden, then in the Blue, then in the Green, but something was lacking. I did not *suit*. So I came home again, I seem to remember with some relief.[73]

That is not from *Diaries* or *Life*, and is carefully chosen as being non-political too, but I'd feel safer if the incident were known. Sylvia kept a deliberate distance from literary gangs, but was widely recognised, for all that. How else could she have conducted those great round robin collections and exhortations during the Spanish Civil War? Why else would the Royal Society of Arts invite her to lecture, or Penguin include her so early in their fiction list? One feels *unsafe* because of all that is missed, because it is not Sylvia but an invention we are offered. In the sense of Faulks's suggestion that literary biographers are spoilt novelists nowadays, it is perhaps more than a Freudian slip that opposite the published title *The Diaries of Sylvia Townsend Warner* there appears under the heading 'By the Same Author' an immodest list of Claire Harman's works – four other editings, of Sylvia and of Robert Louis Stevenson, and her lamentably uncomprehensive biography. We are, after all, in a wholly fictional world. Perhaps it is scarcely surprising, as Simon Watney wrote of Sylvia at the time of Harman's biography:

> Intensely literary, a far leftist, an intellectual to her fingertips, a woman and a lesbian – hardly a combination likely to ensure her reputation in modern Britain. Although British reviewers have praised her recent biography they have all dismissed the subject, either lightly or with vehemence. This is scarcely surprising since, after the 1930s, she abandoned the London literary scene. From the heart of rural England, she wrote with deadly accuracy and wit of the chronic meanness of spirit of British society. That is to say, she cannot be read enough.[74]

Alas, the misconceptions continue – through reviews of *The Diaries*, for instance. Information the book contains is simply accepted as a sum available from which the reviewers can launch themselves out into swamps of theory. This can be simply silly – almost all, for instance, accept Harman's invitation to discuss, school essay fashion, whether diaries are ever written *not* to be published – or actually certifiable. Professor Terry Castle, in the *TLS*[75] claims that what 'saved Warner from herself' *as a writer* who had already produced three extraordinary novels and much great poetry was the marriage to Valentine. Or Anne Chisholm in the Observer[76], whose biography of Sylvia's great friend Nancy Cunard has always seemed to me a model of how to recreate a time, the 1930s, in which you did not yourself live, writes that Sylvia's 'first brilliant success was never quite repeated' meaning, clearly, artistic and not commercial success: has she perhaps not read the later books? The views of Pinney, Maxwell and Harman have become, so far as both Media and Academe are concerned, an incontrovertible orthodoxy. Sylvia was a wit, a short story writer who sometimes extended her talents into longer witty works, Valentine's ultimately tragic lover and, except for a short period of aberration, was apolitical. The end-result is much the same as for Patrick.

Cold War did not begin in 1979 with Trilling and Thatcher. Its long, smeared history goes far far back, well beyond Auden's disowning his magnificent poem 'Spain'. Accumulations of denial, self-denial, redefinition, contradiction, self-contradiction, abolition of both dictionary and common sense, piled up – but slowly: only practice made perfect. Eventually a politics harking back proudly to newly-imagined Victorian Values and the economics of Adam Smith could claim as Thatcherite Revolution what was actually Revanche or Reversal or Reaction: Unchange! passing itself off as Change! What critical position to adopt, how to adopt *any* critical position, in such fogs of nonsense and dispossessions of meaning as have followed must be difficult to those who have known no other weather. And the fog-makers? Dead now, most of them; only these muddled and muddling 'biographers' left to keep on swilling the stuff about. To be kind, I doubt very much if Robert Peel's methodists had any notion of the horrors docility under industrialisation would bring upon their descendants.

> O Lord, what a comfort to be able to get something that isn't just the BBC (which wrote to me the other day, by the way, as Western Regional, politely suggesting I might assist with a little whatnot, and I could not deny myself the rapture of writing back meekly to say that before they entangled themselves further with me they should make sure whether or not I am still on their list of the damned).[77]

So wrote Sylvia in 1946, the bells of victory over fascism still ringing in everyone's ears and Labour in power. Sylvia's experience with a BBC black-list was very common indeed. Montagu Slater, lately head of scripts in the film division of the Ministry of Information, librettist of *Peter Grimes* was, within a few years, unable to get script-work except pseudonymously or by ghosting for others, and published one book at least under another name.[78] Jack Lindsay believed to the end of his days, probably rightly, that a ban had been imposed at the *TLS* on any review of his books.[79] Reggie Smith, drama and sometimes poetry presenter at the BBC and throughout the cold war its token communist, wondered endlessly whether the few old friends he could rescue and bring up for air outweighed his value to the Corporation as 'proof' of non-censorship. Sylvia Townsend

Warner published far more of her persistent 'sniping' in the United States than here. But these of course were the unregenerate, well-known revolutionaries who stood by revolution. What is more interesting, for the moment, is the erstwhile revolutionaries, those who continued to make the films, were all over the journals, filled both air and publishers' lists.

It is here that earlier distinctions really matter – between 'rushing to embrace' and 'needing reason's consent', between a Communist Party of dreams and the Communist Party that (until the mid-1950s, at least) actually was, between a literature regurgitating raw experience and an imaginative literature for active Change, between the emotionally weighted and the intellectually directed. In all those pairings, adherents of the former began, some fifty years ago, to renounce any revolutionary position they may once have held, and the great trail of recusant memoirs, essays, articles and accounts of the 1930s and 1940s began and then was copied – Koestler, Muggeridge, Spender, Symons, Trilling, Bergonzi, Holbrook, Cunningham,[80] shrilling, ten for a shilling – about having been too young to know better, having been hoodwinked, brainwashed, about swallowing reservations in the interests of unity (where others, and at the very time remembered, had managed, like Sylvia in *Summer Will Show* to boost their reservations), about having kept dark on this or that issue (until a convenient Now), about bullying communists who brooked no diversity of view, about a god that failed – but thank god now, they say, we believe in God – about god knows what in the way of personal shame and indignity.

And in parallel to all this, as it were borne away from communism in the baggage of retreat, there came anew the literature of raw experience, hands-on-ism, which grew in extent, direction, level until – via *Dixon of Dock Green* – it even crawled into the House of Lords.[81] Little as they may recognise the fact, or like it, this was a time of authors – comic, sensitive, inventive no doubt, but seldom imaginative – united by 'catching the authentic voice of' or from whose pages 'rose the veritable whiff (or stench) of' or whose 'reality reaches up from the page and grabs the reader'. Even the lowly thriller-writers (and a Ruth Rendell among them can be elevated almost to Orwell-height)[82] must be as experiential as any Zhdanovite[83] – of horse racing, or theatrical backstage, or Roman history, or mediaeval monkery, or international banking or, best of all, of a corrupt police, for make it corrupt in the name of entertainment and surely corruption will matter less. But it's also true of areas apparently more august that approval comes far less often for works of Imaginative Art than for 'detail so well captured' – among the boozy academics of Amis, the lonely spinsters of Anita Brookner, the randy old biddies of Mary Wesley, the pretentious professionals of Iris Murdoch. Kitchensink, Provincial, Redbrick, Royal Court, all are praised for 'authenticity' except, in the latter case, the failed and silenced one among them, the great imaginer John Arden. The final name of this game is Soap, the slithery cleansing stuff, the sagas on the box. Smear the air with it. Butter your friends with it. Wash yourself in a lonely room with it. Suck it and see. (I attended a conference this very year of 1994 in which ex-communists congratulated themselves on *Eastenders* and *Coronation Street* as lineal descendents of Unity Theatre; and so they are. But congratulations? The trouble with experiential writing always is that, by reflecting truthfully the lives of working people, you end by reflecting docility if that is what working people happen to be about: fine when there are great surges of feeling against fascism or for the creation of Welfare, more blunted when there is only broken receptivity for whatever cruelty you are about to receive.) So Soap it is. Work up the lather. Wallow. Economical with the truth of course, leave out 'the whole' and concentrate on the 'nothing but'. Zhdanovism beloved of Stalin, Kitchensink; Thatcherism beloved of Reagan, Soap: theoretical bigotry goes slithering down the pan and into the mainstream.

These are capitalism's twentieth-century desiderata. This is the 'culture' which a younger generation of critics, biographers, spoilt novelists perhaps among them, has breathed, fed upon, digested, grown by and now begins to disgorge in turn. Their elders are less easy to forgive.

Towards the end of her life, perhaps provoked by her own nay-saying introductions to the earlier Virago reprints,[84] Sylvia took strongly against *Lolly Willowes*. ('So poor a welcome for the General Strike. . . . Lolly must of course support the miners, for she was meant to be likeable'.)[85] At the same time she began to approve strongly of *After the Death of Don Juan* – so strongly indeed as to press a second copy upon my wife and myself ('It's politics are so very good') while also recommending it to David Garnett whose politics she loathed. It was the novel that followed immediately upon that sorry Spanish delegation, and is by Sylvia's standards a very narrowly political allegory with Don Juan as 'more of a fascist'[86] against a cross-section of classes in conflict. It is perhaps her only attempt at a 'sectarian novel as a circus with a message', written for the converted and not for Change. Her wanting it liked is understandable enough – a plain desire to be recognised as revolutionary to the end – but her sense of politics and Change was deeper than the surfaces at which *After the Death of Don Juan* operates. Filtering hands-on experience of Spain through a sieve of allegory was not, I think, her genius. Not long after her recommending the book, she said of *The Flint Anchor* (of 1954) that it was 'her work on Hypocrisy – neglected, I can but suppose, because by 1954 the worm of McCarthyism had got into English criticism as well, and corrupted it'.[87]

1954 was also the year of Patrick's rounding off *The Gorse Trilogy* with its brusque but benedictive *Unknown Assailant*, the only book of his that I know to end with characters walking out under an open sky. Both authors have that Prospero air of burying their magic arts, their Art, before departing elsewhere. They are saying what they had always said, for one last time: this society is foul. It need not be. it breeds foulness. It need not. Change it, as we have tried to do. Change.

Notes

1. E.P. Thompson, 'The Transforming Power of the Cross' in *The Making of the English Working Class*. London, 1963, p. 355, (Harmondsworth, 1968, p. 390).
2. The definition is Edgell Rickword's. See Charles Hobday, *Edgell Rickword: Poet at War* Manchester, 1969, for various versions of the concept.
3. Chiefly unavailable are: Patrick Hamilton, *Craven House*, *Impromptu in Moribundia*, *The Duke in Darkness*, *The Governess* (never published); Sylvia Townsend Warner, *After the Death of Don Juan* London, 1938, *The Flint Anchor* London, 1954. Her *Collected*

Poems is actually very selective, the Selected a numbingly 'personal' choice. Poetry collections published in her lifetime are all o.p. Two posthumous collections of short stories (q.v.) are unworthy, the dozen collections in her lifetime all o.p., the Selected Stories London, 1988 gives a somewhat eccentric cross-section of this part of her work, which has nothing like the importance of the novels and poems.
4. Bruce Hamilton, The Light Went Out London 1972; Nigel Jones, Through a Glass Darkly, London, 1991; Sean French, Patrick Hamilton: a biography, London, 1993. Jones is the best of these.
5. Introductions are: J.B. Priestley, Twenty Thousand Streets Under the Sky, London, 1935, and Hangover Square, Harmondsworth; reprint 1974; Claud Cockburn, The Slaves of Solitude Oxford, 1982; Michael Holroyd, Twenty Thousand Streets Under the Sky, London, 1987.
6. Except for Philip Hensher, 'Second to Nun', The Guardian 7 December 1993, the plaudits are strewn through all three biographies (note 4).
7. The celebrating journal is Poetry Nation Review 23, Manchester, 1981; Bea Howe's introduction is to Valentine Ackland, For Sylvia, London, 1985; Wendy Mulford, This Narrow Place, Sylvia Townsend Warner and Valentine Ackland: Life, Letters and Politics, 1930–1951, London, 1988; Claire Harman, Sylvia Townsend Warner, A Biography London, 1989; Sylvia Townsend Warner, Letters, ed. William Maxwell, London, 1982; The Diaries of Sylvia Townsend Warner, ed. Claire Harman, London, 1994.
8. Eric Capon, 'The Strange Case of Patrick Hamilton' in Theatre Today 'Winter Miscellany', London, 1947.
9. P.J. Widdowson, 'The Saloon Bar Society' in John Lucas (ed.) The 1930s: a Challenge to Orthodoxy, Hassocks, 1978.
10. Eleanor Perenyi, 'The Good Witch of the West' in The New York Review of Books, 19 July, 1985; Simon Watney, 'Townsend Warner: Love's Labours Lost' in Village Voice, 23 January, 1980, New York.
11. The novels are Monday Morning, 1925; Craven House, 1926; Twopence Coloured, 1929; The Midnight Bell, 1929, The Siege of Pleasure, 1932 and The Plains of Cement, 1934 (the last three combined as Twenty Thousand Streets Under the Sky, 1935), Impromptu in Moribundia, 1939; Hangover Square, 1941; The Slaves of Solitude 1947; and The West Pier, 1951, Mr Stimson and Mr. Gorse, 1953, Unknown Assailant, 1955 (the last three combined as The Gorse Trilogy, 1992). All London. The stage plays are Rope, 1929; Gaslight, 1939; The Duke in Darkness, 1943; The

Governess (unpublished), 1944; *The Man Upstairs*, 1954. All London except as noted. The radio plays are *Money with Menaces* and *To the Public Danger*, one volume, London, 1939; *This is Impossible*, London, 1942.
12. Drunkenness occasionally in *Twenty Thousand Streets*, combined with Schizophrenia in *Hangover Square*; Silence between classes, *Craven House* and *The Slaves of Solitude* especially, but general; Somnambulism, *The Governess*; Blindness, *The Duke in Darkness*.
13. *Craven House*, pp. 155–6.
14. *Craven House*, p. 213. The notable point here is that, as early as 1926, Hamilton is using the term 'fascist' for political reaction.
15. Richard Eyre, *Utopia and Other Places*, London, 1993.
16. Dominic Hibberd, *Owen the Poet*, London, 1986, Appendix A(7) lists Harold's major suppressions briefly, but the whole book is revelatory.
17. Bruce Hamilton, *A Case for Cain*, unpublished. See French, *Patrick Hamilton*, q.v.
18. Sylvia Townsend Warner and Valentine Ackland, *Whether a Dove or a Seagull*, 1999, New York, 1933, London, 1934.
19. Sylvia Townsend Warner, *Letters*, p. 29, to Oliver Watney.
20. For example, Anita Miller, introduction to *Lolly Willowes*, Chicago, 1980, – e.g. The claim is not infrequent.
21. Valentine Ackland, *For Sylvia*, q.v.
22. Claire Harman, *Sylvia Townsend Warner: a Biography*; Valentine Ackland, *For Sylvia*.
23. Claire Harman, introduction to *Summer Will Show*, London 1987.
24. Lionell Trilling, *The Last Decade*, New York, 1979, pp. 140–1. Quoted in French, *Patrick Hamilton*.
25. The mock-up coffin carried on unemployed workers' demonstrations, chiefly in London, possession of which often led to battles with the police.
26. Valentine Ackland, *Country Conditions*, London, 1936, the only prose book published in her lifetime.
27. Sylvia Townsend Warner to Julius Lipton, 13 November, 1936, unpublished.
28. Hugh Sykes Davies's *Petron* was regarded as the only native surrealist novel; Hansford Johnson's novel was *The Trojan Horse*.
29. This view derives partly from the journals *Left Review, Poetry and the People, Our Time* and *Seven* – not of course from the pronouncements of official party cultural spokesmen – but chiefly from my friendships.
30. Holroyd, introduction to *Twenty Thousand Streets*, 1987, op. cit.

31. Townsend Warner to Arnold Rattenbury, 16 September 1974, unpublished.
32. W.H. Auden, *The Dyer's Hand*, London, 1975.
33. Montagu Slater, *Stay Down Miner*, London, 1936, p. 75. This is the book of reportage, not the play of the same name.
34. Julius Lipton, *Poems of Strife*, London, 1936.
35. Andy Croft, *Red Letter Days: British Fiction in the 1930s*, London 1990. Other critic/historians in this field are Gustav Klaus and Jurgen Enkermann.
36. John Summerfield, *May Day*, London, 1936, reprinted 1984; *Trouble in Porter Street*, London, 1938.
37. Townsend Warner to Julius Lipton, 12 May 1936, unpublished.
38. The fact crops up often in both *Letters* and *Diaries* – as it did in conversation.
39. French, *Patrick Hamilton*, p. 154.
40. Stephen Spender, *New Statesman*, 1 May 1937; *The God That Failed*, 1950; *World Within World*, 1977; *The Thirties and After*, 1978 (which also reprints his 'Notes on the International Congress 1937' from *New Writing 4*, Autumn 1937), all London.
41. Chiefly Charles Hobday and Cuthbert Worsley q.v.
42. Stephen Spender, article in *London Mercury*, August 1937.
43. Wendy Mulford, *This Narrow Place* suggests homophobia.
44. Harman, *Sylvia Townsend Warner* and Worsley q.v. both mention this.
45. Stephen Spender, the *World Within World* version (note 41).
46. Charles Hobday, *Edgell Rickword: Poet at War*.
47. T.C. Worsley, *Fellow Travellers*, London, 1971. The 1984 reprint (Gay Men's Press) has a useful introduction by Paul Binding, good on who's who fact-to-fiction, less so on 1930s politics.
48. Townsend Warner to Edgell Rickword, unpublished in *Letters* but partly quoted in Harman, *Sylvia Townsend Warner* and Hobday, *Edgell Rickwood*.
49. I describe this episode further in 'Total Attainder and the Helots' in *The 1930s a challenge*.
50. R.D. Smith (Reggie), husband of Olivia Manning and central figure in her *Balkan Trilogy*.
51. Julian Maclaren Ross, *Memoirs of the Forties*, London, 1954.
52. Capon, 'The Strange Case of Patrick Hamilton'.
53. Widowson, 'The Saloon Bar Society'.
54. Quoted in French, *Patrick Hamilton*, p. 176.
55. Hamilton, *The Duke in Darkness*, p. 56.
56. *The Governess*, after touring, played briefly at the Embassy Theatre, Swiss Cottage. Immensely thorough searches for all Hamilton texts

were carried out by Brian McKenna towards a doctoral thesis on Hamilton. Not even the Lord Chamberlain's Office has *The Governess* despite its public performance. The radio version, though by Hamilton himself, loses visual, mobile and aural tensions and reads flatly.
57. Claud Cockburn, in his introduction to *Slaves of Solitude* op.cit. claims that Hamilton came under suspicion at communist party headquarters because his portrait of Thwaites was so real. This is Claud at his inventive silliest. He was less often at those headquarters at that time than I, and Hamilton's book was greatly admired there.
58. Sebastian Faulks, 'Get a Life, Elizabeth', *Guardian Weekend*, 5 February 1994.
59. London Review of Books, 2 December 1993.
60. Claire Harman, introduction *Diaries*.
61. Maxwell, introduction *Letters*, Harman, *Autobiography* and introduction to *Diaries*.
62. D.J. Taylor, 'Cry Beyond the Art', *The Independent*, 16 July, 1994.
63. Eleanor Perenyi, 'The Good Witch of the West'.
64. William Maxwell to Arnold Rattenbury, 1 August, 1979.
65. William Maxwell to Arnold Rattenbury, 10 December 1982, 8 April 1983.
66. The given reason is Townsend Warner's own edition of letters between herself and Ackland which is, some day, to be published, but the result is lopsided for all that, enforcing the view of Sylvia as wit above all.
67. Claire Harman, introduction to *Summer Will Show*, London, 1987.
68. Claire Harman, introduction to *The Corner That Held Them*, London, 1988.
69. Conversation with Arnold Rattenbury, as are subsequent bracketed quotations from here on. These conversations were chiefly in the 1960s and 1970s.
70. Townsend Warner to Arnold Rattenbury, 24 August 1944 unpublished. The article referred to appeared in *Our Time*, August 1944.
71. Townsend Warner to Nancy Cunard, 28 April 1944, in *Letters*, Mulford, *This Narrow Place* and Harman *Biography*, all op.cit – very properly.
72. John Carey, 'Days in the Life', *Sunday Times* 12 June 1994.
73. Townsend Warner to Arnold Rattenbury in conversation.
74. Simon Watney, 'Townsend Warner: Love's Labour Lost'.
75. Terry Castle, 'The Will to Whimsy', *The Times Literary Supplement*, 3 June 1994.

76. Anne Chisholm, 'Seal, Salmon and Sylvia', *Observer Review*, 19 June 1994.
77. Townsend Warner to Nancy Cunard, 1946, unpublished.
78. Richard Johns (Montagu Slater), *Man with a Background of Flames*, London, 1954.
79. Jack Lindsay, *Life Rarely Tells*, Harmondsworth, 1982. Contains the three volumes of autobiography. It is the last of these, *Fanfrolico and After*, that is relevant here.
80. Valentine Cunningham, *British Writers of the Thirties*, Oxford 1988. Much praised, this work omits all mention of Hamilton and O'Casey and is scathing about Sylvia Townsend Warner.
81. Ted Willis, one-time author (with a committee) of *Buster*, a Unity Theatre hit, ended up as Lord Willis. In general, a spokesman for what I have called experiential writing about and by 'the ordinary man', he was one of the few practicing Zhdanovites in the communist party.
82. Julian Symons has sedulously advanced the claims of both Orwell and Ruth Rendell to high Art.
83. Zhdanov (see also note 81) was Stalin's personal Arts spokesman.
84. Townsend Warner, in old age, wrote slightly twee accounts of the writing of *Lolly Willowes, Mr Fortune's Maggot* and *The True Heart*, used as introductions to the Virago reprints of 1978.
85. Conversation with Arnold Rattenbury. See note 69.
86. Townsend Warner, *Letters*, where she also calls the book 'a parable of the political chemistry of the Spanish War', not the sort of claim she made for anything else. While this chapter was being prepared appeared *Sylvia and David: the Townsend Warner/Garnett Letters*, ed. Richard Garnett, London, 1994. In respect of this chapter's main argument, it should be noted that here again is a huge gap – of twenty-three years – through the centre of Sylvia's life.
87. Townsend Warner to Arnold Rattenbury in conversation – the same occasion, incidentally, as the conversation about the absence of novels after *The Flint Anchor*. See also *Poetry Nation Review*, 23, 1981.

11 '... itself irradiated by the thing it attacks': Lawrence Ferlinghetti's 'One Thousand Fearful Words for Fidel Castro' and its political contexts

R.J. Ellis

I

Lawrence Ferlinghetti's poem 'One Thousand Fearful Words for Fidel Castro' was written in late 1960 in San Francisco and published in January 1961.[1] It was brought out by Ferlinghetti's small press, City Lights as a pocket-sized 'broadside' containing just this one poem, in a format similar to that of his Pocket Poets Series, which had been designed to enable purchasers easily to slip the booklets into their pockets, and priced cheaply enough to encourage them to do so.[2] The poem was made readily available by being sold at rallies in support of Fidel Castro's Cuba. Ferlinghetti had in fact dubbed his poetry 'street poetry',[3] and described 'One Thousand Fearful Words' as one of his 'broadside' poems; as such he launched the poem in a public performance at a 'Fair Play for Cuba' rally in San Francisco in January 1961.[4] It was designed to be recited, and was frequently read aloud at poetry readings in various venues in San Francisco. The poem thus, conventionally, possesses a refrain, 'I see no way out/ . . . /in the course of human events',[5] which centrally and ominously defines the fearfulness of which the poem's title speaks.

The historical source of this fearfulness is plain enough, and helps contextualise its public and aural search for immediacy: both of performance and of reception – in what might be described as a search for a wide hearing. Cuba, at the time of this poem's composition, was coming under substantial pressure from the United States. Castro had only recently assumed control of the island. The 'invasion' by Castro, 'Che' Guevara and others aboard the 'Granma' had occurred in 1956, Batista's dictatorship had been overthrown in January 1959, and Castro had assumed quasi-dictatorial control of the position of Prime Minister in July 1959.[6] Throughout this period, the United States government's primary concern – it might fairly be described as an obsession – was the extent to which Castro should be identified as a communist fellow traveller or sympathiser. This concern had been so ferociously articulated in the US's diplomatic contacts with Castro's government that it had become increasingly commonly interpreted by Cubans as foreign interference in Cuba's internal affairs, thus alienating Cuba from the United States, exacerbating tensions between the two countries and, in a bald irony, causing Cuba to turn to other sources of foreign support and assistance at a difficult time in its development, both politically and economically. Given the Monroe and Truman doctrines, which together defined the US's worldwide opposition to Communism and Latin America as a hemispheric zone of influence fundamental to US interests (and by implication, not a concern of its Western allies), the only possible alternative source of support was the USSR. Yet by turning in this direction Cuba intensified the circle of mistrust and tension between itself and the United States: July 1960 had seen the introduction of a raft of US economic sanctions which had already been preceded by a military embargo.[7]

It is this nexus that in part inhibits me from making any claim about the possession of prescience by this poem. It predicts the US will 'get' Castro just a few months before April 1961, when the 'Bay of Pigs' invasion by Cuban exiles relying on US military equipment and substantial CIA support did indeed try to 'get' him.[8] However, even taken alone, the Monroe and Truman doctrines made entirely predictable the idea that the United States would seek to do something about Castro's growing contacts with Soviet Russia. Moreover, the rapidly growing military support for Cuban exiles on the US government's part was in the process of being reported, albeit patchily, in a few (mostly radical) US journals – noteworthily, *The Nation*, which is where Ferlinghetti read about these developments.[9] How much about this military support was generally known in the United States is unclear. It will be my contention that Ferlinghetti's poem moves in this terrain of uncertainty, aiming itself at more than one level of knowledge concerning the extent to which the US government was committed to 'get[ting]' Castro 'in the course of human events'.

A key fact is that the poem does not consist of 'One Thousand . . . Words' because Ferlinghetti 'left room for a happier ending, in case the relentless hostility of government and press in the U.S. should somehow not triumph in the end'. This explanation appeared on the back of the original City Lights broadside, in a note which also explained that 'The poem in its present form was first read by Ferlinghetti at a rally in San Francisco one week before the end of the Eisenhower Era', further placing the poem in its precise political context: the threshold of Kennedy's inauguration.[10] The version reprinted here is a subsequent version consisting of 749 words, which appeared (after a second version appearing in *Evergreen Review* in May/June 1961), in the collection *Starting from San Francisco*, published by New Directions later in 1961. This is the most readily available version; the differences from the original are minor and are possibly a consequence of its evolving oral identity.[11]

At readings, of course, the poem would be discovered by the listener at this immediate and aural level; Ferlinghetti has therefore pitched it at one basic level as easily accessible. Its registers are colloquial and vernacular and it offers some very widely known cultural allusions: to the 'Declaration of Independence' and Abraham Lincoln's presidency, set as learning tasks for virtually every US schoolchild, and to artefacts of American leisure (pool tables, transistor radios, pinball machines, nickelodeons, Cadillacs). By bringing the topic into the terrain of the everyday the poem invites the listener to consider how the two impinge on one another. By juxtaposing US policy towards Cuba with 'paisanos playing pool', for example, the poem suggests the way in which the multiple pleasures of US cultural amusements provide constant depoliticising distractions which are at the same time symptoms of the affluent consumption patterns that mark out the United States as a privileged Western nation of enormous, seductive power. Thus the cowboy ballad's jukebox 'groan[ings]' about ' "a Cadillac" ' which he has 'got himself' are sandwiched between a reference to Fidel sinking like a billiardball in a 'felt pocket', 'in the course of human events', and the starkly made point that Cuba's economic conditions do not allow access to such luxury goods: 'He didn't get it in Cuba, baby'. The framing references to the 'Declaration of Independence' are intended to jolt the listener into a recognition of the interrelationship between these 'human events'. This is elaborated upon by a constant return to Jefferson's document as a quasi-refrain. Through this choral return to the Declaration of Independence Ferlinghetti's listeners are led to confront the question as to what independence/dependence is at stake, and as to what relationship there might exist between the US's American revolution against British imperialism and the Cuban revolution. In the example I am here focusing on, at the end of the first stanza, the phrase 'in the course of human events', sandwiched as it is between the image of Castro sinking down a pocket – a billiardball directed by an unnamed hand – and the 'cowhand' moaning about Cadillacs, begins to establish a referential frame setting 1960s US control and wealth besides the US's revolutionary origins and historical aspirations. This paves the way for more sustained later allusions. By constantly interlacing the US's economic powerplays in the early 1960s with references to the US's rejection of British imperial control in the War of Independence in the 1770s, these imply that a present-day imperialism lurks within the economic blockade of Cuba. Thus, the ideological representation of these sanctions against Cuba as an anti-Communist crusade is peeled away. The reference in stanza seven to Abraham Lincoln, 'his' enormously costly Civil War, and 'Liberat[ion]' in turn allies all this, referentially, to the issue of slavery and its abolition: the heavy irony of 'since no one was shot in his [Lincoln's] war' causes the listener to confront the issue of just what can constitute justifiable violence.

The poem not only raises such key considerations but also, as it develops, nudges the listener towards intenser contemplation of these most difficult of political issues. Ferlinghetti's reference to his not having 'quite finished Camus' *Rebel*' invites the listener to discover what it is that Camus postulates in that his text's closing pages concerning rebellion and independence.[12] The listener is thus invited to consider further the political debate set up concerning power, control and independence so central to Cuban motives in rejecting US diktats about its foreign and domestic policies – a rejection driving Cuba into ever closer alliance with the USSR.[13] The poem invites the listener to become a reader, quite literally – and to read on. Put baldly, 'Have *you* read Camus' *The Rebel*?' is the implicit question, but if the answer is already 'Yes' the poem offers a second level of debate. An example here would be the way that reference to Lincoln leads on in the next (and final) stanza to reference to Whitman's elegy to the death of Lincoln 'one of [Castro's] boyhood heroes', 'When Lilacs Last in the Dooryard Bloom'd'.[14] This draws into centre-frame the issue of assassination. Here one might more confidently suggest the poem possesses insight: the CIA-inspired assassination attempt on Castro by Marita Lorenz in 1960 was not generally known at the time Ferlinghetti wrote his poem.[15] This is one source of the poem's fearfulness, but the reference also draws upon the recognition that to liberate slaves is to make powerful enemies who will oppose you even after your success, and provides another dimension to the ramifications of the powerplays the poem explores: the transposition of the quotation 'I give you my sprig of lilac' as 'I give you my sprig of laurel' is carefully judged here, intimating as it does the idea of victory being able to endure beyond the death of Castro, and the glossing of the paradox 'your futile trip is done/yet is not done/ and is not futile' of the preceding lines. The whole issue of the place of rebellion in history is thus opened up, and dialectically feeds into the quotation from Camus.

Thus the poem operates at differing levels of complexity, and it is worthwhile notating how these operate beyond the basic level at which the poem can be heard and understood. We are dealing with levels of listening and reading that greatly concerned Ferlinghetti at this time:[16] it is significant that the first edition of *Starting* included as an insert inside its back cover a disc containing recordings of three of the collection's 'broadsides'. The poem works at different levels of sophistication, and I have chosen to enumerate these on a three-point scale (A – C), within which the poem moves. Level A represents the most direct and surface (commonly understood) allusions. Level B represents allusions which would be more-or-less readily available to most readers of the poem, and to some, perhaps most, listeners at an oral performance. Level C represents allusions depending on relatively specialised or restricted knowledge.

Ferlinghetti was not only an active member of the Fair Play for Cuba Committee in San Francisco, but he also encountered a large number of Latin American poets (including Cubans) at the Writer's Conference in Concepcíon, Chile in January 1959 and, most importantly, he visited Cuba in December of 1960 and met with several young Cuban poets through the auspices of the Cuban Writers' Union. He had also recently discovered he had Caribbean ancestors and survivng Caribbean relatives and this enhanced his interest in Caribbean affairs. (He visited some of his relatives in the Virgin Islands on his way to Cuba in 1960.[17]) His journals indicate that Ferlinghetti was impressed by what he saw in Cuba: 'All I have seen so far indicates Havana, and Cuba in general, are much better off economically than all other Caribbean countries' (4 December 1960).[18] This knowledge, however, does not lead Ferlinghetti into composing a disguised, didactic history lesson. Instead he creates a poem that operates, on one level of allusion, on the assumption that his readers/listeners possess good knowledge of this history, while simultaneously the poem can be coherently followed without any such detailed knowledge, since these allusions are rooted within more broadly available cultural referents, such as the United Fruit Company's general identity as a rapacious multinational.

A second underlying assumption here is that an aural encounter with the poem provides less time for reflection, and thus reduces the likelihood that all its allusions will be recognised. In reading, Ferlinghetti used pauses and emphases in careful modulations in order to provide audiences with the best opportunity to process the poem's allusions, but the multi-level allusion-structure is in itself an attempt to negotiate the inevitable disparity between aural and visual (reading) reception, by enabling the poem's protest concerning US policy towards Castro's Cuba to operate on different levels. This is what I now hope to establish.

> I am sitting in Mike's Place trying to figure out
> what's going to happen
> without Fidel Castro

(i) Mike's place: A/B: a cafe frequented by Ferlinghetti and a number of other Bay area poets. This introduction of an everyday feature of San Franciscan life establishes the basic dialectic between Cuba's development and US interests. More accessibly, the name 'Mike's Place' is commonplace and vernacular-sounding, in itself. (Ferlinghetti had previously set other poems of his in Mike's Place – such as 'Autobiography' in *A Coney Island of the Mind*.[19])

> It's going to be a tragedy
> I see no way out
> among the admen and slumming models

(ii) admen and slumming models: B: in 1961 the so-called San Francisco Renaissance, an explosion of interest in poetry and poetry writing, was in full swing, and the Beats were attracting the attentions of the commercial and fashion worlds (– the Beatnik look). Ferlinghetti's choice of admen and models is further significant in that it introduces the theme of careless consumption and its impediment to political engagement. Also obliquely raised: C: the issue of cultural appropriation, which becomes a central burden of the poem.

> and the brilliant snooping columnists
> who are qualified to call Castro psychotic
> because they no doubt are doctors
> and have examined him personally
> and know a paranoid hysterical tyrant when they see one
> because they have it on first hand
> from personal observation by the CIA
> and the great disinterested news services

(iii) from 'brilliant snooping columnists' to 'news services': A: it was a commonly held view in the US government at the time that Castro was mentally unstable; the commonest accusation was that he was a 'paranoid hysteric'; the CIA helped actively promulgate this view. ('Evidence' for this was, among other things, the fact that he wore two wrist-watches.[20]) This view was commonly adopted by the media in the latter part of 1960.

> And Hearst is dead but his great Cuban wire still stands:
> "You get the pictures, I'll make the war"

(iv) from 'Hearst is dead' to 'I'll make the war': A/B/C: Hearst's 'wire' (February 1897) in fact read: 'You furnish the pictures and I'll furnish the war.' The misquote here reproduces the popularly remembered version. The telegraph was sent to the artist and cartoonist Frederic Remington, who responded by sending back a drawing of a young Cuban woman stripped naked and surrounded by police. This allegedly depicted an incident in which Spanish police had detained three Cuban women on the US ship Olivetti in search of secret documents as part of Spanish attempts to put down the Cuban war of independence. The drawing was printed in the *New York Journal*, purchased by Hearst in 1895 when embroiled in a circulation war with Pulitzer's papers. Above the drawing appeared the banner headline 'Does Our Flag Protect Women?' (12 February 1897). In fact, when they arrived in the United States, the women denied being searched by men, but the cartoon created a storm. War between the US and Spain came in 1898, after constant stoking by Hearst's and Pulitzer's papers. The *Journal*'s headline of 9 May 1898 read: 'HOW DO YOU LIKE THE JOURNAL'S WAR?' This issue sold a million copies. Beyond this recall of the U.S. media's mendacity, however, the reference to the war of 1898 introduces the role of interference in Cuba in the making of US political careers. Theodore Roosevelt (then Assistant Secretary of the Navy), had consistently attacked President McKinley for hesitating over Cuban intervention. McKinley had finally gone to war at a time when the Spanish were already, according to their diplomatic representations, prepared to withdraw peaceably. Roosevelt then led the volunteer cavalry regiment the Rough Riders into some high-profile heroics in the resulting war. Soon afterwards, he was elected Governor of New York State. By the end of 1904 he was President. Roosevelt also promulgated the so-called Roosevelt Corollary to the Monroe doctrine in 1904, which effectively gave the US the power to police Latin America: this further reinforced the Platt Amendment of 2 March 1901 which allowed for US intervention in Cuban affairs 'to maintain the independence of Cuba, and to protect the people thereof'.[21] Both Roosevelt's partly Cuban-based political successes and the Platt Amendment can be related to the 1960 Presidential campaign. During this campaign Kennedy had attacked Eisenhower for not taking a more active line of resistance to what he presented as Communist infiltration of Cuba. Kennedy had also allowed his own war record to form part of his electoral platform when defeating Nixon. He was to be inaugurated in January 1961, just after Felinghetti's poem was published as a broadside (see below).[22]

> I see no answer
> I see no way out
> among the paisanos playing pool

(v) paisanos: A: the use of this Spanish-American word draws attention to the imperialist thread running through Latin American history, and the competition between Spain and the United States that had culminated in the Spanish American war over Cuba (see note iv, above). That the paisanos play pool economically reinforces the theme of cultural appropriation.

> it looks like Curtains for Fidel

(vi) Curtains for Fidel: A: the capital 'C' draws attention to the pun, which refers to the Iron Curtain and hence Communism. In performance, Ferlinghetti usually 'capitalised' the word through oral emphasis.

> They're going to fix his wagon

(vii) 'fix his wagon': A/B: this phrase invokes the exploitation of the vernacular in the populist rhetoric of politicians 'on the stump' during election campaigns.

> in the course of human events

(viii) 'in the course of human events': A/C: a reference to the Declaration of Independence, building on the Imperial theme (see above). However, *Human Events* is also a right-wing periodical which was, throughout the period 1957–61, denouncing the US government's failure to strike at Castro because he was, in that organ's analysis, a 'Communist'. See, for example, Spraille Braden's 'Communist in the Caribbean', *Human Events*, 17 August 1957.

> In the back of Mike's the pinball machines
> shudder and leap from the floor
> when Cuban Charlie shakes them
> and tries to work his will
> on one named "Independence Sweepstakes"

(ix) from 'Cuban Charlie shakes them' to ' "Independence Sweepstakes" ': A/B: large numbers of Cuban supporters of Batista's regime fled Cuba as Castro took over: wealthy capitalist entrepreneurs, members of the army and secret police guilty of atrocities and other crimes, and other Cubans opposed to the revolution. Charlie is cheating at pinball, here, in an attempt to control the progress of 'Independence': independence is indeed at stake.

> Each pinball wandered lonely as a man

(x) 'Each pinball wandered lonely as a man': B: the misquote here makes explicit the analogy between Castro and a ball in a US bar amusement game, suggesting vividly the signficance of US public interest; but it also highlights Ferlinghetti's allegiance in this broadside to the revolutionary, public and political in the Romantic legacy, rather than the nature poetry of the Lakeside Wordsworth, wandering 'lonely as a cloud'.[23] The purpose, if you like, is to dispel 'clouds' and show the human issues at stake.

> siphons thru and sinks
> no matter how he twists and turns
> A billiardball falls in a felt pocket
> like a peasant in a green landscape

(xi) 'a peasant in a green landscape': B/C: the majority of casualties in the Cuban revolution had been peasants (some as conscripts in Batista's army, sometimes via Batista's army's atrocities, some as guerrilla casualties; Castro's army has been characterised as a peasant army).[24]

> On the nickelodeon a cowboy ballad groans
> "Got myself a Cadillac" the cowhand moans
> He didn't get it in Cuba, baby

(xii) from ' "Got myself a Cadillac" ' to 'didn't get it in Cuba': A/C: the Cadillac is an obvious icon of US consumerism. However, it is also true that in the late 1950s the highest concentration of Cadillacs in any city in the Americas was to be found in Batista's Havana, which served as a playground for the American rich and the Cuban aristocracy. Imports of Cadillacs ceased immediately after Castro's revolution.[25]

> Outside in the night of North Beach America
> the new North American cars flick by
> from Motorama
> their headlights never bright enough
> to dispel this night
> in the course of human events

(xiii) 'this night/in the course of human events': A: this third reference to the Declaration of Independence clarifies the idea that the US is on the verge of darkening not only Cuban history, but in a key sense its own cultural legacy. The poem's refrain is both accessible and resonant.

> Three creepy men come in
> One is Chinese
> One is Negro
> One is some kind of crazy Indian
> They look like they may have been
> walking up and down in Cuba

(xiv) 'One is Chinese . . . up and down in Cuba': A/B: this 'brotherhood' economically draws together the strands of American and Cuban history. The 'crazy Indian' refers not only to the US imperialist conquest of Native American civilisation and the psychoses that commonly resulted among the conquered, but also to the Native American 'Indian' peasants who supported Castro and suffered reprisals from Batista. The 'negro[es]' have similar, obvious, Cuban and US referents. The Chinese, as well as being a persecuted minority of particular importance in the Bay

Area, were also as a nation the only other main source of international support for Castro. Ferlinghetti here aims to establish further that his listeners/readers have all around them reminders of the imperialist and exploitatory dimensions of the Cuban question – the interrelatedness of the issue in historical terms.

> but they haven't
> All three have hearing aids
> It's a little deaf brotherhood of Americans
> The skinny one screws his hearing aid
> in his skinny ear
> He's also got a little transistor radio
> the same size as his hearing aid box
> For a moment I confuse the two

(xv) 'For a moment I confuse the two': B/C: a recurrent concern of the poets and writers of the San Francisco Renaissance, and of the Beats, was the multiplicity of media inputs of consensual ideas and their consequent hegemonic grip upon the popular imagination. A classic statement of this can be found in Kerouac's *On the Road*, in the image of Sal Paradise 'osmotic[ally]' absorbing the messages of two Hollywood movies endlessly repeated in continuous showings in an all-night cinema in Detroit.[26]

> The radio squawks
> some kind of memorial program:

(xvi) 'memorial program': A: the most extensive reference to the Declaration of Independence follows this phrase, which plainly intimates the idea that this declaration is now, in Eisenhower's and Kennedy's post-war America, effectively dead, and thus in need of commemoration.

> He's tuned in on your frequency, Fidel
> but can't hear it
> There's interference

(xvii) 'He's tuned in on your frequency, Fidel/but can't hear it/There's interference': A/B/C: Castro (and Guevara) recognised the power of the media; Castro, after his 1956 invasion and his

'. . . ITSELF IRRADIATED BY THE THING IT ATTACKS' 257

flight to the Sierra Maestra, established *Radio Rebelde*, broadcasting 'from the Territory of Free Cuba' from 24 February 1958 onwards.[27] After his accession to power Castro regularly took to TV (ownership of sets was startingly high compared to the rest of Latin America), and set up a powerful short-wave radio station to broadcast his revolutionary messages to the rest of Latin America.[28] Those seeking to listen to these programmes in the US regularly experienced abnormally high levels of interference.

> They're going to fix you, Fidel
> with your big Cuban cigar
> which you stole from us

(xviii) 'your big Cuban cigar/which you stole from us': A/C: Castro's smoking of Cuban cigars was a complicated ideological act. One main source of Cuba's economic problems was its dependence on cane sugar production: beet sugar production had stolen key segments of its potential market, and an important 40 per cent of cane sugar production in Cuba was controlled in Batista's Cuba by US sugar companies. Castro socialised sugar production but also regarded the development of Cuba's tobacco industry as one way out of Cuba's precarious monocultural dependence on sugar. However, the industry's corrupt and Batista-backed unions had in the past slowed down the introduction of mechanisation to cigar rolling so effectively that much cigar production had been transferred to the US mainland, the cigars sometimes being then re-exported back to Cuba. As trade embargoes descended, Cubans ceased to re-import cigars, and Cuban tobacco ceased to reach America; but at the same time Cuba lost some, and then all, of its US markets. Ironies here are replete, and Ferlinghetti's own use of irony here draws on and alludes to this complexity. More accessibly, the 'big[ness]' of Castro's cigar carried phallic overtones, with Castro being effectively represented in the US media as a challenge to the USA's manhood and conveys how US capital had lost its former, autocratic controlling interest in Cuban affairs.[29]

> and your army surplus hat
> which you probably also stole
> and your Beat beard

(xix) 'your Beat beard': A/B/C: this link between Castro's revolt and that of the Beats unites the ideological inflexibility with which the United States categorised Castro and his revolution as ineradicably Communist (despite Castro's own, repeated and probably accurate denials and prevarications and his ideological cloudiness)[30] with its domestic intolerance of non-conformity, that made the Beats into pariahs and monstrous media cartoon freaks. This link may be less forced than it seems: the guerrilla army's members had a high proportion of beards, which helped signal to Cubans their difference from preceding Cuban armies. The Cuban Revolutionary government, including Castro, also marked their difference from their oppressive predecessors, at least early on, by their preparedness to react with 'spontaneity' to events and encounters, rather than holding to any monolithic programme, thus enabling them to be identified as 'honest'.[31] Spontaneity and beards were also hallmarks of the Beat stereotype. Both Fidel's revolutionary government and the Beats alienated the establishment but drew popular youth support.[32] The CIA actively discussed the idea of spiking Castro's drinks with a depilatory substance designed to make his beard fall out.

> History may absolve you, Fidel
> but we'll dissolve you first, Fidel

(xx) 'History may absolve you . . . dissolve you first': B: the reference is to Castro's courtroom speech in defence of his actions on 16 October 1953, *History Will Absolve Me*, following his arrest after the failure of the Moncada barracks attack that year. By linking this speech to the Declaration of Independence via the play on the word 'dissolve' Ferlinghetti is further linking the Cuban to the American Revolution and seeking to defamiliarise the US media's and US government's portrayals of Castro's Cuba. Castro himself referred to the 1776 Declaration of Independence in *History Will Absolve Me*, and quoted from it at length. The Manifesto of Castro's party (the 26 July Movement, named after the Moncada revolt) issued in November 1956, argued that 'By democracy, the 26 July Movement still considers the Jeffersonian philosophy valid'.[33]

> It's going to be a Gas
> As they say in Guatemala

(xxi) 'a Gas . . . in Guatemala': B: the overthrow of the revolutionary government in Guatemala during 1953–4 was regarded by many in the US government as a model of the way in which the same operation should be carried out in Cuba. The actual preparations for the Bay of Pigs invasion had many features in common: for example, the training of Guatemalan pilots to fly US army planes was seen as exemplifying what should be set up to overthrow Castro. The training camps used to prepare Cuban exiles for attacks on Castro's Cuba that were being exposed in the US radical press during 1960 were located in Guatemala.[34]

> It's a midnight murder or something
> Some young bearded guy stretched on the sidewalk
> with blood sticking out

(xxii) 'Some young bearded guy': A: the interpellative power of the consensual intolerance of dissent was well dramatised by a number of attacks on young males in the Bay Area because of their 'Beat' appearance. This links up with note xix.

> That's what happens, Fidel
> when in the course of human events
> it becomes necessary for one people to dissolve
> the bonds of International Tel & Tel
> and United Fruit

(xxiii) 'the bonds of International Tel & Tel/ and United Fruit': B/C: United Fruit was one of the main US investors in the Cuban sugar industry (see note xviii), but its repressive role in Californian (and other states') labour relations would also be picked up by many listeners/readers. International Telephone & Telegraph were large investors in the Cuban telephone utility, which was famous for being unreliable and expensive. A World Bank report had arraigned it in Batista's time for extracting 'a good dividend at the expense of maintenance and replacement of equipment'.[35] Batista had infamously allowed the Cuban Telephone Company (owned by US capital) recently to raise its already over-high rates as a result of pressure from a US ambassador.[36] As thanks, he was given a solid gold telephone, which after the revolution was displayed in Havana. All this came close to the hearts of some Cubans because they used the telephone 'phenomenally'.[37]

> Fidel
> How come you don't answer anymore
> Fidel
> Did they cut you off our frequency
> We've closed down our station anyway

(xxiv) 'We've closed down our station anyway': A/B: massive US disinvestment in Cuba was in full flood in 1961.

> like a good Liberal
> I hadn't quite finished reading Camus' Rebel
> so I couldn't quite recognise you, Fidel

(xxv) 'I hadn't quite finished reading Camus' *Rebel*: C: It is plain that Ferlinghetti intends us to refer Castro's Cuban revolution to Camus' contention that 'Finally, it is those who know how to rebel, at the appropriate moment, against history who really advance its interests . . . rebellion cannot exist without a strange form of love' (pp. 266–8).[38]

> walking up and down your island
> when they came for you, Fidel
> "My country or Death" you told them

(xxvi) ' "My Country or Death" ' I am unsure if this was ever uttered by Castro. If Ferlinghetti is right in stating that it was, it would have been at the time that Castro was arrested and imprisoned for his part in the Moncada Barracks uprising in 1953. This would perhaps explain why one slogan of the Cuban revolution was 'Liberty or Death'. These slogans were a key part of the symbolism of the Revolution.[39] *History Will Absolve Me* contained the phrase 'Finally with death, life begins' – a quotation reproducing one of José Martí's epigrams. Martí ('the Apostle') was seen by most Cubans as the exemplar of the spirit of Cuban independence, due to his role in enabling and then participating in the war of independence from Spain, begun in

1895. Consequently, many of the 1956/9 Revolution's slogans were Martí's epigrams.[40] Ferlinghetti's use of this phrase also links up to Patrick Henry's assertion, 'I know not what course others may take; but as for me, give me liberty or give me death', in his speech in support of an American revolution against the British at the Virginia Convention in September 1774. Plainly the Cuban revolutionary slogan references this and further advances the link Ferlinghetti is seeking to establish between everyday North American life in 'Mike's Place' and the Cuban Revolution.

> Well you've got your little death, Fidel
> like old Honest Abe
> one of your boyhood heroes

(xxvii) 'Honest Abe/one of your boyhood heroes': B/C: In its Manifesto and Statement of November 1956, the 26 July Movement stated 'By *democracy*, the 26 July Movement . . . fully subscribes to Lincoln's formula of a "government of the people, by the people and for the people" '.[41]

> who also had his little Civil War
> and was a different kind of Liberator
> (since no one was shot in his war)

(xxviii) 'since no one was shot in his [Lincoln's] war': A: the heavy irony here causes an abrupt estrangement of the media-promulgated demonic portrait of Castro: plainly, the American Civil War was one of the bloodiest in the history of the world, and makes the irony's point succinctly and brutally: lack of bloodshed is not in itself virtuous, and vice versa.

> and also was murdered
> in the course of human events

(xxix) 'and also was murdered': A: the link between Abraham Lincoln's assassination and Ferlinghetti's fears for Castro are pointed.

> your futile trip is done
> yet is not done
> and is not futile
> I give you my sprig of laurel

(xxx) 'your futile trip is done . . . sprig of laurel': A/B/C: the sense of the Cuban revolution, and Fidel's contribution to it, is reinforced on three levels. The literal level, advancing the idea of the perseverance of the revolution, is directly stated in the paradox 'done/ . . . not done'. The second level offers a reference to Whitman's elegy for Abraham Lincoln, where the misquotation interlaces images of victory into the original line ('I give you my sprig of lilac') – 'lilacs' being replaced by the laurels of victory – which link up to Whitman's celebration of an aspiring future for a reunited slave-free Union emerging after the slaughter of the Civil War in 'When Lilacs Last'. The third level re-invokes Camus' *The Rebel* (see note xxv): 'At the moment of supreme tension there will leap into flight an unswerving arrow, a shaft that is inflexible and free' (p. 270). This is Whitman's victorious resolution to his elegy – that revolutionary achievements will endure: but that his poem *is* an elegy ominously reminds us of Ferlinghetti's fearfulness as he contemplates Castro's future with a similar sense of victoriousness. It is a complex ambivalence of mood matching both Whitman's sense of victory and loss, and Camus's final rescuing of optimism about rebellion's potential from the jaws of pessimistic dismay.

II

Although my attempt to divide the poem into various levels has at times necessarily become rather arbitrary, it is clear that as the poem progresses its allusions grow in complexity. Its audience is effectively being drawn into an increasingly sophisticated recognition of the complex processes by which Castro is in danger of being 'got', how this recognition rooted in the everyday lives of United States citizens, and how intractable political issues are thus at stake. In the process of establishing this, my analysis has, of course, depended heavily on perhaps somewhat naive assumptions about authorial intentionality. I do not intend to disown this approach, but it is worth stressing that there is within the poem a level of discourse, and an analytic line that derives from it, which must complicate the ideas so far advanced about the identity of Ferlinghetti's radical project.

This complication depends upon a recognition of the poem's location within a matrix of national and regional discursive representations of the identity and potential of political dissent. For example, the poem eventually appeared in the collection of Ferlinghetti's poems published by New Directions in 1961, *Starting from San Francisco*. On the cover of this volume the significance of this West Coast 'starting' point is commented upon, and it is picked up on in the title poem, which depicts the poem's persona travelling 'All night Eastward' from San Francisco (p. 5). This reverses the conventional quest-direction for American self- and national definition (the collapse of the two into one another – self/nation/self – is part of the mythic turnstile of US patriotism). Thus, when Ferlinghetti ends 'One Thousand Fearful Words' by noting that the poem was composed in San Francisco, he is unavoidably alluding to the discursive representation of the West Coast as offering a very particular, regional perspective on America's national and international aspirations. This argument is well rehearsed by such commentators as David Wyatt, Kevin Starr, Daniel Hoffman and William Everson.[42]

The recurrent argument is that the West coast offers a particularly liberating and pluralist perspective: it is furthest removed from the hegemonic grip of White Anglo-Saxon Protestant, and particularly Puritan and male East Coast (New England derived) culture; it attracted rebels, outcasts and adventurers (for example, during the gold rush of 1849), who would be the least susceptible to, and the most sceptical about, such consensual appropriation; it became populated as a territory and subsequently as a State at a time when immigration was occurring from far more diverse sources than the original north-western Protestant parts of Europe; its West Coast location led to substantial immigration from the Far East, particularly China and to a lesser extent Japan; it already possessed a substantial population – of indigenous Indians, but also Spanish/Mexican-Americans. The resulting cultural pluralism and non-conformity thus fostered political dissent. Ferlinghetti's (and Nancy Peters') explorations of San Franciscan and Californian cultural history in *Literary San Francisco* recurrently draw attention to the significant presence of political radicals in California.[43] Thus San Francisco might be represented as the 'natural' starting point for radical critiques of contemporary America.

However, greater stress should be placed on the particular socio-political climate created by then recent events in political history. 1961 comes only sixteen years after the end of World War Two, during which large numbers of conscientious objectors and political dissidents (usually anarcho-pacifists) had been transported to conscientious objector camps in Northern California, Oregon and other West Coast locations fairly remote from the US populace. Many young intellectuals who opposed war were sent to these camps, along with older war resisters, and the camps proved to be fertile ground for the development of pacifist and anarchist ideas. One in particular stands out: Waldport Camp in Oregon. Here, artistic expressions of the anarcho-political voice became particularly well developed. As William Everson explains; 'The churches early began setting up special schools in certain camps so men interested in a given project could transfer there and participate in that activity . . . At Waldport we organised an Arts project and were accepted. On the basis of this we began to attract artists from camps all over the country.'[44] Thus, during the course of the war, Everson's own establishment of *The Untide* (1942-3, edited with C.R. Bunyan, Everett Groff and Don Kimmel) and the Untide Press (which published such works as Everson's anti-war *X War Elegies* and Kenneth Patchen's *An Astonished Eye Looks Out of the Air* in 1943) came to be complemented by publication of two little magazines, *The Illiterati* (transferring from Cascade Locks camp, Wyeth, Oregon in 1943 and lasting intermittently until 1955) and *Compass* (1942-5, transferring from a camp in Maryland).[45] *The Illiterati*'s objectives perhaps make clear the atmosphere at Waldport: '*The Illiterati* proposes: creation, experiment and revolution to build a classless, free society; suspects: tradition as a standard and eclecticism as a technique; rejects war and other forms of coercion by physical violence in human associations.'[46]

A strongly political and oppositional tradition was thus drawn upon, articulated and developed by poets, writers and intellectuals in Waldport and the loose nexus of West Coast camps. Commentators and participants have repeatedly mentioned this process,[47] but it needs considerable stress in order to define clearly the way that, in the post-war period, the idea of poetry as possessing, and to some extent needing to possess, a public and political role both gained and in part derived from a particular anarcho-pacifist impetus. This sort of emphasis runs counter to the customary assertion that an apoliticism gripped America's cultural and intellectual life after the Hitler–Stalin pact, the exposure of Soviet war atrocities, the rapid deterioration of East–West relationships and the first indications of the Cold War. This was never wholly the case across America, and now it proved to be particularly untrue on the West Coast. When the war ended, a number of the camps' internees chose to remain on the West Coast, and many of them gravitated to the Bay Area and particularly to San Francisco. Here they encountered an existing radical and dissenting intellectual and artistic community, prominent within which was Kenneth Rexroth, whose rebel credentials stretched back into the Twenties (and the Chicago Renaissance).[48] As Rexroth himself put it, during the period that spanned the establishment of the internment camps, their inmates' discharge and post-war activities in San Francisco, 'Something was definitely being built up'.[49] The resulting interchanges of ideas helped create a genuine intellectual excitement, which aroused the interest of other intellectuals and writers, for example Robert Duncan, who had become quite closely involved with Charles Henri-Ford's surrealist circle and their little magazine, *View* (1940–47).

I do not want to fall into the trap of simply dismissing the original political inspirations which lay behind surrealism (encapsulated, to put it rather crudely, in its antagonism towards bourgeois propriety), but by the mid-1940s the movement's aesthetic programme had become predominant in New York's surrealist circles, particularly once the war had ended. The young Duncan became impatient with this artistic climate and took off for San Francisco, from where he denounced *View* for 'the tone of irreverence which is [its] trademark . . . come . . . to its crisis when articles by serious anarchists, Chiarmonte and Goodman, are presented along with the cud of *fin de siècle* radicalism'.[50] Not long after, Philip Lamantia was to undertake a similar transcontinental migration.

The publication of the little magazine *The Ark* in 1947, edited by Sanders Russell, in which Duncan's attack on *View* appeared, provides a particularly important watershed in this process. This anthology-like single-issue little magazine published work by

Everson, Patchen, Rexroth, James Laughlin, Richard Eberhart, Paul Goodman, William Carlos Williams, Duncan, Lamantia, Richard Moore and Thomas Parkinson, among others, alongside essays on anarcho-pacificism by George Woodcock ('What is Anarchism?') and Ammon Hennacy ('Christian Anarchism'). Publication of *The Ark* from out of San Francisco's anarchist circles dramatises two things conveniently for me. First, the way in which the artistic community in San Francisco was developing into a publishing community, establishing a mode of cultural production independent from academic or commercial outlets. Secondly, the way in which this process was also locked into a political network which, far from being an original West Coast phenomenon, stretched across America and beyond. Another geographic process, altogether more accidental – for example, to do with government decisions about where to isolate conscientious objectors in labour camps – is at work. This is not to deny that there was some sense of relaxed freedom in San Francisco, as, for example, Rexroth argues (and many after him).[51] The representation of the West Coast as a special environment fostering dissent holds most validity when read as a modern myth which chiefly (but not exclusively) plays some sort of *post hoc* rather than formative role in helping foster a particularly pronounced anarcho-pacifist cultural environment in San Francisco and the Bay Area.

I want now to move to the publications of *Ark II, Moby I* and *Evergreen Review*, Vol. 1, No. 2 Edited by James Harmon (an ex-inmate of Waldport) and Michael McClure, *Ark II Moby I* revived *The Ark*'s anthologising instincts in 1956/7, but now also displayed a new influx of writers who had been attracted to the Bay Area. *Ark II Moby I* thus brought all these developments together: by deliberately linking back to *The Ark* through its title and some shared contributors (Eberhart, Duncan, Rexroth and Russell), it established continuity; by publishing writers such as Allen Ginsberg and Gary Snyder it perspicaciously underlined the significance of the famous Six Gallery Reading of 13 October 1955, which symptomatically marked not only a very public flowering of San Francisco poetic activity but also the emergence of the Beats[52]; by publishing Jonathan Williams, Ed Dorn, Denise Levertov, Robert Creeley and Charles Olson it linked up these cross-seminations to the seminal cultural and artistic activity found at Black Mountain College and/or in *Black Mountain Review* (1954–7). *Evergreen Review*, Vol. 1, No. 2 (Summer 1957), complemented *Ark II Moby I* by bringing a similar anthologising reflex to bear on what it called the 'San Francisco Scene', but grafted onto this a nationwide distribution and very large sales (it was distributed by the New York publishing house, Grove Press). It featured, among others, Ginsberg (the text of '*HOWL*'), Rexroth, Duncan, Josephine Miles, Michael McClure and Kerouac, and the large sales and fame attracted to it marks as well as anything the way in which what had been 'built up' in the late 1940s and 1950s now had emerged into full public and media view. (*Evergreen* claimed a circulation of 25,000.[53])

Lawrence Ferlinghetti had poems published in both *Ark II Moby I* and *Evergreen Review*, Vol. 1, No. 2, and this indicates his own increasingly seminal role in these interactive developments, particularly via three linked enterprises: his City Lights Bookshop, co-established with Pete Martin in 1953; the little magazine *City Lights*, first edited by Martin in 1952 and co-edited with Ferlinghetti, when they joined forces to set up City Lights Bookshop (until 1955 when Martin returned to New York); and his City Lights Books, founded in 1955 and publishing Rexroth and Patchen almost immediately.[54]

III

It now becomes chronologically necessary to employ the label San Francisco Renaissance, a term which I will deploy in its broadest and (somewhat awkwardly) portmanteau sense, to mark the gathering up of all the foregoing into one (albeit loosely linked) nexus. Though the accompanying geographical specificity is still somewhat misleading, an anarcho-pacifist artistic momentum was operating, and Ferlinghetti was centrally positioned in these developments. His publication of Ginsberg and Corso besides Rexroth, Denise Levertov and Patchen in the 1950s is accurately indicative of this.[55] Even more important, however, was his decision to publish '*HOWL*' *and Other Poems* as Number Four in his Pocket Poets Series in 1956, since in 1957 this book was to become subject first to US custom's seizure and then police prosecution (one reason why, in its support, *Evergreen Review*

Vol. 1, No. 2, chose to publish the poem). This, and the successful defence of the book by the American Civil Liberties Union in a protracted courtroom battle, made Ferlinghetti, as well as Ginsberg, famous both in California and from coast to coast. Ferlinghetti's rise to prominence in the San Francisco Renaissance thus proved quite rapid. He had arrived in San Francisco in 1950, after completing successful studies at the Sorbonne and before that participating voluntarily in a very minor way in the Second World War as a naval officer, following a sheltered and lonely childhood removed from contact with his biological family. While in the navy he had also spent some time in New York, and by his own account had his eyes opened to a whole terrain of political philosophy he had never encountered before – an experience he dramatised by claiming that at that time, 1941, he did not know what a conscientious objector was'.[56]

Ferlinghetti's encounter with the strong strand of anarcho-pacifism in San Francisco, as he joined the Rexroth circle in 1952, was complex: he had fought against fascism, but had also visited Nagasaki shortly after the atomic bomb had exploded there, and had seen 'hands sticking out of the mud . . . hair sticking out of the road – a quagmire – people don't realise how total the destruction was'.[57] Ferlinghetti thus fitted very well into the international orientations of the Rexroth circle, but was less centrally aligned towards, though not simply averse to its anarcho-pacifist commitment. Thus Ferlinghetti's study, while in France during the period 1948 to 1950 at the Sorbonne, of the existential writings of Sartre and Camus, which had led him to understand both these writers as concerned to be politically engaged: as he put it, 'Sartre . . . has always hollered that the writer should be committed. *Engagement* is one of [Sartre's] favorite words'[58] (Fantasy Records Cover note in Smith).

'One Thousand Fearful Words' needs to be placed within this interactive socio-cultural frame, and its underlying political geography of sorts. That my metaphor here is mixed perhaps indicates the complexity of the interactive cultural processes both complementing and conflicting with each other. Ferlinghetti's poem is located within and draws upon the resulting debates and seeks to establish a dialectic by which to resist the processes of *post hoc* mythologisation. This complex engagement stems from a refusal to tolerate easy acceptance of the kind of thinking to be found in David Meltzer's assertion in his book *The San Francisco Poets* that 'The poet is a revolutionary because he is constantly subverting corrupt institutional languages. He can make the life-denying rhetoric of political power void'.[59] This confident belief that poetry writing is somehow *per se* political directly contradicts the statement by a young poet made to Ferlinghetti in January 1960: 'In Chile at a Writers' Conference last January, [a] Cuban delegate said that Cuban writers are Revolutionary poets whereas American poets are Rebel poets.' Ferlinghetti remembered this statement sufficiently well to record it in his Cuban journal in December 1960.[60] It seems to me these sentiments chime well with the reactions of Cuban and other Latin American poets to Le Roi Jones on a visit he made to Cuba in 1960 under the auspices of the Fair Play for Cuba Committee:

'. . . if they're anti-communist, no matter what kind of foul person they are, you [US] people accept them as your allies . . . That is irrational. You people are irrational!'
I tried to defend myself. 'Look, why jump on me? . . . I'm in complete agreement with you. I'm a poet . . . what can I do? I write, that's all, I'm not even interested in politics.'
She [Senora Betancourt] jumped on me with both feet as did a group of Mexican poets later in Habana. She called me a 'cowardly bourgeois individualist.' The poets, or at least one wild-eyed Mexican poet, Jaime Shelley, almost left me in tears, stomping his foot on the floor, screaming: 'You want to cultivate your soul? In that ugliness you live in you want to cultivate your soul? Well, we've got millions of starving people to feed, and that moves me enough to make poems out of.'[61]

More than incidentally, Ferlinghetti would certainly have read this seminal essay by Le Roi Jones Baraka at about the time he was working on 'One Thousand Fearful Words', since it first appeared in *Kulchur* in 1960 (Vol. 1, No. 2, pp. 54–89) and was then continued in *Evergreen Review* later in 1960, in an issue of the review including Ferlinghetti's own 'Hidden Door' (Vol. 4, No. 15, pp. 91–3). Cuba posed real issues in terms of the poet's position *vis-à-vis* political engagement, of deep concern to Ferlinghetti. By late 1960 we find him writing the following: '[these] satirical tirades [are] . . . poetry admittedly corrupted by the political, itself irradiated by the thing it attacks'. This actually appeared as a back-cover note to *Starting from San Francisco* by Ferlinghetti, and it requires some attention as a verdict on his broadsides in general and 'One Thousand Fearful Words' in particular.

What Ferlinghetti is suggesting here falls quite close to one line of argument to be found in the work of Michel Foucault, that writing is always already drawn into a discursive network of other works and utterances, thereby relatively *pre*scribing what can be said:

> The frontiers of a book are never clear cut: . . . beyond its internal configuration, its autonomous form, it is caught up in a system of reference to other books, other texts, other sentences: it is a node within a network . . . its unity is relative and variable . . . it indicates itself only on the basis of a complex field of knowledge.[62]

This summary crudifies Foucault somewhat, and anyway in some essays he postulates a more volatile situation within which discourse is available for appropriation: 'discourse is the power to be seized'.[63] 'discourse can be both an instrument and an effect of power, but also a hindrance, a stumbling block, a point of resistance and a starting point for an opposing strategy'.[64] Ferlinghetti's quote on *Starting from San Francisco*'s back cover suggests he is inclined towards the idea of political discourse effectively interpellating the poet into replicating the patterns and terms of existing debates, thereby decisively limiting the interrogative power and penetration of the poetry. In this line of argument, for example, one could suggest that it is entirely predictable that anarcho-pacifism took root on the West Coast because in key respects it complemented the dominant, consensual political discourse in America, which advocated self-reliance, individual autonomy, minimal government interference and a tolerance of others' opinions and beliefs provided they did not trespass upon one's own. The argument would thus contend that the soft-core, politically rather under theorised though well-read anarchism found on the West Coast would never constitute a real fracture from this dominant discourse, since pacifism in itself could by definition not be a route to power.

It can also be seen how adept at cultural appropriation this consensual US discourse could be represented as being, since any rebellion could be contained by being portrayed as just one individual statement, no more and no less than an assertion of legitimate, truly American freedoms – of expression and belief. Thus rebellion could be folded back into the dominant discourse. This aptitude for appropriation had negative consequences for US poets, whose role was consensually identified as celebrating their 'selves' – their freedom of self – hence, possibly, the success of the confessional in US mid-century poetry. Ferlinghetti's dry comment that 'it seems the poet is suspect in politics' (in a 1965 interview)[65] well identifies the way in which the idea of 'free selfhood' can underpin the consensual proposition that the US's traditionally high valuation of the individual was uniquely adept at fostering poetic inspiration: taken care of politically, as it were, poets could follow their muse, as creative writing entered the liberal college curriculum via composition classes.

However, things were of course more complex: poets and writers and other intellectuals on the West Coast and more broadly if less concentratedly across America were exhibiting Foucault's alternative vision of resistance. They came together as a loose nexus of groups and communities and brought a common interrogative perspective to bear upon the dominant consensual values of the USA precisely because, as gays, conscientious objectors and/or left-wingers, they experienced no such freedom of self. Furthermore, this sense of community was being conveyed by way of media attention and censorship attracted to this dissent, as norms were fractured: the *HOWL* trial and other censorship run-ins, such as the *Chicago Review*'s and then *Big Table*'s problems in 1959.[66] For a while, in America, a counter-culture or alternative culture came to be actively discussed, rooted in the same anarcho-pacifist spirit (if not the same knowledge) as that which I have depicted on the West Coast. This helped fuel involvements in the Civil Rights campaigns of the late 1950s and early 1960s and the Vietnam protests of the mid- to late-sixties, as well as the Fair Play for Cuba protests sandwiched in between. The 1960s can be described as a time of some consensual breakdown – of protest and rebellion.

What particularly interests me about Ferlinghetti's 'One Thousand Fearful Words' in this respect is that this poem actually confronts the distinction between protest and rebellion on the one hand and revolution on the other, the very thing the Cuban poets had invited Ferlinghetti to do in Chile in January 1960. In particular Ferlinghetti's poem poses questions about the legitimate place of violence, its position in protest, rebellion and revolt. By alluding consistently and clearly to Jefferson and Lincoln it can be argued that Ferlinghetti is actually advancing further in this poem than his back-cover quotation on *Starting* allows: his 'tirade' may (inevitably) be 'corrupted' and 'irradiated' but it is also *progressing*: to ask the actual hard questions that underlie both US intervention in Cuba and West Coast pacific disengagement. By establishing an allusive network, a 'system of references to other . . . texts' in Foucault's phrase, *consciously*, on its own terms, Ferlinghetti's poem raises in a positive, consensual frame the issues of rebellion against imperialism (Jefferson and the American Revolution) and war against slavery (Lincoln and the Civil War). These US icons are then brought to bear upon US imperialism in Cuba and the Caribbean (from Guatemala to Cuban cigars). Thus Ferlinghetti draws both the uncommitted and the liberal critic into an arena where they are rendered vulnerable to persuasion. He uses what I shall call 'controlled irradiation' to limit the corruption of his argument. This argument is conducted on two levels: the first focuses on highlighting the ways in which US intervention has clear imperialist overtones and how the Cuban revolt bears comparison to earlier US revolutions; the second focuses on Sartre's and Camus' recognitions that ultimately individual authenticity can only be guaranteed by acts that necessarily have collective consequences and that these may and often will require a collectivity in revolt (engagement). The first level confronts any US audience with unresolved contradictions that call US policy towards Cuba into question. Both levels (but particularly the second) pose hard questions for what might be described as liberal anarchists: in his address to the Union Square rally in San Francisco on 7 January 1961, Ferlinghetti specifically asked 'why U.S. writers whose reputations are founded on liberal thinking are silent on Cuba'.[67] Furthermore, in the poem 'One Thousand Fearful Words' that he then spoke, Ferlinghetti goes on to consider the hard consequences: the need, in Camus' words, to rebel but to establish limits to revolt, and the need to recognise and confront the issue of revolutionary killings, weighed against the other forms of murder that flow from taking no action: the issue of assassination (raised by the fate of Lincoln) is central here, as is the fate of 'peasant[s] in a green landscape'.

That 'One Thousand Fearful Words' goes much further than the other 'broadsides' in *Starting* in confronting these political issues is surely related to the facts that it was the last poem Ferlinghetti had written for *Starting* when it was originally published in 1961 and that its subject matter compelled him to confront the issue of revolution and the words of the Cuban poet in Chile. It asks and probes at difficult questions and its resolution suggests that for Ferlinghetti the answer is intelligently, and deliberately without qualification, to support Castro as a revolutionary. Hence, the poem's ironic suggestion that 'no one' had died in Lincoln's Civil War: this is, precisely, a means of confronting liberal pacifism's reservations concerning Castro.

There is also an ironic recognition of the limited efficacy of this support for Castro, in the way that Ferlinghetti, in the penultimate stanza, characterises the poetic persona as, in turn, only after all that of another 'good liberal'. This surely dramatises the sense he has of the still extant constraints on his poem's effectiveness: he is still not a good revolutionary, and his sustained interrogation of the limits of liberal anarcho-pacifism in itself has not transformed anything: in fact, they lead back into a matrix of US cultural references which continue to irradiate the poem. Ferlinghetti was deeply aware of the dominant's interpellative powers. As he argued in *Tyrannus Nix* (1969), it is necessary to recognise the modern State's capacity to exercise 'Marcuse's "repressive tolerance", i.e., the policy of tolerance and/or sponsorship as a self-protection against violence; or as Susan Sontag recently put it, divesting unsettling or subversive ideas by ingesting them (*Ramparts*, June 1969)'.[68] Ferlinghetti took this idea further in an interview in 1969. 'The State, whether Capitalist or Communist, has an enormous capacity to ingest its most dissident elements'.[69] In this respect it is important to note that Ferlinghetti seeks to limit and direct such irradiation. He cannot evade focusing on Castro, so very much the centre of the Cuban Revolution, and by this very process of constituting Castro as a 'hero' some measure of 'irradiation' occurs – Castro is granted heroic individualisation. But the poem refuses to incorporate the iconography of the Cuban Revolution, which harped on the fact that 'twelve' had survived the disastrous landfall of the 'Granma' (in fact there were probably always more than twelve in the Sierra Maestra).

Ferlinghetti's design is not to allow the poem to slide off either into uncritical pro-revolutionary quasi-religious rhetoric and hagiography, or into anarcho-pacifist agonisings which blur into debates about liberal freedoms which will disable support for Castro's Cuba from within, but to remain firmly in the terrain of confronting real political questions about developing effective dissent. Thus the creation of a 'good liberal' persona was aimed at dramatising the problem for the non-silent, 'rebellious' liberals in his audience. The requirement is for a more sustained and radical political debate, leading to confident, uncompromised action drawing in blacks, native Americans and Chinese, the 'skinny brotherhood' of exploited minorities, breaking down the 'radio . . . interference' of the media and the State. Otherwise, ultimately, the opposition to US imperialism will remain too narrowly based. The Bay of Pigs, when it occurred just over three months later, almost proved Ferlinghetti wholly correct.

In fact, Kennedy drew back from full support for the Bay of Pigs invasion, which had been planned by Eisenhower in secret, and of which Kennedy had possessed no knowledge during an election campaign in which he had constantly taunted Eisenhower for being insufficiently aggressive towards Cuban communism. Kennedy found out about the invasion plans shortly after his electoral victory, but even after his inauguration he did nothing to impede continued progress towards invasion. However, his refusal to provide key logistical and military (air and naval) support guaranteed the invasion's failure. One could in fact make out a modest case for the efficacy of liberal protest in all this, since in a sense Kennedy's back-out amounted to a reneging on his campaign promises.[70] The widespread dissent, made manifest through the nationwide work of the Fair Play for Cuba Committee, had a minor but still to be calculated influence upon his change of heart. In turn, Ferlinghetti had played his own minor but not unprominent role in the Committee's work, and the way in which his poem had very clearly on its most accessible aural level laid out the case for pulling back from the destruction of Castro must in turn have had a minor mobilising function.

Here of course we have moved into the realm of the inestimable. But we can say that Ferlinghetti's strategy of multi-level address has enabled him to write a poem capable of a mobilising role, firming up resistance to US interference in Cuba, and rhetorically persuading the disengaged or undecided to join this resistance through 'directed irradiation' while also at the same time doing something far more: asking questions about the very nature of political resistance, its consequences, and hard questions about the violence present in the Cuban Revolution. One can argue that the liberal consensus underpinning the anarcho-pacificism of the alternative culture ensured that, whatever success the counter-culture enjoyed in the late 1960s and early 1970s (for example, over Vietnam) it would not confront these issues or properly resolve them, ensuring ultimately a process of relatively easy appropriation – 'ingestion', in Ferlinghetti's phrase. Thus it is that the poem's diagnosis of economic imperialism still has relevance and its claim that Castro will be got can be seen as correct: the Cuba existing just after the revolution, a country attempting to maintain its autonomy, gave way almost immediately after the Bay of Pigs, to another Cuba, shaped by the political realities laid bare in this invasion, and a Cuba that liberal US opinion, broadly speaking, deserted.[71]

Beyond this, Ferlinghetti's multi-level technique of radical writing deserves consideration as a flexible way of addressing different (but not discrete) constituencies and hence maximising its hearing. Here I believe that my analysis suggests some real success, though it must be conceded that the more sophisticated questions raised by way of the technique of multiple allusion are left somewhat truncated by Ferlinghetti's desire to retain a popular and broad appeal. Ferlinghetti recognised this problem, and saw it as inherent in his objective: in an interview in 1965 he commented: 'The bigger the audience becomes, the more public the poetry becomes; you have to read poetry that has more public "surface" . . . I call them Performance Poems. I practise and work on the tape recorder with them'.[72] This remark, besides lending clear support to my argument that Ferlinghetti deliberately sought a multi-level structure, also points to a sense he has that 'surface' can become predominant. His rehearsals I would present as in part a desire to find ways of reading which pointed to or highlighted the levels residing below the 'surface'.

Certainly, 'One Thousand Fearful Words' runs the risk of surface predominating but, in my estimate, nothing before or since in Ferlinghetti's writing approaches a better balance between surface and multi-level debate. 'One Thousand Fearful Words' stands as a minor point of resistance and starting point for an opposing strategy to both consensual US mid-century values and their liberal, or libertarian anarcho-pacifist critics, by demanding a commitment to the Cuban Revolution both whole-hearted and informed – even if it has to be added that a minor hindrance was all that it remained.

Notes

1. Lawrence Ferlinghetti, *One Thousand Fearful Words for Fidel Castro* (San Francisco, 1961), and a letter to R.J. Ellis (postmarked 14 December 1993).
2. See Neeli Cherkovski, *Ferlinghetti: A Biography* (New York, 1979), pp. 80 ff.
3. Lawrence Ferlinghetti, 'Note on Poetry in San Francisco', *Chicago Review*, 12, 1 (Spring 1958), p. 4.
4. Lawrence Ferlinghetti, *Starting from San Francisco* (New York, 1961), back cover note, and a letter to R.J. Ellis (postmarked 14 December 1993).
5. Ferlinghetti, 'One Thousand Fearful Words for Fidel Castro', *Starting from San Francisco* (New York, 1961), p. 48. Henceforth, references to this work will appear in the text. The title will be abbreviated to 'One Thousand Fearful Words'.
6. Lawrence Ferlinghetti, letter to R.J. Ellis (postmarked 14 December 1993); Hugh Thomas, *Cuba or The Pursuit of Freedom* (London, 1971), pp. 891 ff. I have chosen to reference Thomas in this essay, not only because his account is well-balanced and still well-respected, but also because it was composed within a decade of the events. Hence my use of his first edition. There have been many subsequent accounts such as: Morris H. Morley, *Imperial State and Revolution: The US and Cuba, 1952–1986* (Cambridge, 1987); Louis A. Pérez Jr., *Cuba: Between Revolution and Reform* (Oxford, 1988); Juan N del Aguila, *Cuba: Dilemmas of a Revolution* (Boulder, 1988); Leslie Bethell (ed.), *Cuba: A Short History* (Cambridge, 1993).
7. Thomas, *Cuba*, pp. 1289 ff.
8. Ibid., pp. 1308 ff.

9. Ibid., p. 1304. The news first appeared in *Hispanic American Report* in November 1960; *The Nation*, and then the *Los Angeles Mirror* and the *St. Louis Dispatch* picked up on the story.
10. *One Thousand Fearful Words*, back cover.
11. Lawrence Ferlinghetti, 'One Thousand Fearful Words for Fidel Castro', *Evergreen Review*, 5, 18 (May/June 1961), 59–63; Lawrence Ferlinghetti, 'One Thousand Fearful Words for Fidel Castro', *Starting from San Francisco*, pp. 48–52.
12. Albert Camus, *L'Homme révolté* (1951), trans. (1953) by Anthony Bower as *The Rebel* (Harmondsworth, 1962). See below for a further discussion.
13. For a careful depiction of the process by which Castro was driven to seek Soviet assistance, see Thomas, *Cuba*, pp. 1058 ff.
14. Walt Whitman, 'When Lilacs Last in the Dooryard Bloom'd', *The Portable Walt Whitman* (New York, 1945), pp. 289–99.
15. See David Radosh, 'In Bed with Fidel', *The Observer Magazine*, 7 November 1993, pp. 12–13. Lorenz's assassination attempt on Castro is not universally accepted as real. See Georgie Ann Geyer's *Guerilla Prince* (New York, 1991), for example. I am inclined to accept its validity, or at least that it is symptomatic of CIA policy in the period 1959–60. See also Peter G. Bourne, *Castro: A Biography of Fidel Castro* (London, 1987).
16. Lawrence Ferlinghetti, *A Coney Island of the Mind* (New York: New Directions, 1958), p. 48.
17. Cherkovski, *Ferlinghetti*, p. 136 ff.
18. Ibid., p. 142.
19. Lawrence Ferlinghetti, 'Autobiography', *A Coney Island*, pp. 60–6.
20. See Thomas, *Cuba*, pp. 1208 ff.
21. See Thomas, *Cuba*, *passim*; Leo Huberman and Paul M. Sweezy, *Cuba: Anatomy of a Revolution* (New York, 1960), *passim*. The latter is less reliable than the former, being more of a hagiography, but its publication date indicates its contemporaneity.
22. Robert Scheer and Maurice Zeitlin, *Cuba: An American Tragedy* (Harmondsworth, 1984), p. 37.
23. William Wordsworth, 'Poems of the Imagination: XII', *Wordsworth: Poetical Works* (London and Oxford, 1969), p. 149.
24. Thomas, *Cuba*, pp. 1200 ff.
25. Ibid., pp. 1097 ff.
26. Jack Kerouac, *On the Road* (1957; Harmondsworth, 1972), pp. 230 ff.
27. Huberman and Sweezey, *Cuba*, p. 61.
28. Thomas, *Cuba*, p. 1285.
29. Ibid., *passim*. See also Huberman and Sweezey, *Cuba*, *passim*.
30. Thomas, *Cuba*, p. 1058 ff.

31. Scheer and Zeitlin, *Cuba*, p. 83.
32. Le Roi Jones [Baraka], 'Cuba Libre', *Evergreen Review*, 4, 15, (November/December 1960), *passim*.
33. Scheer and Zeitlin, *Cuba*, p. 60.
34. Thomas, *Cuba*, p. 1276 ff.
35. Ibid., p. 1163.
36. Scheer and Zeitlin, *Cuba*, p. 55.
37. Thomas, *Cuba*, p. 1163.
38. Camus, *The Rebel*. Page references to this text appear in the text during this paragraph and subsequently.
39. Huberman and Sweezey, *Cuba*, p. 133.
40. Thomas, *Cuba*, p. 1462.
41. Scheer and Zeitlin, *Cuba*, p. 60.
42. David Wyatt, *The Fall into Eden: Landscape and Imagination in California* (Cambridge, 1986); Kevin Starr, *Americans and the Californian Dream, 1850–1915* (Santa Barbara, 1981); William Everson, *Archetype West: The Pacific Coast as a Literary Region* (Berkeley 1976); Daniel Hoffman, *The Harvard Guide to Contemporary American Writing* (Cambridge, 1979). Michael Davidson, in his *The San Francisco Renaissance: Poetics and Community at Mid-Century* (Cambridge, 1980) goes furthest to resist this sort of characterisation/caricature, though even he is not completely guiltless. Nor is Ferlinghetti himself, in his and Nancy J. Peters' *Literary San Francisco: A Pictorial History from Its Beginning to the Present Day* (San Francisco, 1980).
43. Ferlinghetti and Peters, *Literary San Francisco, passim*.
44. William Everson, in a Fall 1969 interview with David Meltzer, *The San Francisco Poets* (New York, 1971), pp. 79–80. The account which follows of the development of an anarcho-pacifist community of linked artistic groups on the West Coast depends in part on my own research, but also on Anthony Linick, 'A History of the American Literary Avant-Garde Since World War II', unpublished doctoral dissertation (University of California, Los Angeles, 1964); David Kherdian, *Six Poets of the San Francisco Renaissance* (Fresno, 1967); Ferlinghetti and Peters, *Literary San Fancisco*; Davidson, *The San Francisco Renaissance*.
45. Everson interview, in Meltzer, *The San Francisco Poets*, pp. 80 ff.
46. Anonymous cover notice, *The Illiterati*, No. 4 (Summer 1945), n.p. [cover design].
47. See Linick, 'A History', Davidson, *The San Fancisco Renaissance*, and Everson, interview in Meltzer, *The San Francisco Poets* in particular.
48. See Everson, *Archetype West*. Everson, in the course of describing

Rexroth as a sort of Renaissance man, quotes Thomas Parkinson's contention (made in 1968) that Rexroth provided 'general political orientation' (p. 142).
49. Kenneth Rexroth in a Summer 1969 interview with Meltzer, *The San Francisco Poets*, p. 42.
50. Robert Duncan, 'Reviewing *View*: An Attack', *The Ark* (1947), p. 65.
51. Kenneth Rexroth, 'San Francisco Letter', *Evergreen Review*, 1, 2 (Summer 1957), pp. 5–14. See also note 40, above.
52. Gary Snyder, quoted in Arthur Knight and Kit Knight, *The Beat Vision*, (1987) pp. 4–6, pays homage to the key role of Kenneth Rexroth in creating this environment.
53. Linick, 'A History', p. 168.
54. The first three Pocket Poet booklets were: Lawrence Ferlinghetti, *Pictures of the Gone World* (1955); Kenneth Rexroth, *30 Spanish Poems of Love and Exile* (1956); Kenneth Patchen, *Poems of Humor and Protest* (1956).
55. Denise Levertov, *Here and Now* (San Francisco, 1957).
56. Cherkovski, *Ferlinghetti*, p. 59. Most of the information on Ferlinghetti's life has been derived from Cherkovski or Larry Smith, *Lawrence Ferlinghetti: Poet at Large* (California, Southern Illinois University Press), 1983.
57. Ibid., pp. 39–40.
58. Lawrence Ferlinghetti, cover notes to the recording, '*Tentative Dinner to Promote the Impeachment of President Eisenhower*' and *Other Poems*, Fantasy Records 7004, quoted in Smith, p. 65.
59. Meltzer, *The San Francisco Poets*, pp. 46–7.
60. Cherkovski, *Ferlinghetti*, p. 142.
61. Le Roi Jones [Baraka], pp. 140–41.
62. Michel Foucault, *The Archaeology of Knowledge*, trans. A.M. Sheridan Smith (London, 1972), p. 72.
63. Michel Foucault, 'The order of discourse' in R. Young, ed., *Untying the Text: A Post-Structuralist Reader* (London, 1981), pp. 48–78.
64. Michel Foucault, *La Volonté de savoir* [*The History of Sexuality*, Vol. 1: An Introduction] (1976), trans. R. Hurley (London, 1979), p. 100.
65. 'Lawrence Ferlinghetti: A Candid Conversation with the Man Who Founded the "Beat" Generation', *Penthouse*, 1 (August, 1965), 73.
66. See Linick, 'A History', pp. 220 ff.
67. 'Cuba Policy Protested At S.F. Rally', *San Francisco Sunday Chronicle*, 8 January 1961, p. 11, col. 3.
68. Lawrence Ferlinghetti, *Tyrannus Nix* (New York, 1969), pp. 82–3.

69. Ferlinghetti, interview with Meltzer, *The San Francisco Poets*, p. 136.
70. Thomas, *Cuba*, pp. 1303 ff.
71. Aguila argues that 'by mid-1961' Cuba's had become a culture under siege (p. 57); by the Summer of 1961, 'a new Communist party' had emerged in Cuba, incorporating Castro and the 26 July Movement (Jorge Dominguez, in Bethell, *Cuba*, p. 106).
72. 'Lawrence Ferlinghetti: A candid conversation with the man who founded [sic] the Beat Generation', p. 71.

12 Home alone: re-thinking motherhood in contemporary feminist theatre
Elaine Aston

The media 'hype' surrounding the recent blockbuster *Home Alone* movies has provided a timely hook for the right-wing British government to hang its reactionary family policy on. In the wake of the much publicised real-life 'home alone' dramas, there has followed a mounting campaign against single mothers. Media attention has focused on the controversy surrounding single mothers caught working while leaving their children at 'home alone', and, in the weeks following the Conservative Party Conference (October 1993), young mothers on benefit were singled out by government Ministers for punitive measures. The government's proposal to introduce benefit cuts to mothers who continue to have and to raise children on their own and at the State's expense, is argued in terms of economics. However, the discourse surrounding this issue reflects the ideological and moral bias of reactionary right-wing C/conservative familial values.

It would be easy to blame the lack of a concerted feminist opposition to this Conservative lobbying of single mothers on the widespread erosion of a unified and effective feminist movement. However, this would overlook the problematics which the politics of motherhood posed/poses for feminism. While early feminist reactions to motherhood in the late 1960s and early 1970s allowed women to express their discontent over their maternal 'destiny', it also failed to pursue proposals for the radical transformation of the family in a liberatory programme of social change. This meant that the issue of motherhood in the 1980s needed a more radical focus, rather than the 'out-of-focus' treatment she had previously been accorded.[1]

This short study offers an overview of some of the key issues concerning the changing politics of motherhood in the post-liberationist period, as represented in a specific counter-cultural context: contemporary feminist theatre.

Motherhood and the feminist movement: 1970s

> One of the liberating discoveries feminism brought me in 1969/70 was that it was all right to complain, to be bitter, frustrated, angry: subterranean discontents, previously only spoken about collusively, half-jokingly to other mothers, suddenly erupted.[2]

In its early years, the women's movement created the possibility for women to challenge dominant ideologies of motherhood: to critically de-construct the male-created myths of the joys of the maternal which mothers were conditioned into accepting as the 'norm'. As Adrienne Rich explains:

> I was haunted by the stereotype of the mother whose love is 'unconditional': and by the visual and literary images of motherhood as a single-minded identity. If I knew parts of myself existed that would never cohere to those images, weren't those parts then abnormal, monstrous?[3]

The recognition that women were not 'monsters' for admitting to feelings other than those of self-sacrificing love of their children, was politically represented in the call for a radical transformation of the family unit.

In the early 1970s, an out-crop of issue-based theatre focused on what Rich describes as the process in which one meaning of motherhood 'the potential relationship of any woman to her powers of reproduction and to children' is conditioned by another, 'the institution which aims at ensuring that that potential – and all women – shall remain under male control'.[4] The figure of the mother in socialist-feminist theatre revisioned the class-based model of Brecht's *The Mother*, in order to demonstrate the double alienation of class and gender oppression for women, and to call for a transformation of the bourgeois family.[5]

Strike While the Iron is Hot

Red Ladder's first women's play *Strike While the Iron is Hot* (1974) is typical of this movement in political theatre. *Strike While the Iron is Hot* showed the exploitation of working-class women combining full-time motherhood with low-paid employment. Helen, the central protagonist, begins her first phase of married life as a mother at 'home alone' all day with her children:

> isolated and alone, but your time is not your own,
> Caring always for another, as a wife, and then a mother.
> Always ready, always willing, but it's others do the living.[6]

Later, when she combines factory work with motherhood, Helen finds that she has simply acquired two bosses, and her experience is one of disempowerment both in the private (domestic) and public (workplace) spheres. Helen's monologue which closes the play summarises the demands of the movement, and offers an utopian vision of motherhood, citing the political and legislative changes needed in order to make this socialist-feminist vision reality:

> A world where children can grow up under decent conditions, where women can choose when to have kids, where we have free contraception and, when we need it, abortion. Where women can choose not to have kids and that's just as natural as having them. A world where women really are men's equals, not just with equal pay – that's just equal exploitation – but a world with no exploitation. This means big changes, and only you and I can make them. But if they're needed, can you say we're asking too much?[7]

However, making the 'big changes' remained an utopian vision and not a reality. Socialist-feminist Sheila Robotham, who was not a mother at the time of the earliest feminist meetings, recollects 'the gap between those of us who had children and those of us who had not'.[8] Robotham remembers listening to mothers talking about childcare problems, while secretly wanting to 'pass on to more exciting stuff like the domestic labour debate or the revelance of Rosa Luxemburg or something'.[9] Michelene

Wandor also comments on the 'gap' between feminists with and feminists without children, indicating how it disadvantaged mothers, and how it was responsible for militating against the transformation of the family which, in the first wave of excitement, women thought might be 'just around the corner'.[10] Consequently, the domination of early feminism by 'non-mothers' meant that the radical transformation of the family, as *Strike* proposed, was displaced by the feminist focus on choosing whether to have or not have children (with an emphasis on the not), thereby highlighting the demands for contraception and abortion.

My Mother Says I Never Should

In 1975, The Women's Theatre Group performed *My Mother Says I Never Should*, a theatre-in-education play which dramatises the abortion and contraception demands of the movement in a teenage setting. The play seeks to persuade its target audience of the need for young women to have reproductive control of their own bodies, and to support this message with practical advice on where to go for confidential counselling and help with contraception and abortion. A young woman's right to control her own body and to have a 'better' future, is, however, presented at the expense of the stereotypical mother figure who says 'I never should'. The 'mum' in the play embodies a set of old-fashioned, traditional values of femininity which the daughter rejects. Mum, complete with ironing board, is presented as the dead-end future. Having babies means that you end up being stuck at home like mum 'till you was thirty or forty, and then you'd be past it'.[11]

Reducing the politics of motherhood to the issue of reproductive control (important though it is), represents a danger, however, as Claire Duchen describes in her overview of the women's movement in France (MLF), where it

> reduced women's struggle for liberation to a question of providing individual women with means of choice over individual pregnancies rather than a question of a total re-evaluation of motherhood as a socially enforced role. Even worse, some felt that the campaign contributed to making those who 'chose' motherhood guilty: 'You wanted it, you enjoy it, so get on with it.'

Which leads to the ironic equation 'enslaved motherhood + voluntary motherhood = voluntary slavery.'[12]

Despite Rowbotham's claim that in the early days of the women's movement in Britain it was not proposed that motherhood be rejected outright,[13] pieces like *My Mother Says I Never Should* confronted young women with two opposing equations to choose between 'mother = slavery and no future': 'non-mother = free choice and future'.

Dusa, Fish, Stas & Vi

In the second half of the decade, however, feminism began to address the tension and conflict for women between their political beliefs and the social reality of their lives. Pam Gems's controversial *Dusa, Fish, Stas & Vi* (1976) critiques the 'either/or' decision women face in respect of motherhood. As Fish, the political activist and non-mother, says to Dusa, a mother fighting to get her two children back from her husband:

> There's got to be a new deal for us . . . none of the either/or. 'You, too, can have a career and five abortions in the name of progress.' That's a fashion I'll leave out. We have to break new ground. Together.[14]

The play does not dramatise what the 'new ground' might be, but concerns itself with the problems of living by politics alone.

The drama has four female characters who inhabit a 'space' owned by Fish. The women represent very different positions: Fish the upper-middle class activist; Vi, an anorexic, working-class young woman; Stas who works by day as a physiotherapist and by night as a hostess; Dusa, the mother of two children who has left her affluent husband without means of her own. Fish, the centre of the all-female group, is emblematic of the struggle women experience between their political and emotional lives. The image of the confident feminist who preaches political theory at meetings and campaigns, collides and conflicts with the private woman and the feeelings she has for her male lover whom she loses to another woman. To underline this point, Gems breaks the action of Act One by having Fish speak directly to the audience about Rosa Luxemburg and what she stood for: Rosa

Luxemburg the political woman, and Rosa Luxemburg the private woman, and the 'gap' between these two:

> Rose never married Leo. She never had the child she longed for. The painful hopes in the letters from prison were never to be realised. She writes to him from Zurich about seeing a fine child in a park, and wanting to scoop him up in her arms and run off with him, back to her room. Usually when people write about her nowadays they leave all that out. They are wrong.[15]

Fish articulates her regret at not having had a child in her own relationship when she had the opportunity, but understands it as having to choose between being an empowered political animal (activist = non-mother), or a disempowered, stay-at-home wife/mother (non-activist = mother). Her suicide at the end of the play emphasizes the dilemma which the 'either/or' equation for women in which the political path does not necessarily coincide with their personal, or more specifically, maternal, desires.

Teendreams

This point is dramatised again in *Teendreams*, co-authored by David Edgar and Susan Todd for Monstrous Regiment. First performed in 1979, the play takes a long hard look at feminism in the 1970s, contrasting the aspirations of the movement with the reality of women's lives which seemed to have changed very little over the decade. The central protagonist, Frances, struggles with her political commitment to women's liberation and the reality of her own experiences, those of her colleagues and friends, and the young girls she teaches. The drama is framed by the attempted suicide of one of her pupils, after Frances has tried to influence her teenage dreams, which in turn forces Frances to re-think her own position.

The play is critical of male-dominated left-wing politics and of feminism. Like Fish, Frances comes from a privileged background, and both characters are typical of the critique surrounding the white, middle-class values of the feminist movement which failed to address issues of class, sexuality, race, and motherhood. In Scene Five, set in a squat in 1972, for example, the presence of a teenage working-class mother, Sandra, who is living in the squat to avoid her wife-battering husband, provides a comment on the activist groups who cross the stage space. One such group in the squat provides a meta-theatrical comment on issue-based theatre (potentially parodic, depending on how the scene is directed), as they are seen rehearsing an agit-prop piece: 'Fuck the Family'. Frances and her boyfriend Colin attempt to co-opt them in the fight against the 'Housing Finance Act', but fail because, so it is argued, they have no consideration for feminist issues.

The cross-stage political squabbling takes place, however, around Sandra who is not able to join in the 'Fuck the Family' rehearsal as she is feeding the baby, nor even able to answer the door to Frances and Colin because her hands are full with the infant. Imagistically, the scene demonstrates the mother's position as outside the political arena. The comment is completed at the close of the scene, when pragmatically, just as a disgruntled Frances and Colin are about to leave the squat, Sandra turns to them for help: for a match to light the primus stove to warm another bottle of milk for her baby.

In Scene Seven, the contradiction, or gap, between what might be politically desirable for women and the reality of their lives is theatricalised in the staging of a consciousness-raising session. The women of different class, work, and domestic backgrounds find that they may be in danger of oppressing other women because of their different experiences and relative levels of affluence, etc. Furthermore, political theory or action does not necessarily, so the scene demonstrates, provide women with solutions, as Sandra's anecdote illustrates:

> S' just *I* know this woman. Who. Became involved, with the abortion thing. And then she got herself in the club, and her bloke, he wanted to get married, have the baby. But she had it terminated. And lost the bloke. And lost the baby . . .
>
> And she didn't feel that liberated. Didn't feel that free, her right to choose. Fact, she felt quite wretched.
>
> Sometimes I think we should, do what we say we should. And start, where women are.[16]

'Us and them': representations of motherhood in the 1980s

By the end of the decade the feminist movement was under attack for its failure to move beyond its middle-class, white, heterosexual origins. The movement was increasingly critiqued by many different groups of feminists, whom it had failed to represent, and forced to re-think its demands and aims. In respect of motherhood, the early feminist emphasis on birth control and on young women not having children, meant that mothers had not been significantly represented on the feminist agenda. As Black activist bell hooks explains in an American context:

> Although early feminists demanded respect and acknowledgement for housework and child care, they did not attribute enough significance and value to female parenting, to motherhood. It is a gesture that should have been made at the onset of feminist movement. Early feminist attacks on motherhood alienated masses of women from the movement, especially poor and/or non-white women, who find parenting one of the few interpersonal relationships where they are affirmed and appreciated.[17]

The class-based and/or colour-based oppression of mothers, as hooks explains, had left them out on the 'margins' of the feminist center. Hence, despite Rowbotham's assertion that the movement in Britain 'rejected the emancipation of the middle-class "career woman" who was forced to remain childless'[18], feminism's failure to foreground motherhood as an issue for different social groups of women meant that there was no effective feminist opposition to her ascendancy in the 1980s. However 'Superwoman's' arrival in the 1980s, which heightened the intrasexual, class-based oppression between women, forced feminists to re-think the need for a transformation of familial structures, overshadowed by the reproductive 'body politics' of the 1970s.

Top Girls

Caryl Churchill's *Top Girls* (1982)[19] is a frequently cited example of the underlying 'us and them' trends in Britain during the 1980s: a climate of increasingly regressive, reactionary, and right-wing politics in which the 'gap' between working-class mothers and childless middle-class career women widens. The opening dinner scene of historical, fictional, and mythical 'top girls' foregrounds the oppressive systems of patriarchy which women have been subjected to throughout centuries. In respect of motherhood specifically, the scene critiques the power of men to take control of their children, as various of the women dinner guests narrate their experiences of mothering and patriarchal intervention in the birthing and care of children. This is emblematised in Griselda's narrative (based on the story of the obedient wife in Chaucer's 'The Clerk's Tale'), whose husband takes her children away from her, and allows her to spend years believing they have been killed, in order to test her faith in him.

This thematic issue is developed in the play's dramatic action, in the confrontation between 'top girl' Marlene and her working-class sister Joyce. In order to be a successful career woman, Marlene relinquishes a personal, emotional and familial life. However, her status and material advances are made at the expense of her sister who has care of Marlene's daughter, Angie. Marlene illustrates how the success of Thatcher's 'top girls' depends upon women participating in systems of male power and inhabiting a masculinist discourse which sets up systems of intrasexual oppression. The 'Superwoman' myth promoted the idea that women might combine successful careers with motherhood, but in reality it alienated most working women from the maternal. Only a minority of women in a 'super' income bracket did not experience this alienation:

> JOYCE: I don't know how you could leave your own child.
> MARLENE: You were quick enough to take her.
> JOYCE: What does that mean?
> MARLENE: You were quick enough to take her.
> JOYCE: Or what? Have her put in a home? Have some stranger/ take her would you rather? . . .
> Turned out all right for you by the look of you. You'd be getting a few less thousand a year.
> MARLENE: Not necessarily.
> JOYCE: You'd be stuck here/ like you said.
> MARLENE: I could have taken her with me.
> JOYCE: You didn't want to take her with you. It's no good coming back now. Marlene,/ and saying –

MARLENE: I know a managing director who's got two children, she breast feeds in the board room, she pays a hundred pounds a week on domestic help alone and she can afford that because she's an extremely high-powered lady earning a great deal of money.[20]

My Mother Said I Never Should

Images of working mothers in dominant and counter-cultural contexts increased throughout the decade.[21] In a theatrical context, Charlotte Keatley's highly successful *My Mother Said I Never Should*, first performed in 1987, represents the question of 'choice' between motherhood and work across four generations of mothers/daughters. Whereas the earlier *My Mother Says I Never Should* by The Women's Theatre Group proposed that young women look forwards and not 'backwards' (i.e. to their mothers) to better their lives. Keatley's drama explores the value of mothers and daughters understanding the choices each makes, and how these are conditioned, (or in Rich's terms, institutionalised), by the society and culture in which they live. The play does not propose a simplistic reification of mother–daughter bonding, but cross-generational understandings of women's lives and experiences. As Keatley herself explains:

> By showing certain moments which are quite similar for many women – moments of saying things like 'Mum, I want to sleep with that man', or 'Mum, I'm going to have a child', or whatever – the same thresholds are reached in every generation, though very different choices will ultimately be made, largely due to the different social expectations directed at women in each generation.[22]

The 'top girl' syndrome of women whose children are looked after by other members of their family while they pursue their careers is also examined in *My Mother Said I Never Should*, in a way which gives more space than in Churchill's drama to the emotional dilemma which mothers in this situation confront. In Keatley's play, third-generation mother, Jackie, is able to get on in her career as an artist because her baby, which she briefly tried to raise on her own, is taken care of by her mother, Margaret. On the one hand, Jackie acknowledges that she could not have combined motherhood and work: 'You know Mummy, the

Gallery and everything. I couldn't have done it without you. You can't be a mother and then cancel Christmas to be in New York.'[23] On the other hand, she lives with the painful experience of being a mother estranged from her child and having to play the role of surrogate sister. As the one mother in the family who is not the primary carer of her child, Jackie creates tension among the other women. This surfaces particularly when her grandfather's estate passes to her rather than to her grandmother or mother: patriarchy recognises her as an 'achiever' career woman, which implicitly under-values the lives of the other women.

The sense of 'achieving', of living 'better' lives is also one, however, which is transmitted through the mother-line: the sense that each daughter must have more opportunities before her. As Margaret argues with her daughter Jackie at the point of taking Jackie's baby, Rosie, into her care: 'You've got to go further than me – and Rosie too. (Quietly.) Otherwise . . . what's it been worth?'[24] However, the play shows how the opportunity for women 'to go further' is constrained by male systems of power, and especially control over reproduction. For example, in a scene staged in Doris's garden, in which mother (Doris) and daughter (Margaret) discuss 'choice' in relation to motherhood and work. Doris challenges her daughter's assumption that her generation automatically desired motherhood:

> DORIS: I had a job once too. I know it was only teaching, but . . . (*Pause. To stop herself.*) there's an odd maroon one [sock] over there, on the grass. (*Pause. Warning Margaret.*) Of course. Father has absolutely no idea. One would never . . . tell him. (*Pause.*) There wasn't any choice then: so I don't know whether it was my need – to love him, if you know what I mean . . . or his desire – for a son. (*Long pause. Doris bends and picks up a sock.*) Horrible colours he likes. Not my choice, maroon . . . Not my choice at all . . . (*Pause.*)[25]

Sarah Daniels

Radical feminist playwright Sarah Daniels has been particularly concerned to expose the ways in which patriarchy conditions and controls women's 'choices'. Her plays in the early 1980s focused specifically on the plight of middle- and working-class mothers in this context, with a view to exposing both the patriarchal domination of women and class-based intrasexual oppression between women.

In her black comedy *Ripen Our Darkness* (1981), Mary, a middle-class mother, is alienated from the masculinist discourse of her husband and sons which controls and dominates the domestic sphere. When she fails to cope with all her domestic chores, her churchwarden husband refers her to a (male) psychiatrist who is prepared to have her committed. Rather than be taken into care on her husband's orders, Mary takes her own life (by putting her head in the gas oven with her husband's dinner: an imaging of her domestic oppression). She wakes up to find herself in the presence of three blaspheming female deities. When given the option of returning to the male-dominated, 'war-ridden shit heap men call earth', she chooses instead to stay at 'home' with 'Mother Almighty'.[26]

The radical feminist impulse of Daniel's theatre, seeks solutions to the oppression of women in all-female communities. Mary's contact with her daughter Anna, who lives away from home in a lesbian relationship, is one oasis in a masculine desert. Similarly, the domestic sequences set in the kitchen of working-class mother, Rene, which parallel the middle-class home scenes, contrast the violence Rene suffers at the hands of her husband with the loving relationship she has with her daughter. Women forming women-only relationships, whether as a lesbian couple or mother–daughter bonding is presented as an alternative to surviving within the bourgeois family unit.

The lesbian relationships in *Ripen Our Darkness* and again in Daniels's later play *The Devil's Gateway* (1983), also provide an antidote to intrasexual oppression as they involve cross-class female coupling. In contrast to *Ripen Our Darkness*, *The Devil's Gateway* is more firmly rooted in the theatricalisation of working-class mothers and their experiences of life in London's East End. Seeking a way out of patriarchally conditioned family life is metaphorically represented in the closing image of the play as the women, from three different generations and two different families, take flight to Greenham Common. It is respect, understanding, and love of women for each other, whether through blood relations, sexual relationships, or friendships, which is seen as vital for women to escape the male conditioning and control of their lives.

'Dead proud': radical mothers in the margins

The radical vision of separatist, women-only communities poses a significant threat to patriarchy – especially with regard to parenting, as evidenced in our government's recent mobilisation of hostility against some of the weakest and most oppressed members of the State (i.e. single mothers on benefit). In many ways, the most radical representations of motherhood to be found in contemporary feminist theatre, are those which dramatise motherhood taking place outside of the traditional, heterosexist family unit. Further, as this final section aims to show, the vision of young mothers bringing up children alone is one which is represented with pride and resistance by young working-class women.

Care and Control

In the late 1970s, and contrary to the trend of limiting the politics of motherhood to the question of choice over an individual pregnancy, *Care and Control* (1977), devised by Gay Sweatshop and scripted by Michelene Wandor, dramatised the need for a radical transformation of the family, through an exploration of the issue of lesbian motherhood and custody cases. Wandor explains how the drama

> ended up raising some searching questions about the dominant assumptions behind family life in order to maintain the status quo of a family pattern which assumes heterosexual monogamous woman at its centre. When women transgress this norm, the law will try to make them toe the line. The play shows how such 'transgression' can range from a mother who chooses a lesbian relationship to a mother who simply wants to live on her own with her child . . . the emphasis is mainly on the female experience . . . the male experience is the least developed area in the play.[27]

The radical feminist impulse underlying the drama demonstrates the oppression of 'unorthodox' mothers by man-made legal and judicial systems, threatened by their non-conformity. As the programme notes for the production explained:

> Single mothers, lesbian and heterosexual, face the same kind of prejudice when they come before the judicial system. A woman is suspect in the eyes of the State when she asserts her right to live independently of men. She is seen as a direct challenge to family life and the traditional sexual roles which the courts uphold.[28]

Out of the four mothers whose personal lives are portrayed in Act One, only one remains with her children, after the custody cases theatricalised in Act Two. The father who remarries and thereby reinforces dominant heterosexist ideology and the family 'norm' is granted 'care and control'. The lone mother who keeps her children does so merely by default: the father has no plans to re-marry and to provide a suitable home, and so on. The socialist-realist style of the domestic scenes and the Brechtian montage of court-room drama combine to demonstrate the hostility of the State towards motherhood practised in a woman-only or women-only units.

The Arbor

Contrary to the middle-class advice of women in the feminist movement in the 1970s, many of whom went on to have children of their own in the 1980s (for further discussion of this point see Rowbotham[29]), some young working-class women chose pregnancy as a source of pride, identity and defiance. The 'girlmother' figure as she is fashioned by young writers in the 1980s[30], is represented not as downtrodden, social outcast, but as a site of radical resistance, within a complex matrix of class- and gender-based oppression. As Angela McRobbie, who has worked and researched extensively with young women, especially young working-class women, comments:

> They [girls] do challenge that which is perceived to be unacceptable, even if the way in which they challenge is not, perhaps in our view, the most immediately damaging, the most 'political'. But every day girls 'talk back' to teachers, to authoritative figures. They don't always let themselves be pushed around by employers, by families and by boys.[31]

In the case of young working-class girls, McRobbie adds that it is essentially difficult for them to escape their oppression, or 'class domination', and 'deviancy' might only result in reinforcing their 'class and gender destiny'. Yet, nevertheless, 'even if in the end oppression did get the better of them . . . they none the less manipulated the structures where they could'.[32]

Andrea Dunbar's *The Arbor*, first written when Dunbar was fifteen and performed three years later at the Royal Court's Young Writer's Festival in 1980, examines teenage pregnancy against a backdrop of Northern working-class life. Dunbar's dramatisation of the hardships facing young working-class women is drawn from her own experiences of life on a Bradford council estate. Originally the play was written as one act, dramatising a young girl's decision to keep her baby; a decision which the girl argues through defiantly with the teacher at a school for unmarried mothers where she has been placed:

> MRS RENNISH: Do you know if that social worker thinks your family cannot cope with this child you're having she may put the baby in care?
> GIRL: My baby won't go in care! You think we're all daft don't you! But I'm not! Nobody will get that baby!
> MRS RENNISH: Don't be so stupid! You won't be able to stop them and it's only for the baby's own good.
> GIRL: I don't care what it's for, nobody's taking it away from me because I aren't thick. I can look after it, not like others who give their babies away for adoption 'cause they can't look after them.
> MRS RENNISH: Well if you want you can have an abortion because you're not three months gone yet, and you don't have to pay for it.
> GIRL: I'm not having an abortion. I don't believe in them anyway, neither does my mum and she won't give the baby up for adoption.[33]

The girl suffers a miscarriage at the close of the act, originally the end of the play, but her loss is not treated with pathos, just as yet another hardship in a life in which brutality is the norm.

Act Two, which Dunbar wrote for the play's transfer to the main stage at the Court, depicts the girl pregnant again in a violent, mixed-race relationship. To save both herself and her baby she seeks asylum in a women's refuge: the pregnant teenager does not cling to a relationship with a boy, but looks for a way out of the (male) violence of her community. The closing image of the two-act version of *The Arbor* leaves the girl temporarily removed from the systems of class- and gender-based oppression. The refuge offers only temporary protection. The girl's violent partner, Yousaf, will be back battering at the refuge door. Yet it does image the possibility, however fragile, of young women surviving alone. In each of the three plays Dunbar wrote before her sudden death in 1990, the final stage picture is one in which, as in Daniels's theatre, women decide that they are better off without men.[34]

Rose's Story

Teenage pregnancy as a source of pride and resistance is foregrounded in Grace Dayley's *Rose's Story*, first performed in 1984 at the Polytechnic of the South Bank. Based on Dayley's own experiences of being a teenage mother in a mother and baby home, the drama centres on the Black pregnant teenager Rose Johnson who is determined to keep her baby. 'As nearly 50% of the women in the cast were unmarried mothers', the issues in the play were particularly important to the performers.[35] Like Dunbar's 'girl', Rose has to stand up to patronising authority figures who treat her as 'stupid' and incapable of keeping and looking after her baby. The idea of an abortion is firmly rejected, and the pregnancy as a source of empowerment is clearly expressed. As Rose explains to her sister, Elaine:

> ROSE: Don't cry Elaine, because I've realised that I will have to become somebody in my own right, no longer listening to everything people try to push down my throat. Do you remember a time when I was the quiet one who never answered back. I used to get trodden on all the time, people could dump their shit on me left, right and centre . . . I know this may sound really silly, but me getting pregnant, is not such a bad thing. I now answer back because I've got to . . . I can't really afford not to . . . Elaine, look at it this way, all this means is that Rose is growing up and I'll have to learn to hold my own . . . the only person I can let try to dump their shit on me now, is the child I'm having . . . so cheer up: things will sort themselves out . . .[36]

Dead Proud

The theatre of young women writers like Dunbar and Dayley is characterised by a rawness reflecting their working-class lives, which are not represented by middle-class theatre. Festivals like the Royal Court's Young Writer's Festival, created a space for young working-class women, who would normally find it impossible to have their work put on in the theatre, to be represented. Ann Considine, co-ordinator of the Second Wave: Young Women Playwrights festival at the Albany Empire Theatre, explains how the purpose of this festival was 'to celebrate and encourage new writing for the theatre from black and white working-class women whose voices are often not heard'.[37] Her introduction to *Dead Proud*, a collection of plays and play extracts from the 1986 festival states:

> This book is about young women's lives. About dealing with a world in which you have little power, where there are often no real choices, where you have to jostle to be heard. *Dead Proud* is a preview of work from a new generation of women artists. Their voices challenge the voice of experience: their writing as varied in style and character as they are.[38]

In the title play, *Dead Proud* by Angie Milan, a teenage mother decides to keep her baby, while alongside it, *Backstreet Mammy*, by Roselia John Baptiste, portrays a sixteen-year old black girl who chooses to have an abortion. Considine notes that what is important about the different decisions made in these two plays is that each young woman is 'taking steps to become independent'.[39] In each case the decisions are made independently of men who prove unreliable and delinquent. Whether these young working-class women express their vision of independence as single mothers, or through having abortions, their writing is characterised by 'a spirit of resilience and toughness'.[40] It is the 'spirit of resilience and toughness' which determines the radicalism of this new writing, reflecting an attempt to make choices in a world where virtually none exist, and where, as McRobbie explains, oppression may well get the better of you. This is a far cry from the middle-class values of early feminism. The politics of these young women and mothers out in the 'margins' is a politics of survival.

By way of conclusion, this point may be summarised with an illustration from *Teendreams*. Written in 1979, the play looks back at the 1970s (as previously explained), but also closes with a young generation of working-class women on the threshold of the 1980s. In one of the final scenes, Denise, a young working-class single mother, describes her life with her baby, Paul:

> I used to be a juvenile delinquent . . .
>
> But then I got this accident. Well, tell a lie, in fact, was kind of planned. You jump the list, for council flats, if you're a mother. Get away from home.
>
> I haven't seen the bloke. An age. Think he's in Borstal. Was a wash out, anyway. And on your own, can screw the SS that much more.
>
> So what d' I do? Not nothing much, in fact. Get by. Keep going. Paul and me, and take no shit from any one. A lot, in fact.
>
> I'm a fucking superior mother.[41]

'Screwing' the State for benefit is precisely what alarms the government now, as the number of women like Denise has continued to rise throughout the 1980s and 1990s. However, if the government objects to the number of 'fucking superior mothers', then it must, the dramatist suggests, recognise that it has largely helped create them. As it is, the play shows us a fifteen year regime of 'us and them' – a 'major' record of achievement of which the government can be 'dead proud'.

Notes

1. E.A. Kaplan, *Motherhood and Representation* (London and New York, 1992), p. 3.
2. M. Wandor, quoted in V. Beechy, *The Changing Experience of Women: Unit One* (Milton Keynes, 1982), p. 16.
3. A. Rich, *Of Woman Born* (London, 1977), p. 23.
4. Ibid., p. 13.
5. See M. Wandor, *Look Back in Gender* (London and New York, 1987), p. 91.
6. Red Ladder, *Strike While the Iron is Hot*. In M. Wandor (ed.), *Strike While the Iron is Hot* (London, 1980), p. 29.
7. Ibid., p. 62.

8. S. Rowbotham, 'To Be or Not To Be: The Dilemma of Mothering', *Feminist Review*, 31, 1989, 82–93, p. 83.
9. Ibid.
10. Wandor, quoted in Beechy, *The Changing Experience*, p. 16.
11. Women's Theatre Group, *My Mother Says I Never Should*. In Wandor *Strike While the Iron is Hot*, p. 136.
12. C. Duchen, *Feminism in France: From May '68 to Mitterand* (London and New York, 1986), p. 60.
13. Rowbotham, 'To Be or Not To Be', p. 85.
14. P. Gems, *Dusa, Fish, Stas & Vi*. In M. Wandor (ed.) *Plays by Women: One* (London and New York, 1982), p. 69.
15. Ibid., p. 55.
16. D. Edgar and S. Todd, *Teendreams* (London, 1980), p. 18.
17. b. hooks, *Feminist Theory: From Margin to Center* (Boston, 1984), pp. 134–5.
18. Rowbotham, 'To Be or Not To Be', p. 86.
19. First performed in 1982. Reference is to C. Churchill, *Top Girls*, revised edition (London and New York, 1984).
20. Ibid., pp. 79–80.
21. See Kaplan, *Motherhood and Representation*, pp. 188–90.
22. C. Keatley, 'Art Form or Platform?: On Women Playwrighting', *New Theatre Quarterly*, 22, May 1990, 128–140, p. 131.
23. C. Keatley, *My Mother Said I Never Should*, revised edition (London and Portsmouth, 1990), p. 45.
24. Ibid., p. 15.
25. Ibid., p.17.
26. S. Daniels, *Ripen Our Darkness and The Devil's Gateway* (London and New York, 1986), pp. 35–6.
27. Wandor, *Strike While the Iron is Hot*, p. 13.
28. Ibid., p. 64.
29. Rowbotham, 'To Be or Not To Be', p. 84.
30. A description which Rose, young, black and pregnant, uses to describe herself in G. Dayley, *Rose's Story*. In M. Wandor (ed.) *Plays By Women: Four* (London and New York 1985), p. 65.
31. A. McRobbie and T. McCabe, *Feminism for Girls* (London, 1981), p. 18.
32. Ibid., pp. 18–19.
33. A. Dunbar, *Three Stage Plays* (London and New York, 1988), p. 11.
34. For further details of Dunbar's plays, see E. Aston, 'Girls on Stage: Contemporary British Women's Theatre and the Teenage Question', *Modernes Theatre*, 8, 1993, 152–63.
35. Dayley, *Rose's Story*, p. 80.

36. Ibid., p. 72.
37. A. Considine and R. Slovo (eds), *Dead Proud* (London, 1987), p. 3.
38. Ibid., p. 2.
39. Ibid., p. 1.
40. Ibid., p. 3.
41. Edgar and Todd, *Teendreams*, p. 49.

Appendix: Documents

The documents that follow have been chosen in order to indicate something of the contexts out of which moments of radical writing come. I have not however attempted to provide documentary evidence for the subjects raised by each and every one of the chapters in this book. The chapters themselves provide such evidence. My aim has been to provide material which will allow the users of the book to locate its main concerns in issues which the documents point towards and, occasionally, address at length.

Document 1

The Worcester Cathedral Misericord reminds us that for centuries before Milton wrote *Paradise Lost* the rights of labour had been a matter of political concern; and that such rights were thought to be a matter of concern to a just God.

Document 2

The illustrations and extracts from the *Mirabilis Annus* pamphlet, relating to Maureen Bell's Chapter 3, provide evidence both of women's publishing and of the way in which republicans argued that god's intervention in worldly affairs showed his opposition to the rule of kings.

Document 3

Charles Hobday's Chapter 4 on the sansculotte poets John Freeth and Joseph Mather deals with writers whose work has never been made generally available. It therefore seems both desirable and necessary to provide examples of their work as well as bibliographies of both. The poems chosen here are discussed in some detail in Chapter 4 itself.

Document 4

Charlotte Smith's sonnet 'Written on the Sea-Shore', October 1784 is of relevance to Loraine Fletcher's Chapter 6 on 'Four Women Jacobin Novelists', especially in its depiction of the woman speaker as oppressed by fate, which may of course include the fate of being a writer in a society where writing was considered to be a male profession even if women were allowed their place as enthusiastic amateurs.

Document 5

For this reason I have chosen to follow Charlotte Smith's sonnet with an extract from Maria Edgeworth's *Letters for Literary Ladies*. Edgeworth published these *Letters* in 1795 and the extract that follows is taken from the first of these, entitled 'Letter from a Gentleman to his Friend, Upon the Birth of A Daughter'. The satiric edge makes several keen cuts against male complacency especially those revealed in assumptions about women's education and the dangers of allowing women to take to the literary life.

Document 6

The next document is taken from a pamphlet published in 1836. Its author was William Lovett (1800–77), a leading figure in working-class political movements during the nineteenth century and one of those who formulated the demands that were to make up the Chartist movement. The document is therefore of especial relevance to Steve Devereux's Chapter 7 but its insistence on the need for universal suffrage for workmen was bound to lead to working women's demand to be included in the suffrage, a demand which is looked at in Pauline Polkey's Chapter 8.

Document 7

Douglas Goldring's essay on the poets of the First World War was written as that war ended and before the poetry of Wilfred Owen, Isaac Rosenberg, Edward Thomas or the important war poetry of Ivor Gurney had been published. But Goldring's attack on the 'Public School Spirit' is remarkable, both for its understanding of how that spirit contributed to, and indeed, largely prompted, war poetry as ardent as it was innocent (and often absurd) and for sounding the note of radical disaffection with the social and political *status quo* which would be increasingly heard in the post-war years. Goldring was a pacifist and socialist, a poet, novelist, dramatist and memoirist, whose *Odd Man Out: The Autobiography of a 'Propaganda Novelist'* (London, 1935) is well worth reading. The essay is relevant to Chapters 9 and 10.

Document 8

Lawrence Ferlinghetti's 'One Thousand Fearful Words for Fidel Castro' is the poem on which Chapter 11 is based.

DOCUMENT 1

The Worcester Cathedral Misericord

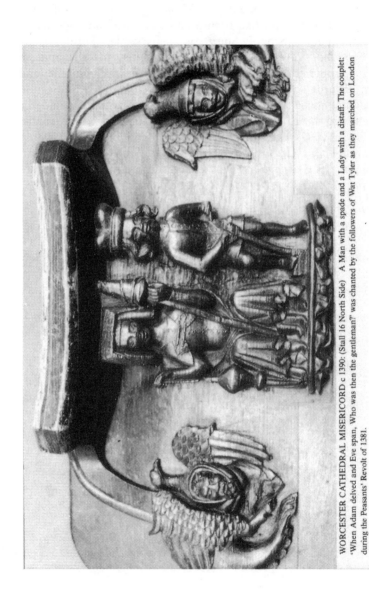

WORCESTER CATHEDRAL MISERICORD c 1390: (Stall 16 North Side) A Man with a spade and a Lady with a distaff. The couplet: 'When Adam delved and Eve span, Who was then the gentleman?' was chanted by the followers of Wat Tyler as they marched on London during the Peasants' Revolt of 1381.

(Reproduced by permission of the Dean and Chapter of Worcester.)

DOCUMENT 2

ΕΝΙΑΥΤΟΣ ΤΕΡΑΣΤΙΟΣ
MIRABILIS ANNUS,

OR

The year of Prodigies and Wonders, being a faithful and impartial Collection of several Signs that have been seen in the Heavens, in the Earth, and in the Waters; together with many remarkable Accidents and Judgments befalling divers Persons, according as they have been testified by very credible hands; all which have happened within the space of one year last past, and are now made publick for a seasonable Warning to the People of these three Kingdoms speedily to repent and turn to the Lord, whose hand is lifted up amongst us.

Isaiah 5. 11, 1². *Wo to them that rise up early in the morning that they may follow strong drink, that continue until night till wine inflame them, and the Harp and the Viol, the Tabret and the Pipe, and Wine are in their feasts, but they regard not the Work of the Lord, neither consider the operation of his hands,* Psal. III. 2. *The works of the Lord are great, sought out of all them that have pleasure therein.*

Revel. 15. 4. *Who shall not fear thee O Lord, and glorifie thy Name, for thou onely art Holy, for all Nations shall come and worship before thee, for thy judgements are made manifest.*

Omnia hæc signa sunt imminentis iræ Dei quam necesse est quocuo modo possumus ut & annunciemus & prædicemus & deprecemur, *Tertul. ad Scap* p. 89.

Quod signum erit iræ Dei impiis, erit signum perfectæ Redemptionis filiis Dei, *Zanch. de oper. Dei*, Tom. 3. p. 335.

Printed in the Year 1661.

DOCUMENT 2 continued

DOCUMENT 2 continued

ΕΝΙΑΥΤΟΣ ΤΕΡΑΣΤΙΟΣ: mirabilis annus, or the year of prodigies and wonders . . .

The Preface

. . . The things that are here presented to the Reader are *various*, and *remarkable*, the particulars seen in the Heavens are in number fifty four, those in the Earth twenty three, those in the Waters ten, the Accidents and Judgements befalling several persons twenty seven, all these, which have been collected but by a *few hands*, (there being we are perswaded many more which have not come to our knowledge) have happened within the compasse of a *year*, the like we believe a *whole age* hath scarce produced in times past, the Lord therein shewing great mercy and compassion to the people of these Nations, that though he hath suffered this year so many *hundreds*: if not *thousands* of our able godly, *preaching Ministers* to be *removed into corners*, yet the defect of their Ministry hath been *eminently* supplied by the *Lords* immediate preaching to us from *Heaven*, in the great and wonderful works of his Providence, which *Eusebius* calls Τα Του-εου κγρύγμαΤα *Gods Sermons*, which this year come to more then two in a week according to the foregoing *calculation*.

And if (according to the opinion of learned men, such as *Luther, Voetius, Weems*, &c) Prodigies and signs are *especially* for the sakes of *wicked and ungodly men, Aarons Rod budded for a token against the Rebels*. Then from the vast disproportion of their number this year, to what they were for many years together in the times foregoing, we may easily guesse at the prodigious increase of the most bruitish prophannesse, Atheism, uncleannesse, murders, blasphemy and superstition that *this single year* hath produced, beyond all the presidents which former times have acquainted us with. And surely by these hainous and unparralel'd enormities, the *Jealous* God hath been exceedingly provoked, and by his remarkable and strange Signs in the Heavens, the Earth, and the Waters, doth in a most dreadful manner Alarm the ungodly world; they are not onely the *Messengers*, but *Harbingers* also of Divine indignation, to such as are *obstinate* in their wickedness, *who say in their hearts there is no God*, and lead a life worse then that of the people in the time of *Noah*.

We shall not dare to be possitive in a particular application of all, or any of the portents mentioned in the following History, knowing it would relish of too much boldnesse and presumption to peep into the Ark of Divine Secrets. We shall in this case subscribe to the judgement of the Learned *Voetius*, who accounts it no lesse then a *Nefas* to apply Prodigies to particular persons, *sine extraordinario & peculiari* χαρίμαTα which we do not in the least pretend unto; therefore according to the caution given by the same Author, we shall avoid *Cacœthes illud* as he calls it, and conclude with *Balduin, praestat ergo talia in scientio & Spe committere Deo quam divinando temeritatem prodere; It is better in science and hope, to leave things of this nature to God, then by attempting to prognosticate any thing from them, thereby to betray our own rashnesse.* Onely we shall be bold to hint thus much, that accidents of this kind do portend the futurition or manifestation of some things as yet not existent or not known, which usually carry in them some kind of agreement and assimulation to the Prodigies themselves, as (according to the opinion of some learned men) *the raining of bloud* may signifie much slaughter, *the noise of Guns and the apparition of Armies in the Air*, wars and commotions, *great inundations*, popular tumults and insurrections, yet still we must know that God is unsearchable in his wayes, and our most *critical* and *exact* observations, together with our best experiences will not capacitate us *fully* to trace him through the Maze and Labyrinth of hid providences, his way being as *Solomon* speaks, *like the way of a ship in the sea*. However, that the following discourse might be the more profitable (so far as the Scriptures with the modest conjectures of the most sober amongst the learned will warrant us) we shall here briefly insert a few of those *general* things which commonly prove the *issues and events* of such *prodigious apparitions* as the ensuing History gives us an account of.

1. They do usually sore signifie some remarkable *changes* and *revolutions* which bring with them very sad *calamities* and *distresses* to the generality of the people, amongst whom they happen; *our Saviour* himself shews us a *necessary* connexion between *signs in the sun and in the Moon, and in the stars, and upon the earth distresse of Nations with perplexity*. Great are the influences which these things have in a natural way upon States and Kingdoms in the world, it being a received Maxim amongst the meer *Naturalists*, that some considerable mutations and concussions are the usual products of them, but certainly their vertue and Operation is far greater, as they are *ordained of God* to portend and signifie the most dreadful and important Revolutions of his providence. These did our *Saviour himself* institute and appoint as the certain Signs and immediate forerunners of that sore destruction so often threatned, and at last so severely executed by *Titus Vespasian* upon *Jerusalem*. Great honour is Likewise given to them by Christ in that he reckons them amongst the *Portents* and *Presages* of his second coming. We shall therefore conclude this with those Instances which the *Reverend* and *Learned* Dr *Jackson* hath furnished us with, *viz*. That Testimony of *Herodotus* (who lived before *Alexander the Great*, but after *Cyrus* had taken the City *Babylon*) his words (as they are quoted by the said

Author) are these *quoties ingentes sunt eventuræ Calamitates vel Civitati, vel Nationi solent Signis prænunciari*, extraordinary calamities whether such as befall Cities or peculiar Signiories are alwaies fore shewen by some sign or other. His other instance is that of *Matchiavel*, of whom he saies, that he was a man as free from *Superstition* or vain *Credulity* as any other Writer that hath been born and bred amongst *Christians*; yet he out of his own Reading and Experience hath made the same induction with *Herodotus*, but somewhat more full, *ut causam facile me confitebor ignorare ita rem ipsam cum ex antiquis, tum novis exemplis agnoscere oportet, & confiteri omnes magnos motus, quicunque aut urbi aut regioni evenerunt, vel a conjectoribus vel a revelatione aliqua Prodigiis, aut Cælestibus Signis prædici aut prænunciari solere*, As I must needs confesse my self ignorant of the cause, so the thing it self I cannot but acknowledge to be true, both from antient and modern examples, that the motions and changes which have at any time happened either to Cities or Countryes, have still been foretold or pre declared either by some Southsayers, or else by some discoveries from Prodigies or Signes in the Heavens; And afterwards the same *Machiavel* affirms, that the severall *Changes* which happened in *Italy* in his time, were still presaged by divers remarkable *Signes* and *Prodigies*, whereof he gives particular instances in the Chapter before cited.

2. They do bode very much misery and calamity to the *prophane* and *wicked* part of the World (except a through and seasonable repentance and turning to God do intervene) the *Mene Tekel* on the Wall did signifie evil to *Belshazzar*, who though he knew all that God had done to his *Father, yet humbled not his heart, but lifted up himself against the Lord of Heaven*, and by his *presence at least* did keep up and encourage *drunken and debauched meetings*, wherein the *Vessels of the Temple* (the spoiles of the Lords people) were *prophaned*, the *High God blasphemed, and the Gods of Gold, and of Silver, of Brass, of Iron, of Wood and of Stone were praised* and magnified; and sayes the Text in *that same hour came forth fingers of a mans hand, &c.* So that God by a prodigie doth sharply reprove the debauchery of this King and his Concubines, with the rest of his *Associates*, and thereby also declares the sudden period and determination of his *Kingdom*.

But amongst the *Hellish* rout of prophane and ungodly men, let *especially the Oppressors* and *Persecutors of the True Church* look to themselves, when the hand of the Lord in strange Signes and Wonders is lifted up among them for *then* let them know assuredly *that the day of their Calamity is at hand, and the things that shall come upon them make hast* The totall and finall overthrow of *Pharoah* and the *Ægiptians* (those cruell Task-Masters and Oppressors of the Israelites) did bear date not long after the *Wonderfull* and *Prodigious Signes* which the Lord had shewn in the mid'st of them; Neither could the Nation of the *Jews (who were both the betrayers and murderers of the Lord of Life and Glory*; and did persecute his *Apostles* and *Disciples from City to City)* escape those sad and dreadfull effects of the *Signes* and *Prodigies* which Christ long before foretold and forewarned them by, and were indeed according to our Saviours Predictions, the doleful Messengers of the approaching ruine both of *themselves,* their *City* and *Temple*: O that therefore all the Enemies of *Sion* (who make it their work to *tread the Holy City under foot)* would betimes before the effects of this years wonders take place against them, truly repent, and be ashamed of all their enmity against the faithfull Servants of the *most High God,* least his wrath break forth *and their be none to deliver.*

3. They do usually Prognosticate very much good to the *Sober* and *Religious* part of the World, that which severely threatens the ruine and destruction of others, doth clearly portend the security and preservation of their interest.

Those signall Predictions of *Pharoahs* and the *Ægyptians* overthrow did yet assure the *Israelites* of *their* speedy deliverance and departure *out of the House of bondage*; Therefore when the Psalmists had largely discoursed of those *Signes* which God did show in *Ægypt,* he concludes with these words, *he made his own people to go forth like Sheep, and guided them in the Wilderness like a Flock, and he led them on safely so that they feared not, but the Sea over-whelmed their enemies,* yea the very first discovery that ever the Lord made of saving that *People,* was by the *Prodigie* of a burning bush. *David* also speaking of great *Earthquakes* sad and dark *Eclypses,* terrible *Storms,* strange *Fiery Meteors* in the Heavens, dreadfull *Thunders* and *Lightnings, &c.* makes the end of all this to be nothing else but his own *Deliverance*; Therefore he sayes in the close of all, *he sent from above, he took me, he drew me out of many Waters, he delivered me from my strong Enemy and from them that hated me, for they were too strong for me.* The greatest blessing likewise that ever the Church received, *viz.* (the birth of our Lord Jesus Christ (who came into the world on purpose *to save his people from their sins*) was ushered in with the appearance of a strange and unusuall Star in the *East,* whereof *Chalcidius* in his Comment upon *Plato's Timœus* takes great notice because it signified the coming down of a *God* in favour to the Salvation of men, as Dr. *Hammond* hath well observed in his Comment on *Mat.* 2.2. Those very *Signes* also which according to *Christs* prophesie did point at the miserable *Desolation* of *Jerusalem* did notwithstanding presage the giving of the *Holy Ghost* to the *Apostles,* and the first *Gospel Church,* as *Peter* himself affirms in his *Apology* for the *Disciples.* And indeed these strange *Prodigies* were long before by the Prophet *Joel* prophesied of, as the *Harbingers* of that new and Spiritual dispensation under the Gospel according to his *excellent connection, I will powre out my Spirit upon all flesh, And I will shew wonders in the Heavens, &c.* Which Peter in the forementioned *Scripture* makes to be fulfilled in that *wonderfull* effusion of the *Spirit* on the day of *Penticost.*

Yea further, our Lord *Jesus Christ himself,* when he speaks of the severall *Signes* that shall preceed his *second coming,* (at the sight whereof *all the Tribes of the Earth shall mourn*) yet encourages *his people to lift up their heads with joy, because their Redemption draweth nigh* . . .

Several Prodigies and Apparitions seen in the Heavens from August the 1. 1660. to the latter end of May, 1661.

(Margin notes from the original document are set in square brackets after each section.)

I.

Several persons who were reaping Wheat in a Field about a quarter of a Mile from *Hertford,* near six of the Clock in the Evening, *August* 1. 1660. espyed two Suns in the Firmament, the One West, the Other more Northerly at some distance each from other; they were as they judged of equal height and bignesse, and beams did issue from both, only that more Northerly shone not so bright as the other. They continued in their view near half an hour, and then were both overshadowed by a cloud. This is Testified by honest credible persons who were eye-witnesses.

These παργλιος, *as the Greeks call them, do naturally portend much moisture and rainy weather.*

God ordaines them (as some learned men conceive) to signifie severall Judgments, as War, Famine and Pestilence. Some do affirm, they portend the fall of Great Men from their power, who rule with pride and disdain. They also signifie (as others do conjecture) disturbances and innovations in matters of Religion.

There were two Suns seen in England *at one time, shining at a good distance from each other in the beginning of Queen* Maries *reign:* See Bakers *Chron.* p.346.

Several Suns were seen near Prague, *about the time of the dreadful persecution which the Protestants sustained there from the hands of the bloody Papists.* See Bohem. Hist. p.355.

[Two Suns seen near *Hertford, Aug.* I. 1660. *Naturaliter portendunt & prœnunciante Pluvios.* Zanch. *de operibus Dei,* p. 348. *Parhelius est magnum pluviarum signum.* Her. Trismeg, *l.* 5. *p.* 473. *Ex Dei autem ordinatione varia ejus Judicia, vel Bella, vel Fames,* &c. Zanc. *ibid.* Pucerus, *Lib.* Metorolog. *p.*

340. *As it happened *Anno* 1156. 2 Suns appear'd, prognosticating the death of *Tho. Becket* Arch B. of *Cant.* an insolent proud Prelate. *Lycost.* p. 412.]

II.

In the same month also was seen at *Stratford Bow* near *London*, the likenesse of a great Ship in the Air, which by degrees lessened till it came to be as small as a mans Arm, but kept its form all the while, and at last disappeared. This is testified by an able Minister living not far from the place; who received the Information from the spectators themselves.

[The likenesse of a Ship seen in the Air at *Stratford Bow* near *London*.]

III.

About the same time at *Southo* in *Huntingtonshire*, was seen before Sun-rising, in the West and by North, a Rain-bow of a blood-red colour, it gave forth brightnesse, as if the Sun had been rising in that part of the Heavens, after it had continued for a while, a great red cloud by degrees swallowed it up. This is testified by a very credible person who lived not far from *Southo*, and did speak with several who were eye-witnesses.

[A Rain-bow of a blood-red colour seen before Sun-rising, at *Southo* in *Huntingtonshire*.]

IV.

A Gentleman of good quality, and an Officer of Eminency in the late Kings Army, & now a Justice of Peace in his Country, having occasion to be at *London* about the month of *September*, 1660: as he was going over *Smithfield* about ten of the Clock at night to his Lodgings in *Bartholomews* close, perceiving several people looking up into the Heavens, did himself also look up & espied towards the South-west a bright Star of a more then ordinary bignesse, and encompassed with six lesser Stars; whilst he with several others, were with some Admiration beholding them, they all fell down perpendicularly and vanished. This Gentlemans Lady being at the same time in her Lodgings and looking out at the window, expecting her Husbands coming, saw the same thing, with all the circumstances of it, a person of very good credit received this Information from both their mouths.

[Seven Stars seen to fall down perpendicularly. It is a thing rarely heard of, that such exhalations should move perpendicularly, but rather obliquely which is their natural motion. *Vid. Herm. Trismeg. l.* 5. *p.* 518.]

V.

At *Hull* about two of the Clock in the morning, *Octob.* 3. 1660. the Souldiers upon the Guard at the South Blockhouse, saw the Appearance of a great Body of Fire at South-east, the form of it (to use the Spectators own terms) was as big at one end as a great Sheet, from which went a narrow stream of fire, which they judged to be many yards long; it gave such a light, that according to their report (though immediatly before & after it was very dark) yet they could see to read a very smal print, or take up a pin from off the ground; [t]his continued about the space of half an hour and then vanished.

The same morning also one Travelling from *Lincolnshire* towards *Hull* saw a very great light in the sky, whereby he could perfectly discern his way, though before it was exceeding dark; this upon his arrival at *Hull* that day, he affirmed to divers persons there. And the whole Relation is signified by Letters from several eminent Men in *Hull* who spake with the eye-witnesses, as also by some Inhabitants in *London*, who upon occasion have been at *Hull* since that time, and there from very good hands have received credible and satisfactory Information concerning the premises.

[A great body of fire seen at H*ull Octob.* 3. 1660.]

VI.

October 5. 1660, between 11 and 12 of the clock at night, was seen near the New Artillery ground, a very fair Rainbow with the usual colours in it, that did seem to stand directly over the Moon, which at that time did shine extraordinary bright. The Information we received from a very credible person who was an eye witnesse.

Pliny *makes it to be an impossible thing in nature, that a Rain-bow should be at any time seen in the Night, though he confesseth that* Aristotle *doth affirme, that once such a thing happened, but it was when the Moon was at Full.* But if what Aristotle *says were true, (which* Pliny *much questions) yet still what hath been above related concerning the Rain-bow seen in the night when the Moon was not at the Full, must needs be acknowledged to be no ordinary thing: the meaning* and import whereof, the Lord may in due time discover; which we pray that he will turn for good to all that tremble at his Word and Works.

[A Rain-bow seen between 11 and 12 of the clock at night, *Octob.* 5. 1660. *Plin. Nat. Hist. l.* 2, *c.* 59. *Zanch.* says that this *Iris Lunarii* differs from the other in respect of the colour; for in this he sayes there is but *unus tantum color albus nimirum. Vid.* Zanch. *de operibus Dei, p.* 353. He sayes it portends *longam tempestatem annumq[ue] instabilem. ibid. p.* 356.]

VII.

A Person of very good Note and Credit living at *Hertford*, awaking about 4 of the clock in the morning, *Octo*. 11. 1660. perceived a flashing like fire against his window, and fearing some house near him had been on fire, he immediately arose and went to his window, and looking up perceived a Star about the bignesse of the palm of his hand, it had a dusky Circle about it, two straiks near half a yard long a piece went through the midst of it, which both above and below did send forth continually great Flashes of Fire; it stood directly North and South, and on the South side of it, was a point about half a quarter of a yard long, this continued for some hours and then disapeared; it was seen also by several other credible persons at *Hertford*, from whom this Relation comes.

[A strange Comet seen at *Hertford, Octob*. 11. 1660]

VIII.

Much about the same time was seen by several persons neer *Hornsy* a Flame of fire in the form of a Dart; which according to the apprehensions of the spectators hung directly over the City of *London*.

[A Meteor in the Form of a Dart seen hanging over *London*. This is by the Philosopher called *Bolis*. *Vid*. *Magiri*. *Physol*. *l*. 4. c. 2.]

IX.

In *Woodstreet, London*, upon the 12. of *Octo*. 1660 about four of the clock in the afternoon was seen by several of the Inhabitants there, a fiery Meteor in the form of a Ship streamer, or as others apprehended of a Beesome, with the great end formost about two yards in length; it passed with a very swift motion from West to East, And as some of the spectators do affirm, it made a great noise as it passed by, immediately upon it followed another of the same form, but not of the same bignesse. The Information comes from eye-witnesses.

Such a prodigious sign in this Form, though of longer continuance, appeared in Anno 1550. *when the persecution began to wax hot in* Scotland *against the professors of the Truth*. *Vid*. *Clarkes* Prodigies, *p*. 490.

[2 Meteors like a Ship-streamer or a Beesom seen in *Woodstreet, Octob*. 12. 1660.]

X.

At *Shenley* in *Hertfordshire*, (*Octob*. 17. 1660. being the day wherein Colonel *Scroop*, Col. *Jones*, and some Others were Executed at *Charing-cross*) was seen in the Aire towards the Evening, the Sky being very clear, the appearance of five naked Men exceeding bright and glorious, moving very swiftly, and after a little time a great Hill intercepted the sight of them. The Report of this was received from an Eye-witness, who is not in the least suspected to be a Phanatique, but hath given evident proof of the contrary; he doth constantly affirm the Truth of it, and offers to confirm it by his Oath.

[Five naked men seen in the Air at *Shenley, Octob.* 17, 1660.]

XI.

Not long after this, *viz.* the same day when the Quarters of the several Executed persons were set upon the Gates of the City, there appeared at Noon-day a bright Star over *Algate*, for two or three hours together, and continued so for four or five days; Of this many hundreds in the City passing that way, together with the adjacent Inhabitants were daily spectators during the time before specified.

[A bright Star appearing at noonday over the Quarters which were set up upon *Algate*.]

XII.

Also at *Bishops-gate* there appeared seven Pillars of smoke, (one wherof was bigger then the rest) ascending from the Seven quarters, which were first set up upon the Gate; they reached up towards Heaven as high as the beholders could well discern.

[Seven Pillars of Smoke seen ascending from the *Quarters* over *Bishopsgate*. Two Quarters more having been since set upon the same Gate.]

XIII.

At *Titsle* in *Surrey, Octob.* 29. 1660. about 8 or 9 of the clock in the Evening, there appeared in the Heavens three Moons of equal bignesse and brightnesse at a little distance from each other: The Relation comes from eye-witnesses, who were many, and some of good note and quality.

In Ireland; *Anno* 1342, *October* 11. *the Moon being* 11. *daies old, were seen at* Dublin *two Moons*: Camb. Brit. *Ireland, p.* 188. *Also in the moneth of* March, *Anno* 1551, *in the year wherein the Duke of* Somerset *was beheaded, and the Disputes were in* Germany *about Religion, and the French made war with the Emperour, three Moons were seen together here in* England: The *like happened also* Annis 1644, 1645, 1646, 1647. The *like happened a little before the bloody Wars between the* Romans *and* Carthaginians *brake forth.* Livius *Hist.*

[Three Moons were seen at *Titsie* in *Surrey, Octob.* 29. 1660.]

XIV.

Three persons Inhabitants of *Austy* in *Hertfordshire* going before Day, *Octob.* 30. 1660. with Malt-horses to *Ware* Market, were on a sudden smitten with a great and terrible Flash of Lightning; after which the Air continued very light, and grew brighter and brighter, and they looking from whence this great light should come, saw, as they conceived, full East before them a very dreadful Fire, and concluded that some House at *Meisden* had been on Fire; but they having not ridden much further perceived the fire in a great body to ascend, and the Sky opening to receive it; and as it went up, three Stars one immediately after another fell down from it perpendicularly; and when they fell, the Earth seemed lighter then at any time by the brightest Moon-light: Some part of the body of fire which ascended, remained yet in their view, and after a little space it turned into the direct form of a sickle with a handle, and afterwards it grew much like to a syth, and continued in that form till the day light swallowed it up: The spectators are very Credible Persons from whom this Relation comes.

[A fiery Meteor seen near *Misden* in *Hertfordshire*, from which did fall down perpendicularly 3 Stars, whereby the Earth was exceedingly enlightened. The Meteor afterwards turned into the form of a Sickle and then into the Form of a Sythe.]

XV.

The same Morning also some going before day with their Carts from about *Hadham* side in *Hertfordshire* to *Ware*, saw a body of fire in the Sky of divers colours like the Rain-bow, which presently turned into the perfect form of a Dragon, and immediately fell down to the ground, and by the fall of it the Earth was so lightned, that they could have seen a penny upon the ground as the spectators themselves do affirm, from whom we have this whole Relation.

This kind of Meteor is called by the Philosopher Draco Volans. *And about the time of the* Bohemian *Persecution, viz in the year* 1924 [sic] *such a fiery Dragon was seen throughout all* Bohemia *and* Silesia, vid. Bohe. Hist. *p.356. The like also was seen in* Scotland November 25. 1656. *which was confirmed by several Letters from thence at that time a true and full description of it; together with the Portends thereof you have in a Book called* Miraculum Signum Cœleste, *page* 28. 29, *&c.*

[A fiery Meteor in the form of a Dragon seen between *Hadham* and *Ware*, *Octob.* 30. 1660.]

XVI.

The same morning likewise before Day when it was very dark, five Neighbours going from *Hertford* to *London*, did alight by the way and walked to get themselves a heat, & as they were getting up upon their Horses again, there came a sudden Flash of Fire which made it so light, that they could perfectly descern as at noon day any thing upon the ground, their Horses also seemed to be all on fire; but within a little space this body of fire rose up again into the Aire, with a Tayl about a Pole long and went Eastward, where at last it fixed it self in the Sky like a Star.

[A body of fire ascending into the Air till it fixed it self in the Sky like a Star seen between H*ertford & London, Octob.* 30. 1660.]

XVII.

Upon the same morning very early, the Waggoner of *Wickham* in the county of *Bucks* came towards *London* with his Waggon and divers Passengers in it, about a mile from *Wickham* they all saw to their great afrightment, the Heavens open, and a large Ball of fire about the bigness (to use the Relaters own phrase) of a great Kittle, in a terrible manner descending and falling as they conceived, upon a Gentlemans house near a quarter of a mile from them, and they verily thought, because the fire brake in pieces on the house, it had been set on fire by it, but afterwards they found it to be otherwise: immediately upon this they saw another ball of fire descending in the same manner with the former, which fell upon a Wood very near to the Road wherein they were travelling, and they conceived that the whole Wood had been in a flame: A third ball also came down and fell upon the Earth and was broken into several pieces; during this time which was about the space of half an hour the Air was exceeding light, so that the Passengers in the Waggon could perfectly discern each other, and see to read an ordinary Print, but immediately after it was as dark as before. This Relation comes from some of the aforesaid Passengers, and particularly from the Waggoner and his Wife.

[A Ball of fire was seen to come out of the Heavens and fell upon a Gentlemans house. Another fell upon a Wood. And a third upon the Ground. These were seen *Oct*, 30 1660.]

For help in translating the Greek and Latin, Maureen Bell wishes to thank Matthew Fox, of the Dept. of Classics, the University of Birmingham.

DOCUMENT 3

Two poems by John Freeth

The Colliers' March

For details of the incident described in this ballad see page 73.

The summer was over, the season unkind,
In harvest a snow how uncommon to find;
The times were oppressive and, well be it known,
That hunger will strongest of fences break down.

'Twas then from their cells the black gentry stepped out
With bludgeons, determined to stir up a rout;
The prince of the party, who revelled from home,
Was a terrible fellow, and called Irish Tom.

He brandished his bludgeon with dexterous skill
And close to his elbow was placed Barley Will.
Instantly followed a numerous train,
Cheerful as bold Robin Hood's merry men.

Sworn to remedy a capital fault
And bring down the exorbitant price of the malt,
From Dudley to Walsall they trip it along
And Hampton was truly alarmed at the throng.

Women and children, wherever they go,
Shouting out, 'Oh the brave Dudley boys, O';
Nailers and spinners the cavalcade join,
The markets to lower their flattering design.

Six days out of seven poor nailing boys get
Little else at their meals but potatoes to eat;
For bread hard they labour, good things never carve,
And swore 'twere as well to be hanged as to starve.

Such are the feelings in every land,
Nothing Necessity's call can withstand;
And riots are certain to sadden the year
When sixpenny loaves but three-pounders appear.

The Troubles of France

This ballad, written in the autumn of 1789, refers to George III's first visit to Weymouth in the previous June, the release of the Earl of Massereene (an Irish peer imprisoned for debt in La Force) by the people of Paris on 13 July, the storming of the Bastille on the following day, the National Assembly's attempt in September to raise money by a 'patriotic contribution', and its decision on 2 November to nationalize church property.

Behold Britain's Monarch grown fond of the deep,
    To and fro on the waves take a dance;
Secure, while his subjects are taking a peep,
    A peep at the troubles of France.

The Monsieurs are rouz'd who have long been abus'd,
    And liberty-hall is the cry;
Their unshaken zeal with their blood will they seal,
    Determin'd to conquer or die.

Each province around is fir'd with the sound!
    Scarce her life can the QUEEN call her own;
The TIERS ETAT give the NOBLES a sweat,
    And the KING a mere cypher is grown.

To Lord Massarene, how delightful the scene,
    When the BASTILE strong doors open flew;
For the deep dreary way where the IRON MASK lay,
    No soul without horror could view.

How furrow'd with care in this den of despair,
    Must the brow of the wearer have been;
But chang'd is the day for I'll venture to say,
    The like ne'er again will be seen.

Other states soon will aim to play the same game,
    Which FRANCE in AMERICA learn'd;
The TRIPLE CROWN shakes and the Emperor quakes,
    To see how the tables are turn'd.

Boldly at it they set and the National Debt
    Diminish'd will speedily be;
Much the CHURCH has to fear, for the clergy they swear,
    The state of that burden shall free.

The cause to uphold how free and how bold,
    Assembled the artisans' Wives;
Their jewels they gave and their country to save,
    Are ready to hazard their lives.

May PITT from abroad learn of taxing the mode,
    And should future plans be devis'd,
When he craves further aid tell him boldly that Trade
    Already too much is excis'd.

Peace and friendship's my wish, and may they their deserts
    Always meet, who intrude on the ground;
And BRITAIN for ever in arms and in arts,
    Of all states the foremost be found.

Three poems by Joseph Mather

The File Hewer's Lamentation

Ordained I was a beggar,
And have no cause to swagger;
It pierces like a dagger –
    To think I'm thus forlorn.
My trade or occupation
Was ground for lamentation,
Which makes me curse my station
    And wish I'd ne'er been born.

Of slaving I am weary,
From June to January;
To nature it's contrary,
    This, I presume, is fact.
Although, without a stammer,
Our Nell exclaims I clam her,
I've wield my six-pound hammer
    Till I am grown round-backed.

I'm debtor to a many,
But cannot pay one penny;
Sure I've worse luck than any,
    My sticks are marked for sale.
My creditors may sue me,
And curse the day they knew me;
The bailiffs may pursue me,
    And lock me up in jail.

As negroes in Virginia,
In Maryland or Guinea,
Like them I must continue
   To be both bought and sold.
While negro-ships are filling
I ne'er can save one shilling
And must – which is more killing
   A pauper die when old.

My troubles never ceased,
While Nell's bairn-time increased;
While hundreds I've rehearsed,
   Ten thousand more remain;
My income for me, Nelly,
Bob, Tom, Poll, Bet and Sally,
Could hardly fill each belly,
   Should we eat salt and grains.

At every week's conclusion
New wants bring fresh confusion,
It is but mere delusion
   To hope for better days,
While knaves with power invested,
Until by death arrested,
Oppress us unmolested
   By their infernal ways.

A hanging day is wanted;
Was it by justice granted,
Poor men distress'd and daunted
   Would then have cause to sing –
To see in active motion
Rich knaves in full proportion
For their unjust extortion
   And vile offences swing.

Watkinson and his Thirteens

For the events which gave rise to this song see page 79.

> That monster oppression, behold how he stalks,
> Keeps picking the bones of the poor as he walks,
> There's not a mechanic throughout this whole land
> But more or less feels the weight of his hand;
> That offspring of tyranny, baseness and pride,
> Our rights hath invaded and almost destroyed.
> May that man be banished who villainy screens,
> Or sides with big Watkinson and his thirteens.
>
> *Chorus*
> And may the odd knife his great carcase dissect,
> Lay open his vitals for men to inspect,
> A heart full as black as the infernal gulf,
> In that greedy, blood-sucking and bone-scraping wolf.
>
> This wicked dissenter, expelled his own church,
> Is rendered the subject of public reproach;
> Since reprobate marks on his forehead appeared,
> We all have concluded his conscience is seared.
> See mammon his God and oppression his aim,
> Hark! how the streets ring with his infamous name,
> The boys at the playhouse exhibit strange scenes
> Respecting big Watkinson and his thirteens.
>
> Like Pharaoh for baseness, that type of the evil,
> He wants to flog journeymen with rods of steel,
> And certainly would, had he got Pharaoh's power:
> His heart is as hard and his temper as sour.
> But justice repulsed him and set us all free
> Like bond-slaves of old in the year jubilee.
> May those be transported or sent for marines
> That works for big Watkinson at his thirteens.
>
> We claim as true Yorkshiremen leave to speak twice,
> That no man should work for him at any price,
> Since he has attempted our lives to enthral,
> And mingle our liquor with wormwood and gall.
> Beelzebub, take him with his ill-got pelf,
> He's equally bad, if not worse than thyself.
> So shall every cutler that honestly means
> Cry 'Take away Watkinson with his thirteens.'

But see, foolish mortals! far worse than insane,
Three-fourths are returned into Egypt again.
Although Pharaoh's hand they had fairly escaped,
Now they must submit for their bones to be scraped.
Whilst they give themselves and their all for a prey,
Let us be unanimous and jointly say:
Success to our sovereign who peaceably reigns,
But down with both Watkinson's twelves and thirteens.

Raddle-Neck'd Tups

'Raddle-neck'd tups' = red-necked fools. For the Norfolk Street riots referred to in this song see page 81. 'Cerberus' was Colonel Athorpe, J. P., commander of the local volunteers. General Pichegru commanded the French Army of the Rhine and Moselle in 1795–6.

Among some infernal productions
   Consistent with Norfolk-street news,
Black Cerberus pick'd up his instructions,
   And came a recruiting for blues.
My grandmother told me last winter,
   But hop'd I'd her dotage excuse,
They were by a democrat printer
   Call'd 'Raddle-neck'd Tups' and not blues.

My name is Timothy Careless,
   I sprang from a vagabond Jew,
I'm subtle, blood-thirsty, and careless,
   Exactly the thing for a blue.
To fighting I am but a stranger,
   Its consequence I never knew,
I take to my heels when in danger,
   And just skulk away like a blue.

My thoughts in succession are evil,
   My clothes are both ragged and few.
Last week I shook hands with the devil,
   And then volunteer'd for a blue.
Like him that leads up our banditti
   To Beelzebub I will be true,
I'll show no love, remorse, or pity
   And that's just the part of a blue.

'Tis true we're the slaves of oppression.
   The sensible slaves to subdue;
While curs'd villainy rides in procession,
   Protected by hell-hounds in blue.
The poor must all be kept under,
   Held down as it were with a screw,
The rich with impunity plunder,
   And boast of assassins in blue.

The fate of the *swine* we'll determine,
   Repeated insults they shall rue,
They think us detestable vermin,
   More fitted for halters than blue;
When tyranny offers a bounty
   The Norfolk-street feats we'll renew,
And slay all the pigs in the county
   That grunt at us, butchers in blue.

If I be convicted of murder
   A jury will pull me clear through,
They'll say "'twas maintaining good order,"
   And tell me I am a true blue.
Mad Cerberus was our commander
   When Sorsby and Bradshaw we slew,
We took him for great Alexander,
   He played such exploits in his blue.

But ah! if the French should invade us,
   How must we approach Pichegru?
In Wharncliffe our chief man parade us,
   For none durst be seen in his blue.
B-s-t in the hole of some badger,
   I would raise an uncommon stew:
In like manner I durst lay a wager
   Would be every hero in blue.

Till brave Sans-Cullotes returned homewards
   We should not wear out many shoes;
The strongholds of foxes and polecats
   Would be sanctuaries for blues.
Should interest become a temptation,
   I would, with my infernal crew,
Sell loyalty, sovereign, and nation,
   And go to old Nick like a blue.

Bibliography

Anthologies containing poems by Freeth and Mather

Roy Palmer (ed.), *A Touch on the Times. Songs of Social Change, 1770–1914* (Harmondsworth, 1974).
Roger Lonsdale (ed.), *The New Oxford Book of Eighteenth Century Verse* (Oxford, 1984).

John Freeth

John Alfred Langford, *A Century of Birmingham Life, 1741–1841*, 2 vols (Birmingham, 1868).
'John Freeth: The Birmingham "Ballad Maker" ', *Mid-England*, 1, (Birmingham, 1880).
Stanley W. Light, 'Poet John Freeth: A Dibdin of Old Birmingham', *The Central Literary Magazine*, December 1960 (Birmingham).
John Money, *Experience and Identity: Birmingham and the West Midlands, 1760–1800* (Manchester, 1977).

Joseph Mather

John Wilson (ed.), *The Songs of Joseph Mather* (Sheffield, 1862).
W.H.G. Armitage, 'Joseph Mather: poet of the filesmiths', *Notes and Queries*, 195 (1950).
John Holland and James Everett, *Memoirs of the Life and Writings of James Montgomery*, 7 vols (London, 1854–6).
R.E. Leader, *Sheffield in the Eighteenth Century* (Sheffield, 1901).
Mary Walton, *Sheffield: Its Story and Its Achievements* (Sheffield, 1948).

The Political Background

E.P. Thompson, *The Making of the English Working Class* (London, 1963).
Gwyn A. Williams, *Artisans and Sans-Culottes. Popular Movements in France and Britain during the French Revolution* (London, 1968).
Albert Goodwin, *The Friends of Liberty: The English Democratic Movement in the Age of the French revolution* (London, 1979).

DOCUMENT 4

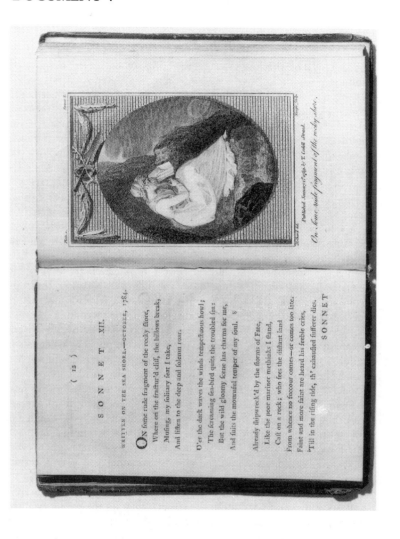

Published January 1789 by T. Cadell Strand.
On some rude fragment of the rocky shore.

(12)

SONNET XII.

WRITTEN ON THE SEA SHORE.—OCTOBER, 1784.

On some rude fragment of the rocky shore,
 Where on the fractur'd cliff, the billows break,
Musing, my solitary seat I take,
 And listen to the deep and solemn roar.

O'er the dark waves the winds tempestuous howl;
 The foaming sea-bird quits the troubled sea:
 But the wild gloomy scene has charms for me,
And suits the mournful temper of my soul.

Already shipwreck'd by the storms of Fate,
 Like the poor mariner methinks I stand,
 Cast on a rock; who sees the distant land
From whence no succour comes—or comes too late,
Faint and more faint are heard his feeble cries,
'Till in the rising tide, th' exhausted sufferer dies.

SONNET

DOCUMENT 5

Letter from a Gentleman to his Friend

... Let us not then despise, or teach the other sex to despise, the traditional maxims of experience, or those early prepossessions, which may be termed prejudices, but which in reality serve as their moral instinct. I can see neither tyranny on our part, nor slavery on theirs, in this system of education. This sentimental or metaphysical appeal to our candour and generosity has then no real force; and every other argument for the *literary* and *philosophical* education of women, and for the extraordinary cultivation of their understandings, I have examined.

You probably imagine that, by the superior ingenuity and care you may bestow on your daughter's education, you shall make her an exception to general maxims; you shall give her all the blessings of a literary cultivation, and at the same time preserve her from all the follies, and faults, and evils, which have been found to attend the character of a literary lady.

Systems produce projects; and as projects in education are of all others the most hazardous, they should not be followed till after the most mature deliberation. Though it may be natural, is it wise for any man to expect extraordinary success, from his efforts or his precautions, beyond what has ever been the share of those who have had motives as strong for care and for exertion, and some of whom were possibly his equals in ability? Is it not incumbent upon you, as a parent and as a philosopher, to calculate accurately what you have to fear, as well as what you have to hope? You can at present, with a sober degree of interest, bear to hear me enumerate the evils, and ridicule the foibles, incident to literary ladies; but if your daughter were actually in this class, you would not think it friendly if I were to attack them. In this favourable moment, then, I beg you to hear me with temper; and as I touch upon every danger and every fault, consider cautiously whether you have a certain preventive or a specific remedy in store for each of them.

Women of literature are much more numerous of late than they were a few years ago. They make a class in society, they fill the public eye, and have acquired a degree of consequence and an appropriate character. The esteem of private friends, and the admiration of the public for their talents, are circumstances highly flattering to their vanity; and as such I will allow them to be substantial pleasures. I am also ready to acknowledge that a taste for literature adds much to the happiness of life, and that women may enjoy to a certain degree this happiness as well as men. But with literary women this silent happiness seems at best but a subordinate consideration; it is not by the treasures they possess, but by those which they have an opportunity of displaying, that they estimate their wealth. To obtain public applause, they are betrayed too often into a miserable ostentation of their learning. Coxe tells us, that certain Russian ladies split their pearls, in order to make a greater display of finery.

The pleasure of being admired for wit or erudition, I cannot exactly measure in a female mind; but state it to be as delightful as you can imagine it to be, there are evils attendant upon it, which, in the estimation of a prudent father, may overbalance the good. The intoxicating effect of wit upon the brain has been well remarked, by a poet, who was a friend to the fair sex: and too many ridiculous, and too many disgusting examples confirm the truth of the observation. The deference that is paid to genius, sometimes makes the fair sex forget that genius will be respected only when united with discretion. Those who have acquired fame, fancy that they can afford to sacrifice reputation. I will suppose, however, that their heads shall be strong enough to bear inebriating admiration, and that their conduct shall be essentially irreproachable; yet they will show in their manners and conversation that contempt of inferior minds, and that neglect of common forms and customs, which will provoke the indignation of fools, and which cannot escape the censure of the wise. Even whilst we are secure of their innocence, we dislike that daring spirit in the female sex, which delights to oppose the common opinions of society, and from apparent trifles we draw unfavourable omens, which experience too often confirms. You will ask me why I should suppose that wits are more liable to be spoiled by admiration than beauties, who have usually a larger share of it, and who are not more exempt from vanity? Those who are vain of trifling accomplishments, of rank, of riches, or of beauty, depend upon the world for their immediate gratification. They are sensible of their dependence; they listen with deference to the maxims, and attend with anxiety to the opinions of those, from whom they expect their reward and their daily amusements. In their subjection consists their safety; whilst women, who neither feel dependent for amusement nor for self-approbation upon company and public places, are apt to consider this subjection as humiliating, if not insupportable: perceiving their own superiority, they despise, and even set at defiance, the opinions of their acquaintance of inferior abilities: contempt, where it cannot be openly retorted, produces aversion, not the less to be dreaded because constrained to silence: envy, considered as the involuntary tribute extorted by merit, is flattering to pride: and I know that many women delight to excite envy, even whilst they affect to fear its consequences: but they, who imprudently provoke it, are little aware of the torments they prepare for themselves. – "Cover your face well before you disturb the hornet's nest," was a maxim of the *experienced* Catherine de Medici.

Men of literature, if we may trust to the bitter expressions of anguish in their writings, and in their private letters, feel acutely all the stings of envy. Women, who have more susceptibility of temper, and less strength of mind, and who, from the delicate nature of their reputation, are more exposed to attack, are also less able to endure it. Malignant critics, when they cannot attack an author's peace in his writings, frequently scrutinize his private life; and every personal anecdote is published without regard to truth or propriety. How will the delicacy of the female character endure this treatment? How will her friends bear to see her pursued even in domestic retirement, if she should be wise enough to make that retirement her choice? How will they like to see premature memoirs, and spurious collections of familiar letters, published by needy booksellers, or designing enemies? Yet to all these things men of letters are subject; and such must literary ladies expect, if they attain to any degree of eminence. – Judging, then, from the experience of our sex, I may pronounce envy to be one of the evils which women of uncommon genius have to dread. "Censure," says a celebrated writer, "is a tax which every man must pay to the public, who seeks to be eminent." Women must expect to pay it doubly.

Your daughter, perhaps, shall be above scandal. She shall despise the idle whisper, and the common tattle of her sex; her soul shall be raised above the ignorant and the frivolous; she shall have a relish for higher conversation, and a taste for higher society; but where is she to find, or how is she to obtain this society? You make her incapable of friendship with her own sex. Where is she to look for friends, for companions, for equals? Amongst men? Amongst what class of men? Not amongst men of business, or men of gallantry, but amongst men of literature.

Learned men have usually chosen for their wives, or for their companions, women who were rather below than above the standard of mediocrity: this seems to me natural and reasonable. Such men, probably, feel their own incapacity for the daily business of life, their ignorance of the world, their slovenly habits, and neglect of domestic affairs. They do not want wives who have precisely their own defects; they rather desire to find such as shall, by the opposite habits and virtues, supply their deficiencies. I do not see why two books should marry, any more than two estates. Some few exceptions might be quoted against Stewart's observations. I have just seen, under the article "A Literary Wife", in D'Israeli's *Curiosities of Literature*, an account of Francis Phidelphus, a great scholar in the fifteenth century, who was so desirious of acquiring the Greek language in perfection, that he travelled to Constantinople in search of a *Grecian wife*: the lady proved a scold. "But to do justice to the name of Theodora," as this author adds, "she has been honourably mentioned in the French Academy of Sciences." I hope this proved an adequate compensation to her husband for his domestic broils.

Happy Mad. Dacier! you found a husband suited to your taste! You and Mons. Dacier, if D'Alembert tells the story rightly, once cooked a dish in concert, by a receipt which you found in Apicius and you both sat down and ate of your learned ragout till you were both like to die.

Were I sure, my dear friend, that every literary lady would be equally fortunate in finding in a husband a man who would sympathize in her tastes, I should diminish my formidable catalogue of evils. But, alas! M. Dacier is no more; "and we shall never live to see his fellow." Literary ladies will, I am afraid, be losers in love, as well as in friendship, by the superiority. – Cupid is a timid, playful child, and is frightened at the helmet of Minerva. It has been observed, that gentlemen are not apt to admire a prodigious quantity of learning and masculine acquirements in the fair sex; – we usually consider a certain degree of weakness, both of mind and body, as friendly to female grace. I am not absolutely of this opinion; yet I do not see the advantage of supernatural force, either of body or mind, to female excellence. Hercules-Spinster found his strength rather an incumbrance than an advantage.

Superiority of mind must be united with great temper and generosity, to be tolerated by those who are forced to submit to its influence. I have seen witty and learned ladies, who did not seem to think it at all incumbent upon them to sacrifice any thing to the sense of propriety. On the contrary, they seemed to take both pride and pleasure in showing the utmost stretch of their strength, regardless of the consequences, panting only for victory. Upon such occasions, when the adversary has been a husband or a father, I must acknowledge that I have felt sensations which few ladies can easily believe they excite. Airs and graces I can bear as well as another; but airs without graces no man thinks himself bound to bear, and learned airs least of all. Ladies of high rank in the court of Parnassus are apt, sometimes, to claim precedency out of their own dominions, which creates much confusion, and generally ends in their being affronted. That knowledge of the world which keeps people in their proper places they will never learn from the Muses.

Molière has pointed out, with all the force of comic ridicule, in the *Femmes Savantes*, that a lady, who aspires to the sublime delights of philosophy and poetry, must forego the simple pleasures, and will despise the duties of domestic life. I should not expect that my house affairs would be with haste despatched by a Desdemona, weeping over some unvarnished tale, or petrified with some history of horrors, at the very time when she should be ordering dinner, or paying the butcher's bill. – I should have the less hope of rousing her attention to my culinary concerns and domestic grievances, because I should probably incur her contempt for hinting at these sublunary matters, and her indignation for supposing that she ought to be employed in such degrading occupations. I have heard, that if these sublime geniuses are awakened from their reveries by the *appulse* of external circumstances, they start, and exhibit all the perturbation and amazement of *cataleptic* patients.

Sir Charles Harrington, in the days of Queen Elizabeth, addressed a copy of verses to his wife, "On Women's Vertues": – these he divides into "the private, *civill*, and heroyke", the private belong to the country housewife, whom it concerneth chiefly –

> The fruit, malt, hope, to tend, to dry, to utter,
>   To beat, strip, spin the wool, the hemp, the flax,
>   Breed poultry, gather honey, try the wax,
> And more than all, to have good cheese and butter.
> Then next a step, but yet a large step higher,
>   Came civill vertue fitter for the citty,
> With modest looks, good clothes, and answers witty.
> These baser things not done, but guided by her.

As for heroyke vertue, and heroyke dames, honest Sir Charles would have nothing to do with them.

Allowing, however, that you could combine all these virtues – that you could form a perfect whole, a female wonder from every creature's best – dangers still threaten you. How will you preserve your daughter from that desire of universal admiration, which will ruin all your work? How will you, along with all the pride of knowledge, give her that "retiring modesty", which is supposed to have more charms for our sex than the fullest display of wit and beauty?

The *fair Pauca of Thoulouse* was so called because she was so fair that no one could live either with or without beholding her – whenever she came forth from her own mansion, which, history observes, she did very seldom, such impetuous crowds rushed to obtain a sight of her, that limbs were broken and lives were lost wherever she apeared. She ventured abroad less frequently – the evil increased – till at length the magistrates of the city issued an edict commanding the fair Pauca, under the pain of perpetual imprisonment, to appear in broad daylight for one hour, every week, in the public market-place.

Modern ladies, by frequenting public places so regularly, declare their approbation of the wholesome regulations of these prudent magistrates.

Very different was the crafty policy of the prophet Mahomet, who forbad his worshippers even to paint his picture. The Turks have pictures of the hand, the foot, the features of Mahomet, but no representation of the whole face or person is allowed. The portraits of our beauties, in our exhibition-room show a proper contempt of this insidious policy; and those learned and ingenious ladies who publish their private letters, select maxims, secret anecdotes and family memoirs, are entitled to our thanks, for thus presenting us with full-lengths of their minds.

Can you expect, my dear sir, that your daughter, with all the genius and learning which you intend to give her, should refrain from these imprudent exhibitions? Will she "yield her charms of mind with sweet delay"? Will she, in every moment of her life, recollect that the fatal desire for universal applause always defeats its own purpose, especially if the purpose be to win our love as well as our admiration? It is in vain to tell me, that more enlarged ideas in our sex would alter our tastes, and alter even the associations which now influence our passions. The captive who has numbered the links of his chains, and has even discovered how those chains are constructed, is not therefore nearer to the recovery of his liberty.

Besides, it must take a length of time to alter associations and opinions, which, if not *just*, are at least *common* in our sex. You cannot expect even that conviction should operate immediately upon the public taste. You will, in a few years, have educated your daughter; and if the world be not educated exactly at the right time to judge of her perfections, to admire and love them, you will have wasted your labour, and you will have sacrificed your daughter's happiness: that happiness, analyze it as a man of the world or as a philosopher, must depend on friendship, love, the exercise of her virtues, the just performance of all the dutes of life, and the self-approbation arising from the consciousness of good conduct.

> I am, my dear friend,
> Yours sincerely.

DOCUMENT 6

Fellow Countrymen,

The Members of the Working Men's Association believing that a great and doubtful crisis is at hand, and that its result for evil or for good will principally depend on the mutual understanding among our own class, deem it to be their duty to address you on this important occasion. And in addressing you they are desirous of honestly and fearlessly avowing their sentiments regarding the great principle of right and justice, however in practice it may affect the selfish projects of any party in the state. We would willingly cast the mantle of oblivion over our past history—we would even endeavour to erase from our memories the atrocities, the persecutions, and the injustice, that for ages have been perpetrated against our class, if a disposition was even now evinced, on the part of our rulers, to commence the reign of JUSTICE and HUMANITY. And in expressing these our own feelings, we believe we express the feelings of every well-constituted and intelligent mind.

But, fellow countrymen, judging from the marshalling of forces and threats of defiance, we fear a similar disposition is not found among the various factions, whose continual strife for power and plunder is the curse of our country; their aim is to perpetuate the reign of wrong, and to consolidate their power at the expense of justice.

The strength, however, of any one of those parties will depend, fellow workmen, on us, on our united exertions to prevent the supremacy of any party, and to contend for the annihilation of all. Under a just system of government there would be but one party, *that of the people*; whose representatives would be actuated by one great motive, *that of making all the resources of our country tend to promote the happiness of all its inhabitants.*

Far different, however, are the views of those who now govern England, nay (with few exceptions) of those of their constituents who give them the power to govern. Each seems actuated by an exclusive interest; and exclusive privileges seem, in their estimation, the wisest legislative measures.

Will it, think you, fellow countrymen, promote our happiness—will it give us more comforts, more leisure, less toil, and less of the wretchedness to which we are subjected, if *the power and empire of the wealthy be established on the wreck of title and privilege?*

Yet to this end we believe, is the tendency of the present contest now waging between the two great parties both in and out of parliament—between the agricultural and privileged classes on the one hand, and the monied and commercial classes on the other. If the past struggles and contentions we have had with the latter to keep up our wages—our paltry means of subsistence;—if the infamous acts they have passed since they have obtained a portion of political power form any criterion of their disposition to do *us* justice, little have we to expect from any accession to that power, any more than from the former tyrants we have had to contend against.

There are persons among the monied class, who, to deceive their fellow men, have put on the cloak of reform; but they mean not that reform shall so extend as to deprive them or their party of their corrupt advantages. Many boast of freedom, while they help to enslave us; and preach *justice*, while they assist the oppressor to practice wrongs and to perpetuate the greatest injustice towards the working millions. Others among them are fertile in devising endless plans for strengthening their own interests, or for hoodwinking their constituents for the time being into a belief of their sincerity for the public weal. Many are for step-by-step improvement; they are characterized by their earnest solicitude *gradually to enlighten us*, lest we should see our political degradation too soon, and make any advance towards depriving them of their exclusive prerogative of leading us from year to year through the political quagmire, where we are daily beset by plunderers, befooled by knaves, and misled by hypocritical imposters.

These persons, under various pretences, and with a show of liberality, daily enlist in their ranks some portion of our deluded countrymen; and by opposing them to each other, accomplish their objects of deceiving and fleecing the whole. So long as we continue to be duped by some new political chimera, which they have ever at hand to amuse us,—so long as we continue to seek political salvation through the instrumentality of others, instead of our own exertions, so long will *party* be triumphant, will corrupt legislation prevail, will private peculators and public plunderers flourish, and so long must we continue to be the mere supplicating cringing vassals of a proud, arrogant, speech-making few; whose interest it is to keep us the mere toiling charity-ridden set we are, the unhappy dupes of the idle and the designing.

Fellow countrymen, have you ever enquired how far a just and economical system of government, a code of wise and just laws, and the abolition of all the useless appendages of state would affect the interests of the 658 members of the House of Commons? If you have not, begin now to enquire, and you will soon lose any vain hopes you may entertain from that house as at present constituted. Nay, if you pursue your enquiries in like manner respecting the present constituents of that house, to see how far their interests are identified with yours, how far just legislation and efficient reform would deprive them of their power to grind and oppress you, you would be equally hopeless of benefits from that quarter. To satisfy yourselves in this respect, propose for your own judgment and reflection the following questions:—

Is the FUNDHOLDER, whose interest is to preserve the debt and burthens of the country, and who revels in extravagance on the cheap productions of labour, a fit representative for us?

Is the LANDHOLDER, whose interest leads him to keep up his rents by unjust and exclusive laws, a fit representative for working men?

Are the whole host of MONEYMAKERS, SPECULATORS, and USURERS, who live on the corruption of the system, fit representatives for the sons of labour?

Are the immense numbers of LORDS, EARLS, MARQUESSES, KNIGHTS, BARONETS, HONORABLES, and RIGHT HONORABLES, who have seats in that house, fit to represent our interests? many of whom have the prospect before them of being the *hereditary legislators* of the other house, or are the craving expectants of place or emolument, who shine in the gilded circle of court, or flutter among the gaieties of the ball room, who court the passing smile of royalty, whine at the ministers of the day, and when the interests of the people are at stake, are found the revelling debauchees of fashion, or the duelling wranglers of a gambling house.

Are the multitude of MILITARY and NAVAL OFFICERS in the present House of Commons, whose interest it is to support that system which secures them their pay, and whose only utility is to direct one portion of our brethren to keep the other in subjection, fit to represent our grievances?*

Have we fit representatives in the multitude of BARRISTERS, ATTORNEYS, SOLICITORS, and all those whose interests depend on the dissensions and corruptions of the people; persons whose prosperity, depending on the obscurity and intricacy of the laws, seek to perpetuate the interests of *"their order"* by rendering them so unmeaning and voluminous that none but *law conjurers* like themselves shall understand them, and therefore their *legal* knowledge (that is, of *fraud* and *deception*) generally procure them seats in the legislature, and the highest offices knavery and corruption can confer.

Is the MANUFACTURER or CAPITALIST, whose exclusive monopoly of the combined powers of wood, iron, and steam, enables him to cause the destitution of thousands, and who has an interest in forcing labour down to the *minimum* reward, fit to represent the interests of working men?

Is the MASTER, whose interest it is to purchase labour at the cheapest rate, a fit representative for the WORKMAN, whose interest it is to get the most he can for his labour?

Yet such is the description of persons composing that house, and such the interests represented, to whom we, session after session, address our

---

* There are a few honourable exceptions in this class (and it may be in others) of persons whose benevolence prompts them to seek justice in opposition to their interests.

humble petitions, and whom we in our ignorant simplicity imagine will generously sacrifice their hopes and interests, by beginning the great work of political and social reformation.

Working men, enquire if this be not true, and then if you feel with us, stand apart from all projects, and refuse to be the tools of any party, who will not, as a *first and essential measure*, give to the working classes EQUAL POLITICAL AND SOCIAL RIGHTS; so that they may send their own representatives from the ranks of labour into that house to deliberate and determine among *all those other interests*, that the interests of the labouring classes, of those who are the foundation of the social edifice, shall not be daily sacrificed to glut the extravagances and luxuries of the few. If you feel with us, then you will proclaim it in the workshop, preach it in your societies, publish it from town to village, from county to county, and from nation to nation, that there is no hope for the sons of toil, till those who feel with them, who sympathise with them, and whose interests are identified with theirs, have an *equal right* to determine what laws shall be enacted or plans adopted for justly governing this country.

To this end, fellow workmen, are wanted, a FREE PRESS, UNIVERSAL SUFFRAGE, the Protection of the BALLOT, ANNUAL PARLIAMENTS, EQUAL REPRESENTATION, and no PROPERTY QUALIFICATION for members.

To the attainment of these essentials, embracing one great object—EQUAL POLITICAL RIGHTS—you must direct the sole attention of those representatives who call themselves RADICAL REFORMERS. Suffer them not, as far as your influence extends, to divert attention away to other projects of minor importance; test their sincerity by their dropping all paltry questions of policy or expediency, and contending with all their energies and talents for the attainment of this our only hope. Let no specious, eloquent, or delusive sophistries divert you from your purpose. Spurn the hypocritical pretensions of those who presume to sympathize with your wretchedness, but who would deny you, or delay, the only means of improving it by wise and just legislation. Equally despise the man who would refuse you the franchise on the plea of your ignorance, when your corrupt legislators seek to perpetuate that ignorance by the most infamous of laws, and whose interest it is to do so as long as they can gratify their plundering propensities with impunity. If knowledge is to be the qualification for political right, it is questionable whether you are not equally eligible with the paltry number of electors who have virtually the power of determining what laws shall be imposed on twenty-four millions of people. That you may have some standard by which to judge of the present rotten, unequal, and unjust state of the franchise of the United Kingdom, our Association have taken considerable pains to compile the following document, by which you will see that, notwithstanding there are 6,023,752 males above the age of twenty-one, that there are only 839,519 persons who have any portion of political right; and that owing to the *unequal* state of the representation, about one-fifth of that number have the power of returning the majority of the House of Commons. Nay, further, that owing to the present mode of registration, coupled with the ignorance or blunderings of the tools employed in an object so important, the real numbers, if they could be correctly estimated, would be considerably less even than this fifth. And these being the constituents of the smaller boroughs, must be regarded as persons more likely to be influenced or corrupted by their lords and masters than if they belonged to larger constituencies. Thus this miserable fraction of the people, whose interest may be opposed to the millions, have the power of forcing on them what laws, what despotic ordonnances they may think proper. Can we wonder then at the injustice and gross profligracy that pervade every department of the state, when the real power of the country is so limited? Read, therefore; think fellow countrymen; and enquire if it be not high time to arouse from your political apathy, and trusting to your own honest exertions, to firmly resolve, that as your power and energies forced the Whig Reform Bill, so by similar or still more powerful exertions you will force a real Radical Reform, by which all may be benefited.

No doubt there are persons of great political power and high standing in public opinion, who, while despising these sentiments (supported as they are by facts) will endeavour to persuade you that we are violent theorists, destructives, and levellers of the constitutional order of things; that our aim is revolution, that our object is plunder, and thereby they will seek to frighten the timid among you out of the propriety of their reason and better judgment. Fellow men, do not be deceived; we are working men like yourselves; we seek not any privilege or benefit that cannot be shared with the poorest amongst you. We seek just legislation as a means of adding to *the happiness of every human being*. While we feel intensely we may express ourselves warmly; but our knowledge of human nature can make allowances even for the feelings of our oppressors towards us; we therefore, wish, with all the anxiety of fathers, husbands, and brothers, that all classes and all creeds would see the necessity of uniting for the attainment of our objects peaceably—and not by delay and by oppression, risk the sullying of our beloved country by violence or revolutions. But that each benevolent heart and head would seek to forward our truly benevolent end, that of obtaining a legislature equally representing all interests, chosen by a free people, composed of the wise and the good of every class, and actuated by an enthusiastic desire to promote the happiness of every human being.

DOCUMENT 7

The War and the Poets

Not the least curious among the minor phenomena of the World War was the flood of war verse, by "soldier poets" and others, which found its way into print in England after the lamented death of Rupert Brooke. Poetry, we were assured, was booming. Lying about in every smart London drawing-room you would find the latest little volume, and at every fashionable bookshop the half-crown war poets were among the "best selling lines". We were asked to believe that the European War—unlike all its predecessors known to history, not one of which has ever inspired any art worth mentioning—had really brought to light a wealth of poetic talent. The publishers, faced by the problem of the paper shortage and the resulting necessity of selling very small books at very high prices if they were to make two ends meet, naturally did their bit towards encouraging "the muse in arms". The literary gentlemen who sat in their armchairs and rhapsodised—in the interests of propaganda—about the beauties of war, aided and abetted them with real fervour. An atmosphere was quickly and easily created favourable to the sale of verse, and the always gullible English public, flattered by the remarks in the Press about its "revived interest in poetry," disbursed its shillings with a lavishness only equalled by its lack of discrimination.

There remained, however, a few obstinate people who declined to allow their critical faculties to be chloroformed by popular sentiment, who continued to believe that although death on the field of battle might gain for the hero instant admission to Valhalla, it was not necessarily a qualification for Parnassus. Such ironsides clung to the notion that it is quality, not quantity, which makes a golden age of literature. And looked at from their point of view, it must be admitted that the influence which the Great War has had on the art of poetry seems to have been as unfortunate as its influence on the sister art of criticism.

The English war poets appear to divide themselves roughly into three sections. The first, and by far the largest section, includes the work of subalterns, fresh from the Public Schools, whose verse is as second-hand and as imitative in form as in sentiment. Then come the few from whom the tragedy of the years since 1914 has wrung a real *cri de cœur*, an honest statement of emotional experience in verse form. Finally we have the older professional poets and the journalists in verse, who have "carried on" as best they might.

If any student of English life wishes to gain an insight into the real meaning of the Public School spirit, that poisonous anachronism on which our country still prides herself, he cannot do better than study a handful out of the countless volumes of war verse which it has produced. For our Public School system, in its effort to turn out every little Englishman "a thoroughly manly young fellow," succeeds brilliantly in stunting the growth of his thinking apparatus. It preserves him as an intellectual adolescent living in a fairyland of chivalrous illusion, with a blind trust in the doctrines enunciated by the reactionary newspapers. Many of these Public Schoolboy soldiers must have gone straight from the cricket-field and the prefect's study to the trenches, in a kind of waking dream. Their mental equipment for withstanding the shock of experience was as useless as the imitation suit of armour, the dummy lance and shield of the actor in a pageant. It was their false conception of life, their inability to look at facts except through tinted glasses of one particular colour, which rendered the poems of so many young subalterns so valueless as literature, so tragic and accusing as human documents. For they accuse the age which permitted and gloried in an educational system so monstrously unfair to its victims, and they accuse the schoolmasters who have acquiesced in perpetuating it.

I quote the lines which follow because they are eminently characteristic of the note of scores of books of the kind to which I have just referred. They were picked out for special praise by one of our head masters, in an issue of *The Poetry Review*—

> "Malvern men must die and kill,
> That wind may blow on Malvern Hill;
> Devonshire blood must fall like dew,
> That Devon's bays may yet be blue;
> London must spill out lives like wine,
> That London's lights may ever shine."

This is precisely the doctrine of the "You-go-first" or "Comb-them-all-out-except-me" press, accepted with a blind and touching credulity, and it is certainly not intended to be the scarifying satire which, in effect, it is. It is the kind of thing which during the War was accepted as poetry, even by a journal ostensibly devoted to that art; which the reviewers chose for commendation, and the reading public presumably appreciated.

For the second section into which I have divided the war poets—the section containing those who have something to say, and therefore the only one that really matters—I must confess I have found only a very small group who claim admittance. Alan Seeger, Wilfred Sorley, and one or two others were moved at moments to sincerity, and some honest and effective verse has been written by Siegfried Sassoon, Robert Graves and Osbert Sitwell.

Of these three Robert Graves is the most fanciful, the least introspective and reflective, the least savage. His poem, "It's a Queer Time," strikes his characteristic note of whimsical resignation. It is a curiously touching poem, and in places curiously vivid—

> "Or you'll be dozing safe in your dug-out—
> A great roar—the trench falls and shakes about—
> You're struggling, gasping, struggling, then . . . hullo!
> Elsie comes tripping gaily down the trench,
> Hanky to nose—that lyddite makes a stench—
> Getting her pinafore all over grime.
> Funny! Because she died ten years ago!
> It's a queer time."

Mr. Graves has a gentle voice, naturally gay and cheerful, and always his own. He does not probe or question; when the actual becomes unbearable he flies away on the wings of his fancy. Mr. Sassoon, on the other hand, deals chiefly with the actual. His verse is wrought out of the stuff of life, and throughout it all is heard a cry of agony, an agony of compassion. He has not a trace of Mr. Graves' resignation. Indeed the natural rage of a sensitive man at the horrors and stupidity of war—which level of literary merit, but it cannot be said that the War inspired them to surpass themselves. Among the younger men, Mr. Robert Nichols, who had the advantage of a fair technical equipment, achieved a popular success with his much-praised *Ardours and Endurances*. After his experiences in the trenches he tried nobly to rise to the occasion, and his poem "The Assault" is the principal result of his efforts. Considered in cold blood, however, it is an empty and pretentious piece of work, too laboured, too patently worked out in accordance with some brand-new "stuntist" theory to be at all impressive. The dabs and splashes of colour, the onomatopæic rendering of gunfire, fail to interest, because the thought underlying the poem is commonplace. (In a year or two, if the human race is to continue at all, let us hope it will have become an absurd memory.)

> "Ha! Ha! Bunched figures waiting.
> Revolver levelled quick!
> Flick! Flick!
> Red as blood.
> Germans. Germans.
> Good! O good!
> Cool madness."

It was characteristic of our war-time criticism that this masterpiece of drivel, instead of exciting derision, was hailed as a work of genius and read with avidity. On the whole Mr. Nichols is much more sincere and more effective when he is writing about other things than war, and occasionally, as in his poem "The Tower," he achieves beauty of atmosphere and description.

Captain Gilbert Frankau's war poems are topical; they are smart, descriptive journalism done into the slickest modern verse, and their competence lifts them head and shoulders above ninety per cent of the verse of his brothers in arms. Captain Frankau's talents are considerable and under perfect control, so that whether he is writing about night clubs or trench-lights he is always, as the pressmen say, "in the news". He does not attempt to be profound.

Perhaps the real test of the influence of the war on recent poetry—an influence alleged by our sentimentalists to have been so profoundly inspiring and invigorating—is to be found, not in a study of the younger men, but in an examination of the output during the period of hostilities, of the older poets whose reputations, in 1914, were already established. Did the War actually infuse fresh energy into our surviving Victorian or Edwardian singers? If it did, the masterpieces have been cruelly withheld from a public all agog to receive them.

William Watson, it is true, wrote a sonnet to Lord Northcliffe and one or two other pieces inspired by current events. He received a knighthood, but his literary reputation has not thereby been increased. Rudyard Kipling exhibited the bankruptcy of his point of view in several archaic bleats, so feeble in thought and style that a practical joker was easily able to hoax one of the leading newspapers into publishing a burlesque of them. And yet, in the piping days of peace, it was Kipling who, more successfully than any other writer, preached the gospel of commercial and militarist Imperialism in Great Britain! Mr. John Masefield, whom one might have imagined the smell of blood would have intoxicated, produced nothing of literary importance, but threw himself with fervour into propagandist journalism intended for consumption in America. Mr. Hardy gave us a few morose and gloomy verses; Mr. Bridges, our Poet Laureate, showed signs of marked discomfort at the realisation of the part he was expected to play; and several other great ones attempted the top note and cracked on it badly. A survey of the poetic output during the War of the established English poets forces one to the conclusion that only those who—like Mr. de la Mare and Mr. D. H. Lawrence—deliberately kept their minds and thoughts on a higher plane, managed to escape its vulgarising influence. During the last year of the War three volumes of new verse by well-known writers made their appearance—*Motley, and Other Poems*, by Walter de la Mare, *Look!*

We Have Come Through! by D. H. Lawrence, and *On Heaven, and other Poems*, by Ford Madox Hueffer. Of these three poets, I believe only Mr. Hueffer served in the trenches. It is an unfortunate fact that of the three it is his work alone which shows marked signs of deterioration. *On Heaven, and other Poems*—the only volume which has come from Mr. Hueffer's pen for some time—is a sad descent, at any rate so far as the war verses in it are concerned, from the general level of his *Collected Poems*. Somehow, in putting on khaki, he seems, like so many other men in the early forties, to have resumed, as far as possible, the outlook of the Public Schoolboy. The tone of his war poems to some extent suggests the "old boy" on a school speech-day, and to one at least of his admirers it was a shock to see a mind which in the recent past had been as active, as daring, as sensitive, as fresh as Mr. Hueffer's, becoming a middle-aged mind. And yet the "old boy" attitude is of the very essence of middle age; it is a deliberate orgy of reaction. Middle age is acquiescent where youth is rebellious. Middle age is intent on recovering the thrill of a dead romance, on reviving an old glamour, while youth "reasons why," strives to break free from the bondage of the past, and peers eagerly into the future for a glimpse of that glamour which surrounds to-morrow. To middle age "to-morrow" must be the same as yesterday, or it will be indignantly disowned. Youth will have no more of yesterday.

The Great War, which to middle age seemed something infinitely heroic and noble—more noble even than the Eton and Harrow cricket match—to youth more often appeared merely as a tragic farce, an insane contest between rival bands of slaves organised by rival profiteers.

Nothing gives a more dismal indication of the change which has come over Mr. Hueffer's mind than the fact that the qualities of his war poems are almost exclusively those which belong to average descriptive reporting. The artist in him is submerged in the newspaper man, and he hits the bull's eye of "topicality" every time. He can write of wangling leaves from the adjutant, and of machine guns going "wukka wukka" in a way to cause a thrill in the bosom of Mr. Kipling's admirers—

"And far away to the left
Wukka wukka.
And sharply,
Wuk . . . wuk."

Perhaps the true hero of this war was some poor devil who was struck down by a 'wukka-wuk" while a roar of derisive laughter broke out of him. Could only such a great Dionysian laugh now re-echo through the world, the whole silly business might be seen, as by a lightning flash, in just perspective.

The further Mr. Hueffer gets away from the War and popular emotionalism, the more his hand remembers its old cunning. In one poem he begins to sketch some remote and beautiful landscape—

"The seven white peacocks against the castle wall
In the high tree and the dusk are like tapestry,
The sky being orange, the high wall a purple barrier
The canal, dead silver in the dusk,
    And you are far away.
Yet I can see infinite miles of mountains.
Little lights shine in rows in the dark of them. . . ."

But the second verse opens with "Around me are the two hundred and forty men of B Company," etc., and the poem relapses into the kind of slop which, at the moment it was written, it was almost a criminal offence not to admire. The poem which follows it, "The Silver Music," seems to suggest that the War had temporarily obscured Mr. Hueffer's usually keen faculty of self-criticism. It reads like a parody which he might have composed over the telephone for the benefit of a young friend, as an illustration of the kind of verse *The Spectator* would be certain to print—

"Oh! I'm weary for the castle,
And I'm weary for the Wye," etc.

the topographical note, style A. E. Houseman—

"And another soldier fellow
Shall come courting of my dear
And it's I shall not be with her
With my lips beside her ear"

To the young friend's objection: "How could 'I' be with her, unless 'I' were a sort of ghostly gooseberry?" one can almost hear Mr. Hueffer's tired rejoinder: "But, my dear chap, that is just the sort of thing that Strachey *eats!*"

In "One Last Prayer," the musician in Mr. Hueffer asserts himself, and the result is a song which is worthy to rank with "À la Mauresque" in its simplicity and beauty—

"I have only you beneath the skies
To rest my eyes
From the cruel green of the fields
And the cold, white seas
And the weary hills
And the naked trees.

> I have known the hundred ills
> Of the hated wars.
> Do not close the bars,
> Or draw the blind.
> I have only you beneath the stars:
> Dear, be kind!"

But, with this exception, the only poem in the book which reaches the level of the author's best work is the one which gives it its title, and this one was written before the outbreak of war. "On Heaven" seems to have been inspired in the first instance by a desire to show the young American school of poets how very much better an old hand could, if he chose, do their particular "stunt". But once embarked on the poem, the possibilities of the medium seem to have enchanted him, and he has let himself go in an imaginative and emotional rhapsody which is perhaps one of the best things of its kind which has yet appeared. After reading it, one can only hope that Mr. Hueffer's natural force is only temporarily abated, and that his lost youth will soon be restored to him.

Mr. Walter de la Mare's poetry—so pure, so remote—is like an echo from some fairy-land, midway between earth and heaven, to whose gates only poets and children have the key. His melodies are haunting and eerie in their high clarity and strangeness. They are like songs heard at night-time in some deep wood whose paths are chequered by moonlight, whose shadowy thicknesses are thronged with ghosts.

> "Breathe not—trespass not;
> Of this green and darkling spot,
> Latticed from the moon's beams,
> Perchance a distant dreamer dreams;
> Perchance upon its darkening air,
> The unseen ghosts of children fare,
> Faintly swinging, sway and sweep,
> Like lovely sea-flowers in its deep;
> While, unmoved, to watch and ward,
> 'Mid its gloomed and daisied sward,
> Stands, with bowed and dewy head,
> That one little leaden lad."

His feeling for Nature and his love of flowers and birds are not surpassed either by Mr. W. H. Davies or by the late Francis Ledwidge, as the little poem called "The Linnet" is enough to indicate—

> "Upon this leafy bush
> With thorns and roses in it,
> Flutters a thing of light,
> A twittering linnet.
> And all the throbbing world
> Of dew and sun and air
> By this small parcel of life
> Is made more fair;
> As if each bramble-spray
> And mounded, gold-wreathed furze
> Harebell and little thyme,
> Were only hers;
> As if this beauty and grace
> Did to one bird belong,
> And, at a flutter of wing,
> Might vanish in song."

Mr. de la Mare, luckily, was not inspired to write war poems; but the poet's sense of horror at the martyrdom of mankind finds poignant expression in the piece called "The Marionettes"—

> "Let the foul Scene proceed:
>   There's laughter in the wings;
> 'Tis sawdust that they bleed,
>   But a box Death brings.
>
> Gigantic dins uprise!
>   Even the gods must feel
> A smarting of the eyes
>   As these fumes upsweal.
>
> Strange, such a Piece is free,
>   While we Spectators sit,
> Aghast at its agony,
>   Yet absorbed in it!
>
> Dark is the outer air,
>   Coldly the night draughts blow,
> Mutely we stare and stare
>   At the frenzied Show.
>
> Yet heaven hath its quiet shroud
>   Of deep, immutable blue—
> We cry 'An end!' We are bowed
>   By the dread, ' 'Tis true!' "

And so we are brought back again to the conclusion that it is men like Walter de la Mare, D. H. Lawrence, Siegfried Sassoon—men who have either shunned the War altogether in their verse or attacked it with an almost revolutionary fervour—who, since the death of Flecker and of Rupert Brooke, have alone kept alive the art of poetry in England.

The ardours of revolutionary idealism warm and fire the creative impulse like the ardours of romantic love. Perhaps the agonies from which the world is so slowly emerging will produce in England a new Shelley, a new and greater Byron, whose work will enshrine, not a frenzy of hatred and a desire for maniacal destruction, but a passion for a freer and nobler life in the new world which will be built up by the tireless hands of the young men of to-morrow, which will be cemented with the blood of the martyrs, of the despised and rejected pioneers of to-day. The ghastly absurdities of mutual murder can never—at this period of the world's history—be immortalised by the arts. Only the lyrical journalism of a corrupt and lying Press can properly occupy itself with the tinsel glories in which one of the greatest crimes yet committed by the Western races is sought to be wrapped up by those dark forces which were principally responsible for it.

All great art, in every country, must spring ultimately from the heart of the people. In the late War the peoples of Europe suffered a martyrdom almost without parallel in the world's history. Surely when the masses in every country become articulate—through the medium of the great poets, painters and dramatists who must inevitably arise—their utterances will be neither a slavish kissing of the rod, nor yet a slavish adulation of the social system which made their suffering possible.

And if we are to have a renaissance of poetry in England we must have a new criticism to meet it—a savage, rasping criticism, speaking with the bitter notes of an idealism which longs passionately for the best, and will no longer tolerate shams. Criticism must once again become the task of those who have an uncompromising standard of values, of those whose love for what is real and sincere will not permit them to deal gently with what is false, pretentious, empty and ephemeral.

During the War we saw in England the mawkish theory that death on the field of battle automatically made a man a creditable poet, upheld by almost every critic of literature who wished to find a ready market for his wares. They could not, it seemed, do honour to the men who died without making themselves parties to a fraud. No doubt the ghoulish traffic in the verse exercises of dead schoolboys was an excellent business "proposition". No doubt some publishers—by bleeding the bereaved parents to pay for the production of their sons' pathetic little poems, or by gulling the public, with the aid of the sentimental reviewers and critics—managed to make a great deal of money out of it. But it is a damaging reflection on the influence of the War on the British reading public that it should have been a "stunt" which it was possible to work so blatantly.

DOCUMENT 8

One Thousand Fearful Words for Fidel Castro

    I am sitting in Mike's Place trying to figure out
    what's going to happen
    without Fidel Castro
    Among the salami sandwiches and spittoons
    I see no solution
    It's going to be a tragedy
    I see no way out
    among the admen and slumming models
    and the brilliant snooping columnists
    who are qualified to call Castro psychotic
    because they no doubt are doctors
    and have examined him personally
and know a paranoid hysterical tyrant when they see one
    beause they have it on first hand
    from personal observation by the CIA
    and the great disinterested news services
And Hearst is dead but his great Cuban wire still stands:
    "You get the pictures, I'll make the War"
    I see no answer
    I see no way out
    among the paisanos playing pool
    it looks like Curtains for Fidel
    They're going to fix his wagon
    in the course of human events

    In the back of Mike's the pinball machines
    shudder and leap from the floor
    when Cuban Charlie shakes them
    and tries to work his will
    on one named "Independence Sweepstakes"
    Each pinball wandered lonely as a man
    siphons thru and sinks
    no matter how he twists and turns
    A billiardball falls in a felt pocket
    like a peasant in a green landscape
    You're whirling around in your little hole
    Fidel
    and you'll soon sink
    in the course of human events

On the nickelodeon a cowboy ballad groans
"Got myself a Cadillac" the cowhand moans
He didn't get it in Cuba, baby
Outside in the night of North Beach America
the new North American cars flick by
from Motorama
their headlights never bright enough
to dispel this night
in the course of human events

Three creepy men come in
One is Chinese
One is Negro
One is some kind of crazy Indian
They look like they may have been
walking up and down in Cuba
but they haven't
All three have hearing aids
It's a little deaf brotherhood of Americans
The skinny one screws his hearing aid
in his skinny ear
He's also got a little transistor radio
the same size as his hearing aid box
For a moment I confuse the two

The radio squawks
some kind of memorial program:
"When in the course of human events
it becomes necessary for one people
to dissolve the political bonds
which have connected them with another—"
I see no way out
no escape
He's tuned in on your frequency, Fidel
but can't hear it
There's interference
It's going to be
a big evil tragedy
They're going to fix you, Fidel
with your big Cuban cigar
which you stole from us
and your army surplus hat
which you probably also stole
and your Beat beard

History may absolve you, Fidel
but we'll dissolve you first, Fidel
You'll be dissolved in history
We've got the solvent
We've got the chaser
and we'll have a little party
somewhere down your way, Fidel
It's going to be a Gas
As they say in Guatemala

Outside of Mike's Place now
an ambulance sirens up
It's a midnight murder or something
Some young bearded guy stretched on the sidewalk
with blood sticking out
Here's your little tragedy, Fidel
They're coming to pick you up
and stretch you on their Stretcher
That's what happens, Fidel
when in the course of human events
it becomes necessary for one people to dissolve
the bonds of International Tel & Tel
and United Fruit
Fidel
How come you don't answer anymore
Fidel
Did they cut you off our frequency
We've closed down our station anyway
We've turned you off, Fidel

I was sitting in Mike's place, Fidel
waiting for someone else to act
like a good Liberal
I hadn't quite finished reading Camus' Rebel
so I couldn't quite recognize you, Fidel
walking up and down your island
when they came for you, Fidel
"My Country or Death" you told them
Well you've got your little death, Fidel
like old Honest Abe
one of your boyhood heroes
who also had his little Civil War
and was a different kind of Liberator
(since no one was shot in his war)

and also was murdered
in the course of human events

Fidel . . . Fidel . . .
your coffin passes by
thru lanes and streets you never knew
thru day and night, Fidel
While lilacs last in the dooryard bloom, Fidel
your futile trip is done
yet is not done
and is not futile
I give you my sprig of laurel

San Francisco, January, 1961

Selected bibliography

The chapters which make up this book includes references to works of especial relevance to their subject areas and there is no point in itemising them again here. Instead, what follows is a list of works, some general, some of a more specialised nature, which may prove of use to the interested reader. The books are listed in alphabetical order but I have taken care to give titles at sufficient length in order to make plain their contents and major concerns.

Alexander, M., *Women in Romanticism: Mary Wollstonecraft, Dorothy Wordsworth, Mary Shelley* (London, 1989).
Aston, Elaine, *An Introduction to Feminism and Theatre* (London, 1995).
Ayer, A.J., *Thomas Paine* (London, 1988).
Barrow, Margaret, *Women 1870–1928: A Select Guide to Printed and Archival Sources in the United Kingdom* (London, 1981).
Blain, Virginia, Clements, Patricia and Grundy, Isobel (eds), *The Feminist Companion to Literature in English* (London, 1990).
Butler, Marian (ed.), *Burke, Paine, Godwin and the Revolution Controversy* (Cambridge, 1984).
Chesler, Phyllis, *Sacred Bond: Motherhood Under Siege* (London, 1990).
Clemit, P., *The Godwinian Novel* (Oxford, 1993).
Erdman, D., *Blake: Prophet Against Empire* (Princeton, 1969).
Everest, K. (ed.), *Revolution in Writing: British Literary Responses to the French Revolution* (Milton Keynes, 1991).
Hanley, K. and Seldon, R. (ed.), *Revolution and English Romanticism* (Hemel Hempstead, 1990).
Hanscombe, E.G. and Forster, J., *Rocking the Cradle: Lesbian Mothers* (London, 1982).
Jones, V. (ed.), *Women in the Eighteenth Century* (London, 1990).
Kanner, B., *Women in Social History, 1800–1914: A Guide to Research* 2 vols (London, 1988).
Kelly, G., *The English Jacobin Novel, 1770–1805* (Oxford, 1976).

Knight, S. and Wilding, M. (eds), *The Radical Reader* (Sydney, 1977).
Lucas, J., *England and Englishness: Poetry and National Identity, 1688–1900* (London, 1990).
Lucas, J. (ed.), *Literature and Politics in the Nineteenth Century* (London, 1971 and 1974).
Lucas, J. (ed.), *The 1930s: A Challenge to Orthodoxy* (Brighton, 1978).
McCalman, Iain, *Radical Underworld: Prophets, Revolutionaries, and Pornographers in London, 1795–1840* (Oxford, 1993).
Mee, J., *Dangerous Enthusiasm: William Blake and the Culture of Radicalism in the 1790s* (Oxford, 1992).
Mellor, A., *Romanticism and Gender* (London, 1993).
Powell, D., *Tom Paine: The Greatest Exile* (London, 1985).
Rogers, K.M., *Feminism in Eighteenth-Century England* (Brighton, 1982).
Smith, O., *The Politics of Language, 1791–1819* (Oxford, 1986).
Spender, Dale, *Women of Ideas and What Men Have Done to Them* (London, 1982).
Stanley, Liz, *The Auto/biographical I: The Theory and Practice of Feminist Auto/Biography* (Manchester, 1992).
Thompson, E.P., *The Making of the English Working Class* (London, 1963).
Thompson, E.P., *Witness Against the Beast: William Blake and the Moral Law* (Cambridge, 1993).
Todd, J., *Feminist Literary History: A Defence* (Oxford, 1988).
Wandor, M., *Look Back on Gender: Sexuality and the Family in Post-War British Drama* (London, 1987).
Worrall, D., *Radical Culture: Discourse, Resistance and Surveillance, 1790–1820* (Hemel Hempstead, 1992).
Yarrington, A. and Everest, K. (eds), *Reflections of Revolution* (London, 1993).

Index

Auden, W.H. 197–8
Austen, Jane 10, 104
   Emma 124–5
   Mansfield Park 123–4

Bage, Robert 84, 85, 103
   Hermpsrung 84
Barbauld, Anna 84–5
Bennett, Arnold 186–8
   Accident 196–7
   Mr. Prohack 186–8
Berline, Isaiah 3
Blake, William 22, 84, 85, 86, 87, 88–9, 94, 95, 96–7, 100
Burney, Fanny 7, 14
   Evelina 7
Burns, Robert 128

Calvert, Elizabeth 41, 47, 48, 50, 52, 53, 54, 56, 57
Caxton, William 3
Chapman, Livewell 52
Chartists, The 128–49 *passim*
Churchill, Caryl 288
   Top Girls 288–90
Coleridge, S.T. 76, 100
Cooper, Thomas 134
Curtis, Jane 39–45, 40, 42, 43, 44, 57, 58

Daniels, Sarah 291–2
   The Devil's Gateway 292, 296
   Ripen Our Darkness 291–2
Darby, Joan 47
Dayley, Grace 296
   Rose's Story 296
Dickens, Charles 2, 132
   A Child's History of England 2
   Our Mutual Friend 11–12
Diggers, The 24–5
Dover, Joan 45–6, 52
Dryden, John 54
Dunbar, Andrea 295–6
   The Arbor 295–6

Edgar, David 286
   Teendreams 286–8, 297–8
Edgeworth, Maria 328–33
   Letters for Literary Ladies 328–33
Eliot, George 150, 158, 159, 160
Eliot, T.S. 178, 185, 189
   The Waste Land 188, 192

Ferlinghetti, Lawrence 245–76
   'One Thousand Fearful Words for Fidel Castro' (the text) 349–52
Freeth, J. 9, 62–76
   'John Free' 63–6

Poems by Freeth 319–21
Frost, Thomas 139–43, 146
   The Secret 139–43

Gay Sweatshop 293
   Care and Control 293–4
Gems, Pam 285–6
   Dusa, Fish, Stas and Vi 285–6
Godwin, William 84, 100
   An Enquiry Concerning Political Justice 84, 85, 91
   Things As They Are (Caleb Williams) 90–1
Goldring, Douglas 189
   from *Reputations* 339–48
Goldsmith, Oliver 8
Gordon, D.J. 5
Graves, Robert 190–1

Hamilton, Patrick 201–39
   Craven House 204, 205–7, 213, 226
   Duke in Darkness, The 224–6
   Gaslight 223
   Governess, The 225
   Hangover Square 205, 222, 224
   Impromptu in Moribundia 215, 219, 223–4
   Slaves of Solitude, The 225–6
   Twenty Thousand Streets Under The Sky 204, 209, 215, 223, 226
Hays, Mary 102, 111–12
Herzen A. 3
Hogarth, William 8–9
Holcroft, Thomas 103
Huxley, Aldous 192–3
   Antic Hay 192
   Crome Yellow 193

Inchbald, Elizabeth 95, 102, 112–16
   A Simple Story 95, 99, 113–16

Jacobins, The 61–81 *passim*
James, Henry 13
   Awkward Age, The 13
Jones, Ernest 134, 146
   Woman's Wrongs 134–9
Joyce, James 193–5, 196
   Ulysses 194–5

Keatley, Charlotte 290
   My Mother Said I Never Should 290–1
Keats, John 100

Lawrence, D.H. 178–9, 181–2, 183, 184, 185, 193
   England, My England 182
L'Estrange, Roger 50, 53, 55, 57, 58
   Consideration and Proposals for the Regulation of the Press 50, 52
Lewis, Wyndham 195–6
Lindsay, Jack 27
Lovett, William 334–8

Mallock, W.H. 13
Marvell, Andrew 21, 54–5
   'Upon Appleton House' 21
Marx, Karl 26
Masterman, C.F.G. 188–9
Mather, Joseph 9, 77–81
   Poems by Mather 321–5
McRobbie, Angela 294–5
Meredith, George 12
   Ordeal of Richard Feverel, The 12

INDEX 357

Milan, Angie 297
  Dead Proud 297
Milton, John 4, 19–38
  A Masque (Comus) 4, 5, 19–20
  Areopagitica 6, 25
  Paradise Lost 20–38
  Paradise Regained 36
  Tenure of Kings and
    Magistrates 24–5
Moore, George 13
  Literature at Nurse 14
  Mummer's Wife, A 13
More, Hannah 95, 132
Morris, William 14, 180, 225
  News from Nowhere 14

Owen, Wilfred 186

Paine, Tom 10, 84, 87, 88, 91, 100
  Age of Reason, The 93
  Rights of Man 80, 89, 103
Pope, Alexander 7

Ranters, The 25
Red Ladder Theatre Company 283
  Strike While The Iron's Hot 293–4
Reynolds, G.M.W. 132, 133, 134
Riche, Adrienne 282
Rickword, Edgell 195–6
Robinson, Mary 95–6
Rousseau J.-J. 105, 115

Seward, Anna 7
Shakespeare, William 4
  Richard II 4, 21
  Tempest, The 108
Shaw, G.B.S. 27
Shelley, Mary 10

Frankenstein 125–6
Shelley, P.B. 22, 27
Simcox, Edith 150–74
Smith, Charlotte 102, 116–23
  Celestina 117–18
  Elegaic Sonnets 116, 121, 327
  Marchmont 120
  Old Manor House, The
    113–20, 123–4
  Young Philosopher, The
    120–3
Smith, Francis 39, 42, 56
Southey, Robert 76, 108
Swift, Jonathan 7
  Irish Tracts 8

Thomas, Edward 180–1
  'As the Team's Head Brass' 180
Thompson, E.P. 10, 17, 73, 95
Todd, Susan 286
  Teendreams 286–7, 297–8
Townsend-Warner, Sylvia 5, 15, 16, 201–39
  After The Death of Don Juan 231, 239
  Corner That Held Them, The 228, 231
  Flint Anchor, The 230, 239
  Lolly Willowes 209, 210, 238
  Opus 7, 210
  Summer Will Show 211, 212, 218, 228, 237
Turner, Matthew 91
  Answer to Dr. Priestley, An 91

Vizetelly, Henry 13

Wandor, Micheline 283–4, 293–4
Waugh, Evelyn 190, 191
  Vile Bodies 198–9

Wheeler, T.M. 143–5
  Sunshine and Shadow 143–5
Wilde, Oscar 15
  'The Soul of Man Under Socialism' 15
Williams, Helen Maria 84, 85
Wollstonecraft, Mary 84, 85, 86, 90, 91, 93, 95, 102
  Mary, A Fiction 105–7
  Vindication of the Rights of Women, A 84, 86, 92, 97–8, 107–8
  Wrongs of Women, or Maria 105, 107–11
Women's Theatre Group 284
  My Mother Says I Never Should 284–5
Woolf, Virginia 193
Wordsworth, William 76, 106, 128
Wycliffe, William 2–3

Yearsley, Anne 87, 95, 98–9
Yeats, W.B. 184, 185, 189